Communication Theory Today

Edited by David Crowley
and David Mitchell

Polity Press

Copyright © This collection Polity Press 1994
Each chapter copyright © the author

First published in 1994 by Polity Press
in association with Blackwell Publishers

Editorial office:
Polity Press
65 Bridge Street
Cambridge CB2 1UR, UK

Marketing and Production:
Blackwell Publishers
108 Cowley Road
Oxford OX4 1JF, UK

ISBN 0 7456 1046 3
ISBN 0 7456 1289 X (pbk)

British Library Cataloguing-in-Publication Data
A CIP catalogue record for this book is available
from the British Library.

Typeset in 11 on 12pt Garamond
by Acorn Bookwork, Salisbury, Wiltshire
Printed in Great Britain by T.J. Press, Padstow, Cornwall

This book is printed on acid-free paper.

Contents

Notes on Contributors   vii

Acknowledgements   x

1   Communication in a Post-Mass Media World   1
    David Crowley and David Mitchell

Part I: Communication and the Mediation of Social Worlds   25

2   Social Theory and the Media   27
    John B. Thompson

3   Medium Theory   50
    Joshua Meyrowitz

4   A Recursive Theory of Communication   78
    Klaus Krippendorff

Part II: Messages, Meanings, Discourse   105

5   Discourse and Cognition in Society   107
    Teun A. van Dijk

6   Risk Communication and Public Knowledge   127
    William Leiss

7   Talk, Text and History: Conversation Analysis
    and Communication Theory   140
    Deirdre Boden

Part III: Contingency, Reflexivity, Postmodernity   171

  8   The Mode of Information and Postmodernity   173
      Mark Poster

  9   In the Realm of Uncertainty: The Global Village
      and Capitalist Postmodernity   193
      Ien Ang

 10   By Whose Authority? Accounting for Taste
      in Contemporary Popular Culture   214
      James M. Collins

Part IV: Communication and Public Interests   233

 11   Mass Communication and the Public Interest: Towards
      Social Theory for Media Structure and Performance   235
      Denis McQuail

 12   Electronic Networks, Social Relations
      and the Changing Structure of Knowledge   254
      William Melody

 13   Communication and Development   274
      Majid Tehranian

Index   307

Notes on Contributors

Ien Ang Senior Lecturer in Communication Studies at Murdoch University. Author of *Desperately Seeking the Audience* (London: Routledge, 1991); and *Watching Dallas: Soap Operas and the Melodramatic Imagination* (London: Methuen, 1985).

Deirdre Boden Lecturer in Sociology at the University of Lancaster. Author of *The Business of Talk* (Cambridge: Polity, 1994). Co-editor of *Talk and Social Structure* (Cambridge: Polity Press, 1991).

James M. Collins Associate Professor of Communication and Theatre at the University of Notre Dame. Author of *Uncommon Cultures: Popular Culture and Post-Modernism* (New York: Routledge, 1989) and *Architectures of Excess* (New York: Routledge, 1994). Co-editor of *Film Theory Goes to the Movies* (New York: Routledge, 1993).

David Crowley Associate Professor of Communications at McGill University and a member of the McLuhan Program in Culture and Technology at the University of Toronto. Author of *Understanding Communication: The Signifying Web* (New York: Gordon & Breach, 1982). Co-editor of *Communication in History* (New York: Longman, 1990).

Klaus Krippendorff Professor of Communications at the University of Pennsylvania's Annenberg School for Communication. Author of *Information Theory* (Beverly Hills, Calif.: Sage, 1986); and *Content Analysis* (Beverly Hills, Calif.: Sage, 1980). Editor of *Communication and Control in Society* (New York: Gordon & Breach, 1979) and *Studies in Cybernetic Epistemology*.

William Leiss   Professor of Communication at Simon Fraser University. Author of *Risk and Responsibility* (forthcoming, 1944) and *Under Technology's Thumb* (Montreal: McGill–Queen's University Press, 1990). Co-author of *Mandated Science* (Dordrecht: Kluwer Academic, 1988); and *Social Communication in Advertising: Persons, Products and Images of Well-being* (Scarborough: Nelson, 1990). Editor of *Prospects and Problems in Risk Communication* (Waterloo: University of Waterloo, 1989).

Denis McQuail   Professor of Mass Communication at the University of Amsterdam. Author of *Media Performance* (London/Newbury Park, Calif.: Sage, 1992); and *Mass Communication Theory* (London: Sage, 1987). Co-editor of *New Media Politics* (London: Sage, 1986). Editor of the *European Journal of Communication*.

William Melody   Director of the Centre for International Research on Communication and Information Technologies (CIRCIT) in Melbourne. Editor of *The Intelligent Telecommunication Network* (Melbourne: CIRCIT, 1991). Co-author of *Information and Communication Technologies: Social Science Research and Training, vols. 1 and 2* (London: Economic and Social Research Council, 1986).

Joshua Meyrowitz   Professor of Communication at the University of New Hampshire. Author of *No Sense of Place: The Impact of Electronic Media on Social Behavior* (New York: Oxford University Press, 1985).

David Mitchell   Assistant Professor of Communications Studies at the University of Calgary.

Mark Poster   Professor of History at the University of California at Irvine. Author of *The Mode of Information* (Chicago: University of Chicago Press, 1990); and *Critical Theory and Poststructuralism* (Ithaca, NY: Cornell University Press, 1989); and *Foucault, Marxism and History* (Cambridge: Polity Press, 1984).

Majid Tehranian   Professor of Communication at the University of Hawaii at Manoa. Author of *Technologies of Power: Information Machines and Democratic Prospects* (Norwood, NJ: Ablex, 1990); *Letters from Jerusalem* (Honolulu: Peace Institute, 1990); and *Restructuring for Ethnic Peace* (Honolulu: Peace Institute, 1991). Co-editor of *Restructuring for World Peace: On the Threshold of the 21st Century* (Cresskill, NJ: Hampton, 1992).

John B. Thompson   Lecturer in Sociology and Fellow of Jesus College at the University of Cambridge. Author of *Ideology and Modern Culture* (Cambridge: Polity Press, 1990); *Studies in the Theory of Ideology* (Cambridge: Polity Press, 1984); and *Critical Hermeneutics: A Study in the Thought of Paul Ricoeur and Jürgen Habermas* (Cambridge: Cambridge University Press, 1981). Co-editor of *Habermas: Critical Debates* (Cambridge Mass.: MIT, 1982); and *Social Theory of Modern Societies* (Cambridge: Cambridge University Press, 1989).

Teun A. van Dijk Professor of Discourse Studies at the University of Amsterdam. Author of *Elite Discourse and Racism* (Newbury Park, Calif.: Sage, 1993); *Racism and the Press* (London: Routledge, 1991); *News as Discourse* (Hillsdale, NJ: Erlbaum, 1988); *News Analysis* (Hillsdale, NJ: Erlbaum, 1988); and *Communicating Racism* (Newbury Park, Calif.: Sage, 1987). Editor of *Handbook of Discourse Analysis* (4 vols.; Orlando, Fla: Academic Press, 1985). Founder-editor of *TEXT*, and *Discourse & Society*.

Acknowledgements

The editors would like to thank the Graduate Program in Communication Studies at the University of Calgary for the support it has shown for this project – in particular its Director Edna Einsiedel and Lorraine Ellert for her kind assistance. They would also like to thank Phil Vitone and Dans Caspi for discussions of post-mass media, Nina Gregg and Lisa Henderson, the McLuhan Program at the University of Toronto, especially its Director, Derrick de Kerckhove, and InterNet Consulting Group Ottawa.

1

Communication in
a Post-Mass Media World

David Crowley and David Mitchell

The essays that follow are original works, prepared especially for this Polity Press volume. The volume itself is part of an ongoing Polity series addressing the state of contemporary theory in the humanities and the social sciences. While this is the first of the series to venture outside the traditional disciplines, the present text makes no claim to be representative of the field of communications. Rather, the contributors were asked simply to report on scholarship in their own area of communication research, to say what the substantive issues are at present and what themes and directions lie ahead. Where appropriate we asked the contributors to illustrate their arguments with examples from recent research.

In putting the volume together we wanted to be sensitive to the ways in which contemporary studies of communication appear to embrace a widening diversity of approaches and to address audiences that include a number of neighbouring fields and disciplines. The contributors reflect this mix of variety and common ground. Several write from academic fields and institutional affiliations other than communications, affording a sense of how communication issues are approached in the work of other disciplines. Geography figures here as well, in that the authors speak from several regional bases: four each from the United States and Europe, two from Australia, one from Canada, plus the editors.

The manner in which we have divided the essays into sections may appear confusing to some, accustomed to seeing the scholarship represented in terms of content areas and approaches. Content areas and approaches remain useful indicators of the division of intellectual labours, but we wanted to avoid the conceptual locks that these arrangements imply to some, as the product of older theoretical and institutional ententes. Several contributors chose to provide their own narrative context, showing how their work relates to enduring preoccupations such as audiences, persuasion, development, and critique. Others have been less concerned with continuities and affinities in favour of stressing promising directions beyond the traditional confines of the field.

Looking forward into the nineties, the essays do provide some sense of a common terrain. We identify that common ground roughly as follows, with a more detailed discussion below: a growing emphasis on meaning construction and human agency and an entailed need to place inquiry within social and historical contexts; a stronger focus on matters of contingency and the local with respect to interpreting media products; a rising appreciation for post-mass media culture and its relation to modernity, and a more self-consciously recuperative theorizing that reworks and incorporates aspects of earlier formulations.

If contemporary studies of communication exhibit a widening diversity of approaches, in part this phenomenon sends a signal about the discovery of communication and media issues by other areas of scholarship, with the resulting cross-talk. In the last decade we have become more accustomed to finding culturally oriented historians, like Robert Darnton, digging into records of publishers and booksellers for clues about how popular cultures of the day figured in the French revolution; or historically oriented communication scholars, like Carolyn Marvin, exploring the discursive devices of technical journals to see how expert communities used texts to construct professional careers around nineteenth-century electrification; or ethnographically oriented literary theorists, like Janice Radway, citing field notes from encounters with book club editors and romance novel readers as evidence for how these literatures got to be the way they are. Blended genres – and the refiguring of scholarly work that comes with them – have become a fact of academic life, as we borrow methods, exchange theories, and otherwise go about taking tentative looks into each other's subject matter. In the case of communication studies, these new transdisciplinary border conditions also reveal some convergence, notably in the form of a continuing drift away from content control approaches in favour of meaning-constructing ones.[1]

As much as many of these new hybrid approaches emphasize the popular, the mundane, and the everyday, the transdisciplinary appeal of communications also highlights a maturing institutional theme: the recognition of the role media have played in modernity, in earlier industrial development and now in globalization and its various argued transformations – post-industrial, informational, postmodern. Many scholars now purport to see mass media, past and present, occupying a wider canvas, as part of the reproductive apparatus of society, whose capacity to pool, channel, and redistribute all manner of information and entertainment places them institutionally closer to the centre of the project of modernity. As our most public of social theorists, Anthony Giddens, puts it: 'Mechanized technologies of communication have dramatically influenced all aspects of globalization . . . [and] form an essential element of the reflexivity of modernity and of the discontinuities which have torn the modern away from the traditional.'[2] In coming to grips with the housing and rehousing of these technologies historically, the retro-fitting of older practices in society with newer tools and capacities, as well as their enabling and disabling consequences, scholars in several disciplines today try to take account of how these organized technologies and the practices built up around them are interwoven with social organization and social change.

The search for a more encompassing framework for communication is of course nothing new. In the sixties, communication scholars reached back to the Frankfurt School for those early critical theorists who had worked out a concept of the mass culture industry, or alternatively turned to the linguistic models of structuralism and semiotics for a model of media's role in social reproduction. In the seventies, combined with neo-Marxism, these efforts produced a powerful mapping for the transmission of dominance, charted through concepts such as hegemony, cultural imperialism and social discourse. Following cohorts, however, have been less accepting of the direct linkage of messages and meanings that much of this work, and the functionalist perspectives that preceded it, presumed. With methods and sympathies strikingly diverse, these newer groups have begun to open the black box of mundane reality. As John Thompson and Majid Tehranian make clear in the opening and closing essays respectively, the dynamics of globalized distribution of media products and the persistence of localized conditions of reception push the questions of media's relationship to social worlds further into the variety and verity of everyday cultural and cognitive experience. How else can we cope with the unintended consequences of media, or come to terms with their unexpected or counter-intuitive developments as potentially valid sources for insight into others? How else can we deal with the public resistance to Western models of journalism setting up shop in such likely places as post-Cold War Budapest and Prague; or the remarkable popularity of video storytelling in the form of teleroman, telenovela, and other forms of popular indigenous television? As we enter a post-mass media world, how else are we to fathom the startling role of such ad hoc phenomena as the audio cassette in the Iranian counter-modern revolution, the fax machine in the events surrounding the protests in Tienanmen Square, or the role of telecomputing in derailing the Moscow coup, to note only those that bring media to bear on political culture?

However, the final cusp of modernity's century may look in retrospect to be our loss of scholarly confidence in grand schemata and totalizing narratives, let alone transcendental sources of truth, and our new willingness to take closer looks at the relativities of the everyday. This suggests that as scholars of the public process we may be close to putting our efforts where the American pragmatist John Dewey thought we ought to be putting them all along, mounting the sorts of social inquiry where the 'test of consequences is more exacting than that afforded by fixed general rules'.[3]

The new empirics that this 'test of consequences' requires will make stiff demands on communication researchers if post-mass media conditions deepen. After all, one of the features of modernity that has helped secure the knowledge base of communications, allowing the field stable curricula and focused research agendas, has been the persistence of successive central media and central organizations and regulatory regimes in control of those media throughout much of the twentieth century. National media distribution systems – wire services, mass-circulation magazines, network radio and television – developed along with the scope and scale of other mass-production and consumption organizations, as Alfred Chandler acknowledges in *The Visible Hand*.[4] The stable core of central media provided thereby grounds and rationale for new forms of professional knowledge work and opportunity for new professional communities to grow up around these institutions: from early demonstrations of the proactive uses of research to shape public policy, such as the Payne studies on film, through Paul Lazersfeld's entrepreneurial demonstrations that the new audiences of radio listeners and television viewers could be tracked by statistical sampling as easily as readership, to the promotion of indexical standards of media development for monitoring and evaluating the movement from traditional to modern values. All this – and the subsequent questioning of these gambits in the critical reactions that followed – have rested on the stable core of central media.

If, as Jim Collins and others ruefully note, the darker consequences foretold in those following critiques from Frankfurt, Birmingham, and Paris are unaccountably late getting into the station, this may be cold comfort alongside accumulating evidence that the central media themselves may be up against formidable challenges. Audience fragmentation aside (the term itself shows the evaluative allegiance), a flood of alternative approaches stressing ethnography, feminism, response theory, discursive and critical cultural analysis have begun to construct new and divergent conceptions of what audiences are up to. At the same time, developments in information technologies are reconfiguring our modes and means of symbolic interaction.

Electronic writing, computer networking and new electronic byways such as the Internet will test the limits of previous systems of distribution and expression. Regulatory regimes that for decades have succeeded in separating content from carriers, keeping broadcasters, phone companies, and publishers off each other's turf, policing the electronic interactions of ersatz national borders, and making it all serve more or less convincing notions of the public interest, these too appear less stable. *Post-mass media* may not be the most elegant or inclusive label for all of this. Like those other designations of how we think now – post-structural, post-Marxian, post-Freudian, postmodern – these labels testify to our general reluctance and perhaps our inability to break decisively with our received frameworks of knowledge and action.

Like the postmodern metaphor this anxiety over post-mass media need not be entirely negative. If the normative enclosures of our research and the housings of our most stable technologies of mass communication are no longer quite the basis for master narratives that they once were, it is interesting that a common thread running through many of the contributions involves an examination of how older frameworks of communication research can still figure in current projects. But such reflective engagements with past research have not been exactly a hallmark of the past decade or two, constrained in our deliberations as we have been by the policing effects of paradigms, totalizing theories, and reflexive anti-methods.

A number of contributors attempt to redress gaps in theory by stepping outside previous conceptual confinements. John Thompson and Joshua Meyrowitz, for instance, each draw explicitly on the earlier work of media history, notably that of the Toronto circle in the sixties, and the parallel trajectory of ethnomethodology, emphasizing the work of Erving Goffman, in order to challenge several aspects of how social theory and communication theory have dealt with the question of media and social control. All the authors here who address postmodern scholarship take issue with the media-centric focus of mid-century communication models. As Ien Ang observes, the movement from functionalist models of senders and receivers to semiotic models of encoders and decoders has done little to break down the assumption that we need not look beyond these particular enclosures to understand communications in society.

At the same time several contributors remind us that these older formulations themselves contain overlooked possibilities. Klaus Krippendorff, for instance, follows Gregory Bateson's original notion of cybernetics as a social theory – and Margaret Mead's proposal to apply cybernetic description to cybernetic thought itself – as a basis for recursive theory. For another, William Leiss describes how the original Shannon–Weaver 'message transmission model of communication' breaks a number of conceptual impasses when reapplied in new practical settings.

Looking forward into the nineties as all the essays do – into the postmodern, the anti-modern, and the newly modern – raises other issues about how we think now. For all the evidence of our falling away from older orders and our striving for newer ones (the end of the Cold War and the renewed call for a new world information and communication order), the variousness of the global agendas inevitably brings us back, as Denis McQuail, William Melody, and Majid Tehranian in complementary ways insist, to the need for new normative values wherever older ones no longer seem to suffice. McQuail notes the considerable difficulties now attached to defining the public interest in many countries of the West, never mind outside the West. Melody demonstrates how and why many of the older political recipes for furthering the 'public interest' in telecommunications (natural monopoly, cross-subsidization) are no longer viable options in the new geopolitics forming around information technologies. As counterpoint, Tehranian shows us that there are today wider interests in the participatory potential of alternative communication networks than are presently accommodated in conventional notions of either mass media or public interest politics.

Taking considerable liberty with the richness of the work that follows, we suggest that four conceptual thematics figure strongly enough in the book as a whole to warrant giving them some special mention here: mediation, persuasion, contingency, and the public interest. In fact each of these terms covers a cluster of related concepts: the role of communication in the mediation of social worlds; the way that methodology-laden terms like messages, meanings, and discourse track historically our concerns with persuasion; our difficulty in coming to terms with postmodernity, reflexivity, and contingency and their place in our theorizing; and the way that new technologies and new forms of governance oblige us to rethink public interests.

Communication and the Mediation of Social Worlds

Most of us are aware of a certain neglect in social theory with respect to communication, its technological dynamos and wider societal consequences. Admittedly, Marx did speak about the printing press in relationship to the breakdown of feudal institutions, Weber clearly saw writing, the file, and even arguably the telegraph as pacemakers of bureaucracy, and Freud mused about the telephone and its discontents. Even Talcott Parsons ventured a general concept of media (admittedly highly abstract), but surprisingly few have made it a sustaining feature of their narratives on society. The themes are of course never entirely absent from social theory's range. Hanno Hardt has uncovered in nineteenth-century German and American social thought a rich vein of discourse on that century's central medium, the press. Moreover, many communication scholars – and a considerable number of sociologists, social psychologists, and philosophers – still trace their intellectual projects in part to the work of the American pragmatists, Charles Sanders Peirce, George Herbert Mead, Robert Ezra Park, and John Dewey among others, whose lexicon of signs and symbols, reflexive monitoring, reading publics, and public process provided a core set of ideas around social interaction and human agency. Mead had described the development of a social self built up in and through a reflexive monitoring of others, while Park approached the newswork of newspapers in a similar fashion, stressing the iterative character of its relationship to community. In society's growing capacity to pass beyond the local and direct conditions of community via the 'physical tools of communication', Dewey saw the eclipse of the public. Ever the modernist, he believed the commitments of social theory lay precisely in helping identify a public process 'congruous' with those new instrumentalities.

In some ways the optimism and focus of the pragmatists grated on European strains of social thought. Members of the Frankfurt School, setting up shop in the United States during the Second World War, ridiculed Dewey's concept of the public as generalized from the ideal of the school house; they saw it, along with other motifs, like town hall democracy, as residues of a no longer available American traditionalism. Nonetheless, the empirical dimensions of the project begun by the pragmatists has remained vibrant. Interactionists, as the direct heirs of this legacy are generally known, continue to approach human events as the contingent results of mutual monitoring and adjustments, whereby individuals go on by 'taking account' of how others respond, incorporating and anticipating these responses in their own actions. This capacity to construct the relationship of self and others symbolically is where, as Howard Becker would say, the 'symbolic' in symbolic interactionism comes from; a definition of agency that is at once prior to and wider than language, but easily accommodates language as a primary modality. These symbolic and linguistic modes in turn form the basis for complex collective actions. Social worlds, we could say, are the iterative achievement of this shared capacity for reflexive monitoring and symbolic engagement stretched over time and space.[5]

Interactionists have always been attentive to the way in which communication technologies have provided opportunities for the construction of social worlds. There has also been something like a bias – or perhaps a preference and affection for – activist human agents that has worked to keep the interactionist project firmly fixed on field work, providing a rich compendium for how notions such as community, professional knowledge, the arts, or popular cultures reproduce themselves within everyday life.

This emphasis on makings and doings is a hallmark of interactionists and underscores an awkwardness with respect to communication research, where the focus on modern message systems, principally those of the mass media, has produced a sharply contrasted sense of emphasis in the construction of social worlds. The emphasis on messages and social control has been a defining one for communication studies, over and against the subject matter of other social sciences. Among the consequences of an otherwise salutatory focus has been the marginalizing of other strains of thinking about media and society. Notable among these were the media, or medium, theorists, beginning with Harold Innis but including an eclectic gathering of scholars in the sixties – Jack Goody, Marshall McLuhan, Walter Ong, Eric Havelock, among others. They built a model of media in society, consonant with the early pragmatists, that treated communication technologies as intellectual instruments (today we would say cognitive instruments); and much like the later interactionists showed a distinct aversion to the statistical empiricism favoured by the communication studies of that time period.[6]

In a manner that sometimes seemed counter-intuitive to scholars of media message content, these theorists focused on how the tools and devices that made up the primary mode of communication in a society enabled and constrained the organization of that society and the received experience of its subjects. As they saw it, there were three entwined modes of communication mediating interaction: we can interact directly with one another, emphasizing the repertoire of verbal and non-verbal skills; we can utilize those skills within an organized setting, as a coordinated subset of the originals; and we can employ proxies for those skills (such as literacy and numeracy) along with their associated technologies (the printing press, telegraph and telephone, broadcasting, and more recently the computer). These verbal and non-verbal skill sets and their extending technologies alter the ways in which we experience and act in the world; together they affect not just the content of experience, but the scope and scale of what can be experienced. Harold Innis, the most secular of the mediationists, saw a recurrent dialectic in history where one medium asserted primacy in a society, followed by efforts to bypass the social power that gathered around the control of that medium, with the predictable championing of alternatives and the rise of new social actors around those alternatives. With Innis the linkage to the pragmatists was clear: each new mode of communication was associated with tearing individuals and entire forms of life out of their traditional moorings in locality and place and relocating them within larger and more dispersed forms of influence. With modernity, this process of co-location of the self within multiple spaces, identities, and influences intensifies; human agency itself is progressively pulled away from the local and reconstituted within the expanding possibilities of the modern.

In retrospect, the differences that kept the mediationist and the interactionist projects from a closer association with the mainstream of communication research seem less related to the politics of the discipline and more connected to a genuine difference of ontological opinion on the status of social control in media and about how much we could learn about human agency from a strategy focused on the message system itself. With considerable sympathy for these debates, John Thompson explores a number of difficulties inherent in current versions of that social control thesis, notably as found in contemporary models of critical theory, semiotics, and post-structuralism (themselves critiques of original functionalist models). Thompson is particularly critical of what he sees as the weakness of empirical evidence for the direct linkage of messages and meanings and the correspondingly limited notions of human agency and social cognition that result.

John Thompson's approach to these deficiencies provides a linkage to both mediationists and interactionists. In a broadly recuperative strategy, Thompson incorporates three approaches into what he sees as an outline for a social theory of media: the work of Harold Innis and the Toronto circle on a model of technologically mediated social change; Jürgen Habermas's magisterial conception of a historical public sphere, disengaged by Thompson from its Frankfurt roots; and a hermeneutically informed approach to interaction and human agency, which is indebted to Paul Ricoeur, but also makes significant use of a variety of methodological approaches relevant to the study of everyday life.

Joshua Meyrowitz parallels Thompson's reworking of the media control thesis. He makes explicit here his connection with the Toronto circle of media theorists, notably Walter Ong and Marshall McLuhan, demonstrating how their work intersects with Meyrowitz's own explication of an interaction order around television. Meyrowitz calls them 'medium' theorists, in stressing their focus on differential influences that various media have in society, content aside. Meyrowitz also draws importantly on the work of Erving Goffman, whose micro-sociology for many years has resided just on the other side of an invisible boundary from communication studies. Meyrowitz sees Goffman's work as relevant to understanding television's consequence for the maintenance of social worlds, such as that of childhood, and social relationships, such as those between public figures and private citizens.

Thompson also criticizes social theory for trying to discuss issues of power and control without reference to the workings of modern media. Alternatively, he criticizes communication researchers for following research agendas without reference to perennial sociological concerns like power, ideology, and culture. In trying to encourage a conversation between these constituencies, he is uneasy with the problematic equation of media and the exercise of social power. In particular, Thompson questions how we account for the powers associated with surveillance in contemporary society. He finds currently fashionable notions of surveillance (such as those inspired by Foucault's reworked metaphor of the Panopticon) often fail to catch the differences that modern media make in the relationship between power and public visibility. Both Thompson and Meyrowitz find media more double-edged than current theory recognizes: pervasive instruments for the management of visibility, so used by political leadership. But the very process by which media track and regularize this relationship to the powerful, also provides ways and means for the many to monitor the few, rendering the few who command the media's attention much less in control of the 'sense' they wish to convey than they might wish.

The way in which Meyrowitz sees a second generation building on the work of the original theorists of the medium, taking fuller account both of television and of the computer, has parallels with Klaus Krippendorff's pursuit of more recursive models of communications. Krippendorff spans the first generation of formal theories of information, cybernetics, and information theoretics, and the second generation, of which he is a principal proponent. Krippendorff's framework has never been in any sense media-centric. Although he is an important methodologist with respect to content analysis, his theoretical preoccupations have always been about human communication in the widest sense, including its symbolic, biological, and organizational forms. In this essay Krippendorff argues for a radically recursive conception of human communication, which he proposes to recuperate in part from an early cybernetic formulation, sometimes referred to as second-order cybernetics, carried forward through the work of cognitive constructivists, end-linking it, as Margaret Mead would say, with Anthony Giddens's conception of reflexive human agency. Recursiveness has many applications, of course, and not only in communication and systems theory. Linguistics has long made use of the concept to account for language shift; and recursiveness may better account for the meaning-constructing activity of audiences, artists, or individuals than current approaches based on limited notions of intertextual referencing.

Messages, Meanings, Discourse

Persuasion is an enduring theme of the discourse on modern media. So strong are these preoccupations among North American scholars that James Carey, in commenting on the ways the scholarly literature divides up into persuasive effects versus contextual understanding, saw the latter literature arising from a more distinctly European sensibility. This 'effects' versus 'texts' dichotomy may be more muted these days, perhaps the result of blended perspectives and the cross-trade in ideas, but the persuasion model and the linkage to effects remains the closest thing we have to a master narrative about modern media. Whatever its subsequent limitations, in the immediate post-Second World War period the persuasion model held out the promise that information, properly understood, could rationalize management of the increasingly complex environments of modern society.[7]

Teun van Dijk, as a leading proponent of discourse analysis, sees linkages between contemporary concern for social power and these earlier preoccupations with persuasive effects. In his essay van Dijk reworks Harold Lasswell's template (often summarized as Who says What to Whom through What Channels with What Effects) in terms of the reproduction of dominance: 'Who is allowed (or obliged) to speak or listen to whom, how, about what, when and where and with what consequences.'

Van Dijk suggests that the social power issues can be directly connected to the reporting function of mass media. In a mass-mediated society, where most people depend upon media for their information about society at large, the media become dominant sources for the cognitive models that underlie our shared attitudes, ideologies, and strategies for understanding. Discourses in this sense are vehicles for prevailing sentiments in a society. Many inter-ethnic attitudes and tensions, van Dijk believes, are driven as much by just these symbolic dimensions of discourse as they are by direct interaction. Symbolic dimensions contain our shared meanings about other groups (what discourse analysts call social representations) and much of this comes to us through the discourse produced by mass media. Van Dijk agrees further with the information theorists that, in the complexity of modern settlements, the influence of direct forms of information (personal observation, eyewitness reporting of the views of ordinary people, and so on) pales in comparison to indirect forms. We monitor the mass media for information of all sorts and for the ways in which that information projects and maintains models of the world. In turn we use these inputs to inform our mental strategies and to construct our socially shared world views. Models and mental strategies are the building blocks of van Dijk's model of social cognition. When these models and mental strategies come to be widely distributed in society, they account for what we otherwise refer to as social knowledge, ideology, and prevailing attitudes.

How will the information and reporting functions of media play out in the nineties? Van Dijk is particularly concerned with the way in which negative attitudes toward well-defined groups in society can be copied over to more generalized problems, such as immigration. He points in particular to the negative aspects of the staggering levels of population mobility that now characterize large portions of the world. Not only are immense peasant populations being pushed by poverty and opportunity into the cities of North America and Western Europe, but rural populations are being drawn into the mega-cities of India, South East Asia, South America, and Africa.

The construction and design of information matters more as we confront these historically unique situations. Understanding the way that the reporting function of mass media intersects group identities, such as the majoritarian versus minoritarian issues in van Dijk's research, he believes will become leading problems for society in the decade ahead.

Not everyone will be convinced by van Dijk's formalist approach. Media practitioners still question the strong textual bias in discourse theory. In the experience of television producers in particular it is the pictures that drive the creation of the narrative, not the words. Ethnomethodologists and ethnographers will continue to insist that the elite presumptions of media message makers still need to be reconciled with the wilful diversity of activities and meanings constructed around these products. However, in trying to retrieve an older argument that media have effects, are persuasive, and do have consequences, van Dijk's sociocognitive model suggests that the relationship between what he calls the discursive structures of new reporting and the localized effect on the models and mental strategies of readers and viewers demands a fuller accounting than either the effects tradition or the semiotic alternative has been able to offer us so far.

William Leiss approaches both the persuasion model and the linguistic model with a similar sensibility. The debates over theoretical frameworks is secondary to Leiss's preoccupations with the consequences of industrial development and the implications for public knowledge and public responses to the risks associated with that development. Leiss argues for a return to the persuasion metaphor as the only appropriate model for a political process that tries to reconcile the different views and stakes of the diverse publics (governmental, industry, special interest, scientific) involved in risk situations.

Leiss suggests that risks, such as those associated with the environment, health, and disease, require concerned groups to take account of the capacity of mass media to bring such issues before the public. Risk communication, echoing Thompson's cautions, also entails a healthy appreciation of how media display can positively and negatively shape public perceptions.

In an equally unique perspective on messages and persuasion, Deirdre Boden has applied ethnomethodological analysis to the study of talk –

seen as a new variety of historical artifact. Turning the ethnomethodological toolkit onto a historical axis is not only an original way of recu-
perating this approach, it also counters the reductiveness of linguistic
approaches that turn talk into text and operate entirely on this data as if
they were indeed text. Boden makes clear that there are a number of
significant distinctions between text and talk – in both face-to-face and
mediated settings of interaction – and that these should not be lost when
trying to analyse conversations from the past.[8]

In her work Boden makes a number of crucial points relevant to all of
us who, in translating actual interaction into text, reproduce something
like conventional narratives. Boden tries to alert us to the distinct forms
and styles of conversation operative in everyday interaction. Her mapping
of conversational examples shows just how much of normal verbal
interaction is lost by a less detailed transcription of just what was is said.
In working with transcripts from the Kennedy Archives, Boden shows
how conversation analysis can be used to reproduce and explore the
dynamics of telephone-mediated talk. This is vividly displayed in her
treatment of a series of conversations between President Kennedy and
Governor Barnett of Mississippi during the events surrounding the efforts
to enrol James Meredith as the first black American student at the University of Mississippi. Boden's approach opens up another way of
accounting for the role of media in public policy; in this case telephones,
perhaps the most neglected of modern media, and at the same time far-
reaching in implications for making sense of backstage or 'behind the
scenes' evidence.

Her work also provides a valuable caution to historians and others who
work with historical data: that the analysis of archival materials may
present many more challenges these days and many more reasons why a
sensitivity to the media–content relationship may be a valuable addition
to the methodological toolkit of social scientists.

All three scholars, van Dijk, Leiss, and Boden, are sensitive to the
dynamics that transpire between different forms of interaction. In particular, they are conscious of the way that texts are received in processes
which are themselves nested reflexively within wider circulations of talk
and action. This is evidenced in van Dijk's insights into the relations
between news reporting conventions and shared cognitive structures. It is
also true of Leiss's description of how knowledge of risk enters public
consciousness in modern societies in fully mediated ways. In Boden's
work, the reflexive relations between text and talk and between mediated
and unmediated interaction is seized upon as a universal condition of
interaction and not just as a restrictive methodological device for dealing
with the ethnographic function of knowledge.

Contingency, Reflexivity, Postmodernity

A quarter of a century ago Umberto Eco first issued his call for a critical response approach to the reader. Eco argued at the time that we needed to overhaul our ideas about what readers do with texts in line with the deflation of authorial intention and the approaches that went with it. Again in the early eighties, Eco returned to the theme, this time stressing the limits of the narrow cognitism that he saw operating behind the message-centred analysis of mass media. Messages, he suggested, are not necessarily *what* we think they are for others, nor are they as neatly *where* we think they are; especially in our multi-layered media environment, where media report continually on each other and where audiences in turn construct personal and popular culture out of threads and fragments of this wider discourse. Critique may caution us usefully about the agendas behind the message content of media, but cannot by itself move us more deeply into confronting the complexity of the multiplication of media and interactional opportunities of the late twentieth century, what Eco called 'the media squared'. Characteristically, Eco recommended a prudent response: 'All the professors of theory of communications, trained by the texts of twenty years ago (this includes me), should be pensioned off.'[9]

Eco's wry directive acts as counterpoint to James Carey's suggestion in the late seventies that both North American persuasion-based approaches and European meaning-based approaches could usefully start trading stocks of knowledge. Eco's point is to ask whether both approaches are not built upon totalistic views of mass media, and on simplistic notions about how media products are received. Certainly, semiotics deepened our sense of what messages are, and ideological critique provided a sense of what the backstage actors and the machinery looked like – but both are playing today to an audience no longer present.

Mark Poster, Ien Ang, and Jim Collins also have some purchase on the critical semiotic project. But each seeks to recontextualize former enclosures of analysis: senders and receivers, encodings and decodings, mass messages and rational autonomous individuals. Each rejects the explicit dualism here and works towards a kind of duality. That is, each author respects that any attempt we make to comprehend the nature and workings of phenomena like senders/receivers or intentions/receptions will necessarily be contingent and reflexive. Perhaps this caution should be applied to any of our historical musings about media in society – certainly it fits the lie of the land in the current postmodern moment.

As part of this wider project, Poster takes a post-structuralist look at the rise of electronic communication: notably at the refiguration of personal, political, and knowledge relations around the computer. Post-structuralists have criticized the concept of human agency in liberal and Marxist models of society; the former for emphasizing human agency constructed around privacy, the latter for emphasizing exclusively the role of class struggle. Post-structuralists use the concept of the subject constructed in and through language to counter these models. Poster in turn places this post-structuralist model of language within the context of communication, in order to provide an account of how shifts in the technologies of communication change the patterns of language, reconfiguring in turn how the subject experiences and relates to the world. New forms of language arise along with changes in technologies. We can think here of the shifts from oral language to printed language to electronic language. Within each technology shift, new forms of language arise mediating in turn new patterns of communication, with consequences for the subject's relation to the world. Poster identifies the ensemble of relations that results from these shifts as 'the mode of information'. He argues that we commonly underestimate the ways in which patterns of language use have altered social life. Just as the development of print culture promoted a critical distance for the reader that was double-edged (providing a centre of reasoning within the individual, but subjecting the individual to the persuasive powers of a plurality of sources), so too the development of electronic language contains similar ambivalences. On the one hand Poster sees that the networking capacity of computers creates a playful expansion of relations in symbolic form, the equivalent of electronic cafés, encouraging interaction with strangers and the adoption of personas; providing as well a basis for collaborative work, multiple authorship, and new sites and forums for the reform of society. On the other hand, this same electronically constituted world constantly accumulates data, making databases and the information flows themselves crucial new social actors. This creates the potential basis for a technology of power, capable of assembling disparate knowledge on individuals into aggregate knowledge sets largely beyond active human monitoring. This new knowledge, Poster believes, is paradoxical for liberal society because the knowledge itself appears to radically reduce the scope and viability of privacy guarantees for society as a whole.

If Poster sees communications providing a valuable historical context for the post-structuralist emphasis on language and the subject, Ien Ang sees an equivalent value for communication studies in the way critical culture studies deal with another master concept of communication and media theory – the question of the audience. Critical culture studies identify a wide agenda these days; but Ang identifies them most closely with a revisionist project within communication studies, notably the reworking of functionalist models by British cultural Marxists, such as Raymond Williams and Stuart Hall, and introduced back into North

American scholarship through the work of James Carey.

In working with audiences, cultural Marxism has stressed such matters as oppositional readings, the role of social structure and the use of narrative devices in news reporting that position newsmakers and audiences. These efforts in turn intersect with new audience research, empirically represented by the case studies of Tamar Liebes and Elihu Katz, the descriptive semiotics of John Fiske, and finally in audience ethnographies and gender studies with which David Morley, Janice Radway, and Ang herself are associated. While much of this work has been focused on television, there are also lively scholarly projects around the production of culture. As these separate activities have developed there has been a broadening out of what Ang calls the 'indeterminacy of meaning', which she sees leading communication models well beyond current enclosure of senders, receivers, and messages.[10]

One enclosure that scholars have been reluctant to abandon in the last decade is the assumption that meanings, however variable for groups and individuals, are somehow contained at more abstract levels of society. Ang doubts that society can stand as the ultimate container of meanings. That argument runs somewhat as follows: we assume that society creates and maintains the limiting conditions of meaning; that society maintains an orderly perimeter inside of which some measure of meaning indeterminacy is possible (semiotics' so-called play of particulars), but nonetheless a process by which meaning is ultimately contained. In such a world, access, privilege, and hierarchy are the crucial variables in the containment process and therefore the conceptual framework that we use to approach its analysis.

Using the findings of new audience research and audience ethnographies, Ang comes close to inverting this framework, arguing in effect that the semiotic dimension habitually exceeds the capacity of society to contain it. The diversity of meanings and behaviours that we can observe in society in fact should be seen as an achievement of social power, transient as she finds that moment to be. The significance of this argument can best be appreciated with respect to the claim that postmodernity represents an increasing social diversity. Ang accepts the semiotic idea of a dispersal of meanings in the late twentieth century, but she rejects the efforts to equate dispersed meaning uncritically with increasing semiotic freedom.

Like the work of audience ethnography generally, Ang's essay is valuable in questioning the lock that previous conceptions of the audience have had upon how we think about mass culture. Jim Collins also calls into question another lock on mass culture thinking: specifically, the usefulness of the model of encoding and decoding, which has linkage to both the informational and the language-specific approaches to the communication process. Collins wants to see the dualism in that model corrected – and probably in all such formulations that assume that encoding and decoding denote two sides of a single process – in which one side produces messages for the other side's response. The alternative for Collins would retain the model but as a duality in which encoding and decoding must be seen as inherent conditions at any point in the communication process. Collins believes this would be more consistent with the reality of mundane popular culture today where, for instance, intertextual referencing (once strongly associated with the production of elite art and expression) can be found in many genres of media expression, from *Wayne's World*, detective fiction, and cartoons to every other (cultural) 'hotel', as he puts it, where resonant individuals meet to exchange texts and talk.

From different approaches and with contrasting preoccupations, Poster, Ang, and Collins collectively show that there are now so many ways in which interaction is mediated and so many opportunities for breaking outside mass media narratives that it no longer makes sense to struggle fitting communications into dualistic formulations, such as production and consumption, senders and receivers, encoders and decoders. The audience has changed, but so has the program; and for that matter their location and the modalities in which we find them, placing in doubt portions of our once secure apparatus for telling ourselves how meaning in society is produced, circulated, and comprehended.

Communication and Public Interests

Master theories and narratives appear to be in some difficulty these days, not just in scholarly circles and in the West, but on the world stage as well. In their essays, Denis McQuail, William Melody, and Majid Tehranian demonstrate how long and widely held assumptions concerning commun-ication processes, information technologies, and the public interest are currently the subject of wide-ranging international discussion and debate.

The end of the Cold War and the proliferation of alternative delivery systems for virtually all forms of media seem to have brought an end to a number of the old suppositions about media's role in society. Yet, when we look historically at the role of media in society – particularly in Western society – we encounter ample evidence of the essential variety of those roles: profitable industry, instrument of state policies, vehicle of social and political critique, anchor of emancipatory possibilities. McQuail reminds us that when the fledgling discipline of communications began to put this variety of organization and experience under the scrutiny of its new 'science', it tried to effect a respectable value-neutral posture and not muddy the waters with value-laden and ideological concerns. Critical responses to mass media, by contrast, have always sought to reconnect enduring social theoretical concerns with empirical and institutional studies of the media. Beyond the academic containments, the question of media's role in society has long been a part of public political discussion. In most communities where successive forms of media have developed there has been some measure of ongoing debate over the structure and performance of the media. Beginning with the press, the widest standoff has been between those who have insisted that media should be retained as instruments of state power and others who have wanted them left alone as free market players. But by far the most prevalent and convincing perspective has grown from the conviction that media should play a central role in the construction and circulation of *the public interest* – and accordingly should be provided certain protections.

McQuail points out that, with each new development of mass media in Western countries, public discussion has pushed governments to intervene with a variety of protectionist instruments. As long as we had a working consensus on what liberal and pluralist society ought to be like, it was possible to draw up guiding assumptions (balanced reporting, freedom of expression from political or religious censorship, provisions for a plurality of voices, and so on) that could be mobilized to such ends. As long as media were either mass or local in scale and as long as publics were either homogeneous or at least believed to be homogeneous through the successful workings of what van Dijk calls elite discourses then theory and practice and politics more or less coincided.

There is, however, a double edge in this construction of the public interest: that while media must aim to perform this role, their performance is open to public judgement on the same basis. The question aside of whether we still live in these kinds of actual or imagined consensual societies, the assumption that there are common properties holding the interests of various nations together within regions has been opened to considerable debate and revision. We experience difficulties these days talking about the cohesion of nations, especially as we factor in matters of culture; and we accept that the media we find in and around our everyday reality no longer subdivide so easily into local or network scales. Whatever the scope of this drift from former circumstances, the costs of not talking about it in this way – and giving the ground over to the free play of rivalries, political, entrepreneurial, but also ethnic and even racial – are considerable. So the question for the nineties comes around to this: if the world is not the same, and if media are not the same, can we (and should we) still try to speak prescriptively about the role of media in terms of the *public interest?*

All three authors are convinced that we can and must continue to think and act in this way, but that we will need to reorient ourselves to account for the new realities of society and media. McQuail believes the key question is: how will the new *normative expectations* and *processes for accountability* be handled in the future? He finds himself forced to rewalk many of the old pathways – the dangers of corporate concentration, how the quality of news should be evaluated, the relationship of the media to state security, the portrayal of sex, crime, and violence – to try and rebuild them for future passage. McQuail suggests that the reworking of the role of media will need to be framed by a new public interest vocabulary gathered around such matters as freedom, diversity, information quality, social order and solidarity, and cultural order.

Telecommunications is also party to these new realities. Emblematic of this is the development of electronic transfer and storage of data, including office e-mail, and to a lesser extent forms of public information exchange. Electronic networks have emerged as new players in the communication and information infrastructure, giving scope and scale to the services that can be built around their expanded capacity for the circulation of information and messages in society. As these technologies and services rapidly mesh with the role of transnational corporations, we find ourselves closer to actualizing an aspect of the information society, where major portions of our financial, material, and human resources are allocated to information and communication activities and where the marketplace that results is less defined and constrained by prior geopolitical conditions.

These changes raise questions of consequence. As electronic networks become increasingly actors *sans frontière*, how will we deal with the risks and uncertainties bound up with these new forms of information-in-circulation? William Melody believes that these new technologies and the services they provide draw us into a dramatic and largely unintended global social experiment in which the West and the world at large must be prepared to rework the social as well as the economic relations between knowledge and information. At the centre of this experiment are large firms with international operations which, by virtue of their size and orientation, must buy into these new technologies and services. In earlier stages of the information society, theory had predicted that the marshalling of more information would have the effect of optimizing risk and increasing the potential gains in a competitive environment. Today, by contrast, large organizations find themselves contending with 'information overload', exercising less control over complexities within their environments.

To make headway in these circumstances, organizations must invest resources and a large measure of faith in the role of information professionals – the scribal monks of the information age, as Melody calls them – who have the ability to *screen* relevant messages from an environment saturated with information and noise. Melody makes an insightful inversion here: where monks in the scribal age were gatekeepers in a constructive way with a scarce resource, information professionals in an electronic age are gatekeepers in a deconstructive way with an abundant resource. Both scribal monk and information professional exercise what Harold Innis referred to as a monopoly on knowledge.

As the information that circulates in and through electronic networks becomes the raw material of the information age, requiring expertise for navigating these new waters, we will also require critical understanding of the social implications as well. The risk for researchers here, as Melody tries to show, is that without a framework for properly contextualizing these developments we may all too easily be drawn into this ethos of experimentation as the limited promoters of benefits.

Governments face something of the same dilemma. The globalization of markets, in its current form, does not offer an open competitive arena, but one in which nations and regional trading blocks apply incentive and protectionist instruments to back their respective players. Large firms require considerable upkeep on the part of their national or regional backers, and at a time when many of these are suffering under the weight of aggregate deficits. Moreover, there are few guarantees today that large firms raised for international success will not at some point cut themselves loose from these same backers to chase better deals in other venues. In time, the commitments that governments make in these matters will have to be reconciled with their constituents. How will publics assess the return on these selective investments? In concrete terms, what will they see as the real gains or losses for the national economy and for the provision of social services and the enhancement of democratic processes? In the end, Melody insists, the excitement with new communication and information technologies and services will have to be squared with wider public interests.

If Melody's work shows us how the workings of business and communication on an international stage reconnect to forms of the public interest still largely located within national political arenas, it also points up an inherent difficulty in our theoretical frameworks for dealing with these issues. Researchers in this area have operated with an implicitly conceptual dichotomy of communication and information. Melody thinks that typically we treat information as a 'stock' or commodity concept; and communication as a 'flow' or transmission concept. In dealing with telecommunications there is a tendency to merge these two concepts, so that today we engage in an almost seamless discourse about communication and information technologies and services, CITS to the knowledgeable insider. Melody reminds us that when we uncritically blend a commodity metaphor for information with a transport one for communication, we can lose sight of the social impacts that these new technologies and services entail.

To open out this dichotomy and to return our thinking about communication technologies to a broader canvas in which they can be seen as agents of social change and social consequence, Melody suggests a critical concept of network. Current scholarship on social networks and social network analysis moves in the right direction, but is too narrowly conceived at present to encompass the range of actors and circumstances at work. He reminds us that the work of Harold Innis had the requisite scope, focused as it was on the centripetal and centrifugal dynamics between centres and margins of empires, trading blocks, and ideological alliances. Melody connects Innis's framework to the work of the late Dallas Smythe,[11] whose case studies of transnational corporations drew attention to the political and economic dynamics these actors introduced behind the scenes. Melody's argument, like Smythe's, never focuses on the technologies themselves but on how we can go about understanding the social gains and losses arising from our organized engagements with these 'creatively destructive' tools. A concept of networks may help to counterbalance our working dichotomy of communication and information, providing some sense of how markets and players 'without geographical limits' have become significant features of the information economy.

Melody's work points to the uncertainties developed nations are experiencing in their application of the new communication and information technologies as an engine of social progress. In a similar vein – but encompassing the concerns of developing and developed worlds alike – Majid Tehranian maps out the history and breakdown of the core ideas associated with global development and social change. What distinguishes Tehranian's work is a command of the wider play of factors that enter into development issues – and the sea change that has overtaken our theories and practices in recent times. Old normative and ideological rivalries – East–West, North–South, Developed–Underdeveloped, Modern–Traditional – fit awkwardly at best with new global realities. The end of the Cold War, the rise of the new economies of South East Asia, the existence of counter-modernization movements in Western as well as other societies have fractured older geopolitical mindsets and accommodations. Certainly, terms like First, Second, and Third worlds no longer have a clear geographics. In the fracturing aftermath of the Cold War we are more sensitive to the increasing levels of differentiation found within national boundaries, the interwoven patterns of centres and peripheries, and the breakdown of previously stable spatial boundaries. To

come to grips with this we will need to think about it in newly complicated ways. Countries as arguably different as India and the United States,
Tehranian points out, can also be considered similar in the way they
contain differential pockets of development and underdevelopment.
Tehranian believes that it is still useful to make general distinctions
between more developed countries (MDCs) and less developed countries
(LDCs), but that we can no longer assume that either of these two groups
will continue to embrace previous notions of modernization uncritically.

Theoretical knowledge has some parallels here as well. The knowledge
base of development for some time now has been part of this differentiation, proliferating into a series of more limited perspectives, such as
political economy, popular culture, rural development, news flow, and
Tehranian's own perspective of peace and security. In the area of communication and development, the linguistic paradigm has also served to
challenge older approaches, notably the organicist (evolutionary) and the
cybernetic (systems). The result is a revised framework, less media-centric
than previously, in which we find an expanded scope for thinking about
messages and their modes of exchange, and a greater appreciation of
alternative organizational forms, such as tradition and religion, for the
production and dissemination of messages.

Among development theorists, Tehranian's work is noteworthy for its
efforts to show how our concepts of society, communication, and development have been radically conditioned by 'paradigm shifts' in twentieth-
century knowledge production. In the current essay he shows how the
major metaphors, or models, of social change in this century – supernatural, mechanical, organic, cybernetic, and linguistic – have affected our
organized practices: how we approach social development, how we see the
social function of communication, and how we connect these in turn to
public rationality.

Where does all this leave the development project in the nineties?
Tehranian suggests that the hypermodernization option – catching up in
order to assimilate into the world capitalist system – is now widely
questioned. Today, less developed nations conscious of the negative economic and social consequences of Western-exported development are
more likely to choose defensive strategies, such as counter-modernization
(ethical rejection of modernization processes) or selective modernization
(economic development under totalitarian wraps). In the West as well
Tehranian sees related challenges to modernity: on the one hand, de-
modernization movements (cultural revolts built around the rejection of
industrial and information society) and aspects of postmodernism; on the
other hand, fundamentalism and the global rise in religiously predicated
politics.

There is a recuperative dimension to Tehranian's work. He notes the confluence of social and political movements and ideas around new engagements with the public process. He labels this confluence as 'communitarian', in reference to its emphasis on participatory politics (we could think here of the collapse of Eastern European communism), but also in consideration of those broadly corrective approaches to liberalist and Marxist models of social change that encourage multiple pathways to development. In the nineties, Tehranian suggests, this communitarian possibility may represent the best alternative to authoritarian models and practices.

As we said at the beginning, the essays in this volume should not be taken as a proxy for either the past or the future of communication scholarship. The essays, however, do gather around what we have tried to describe as contested themes and issues and may therefore indicate something of the trajectory of the conversations and engagements before us.

Notes

1 See Robert Darnton, *The Kiss of Lamourette* (New York: Norton, 1990); Carolyn Marvin, *When Old Technologies Were New* (New York: Oxford University Press, 1988); Janice Radway, *Reading the Romance* (Chapel Hill: University of North Carolina Press, 1983).
2 Anthony Giddens, *The Consequences of Modernity* (Stanford, Calif.: Stanford University Press, 1990), p. 77.
3 John Dewey, *The Public and its Problems* (Chicago: Swallow Press, 1954), ch. 4. See also Hanno Hardt, *Social Theories of the Press* (New York: Routledge, 1979). A special thanks to Phillip Vitone for ideas and discussions on this and related points.
4 Alfred Chandler, *The Visible Hand* (Cambridge, Mass.: Harvard University Press, 1977).
5 Dewey, *The Public and its Problems*. See especially Max Horkheimer, *The Eclipse of Reason* (New York: Continuum, 1947). There is so much work in the contemporary shadow of the Chicago School tradition that it would be easy to mis-read the focus on empirics of the everyday as a neglect of Park and Dewey's early emphasis on the importance of the new technologies of communication. This would be unfair. Newspapers and television become, for instance in the work of Gerald Suttles, custodial organizations in the construction and maintenance of urban communities; newsrooms become sites in which news narratives are played out as a part of interpersonal and organizational set pieces, as in the phenomenologically informed studies of Gaye Tuchman; or Howard Becker's inclusive project on art worlds, such as film-making, with their complexly coordinated teams of specialized skills. Furthermore, there is a growing engagement between interactionists and critical culture studies on the expanding topic of cultural production. See

for instance Gerald Suttles, *The Social Construction of Community* (Chicago: University of Chicago Press, 1978); Gaye Tuchman, *Making News* (New York: Free Press, 1978); Howard Becker, *Artworlds* (Los Angeles: University of California Press, 1982); Howard Becker and Michal McCall (eds), *Symbolic Interactionism and Cultural Studies* (New York: Stone Symposium, 1990); Hanno Hardt, *Social Theories of the Press* (Beverly Hills, Calif./London: Sage, 1979).

6 See the new Introduction to Harold Innis, *The Bias of Communication* (Toronto: University of Toronto Press, 1991), by Paul Heyer and David Crowley.

7 See James Carey, *Communication as Culture* (Boston: Unwin Hyman, 1988).

8 See Deirdre Boden and Don H. Zimmerman, *Talk and Social Structure: Studies in Ethnomethodology and Conversation Analysis* (Cambridge: Polity, 1991).

9 Umberto Eco, *Travels in Hyperreality* (New York: Harcourt Brace Jovanovich, 1983), ch. 4.

10 See Tamar Liebes and Elihu Katz, *The Export of Meaning* (New York: Oxford University Press, 1990); David Morley, *Family Television: Cultural Power and Domestic Leisure* (London: Comedia, 1986); John Fiske, *Television Culture* (New York: Methuen, 1987).

11 Dallas Smythe, *Dependency Road: Communications, Capitalism, Consciousness and Canada* (Norwood NJ: Ablex, 1982).

Part I

Communication and the Mediation of Social Worlds

2

Social Theory and the Media

John B. Thompson

It must be said that, in the literature of social theory, the media have not received the attention they deserve. The various traditions of social theory have tended to neglect the media and have failed to reflect on the fact that the media have become a central and quite pervasive feature of social life. This tendency can be traced back to the classical social thinkers of the nineteenth century, such as Marx, Weber and Durkheim, whose writings were virtually silent on the question of the media and their role in the development of modern societies. Similarly, if one examines the work of contemporary social theorists, it is difficult to find systematic and extended reflection on the media, even though some of these thinkers are directly concerned with the circulation of symbolic forms in the social world. One is left with the impression that, for most social theorists, the media are like the air we breathe: pervasive, taken for granted, yet rarely thought about as such.

On those occasions when social theorists have turned their attention to the media, they have generally done so in order to pursue a problem that was worked out in advance. Most commonly this problem was that of ideology. For many theorists influenced by Marxism, the media seemed important primarily because they could be regarded as a principal mechanism of ideology, that is, as a mechanism by which a society riven by class divisions was sustained and reproduced. This is the kind of critical perspective one can find, for instance, in some of the work of the early Frankfurt School, work which was path-breaking in its attempt to develop a systematic theoretical reflection on the media. It is also the kind of perspective one finds in the writings of Althusser and those influenced by him.

While this critical perspective is not without interest, there are two major problems with it. The first problem is that it takes too much for granted concerning the individuals who receive media products as part of their day-to-day lives. The kind of critical perspective outlined above tends to focus on media products and tries, by analysing the products themselves, to read off their consequences. It tends to assume, for instance, that individuals who consume standardized and stereotypical products will tend to act in an imitative or conformative way, thereby reproducing a social order which, in terms of the distribution of power and resources, may work against them. But assumptions of this kind cannot be allowed to stand without a much more careful inquiry into the ways in which individuals do, in fact, make sense of media products and incorporate them into their lives. Hence, as I shall indicate later, the notion of ideology still has a useful role to play in the analysis of the media, but only in so far as it is linked more closely to the conditions of reception of media products.

The second problem with the kind of critical perspective outlined above is that it offers an overly negative view of the media and their impact. The media are viewed, to all intents and purposes, as a mechanism of social control – a mechanism by which individuals can be manipulated and controlled, and an unequal social order can be reproduced over time. But this perspective on the media is simply too narrow. It tends to obscure a whole variety of ways in which the media are interwoven with the development of modern societies, from the late medieval and early modern periods to the present day. Broadening the theoretical perspective to take account of the constitutive and transformative character of the media does not imply that a social theory of the media must lose its critical edge. But it does imply that a critical theory of the media can be plausibly developed today only if it is fundamentally recast.

There are, in my view, three traditions of thought which are particularly helpful for the purposes of developing a social theory of the media, although these are traditions which are rarely brought together in the literature. One is the tradition, already alluded to, of critical social theory stemming from the work of the Frankfurt School.[1] I am doubtful whether much can be salvaged from the writings of the early Frankfurt theorists, such as Horkheimer, Adorno and Marcuse.[2] But Habermas's early account of the formation and transformation of the public sphere is a work that still merits careful consideration.[3] Habermas did not view the media in an entirely negative light. Rather, he argued that the development of print media in early modern Europe played a crucial role in the transition from absolutist to liberal-democratic regimes, and that the articulation of critical public opinion through the media is a vital feature of modern democracy. There are other respects in which Habermas's argument is unconvincing, but *The Structural Transformation of the Public Sphere* remains, in my view, a vital resource for the development of a constructive social theory of the media.

A second tradition of thought which is of enduring significance is that stemming from the work of the so-called media theorists, especially Innis and McLuhan. Writing in the 1940s and early 1950s, Harold Innis was one of the first to explore systematically the relations between media of communication, on the one hand, and the spatial and temporal organization of power, on the other.[4] His theory of the 'bias' of communication – simply put, that different media favoured different ways of organizing political power, whether centralized or decentralized, extended in time or space, and so on – was no doubt too crude to account for the complexities of the historical relations between communication and power. But Innis emphasized the fact that communication media as such are important for the organization of power, quite apart from the question of the content of the messages they convey. This approach has been taken up and developed by others – by McLuhan, of course, but also by Meyrowitz, who insightfully combines an analysis of electronic media inspired by McLuhan with an account of social interaction and self-presentation derived from Goffman.[5] This tradition is less helpful, however, when it comes to thinking about the social organization of the media industries, about the ways in which the media are interwoven with the unequal distribution of power and resources, and about how individuals make sense of media products and incorporate them into their lives.

The third tradition is that of hermeneutics, that is, the tradition concerned, broadly speaking, with the contextualized interpretation of symbolic forms.[6] Hermeneutics calls our attention to the fact that the reception of media products always involves a contextualized and creative process of interpretation in which individuals draw on the resources available to them in order to make sense of the messages they receive. It also calls our attention to the fact that the activity of 'appropriation' is part of an extended process of self-formation through which individuals develop a sense of themselves and others, of their history, their place in the world and the social groups to which they belong. Hermeneutics firmly rejects the view of recipients as passive consumers, emphasizing instead the creative, constructive, day-to-day activities in which individuals make sense of media products and relate them to other aspects of their lives and social milieux.

In this essay I want to sketch the beginnings of a systematic social theory of the media. I shall be drawing on the contributions of the three traditions referred to above, but I shall not be concerned primarily with critical commentary. My aims are more constructive and thematic. I shall begin by adopting a broad social-historical approach: how should we conceptualize the role played by communication media in the emergence and development of modern societies? I shall then try to show that the deployment of communication media has had a fundamental impact on the nature of social interaction in the modern world: in short, symbolic exchange is increasingly divorced from the kind of face-to-face interaction which takes place in a common locale. In the third section I shall argue, *pace* Habermas, that the transformation of interaction has far-reaching implications for the kind of public life that is possible in the modern world. Finally, drawing on the tradition of hermeneutics, I want to suggest that some of the key questions of cultural analysis today can be formulated in terms of the interface between globalized media products and localized conditions of appropriation.

This kind of theoretical reflection on the media is important, in my view, not only for social theorists, whose traditional neglect of the media has been at their cost, but also for those who work within the field of media and communication studies. For it may help to counter the tendency to treat the study of the media as a specialized disciplinary concern, bearing little connection to the classical problems of social and political analysis. A social theory of the media may help to situate the study of the media where, in my view, it belongs: among a set of disciplines concerned with the emergence, development and structural characteristics of modern societies and their futures.

Communication and the Development of Modern Societies

I want to begin by adopting a broad social-historical approach to the media and their role in the development of modern societies. In my view, neither the work of media historians nor that of sociologists and social theorists has brought out clearly the significance of the media as a constitutive feature of modern societies. While often illuminating and rich in detail, the work of media historians tends to focus on particular media technologies, such as printing, or particular media products, such as books or newspapers. Most media historians give insufficient attention to the ways in which these media technologies are interwoven with other aspects of social organization and social change. The result is that the history of the media has emerged as a distinct and rather specialized discipline, largely divorced from a broader reflection on the developmental features of modern societies.

Sociologists and social theorists have generally ignored the role of the media when they have offered a broader reflection of this kind. No doubt this oversight is due, to a large extent, to the enduring legacy of classical social thought. Authors such as Marx and Weber emphasized the importance of certain economic and political institutions in the transition from the feudal societies of medieval Europe to the new forms of social organization characteristic of the early modern period. But when it came to describing the transformations that took place in what could loosely be called the 'cultural' domain, the work of Marx and Weber was less convincing and clear. Classical social theorists emphasized certain themes – for example, the demystification of traditional world views, the declining significance of religion and the rationalization of action – which remain controversial and difficult to substantiate. Nevertheless, these themes continue to frame the way in which most sociologists and social theorists today think about the cultural transformations associated with the rise of modern societies.

In order to move beyond this traditional and somewhat unsatisfactory approach, I shall sketch a theoretical framework which will enable us to do justice to the role of the media as a constitutive feature of modern societies. It is helpful to begin by considering very briefly the nature of action and its relation to organized forms of power.[7] Social life is made up of individuals who pursue aims and objectives within social contexts that are structured in certain ways. In pursuing their objectives, individuals draw on the resources available to them; these resources are the means which enable them to pursue their aims and interests effectively, and thereby to exercise some degree of power. For the purposes of analysing broad social trends, it is helpful to distinguish several forms of power, each of which is linked to certain kinds of resources. These distinctions are primarily analytical in character: in reality, the different forms of power commonly overlap in complex and shifting ways. But, by distinguishing explicitly between them, we can gain a clearer view of some of the broad social trends which characterized the rise of modern societies. We can also identify some of the key institutions – or 'paradigmatic institutions', as I shall call them – in which certain kinds of resources were accumulated.

I shall distinguish four main forms of power – what I shall call 'economic', 'political', 'coercive' and 'symbolic' power.[8] Here I shall not discuss the first three forms of power in any detail; I shall take for granted some understanding of them and of the paradigmatic institutions in which, with the development of modern societies, these forms of power were concentrated.[9] In brief, economic power was institutionalized in productive enterprises which were organized primarily on a capitalist basis, and which were oriented increasingly towards large-scale industrial production. Political power was institutionalized in the modern state, which generally assumed the form of a nation-state with clearly defined boundaries and a centralized system of administration. Coercive power was institutionalized in military and paramilitary organizations which, with the development of modern societies, were increasingly concentrated in the hands of territorially based nation-states. Of course, all of these processes of institutionalization have been contested in various ways; all have been, and continue to be, associated with distinctive forms of conflict, manifested in some cases locally and in other cases on a global scale.

Let us now focus on the fourth form of power, what I have called 'symbolic power'. In the recent sociological literature on the development of modern societies, this form of power has received a good deal less attention than the other three. By 'symbolic power' I mean the capacity to use symbolic forms – understood generally as any expression which conveys information or symbolic content – to intervene in and influence the course of action or events.[10] In exercising symbolic power, individuals draw on various kinds of resources which I shall loosely describe as the 'means of information and communication'. These include the technical means of fixing and transmitting information or symbolic content, as well as the skills and forms of knowledge employed in producing, transmitting and receiving it. As with other forms of power, the resources employed in exercising symbolic power can be accumulated in institutions which acquire some degree of autonomy and stability over time.

In what ways did the social organization of symbolic power change with the advent of modern societies in late medieval and early modern Europe? There were two changes which have been well discussed in the sociological and historical literature. One concerns the shifting role of religious institutions. In medieval Europe, the Roman Catholic Church was a central institution of symbolic power, holding a virtual monopoly on the production and diffusion of religious symbols and sustaining close relations with political elites. But, with the development of Protestantism in the sixteenth century, the virtual monopoly of the Catholic Church was shattered. Religious authority became increasingly fragmented among a plurality of sects advocating distinctive lifestyles and claiming alternative paths of access to scriptural truth. Moreover, as European states grew in strength and developed specialized systems of administration, the Church became increasingly peripheral to the exercise of political power.

The fragmentation of religious authority and its declining hold on political power was paralleled by a second shift: the gradual expansion of systems of knowledge and learning that were essentially secular in character. The sixteenth century witnessed a significant development of sciences such as astronomy, botany and medicine. These emerging disciplines stimulated the formation of learned societies throughout Europe and found their way onto the curricula of the more liberal universities. As scientific knowledge was gradually freed from the hold of religious tradition, so too the system of education was prised apart from the Church. Schools and universities became increasingly oriented towards the transmission of a range of skills and forms of knowledge, of which scriptural knowledge was merely a part (and, in most cases, an increasingly diminishing one).

There was, however, a third important shift in the social organization of symbolic power which began in the middle of the fifteenth century, and which to some extent underpinned the two changes just noted: this was the shift from script to print and the subsequent development of the media industries. The technical basis for this shift is well known. By 1450 Gutenberg had developed the techniques of printing and the replica-casting of metal letters far enough to exploit them commercially, and during the second half of the fifteenth century these techniques spread rapidly throughout Europe. This could be described as the beginning of the era of mass communication, even if the terms 'mass' and 'communication' are both somewhat misleading in this context.[11] It was the beginning of an era when symbolic forms could be reproduced and diffused throughout the social world on a scale that was altogether different from that which had existed previously.

The early printing presses were, for the most part, commercial enterprises organized along capitalist lines. Their success and continued survival generally depended on their capacity to reproduce and sell printed materials in a profitable way – that is, it depended on their capacity effectively to commodify symbolic forms. The development of the early presses was thus part and parcel of the growth of a capitalist economy in late medieval and early modern Europe. At the same time, however, these presses became new bases of symbolic power which stood in ambivalent relations with the political institutions of the emerging nation-states, on the one hand, and with those religious institutions which claimed a certain authority with regard to the exercise of symbolic power, on the other. The rise of the printing industry represented the emergence of new centres and networks of symbolic power which were generally outside the direct control of the Church and the state, but which the Church and state sought to use to their advantage and, from time to time, to suppress.

In the early years of printing, the Church actively supported the development of new methods of textual reproduction.[12] The clergy commissioned printers to supply liturgical and theological works, and many monasteries invited printers into their premises. But the Church could not control the activities of printers and booksellers with the same degree of circumspection as it had exercised over the activities of scribes and copyists in the age of manuscripts. There were simply too many printing firms and outlets, capable of producing and distributing texts on too great a scale, for the Church to be able to exercise effective control.

Attempts by religious and political authorities to suppress printed materials were of limited success. Printers found many ways to evade the
censors, and materials banned in one city or region were often printed in
another and smuggled in by merchants and pedlars. Censorship stimulated a vigorous trade in contraband books and pamphlets.

I have been arguing that the development of the printing industry in
late medieval and early modern Europe should be regarded as the
beginning of a fundamental transformation in the social organization of
symbolic power, a transformation which was interwoven in complex ways
with the expansion of a capitalist economy and with the concentration of
political and coercive power in the hands of modern nation-states. The
presses, and the trade in commodified symbolic forms to which they gave
rise, created new networks of information and communication which
could not be fully controlled by the established authorities of Church and
state. But how should we understand the social and cultural impact of this
transformation? What implications did it have for the nature of social
relations and for the individuals who received printed materials as part of
their day-to-day lives? The issues raised by these questions are, of course,
extremely complex, and I shall not try to address them in detail.[13] But by
focusing on one key feature of certain media of communication like print,
we can highlight some of the most important and far-reaching implications of the transformation whose beginnings we have briefly described.

The Transformation of Interaction

In order to assess the impact of new media of communication, it is
important to emphasize that the deployment of communication media
does not consist simply in the establishment of new networks for the
transmission of information between individuals whose basic social relationships remain intact; on the contrary, the deployment of communication media establishes new forms of interaction and new kinds of social
relationships between individuals. Again, it is helpful to view this in a
broad historical perspective. For most of human history, most forms of
social interaction have been face-to-face. Individuals have interacted with
one another primarily by coming together and exchanging symbolic
forms, or engaging in other kinds of action, within a shared physical
locale. Traditions were primarily oral in character and depended for their
existence on a continuous process of renewal, through storytelling and
related activities, in contexts of face-to-face interaction.

With the development of technical media of communication, however, the activities of social interaction and symbolic exchange were
increasingly severed from the sharing of a common locale. Hence, com-

munication media gave rise to new forms of interaction in which information and symbolic content could be exchanged between individuals who did not share the same spatio-temporal setting. Of course, this severing of social interaction from physical locale was not restricted to those forms of mediated communication which became increasingly common from the mid-fifteenth century on: earlier forms of mediated communication, such as those involved in letter-writing or manuscript production, involved a similar separation. But, with the development of media institutions based on print, and subsequently on electronic forms of codification and transmission, it became possible for more and more individuals to acquire information and symbolic content through mediated forms of interaction. Print and other media become increasingly important as a means of informing individuals about events that took place in distant locales and as a way of creating, reproducing and transmitting the symbolic content of tradition.

In order to develop this argument further, I want to distinguish between three types of interaction – what I shall call 'face-to-face interaction', 'mediated interaction' and 'mediated quasi-interaction'. Face-to-face interaction takes place in a context of co-presence; the participants in the interaction are immediately present to one another and share a common spatio-temporal reference system. Face-to-face interaction is also dialogical in character, in the sense that it generally involves a two-way flow of information and communication, so that producers are also recipients and vice versa. Furthermore, the participants in face-to-face interaction commonly employ a multiplicity of symbolic cues – gestures and facial expressions as well as words – in order to convey messages and to interpret the messages conveyed by others.

Face-to-face interaction can be contrasted with 'mediated interaction', by which I mean forms of interaction such as letter-writing, telephone conversations and so on. Mediated interaction involves the use of a technical medium (paper, electrical wires, electromagnetic waves, etc.) which enables information or symbolic content to be transmitted to individuals who are remote in space, in time or in both. Mediated interaction is stretched across space and time, and it thereby acquires a range of distinctive characteristics. For instance, the participants in mediated interaction are generally located in contexts which are spatially and/or temporally distinct. Hence they do not share the same spatio-temporal reference systems and cannot assume that others will understand the deictic expressions they use ('here', 'now', 'this', 'that', etc.). Participants must therefore always consider how much contextual information should be included in the exchange – for example, by putting the place and date at the top of a letter, or by identifying oneself at the beginning of a telephone conversation. Mediated interaction also generally involves a

narrowing of the range of symbolic cues which are available to participants. Communication by means of letters, for example, deprives the
recipients of a range of cues associated with physical co-presence (gestures, facial expressions, etc.), while other symbolic cues (those linked to
writing) are accentuated.

Finally, let us consider the form of interaction that I have described as
'mediated quasi-interaction'. I use this term to refer to the kinds of social
relations established by the media of mass communication (books,
newspapers, radio, television, etc.).[14] Like mediated interaction, this third
form of interaction involves the extended availability of information or
symbolic content in time and space. In many cases it also involves a
certain narrowing of the range of symbolic cues, by comparison with face-
to-face interaction. However, there are two key respects in which mediated quasi-interaction differs from both face-to-face interaction and
mediated interaction. In the first place, the participants in face-to-face
interaction and mediated interaction are oriented towards specific others,
for whom they produce utterances, expressions, etc.; but in the case of
mediated quasi-interaction, symbolic forms are produced for an indefinite
range of potential recipients. Second, whereas face-to-face interaction and
mediated interaction are dialogical, mediated quasi-interaction is monological in character, in the sense that the flow of communication is predominantly one-way. The reader of a book, for instance, is primarily the
recipient of a symbolic form whose producer does not require (and
generally does not receive) a direct and immediate response.

Since mediated quasi-interaction is monological in character and
involves the production of symbolic forms for an indefinite range of
potential recipients, it is best regarded as a kind of quasi-interaction. It
does not have the degree of reciprocity and interpersonal specificity of
other forms of interaction, whether mediated or face-to-face. But mediated
quasi-interaction is, none the less, a form of interaction. It creates a
certain kind of social situation in which individuals are linked together in
a process of communication and symbolic exchange. It is a structured
situation in which some individuals are engaged primarily in producing
symbolic forms for others who are not physically present, while others are
involved primarily in receiving symbolic forms produced by others to
whom they cannot respond, but with whom they can form bonds of
friendship, affection or loyalty.

The distinction between these three types of interaction forms the basis
of an analytical framework which can be used to examine the interactional
features of the social relationships established by the media.[15] Used historically, it can also help us to assess the significance of the development
of new media of communication from the fifteenth century on. Prior to
the early modern period in Europe, and until quite recently in some other

parts of the world, the exchange of information and symbolic content was, for most people, a process that took place exclusively within the context of face-to-face situations. Forms of mediated interaction and quasi-interaction did exist, but they were restricted to a relatively small sector of the population. To participate in mediated interaction or quasi-interaction required special skills – for example, the capacity to write or read – which were largely the preserve of political, commercial or ecclesiastical elites. But, with the rise of the printing industry in fifteenth- and sixteenth-century Europe and its subsequent development in other parts of the world, and with the emergence of various types of electronic media in the nineteenth and twentieth centuries, face-to-face interaction has been increasingly supplemented by forms of mediated interaction and quasi-interaction. To an ever-increasing extent, the exchange of information and symbolic content in the social world takes place in contexts of mediated interaction or quasi-interaction, rather than in contexts of face-to-face interaction between individuals who share a common locale.

The historical rise of mediated interaction and quasi-interaction has not necessarily been at the expense of face-to-face interaction. Indeed, in some cases, the diffusion of media products has provided a stimulus for interaction in face-to-face situations in the way, for instance, that books in early modern Europe were commonly read aloud to individuals who had gathered together to hear the written word,[16] or in the way that television programmes today can serve as a focal point for discussions among family or friends.[17] But the growing importance of mediated interaction and quasi-interaction does mean that social life in the modern world is increasingly made up of forms of interaction which are not face-to-face in character. It has, we could say, altered the 'interaction mix' of social life. Individuals are increasingly likely to acquire information and symbolic content from sources other than the persons with whom they interact directly in their day-to-day lives. The creation and renewal of traditions are processes that become increasingly bound up with mediated symbolic exchange. The very nature of what is public and private, and the ways in which individuals are able to relate to the public domain, are transformed by the extended availability of symbolic forms in time and space. Let us examine this last point in more detail.

The Reconstitution of the Public Sphere

The distinction between the public and the private has a long history in Western social and political thought.[18] It can be traced back to the philosophical debates of Classical Greece and to the early development of Roman Law. However, in the late medieval and early modern periods, the public–private distinction began to acquire new meanings, partly in relation to the institutional transformations that were taking place at that time. If we focus on the meanings that this dichotomy has come to assume in Western societies since the late medieval period, we can distinguish two senses which are of particular importance.

The first sense of the dichotomy has to do with the relation between, on the one hand, the domain of institutionalized political power which was increasingly vested in the hands of a sovereign state and, on the other hand, the domains of economic activity and personal relations which fell outside direct political control. Thus, from the mid-sixteenth century on, 'public' came increasingly to mean activity or authority that was related to or derived from the state, while 'private' referred to those activities or spheres of life that were excluded or separated from it.

We can, however, distinguish a second sense of the public–private dichotomy as it has emerged in Western social and political discourse. According to this sense, 'public' means 'open' or 'available to the public'.[19] What is public, in this sense, is what is visible or observable, what is performed in front of spectators, what is open for all or many to see or hear or hear about. What is private, by contrast, is what is hidden from view, what is said or done in privacy or secrecy or among a restricted circle of people. In this sense, the public–private dichotomy has to do with publicness versus privacy, with openness versus secrecy, with visibility versus invisibility. A public act is a visible act, an act performed openly so that anyone can see; a private act is invisible, an act performed secretly and behind closed doors.

The second sense of the dichotomy does not coincide with the first, but historically there is a complex and shifting relation between forms of government and the visibility or invisibility of power. In the traditional monarchical states of medieval and early modern Europe, the affairs of state were conducted in the relatively closed circles of the court, in ways that were largely invisible to most of the subject population. When state officials appeared before their subjects, they generally did so in order to affirm their power publicly (visibly), not to render public (visible) the grounds on which their decisions and policies were based. In theoretical writings on the *raison d'Etat*, the privacy of decision-making processes was commonly justified by recourse to the *arcana imperii* – that is, the doctrine of state secrecy, which held that the power of the prince is more effective and true to its aim if it is hidden from the gaze of the people and, like divine will, invisible.[20] The invisibility of power was assured institutionally by the fact that decision-making processes took place in a closed space, the secret cabinet, and by the fact that the decisions themselves were only occasionally and selectively made public.

With the development of the modern constitutional state, the invisibility of power was limited in certain ways. The secret cabinet was replaced or supplemented by a range of institutions that were more open and accountable; important political decisions and matters of policy were subjected to debate within parliamentary bodies; and the doctrine of *arcana imperii* was transformed into the modern principle of official secrecy and restricted in its application to those issues regarded as vital to the security and stability of the state. In these and other ways, power was rendered more visible and decision-making processes became more public, although this broad trend was neither uniform nor complete. Those in positions of power found new ways of maintaining invisibility and new grounds for doing so, and the ways in which political power is exercised in modern societies remains in many respects shrouded in secrecy.

Against the backcloth of these distinctions, I now want to consider the ways in which the development of new media of communication – beginning with print, but including the more recent electronic media such as television – has reconstituted the boundaries between public and private life. The basis of this reconstitution is that, with the development of mass communication, the publicness (or visibility) of actions or events is no longer linked to the sharing of a common locale, and hence actions or events can acquire a publicness which is independent of their capacity to be seen or heard directly by a plurality of co-present individuals. The development of mass communication has thus created new forms of mediated publicness which simply did not exist before, and which differ in fundamental respects from the traditional publicness of co-presence.

How should we understand the implications of these new forms of mediated publicness for the ways in which political power is exercised in modern societies? I want to outline the beginnings of an answer by emphasizing that, with regard to the exercise of political power, mediated publicness is a double-edged sword. On the one hand, in the new political arena produced and sustained by the media of mass communication, political leaders are able to appear before their subjects in a way and on a scale that never existed previously. The relationship between political leaders and their subjects increasingly becomes a form of mediated quasi-interaction through which bonds of loyalty and affection (as well as feelings of repugnance) can be formed. Skilful politicians exploit this circumstance to their advantage. They seek to create and sustain a basis of support for their power and policies by controlling their self-presentation and managing their visibility within the mediated arena of modern politics. The use of communication media as a means of managing visibility is not unique to the twentieth century: monarchs in early modern Europe, like Louis XIV or Philip IV of Spain, were well versed in the arts of image-making.[21] But in the late twentieth century, the capacity for using communication media in this way has increased enormously, partly as a result of the massive expansion in the size and geographical spread of audiences capable of receiving mediated messages, and partly because of the development of television, which has accentuated the importance of visibility in the narrow sense of vision (that is, capable of being seen with the eyes) while detaching this visibility from the sharing of a common locale.

While the development of mass communication has created new opportunities for the management of visibility, it has also created unprecedented risks for political leaders. Prior to the advent of mass communication, leaders could generally restrict the activity of managing visibility to the relatively closed circles of the assembly or the court. Visibility required co-presence: one could be visible only to those who shared the same spatio-temporal locale. On the relatively rare occasions when rulers appeared before wider audiences, they generally did so in ways that were carefully staged. The pomp and ceremony of such occasions, the extravagance of the apparel and surroundings, the aloofness of a figure who could be seen but neither heard nor touched nor confronted as an equal: all enabled the ruler to maintain some distance from his subjects while enabling them temporarily to see and celebrate his existence in a context of co-presence. But, for most individuals in ancient or medieval societies, the most powerful rulers were rarely if ever seen. Apart from royal progresses, which were transient and relatively infrequent, most public appearances of the monarch took place in the political centre – in the halls and courts of the palace or in the street and squares of the capital city – and were unavailable to the vast majority of individuals who lived in rural or peripheral regions.[22]

Today it is no longer possible to circumscribe the management of visibility in this way. The mediated arena of modern politics is open and accessible in a way that traditional assemblies and courts were not. Moreover, given the nature of mass communication, the messages transmitted by the media may be received and understood in ways that cannot be directly monitored and controlled by communicators. Hence the visibility created by mass communication may become the source of a new and distinctive kind of fragility: however much political leaders may seek to manage their visibility, the very phenomenon of visibility may slip out of their control and undermine whatever support they may have or seek. The inability completely to control the phenomenon of visibility is a constant source of trouble for political leaders. They must be on their guard continuously and employ a high degree of reflexivity to monitor their actions and utterances, since an indiscreet act or ill-judged remark can, if recorded and relayed to millions of viewers, have disastrous consequences. Gaffes and outbursts, performances that backfire and scandals are some of the ways in which the limits of control are most clearly and strikingly manifested.

More generally, the exercise of political power today takes place in an arena which is increasingly open to view. However hard political leaders may try to control or restrict the visibility of themselves or of particular actions or events, they know they run the risk that they, or the actions or events for which they are responsible, may be seen in ways they did not intend, and hence they must reckon with the permanent possibility of uncontrolled visibility. Actions such as military intervention in Central America or the Gulf, or the suppression of demonstrations in China, South Africa or the West Bank, are actions which take place in a new kind of global arena: they are visible, observable, capable of being witnessed simultaneously and repeatedly by millions of individuals around the world. The exercise of political power is thus subjected to what I shall call 'global scrutiny': that is, it takes place within a global field of vision which is created and structured by the media industries, and which may expose political leaders or regimes to unprecedented risks, as is illustrated by the international condemnation that followed the suppression of the pro-democracy movement in China, the invasion of Kuwait and so on.

In developing this argument about the creation of a new kind of publicness in the modern world, I am putting forward a view which differs quite sharply from the kinds of interpretation which prevail in some of the literature of social and political theory. It differs, for instance, from the interpretation offered by Habermas in his early work on the transformation of the public sphere, and by theorists like Alvin Gouldner and Richard Sennett who were influenced by Habermas.[23] Very briefly, Habermas's argument is that the development of the periodical press – and especially the kind of political journalism which flourished in eighteenth-century England – stimulated the emergence of a distinctive kind of public sphere in early modern Europe, a sphere in which individuals came together in public places, like salons and coffee houses, to discuss the issues of the day. This emerging public sphere provided a basis of potential opposition to, and criticism of, the exercise of state power; it was, in this respect, a key factor in the shaping of modern democratic politics. But with the subsequent development of the media industries, argues Habermas, this emerging public sphere was largely destroyed. The salons and coffee-houses declined in significance, and the media industries became large-scale commercial organizations that were primarily concerned with manipulating consumers rather than stimulating rational debate among citizens.[24]

Habermas's account of the development of the public sphere is of great interest, but his argument concerning its subsequent transformation and decline is, in my view, flawed. The main weakness of the argument is that it fails to take account of the fact that the development of mass communication has transformed the very nature of publicness in the modern world. Habermas's argument is based on a notion of publicness which is essentially spatial and dialogical in character: it is the traditional publicness of co-presence, in which publicness is linked to the conduct of dialogue in a shared locale. This notion is derived from the assemblies of the classical Greek city-states, and it could still be applied with some degree of plausibility to the salons and coffee-houses of early modern Europe. But in adhering to this traditional notion of publicness, Habermas has deprived himself of the means of understanding the new kind of publicness created by mass communication. The media have created a new kind of public sphere which is de-spatialized and non-dialogical in character: it is divorced from the idea of dialogical conversation in a shared locale and is potentially global in scope.

The account I have outlined here also gives us a critical perspective on the work of another influential social theorist – Michel Foucault. Although Foucault did not say anything of interest about the media, he did develop, in *Discipline and Punish*, a distinctive argument about the organization of power in modern societies and about the changing relations between power and visibility.[25] The argument, to put it briefly, is this. The societies of Antiquity and of the Middle Ages were societies of spectacle: the exercise of power was linked to the public manifestation of the strength and superiority of the sovereign. It was a regime of power in which a few were made visible to many, and in which the visibility of the few was used as a means of exercising power over the many – in the way, for instance, that a public execution in the market square became a spectacle in which a sovereign power took its revenge, reaffirming the glory of the king through the destruction of a rebellious subject. But from the sixteenth century on, the spectacular manifestation of power gave way to forms of discipline and surveillance which increasingly infiltrated different spheres of life. The army, the school, the prison, the hospital: these and other institutions increasingly employed the more subtle mechanisms of power that were exemplified so strikingly in Bentham's Panopticon. The spread of these mechanisms gradually gave rise to a kind of 'disciplinary society' in which the visibility of the few by the many has been replaced by the visibility of the many by the few, and in which the spectacular display of sovereign power has been replaced by the normalizing power of multiple gazes.

Foucault's account of the development of new mechanisms of power, especially in the context of specialized institutions like the prison, is helpful and insightful. But his suggestion that the Panopticon provides a generalizable model for the exercise of power in modern societies is much less convincing. Of course, there are some organizations in modern societies which use methods of surveillance: the police, the military and the secret services, above all, but also some other agencies of the state and private organizations which are concerned with the routine gathering of information. It would be quite misleading, however, to focus our attention exclusively on these organizations and to neglect the role and impact of new media of communication. If Foucault had considered the media more carefully, he might have seen that they establish a relation between power and visibility which is quite different from that implicit in the model of the Panopticon. For the media provide a means by which many people can gather information about a few, and a few can appear before many – though now in ways that are very different from the Ancient or medieval spectacle, since they no longer involve the sharing of a common locale.

The Media and Everyday Life

So far I have argued that the development of the media has detached the transmission of information and symbolic content from the sharing of a common locale, and has thereby created a new kind of publicness in the modern world. In this final section I want to emphasize the importance of relating the analysis of the media to the concrete, day-to-day activities through which individuals appropriate media products and incorporate them into their lives. But let me begin by asking another historical question: how has the development of the media affected individuals' modes of experiencing the world and their ways of relating to themselves and others?

Prior to the advent of mass communication, most people's sense of the past and of the world beyond their immediate milieu was shaped primarily by the symbolic content exchanged in face-to-face interaction. For most people, the sense of the past, of the world beyond their locales and of the socially delimited communities to which they belonged, were constituted primarily through oral traditions that were produced and reproduced in the social contexts of everyday life. With the development of the media, however, individuals were able to experience events, observe others and, in general, learn about worlds – both real and imaginary – that extended well beyond the sphere of their day-to-day encounters. The spatial and temporal horizons of understanding were greatly expanded, since it was no longer necessary for individuals to be physically present at the places where, and the times when, the observed actions or events occurred.

The expansion of spatial and temporal horizons enabled individuals to take some distance from the conditions of their day-to-day lives and from the symbolic content of oral traditions. Individuals who were able to appropriate media products – that is, who had the economic and symbolic resources to do so – could open themselves to new kinds of information, images and ideas and could incorporate these reflexively into their own projects of self-formation. The ways in which individuals understood themselves and others, acquired a sense of who they were and their place in the world, learned about other ways of life and how these compared with their own – these and other aspects of self-formation were increasingly mediated by symbolic materials which stemmed from sources other than the traditions handed down through face-to-face interaction.

The broad shift in the symbolic mediation of self-formation and everyday life has been greatly accentuated in recent decades by the advent of television. The relative accessibility of televisual information, the vividness of the images and the speed of transmission have all served to extend and deepen a process in which individual self-understanding is mediated by symbolic materials stemming from distant sources. The very fact that individuals in London or New York or Cairo are able today, at the flick of a switch, to witness events taking place in the streets of Berlin or Beijing or Los Angeles (and vice versa) attests to the fact that they are part of a structured process of symbolic exchange which has become virtually instantaneous and global in scope.

While the exchange of information and symbolic content has become increasingly global in scope, the appropriation of this material by recipients is a process that always takes place in particular social-historical circumstances. The process of appropriation is much more complicated than most traditional social theories of the media assumed. It is an active, creative and selective process in which individuals draw on the resources available to them in order to receive and make sense of the symbolic material transmitted by the media. Through this process, media products, which have been disconnected from their contexts of production, are re-embedded in particular locales and adapted to the material and cultural conditions of reception. The symbolic content of media products may be integrated into the conversational exchanges of face-to-face interaction and may become part of the self-understanding of recipients and their interlocutors.

Given the growing importance of the media in the modern world, I want to conclude by suggesting that many of the key questions of culture and cultural analysis today can be defined in terms of the interface between the information and symbolic content produced and transmitted by the media industries, on the one hand, and the routine activities of everyday life into which media products are incorporated by recipients, on the other. Moreover, as media products circulate on an ever-greater scale, the cultural domain increasingly becomes the site of a continuously shifting boundary between globalized media products and localized conditions of appropriation. This is a boundary which can become a source of tension and conflict as well as a source of information, as the symbolic content of media products may clash with the beliefs and expectations embedded in the routine practices of everyday life. This kind of cultural clash is dramatically illustrated by the Rushdie affair, but the tensions and conflicts stemming from the contextualized appropriation of media products are more common and generally less intense than this example would suggest. Individuals are constantly involved in adapting the contents of media products to the conditions of their own lives and in reconciling, or simply holding in an uneasy balance, messages which conflict with one another and with the values, practices and circumstances of their lives. And the conflicts and tensions stemming from contextualized appropriation may be manifested as self-conflict, since the process of self-formation is increasingly informed by the symbolic content of media products.

By focusing attention on the shifting boundaries between globalized media products and localized conditions of appropriation, and by examining in detail, by means of hermeneutically informed ethnographic inquiry, the ways in which individuals situated in different circumstances make sense of media products and integrate them into their lives,[26] we can avoid the shortcomings of many of the traditional social-theoretical approaches to the media. For many of these approaches – here I include not only the critical theory of Horkheimer, Adorno, and the early Habermas, but also that large body of critical literature which has descended loosely from structuralism and semiotics – tended to ignore the problem of appropriation and to neglect the ways in which individuals actively make sense of the products they receive. These approaches were too quick to infer the consequences of media messages from an analysis of the structure and content of the messages themselves, without reference to the ways in which these messages were taken up, used and understood by the individuals who received them. Hence, these approaches generally presupposed a conception of the relation between media products and recipients which was too crude and deterministic, and which obscured the complex character of appropriation.

To argue that a social theory of the media can avoid the shortcomings of traditional approaches by considering more carefully the process of appropriation is not to suggest, however, that a social theory of the media should abandon the concepts and problems with which social theorists have traditionally been concerned. On the contrary, it is both possible and desirable to reformulate some of these concepts within the framework of a theory which does justice to the distinctive character of the media and their centrality in the modern world.[27] Such a reformulation is desirable not only for those working within social theory, who have much to gain from a sustained reflection on the media, but also for those working within media and communication studies. For the study of the media does not do justice to the importance of its subject matter if it is dissociated from a range of problems which have been and remain central to social and political thought – problems such as the nature and organization of power and ideology, the changing character of public life, the operation of democratic institutions, the formation of the self and the globalizing character of modern social life.[28] Today there is a need for the deepening of a dialogue between disciplines which have too often stood apart, but whose overlapping concerns are everywhere apparent in the very world they seek to understand.

Notes

1 See esp. Max Horkheimer and Theodor W. Adorno, 'The Culture Industry: Enlightenment as Mass Deception', in their *Dialectic of Enlightenment*, trans. John Cumming (New York: Seabury Press, 1972); and Theodor W. Adorno, *The Culture Industry: Selected Essays on Mass Culture*, ed. J. M. Bernstein (London: Routledge, 1991).

2 For critical appraisals of the contribution of the early critical theorists to media and cultural studies, see Douglas Kellner, *Critical Theory, Marxism and Modernity* (Cambridge: Polity Press, 1989), chs. 5 and 6; and John B. Thompson, *Ideology and Modern Culture: Critical Social Theory in the Era of Mass Communication* (Cambridge: Polity Press, 1990), ch. 2.

3 See Jürgen Habermas, *The Structural Transformation of the Public Sphere: An Inquiry into a Category of Bourgeois Society*, trans. Thomas Burger with Frederick Lawrence (Cambridge: Polity Press, 1989).

4 See Harold A. Innis, *Empire and Communication* (Oxford: Oxford University Press, 1950), and *The Bias of Communication* (Toronto: University of Toronto Press, 1951). For a sympathetic assessment of Innis's contribution, see James W. Carey, 'Space, Time and Communications: A Tribute to Harold Innis', in his *Communication as Culture: Essays on Media and Society* (Boston, Mass.: Unwin Hyman, 1989), pp. 142–72.

5 Joshua Meyrowitz, *No Sense of Place: The Impact of Electronic Media on Social Behavior* (New York: Oxford University Press, 1985).

6 See esp. Hans-Georg Gadamer, *Truth and Method* (London: Sheed & Ward, 1975) and Paul Ricoeur, *Hermeneutics and the Human Sciences: Essays on Language, Action and Interpretation*, ed. and trans. John B. Thompson (Cambridge: Cambridge University Press, 1981). On the relevance of this tradition to the study of the media, see Peter Dahlgren, 'The modes of reception: for a hermeneutic of TV news', in Phillip Drummond and Richard Patterson (eds), *Television in Transition* (London: British Film Institute, 1985), pp. 235–49; and Thompson, *Ideology and Modern Culture*, ch. 6.

7 For a more detailed discussion, see Thompson, *Ideology and Modern Culture*, ch. 3. Here I am drawing loosely on a large body of literature in social theory which is concerned with the nature of action and its relation to the

structural features of social organization, and which has sought – rightly, in my view – to move beyond the traditional opposition between 'action' and 'structure', or 'subjective' and 'objective' orientations. See e.g. Anthony Giddens, *The Constitution of Society: Outline of the Theory of Structuration* (Cambridge: Polity Press, 1984); and Pierre Bourdieu, *The Logic of Practice*, trans. Richard Nice (Cambridge: Polity Press, 1990).

8   This schema is similar to Michael Mann's account of what he calls the four sources of social power; see Michael Mann, *The Sources of Social Power*, vol. 1: *A History of Power from the Beginning to AD 1760* (Cambridge: Cambridge University Press, 1986), ch. 1. However, I think that the notion of symbolic power is more appropriate in this context than Mann's concept of 'ideological power'; the concept of ideology, in my view, is best used in a more restricted sense. A more substantial problem with Mann's account is that, in analysing the development of European societies in the late medieval and early modern periods, he gives very little attention to the rise and impact of printing, which is only briefly discussed (see pp. 442–3).

9   These institutions have received some attention in the recent literature of historical sociology. In addition to Mann's *The Sources of Social Power*, see Immanuel Wallerstein, *The Modern World-System*, I: *Capitalist Agriculture and the Origins of the European World-Economy in the Sixteenth Century* (New York: Academic Press, 1974) and *The Modern World-System*, II: *Mercantilism and the Consolidation of the European World-Economy, 1600–1750* (New York: Academic Press, 1980); Charles Tilly, *Coercion, Capital and European States, AD 990–1990* (Oxford: Basil Blackwell, 1990); and Anthony Giddens, *The Nation-State and Violence: Volume Two of A Contemporary Critique of Historical Materialism* (Cambridge: Polity Press, 1985).

10 The term 'symbolic power' is borrowed from Bourdieu; see esp. his *Language and Symbolic Power*, ed. John B. Thompson, trans. Gino Raymond and Matthew Adamson (Cambridge: Polity Press, 1991). However, in using this term I do not wish to imply, as Bourdieu does, that the exercise of symbolic power necessarily presupposes a form of 'misrecognition' (*méconnaissance*) on the part of those who are subjected to it.

11 I have discussed these terms elsewhere; see *Ideology and Modern Culture*, pp. 218ff.

12 See Elizabeth L. Eisenstein, *The Printing Press as an Agent of Change: Communications and Cultural Transformations in Early-Modern Europe*, vols I and II (Cambridge: Cambridge University Press, 1979), pp. 15–16 and ch. 4; and Lucien Febvre and Henri-Jean Martin, *The Coming of the Book: The Impact of Printing 1450–1800*, trans. David Gerard (London: Verso, 1976), ch. 8.

13 In a suggestive book Benedict Anderson argues that the convergence of capitalism and the technology of print in early modern Europe led to the erosion of the sacred community of Christendom and to the emergence of a plurality of 'imagined communities' which formed the bases for the subsequent development of national consciousness; see Benedict Anderson, *Imagined Communities: Reflections on the Origin and Spread of Nationalism* (London: Verso, 1983). However, Anderson's account of the alleged link

48   *John B. Thompson*

between the rise of the printing industry and the development of national consciousness is rather vague and unconvincing. There is a considerable gulf – historical as well as conceptual – between the emergence of a plurality of reading publics in sixteenth-century Europe, on the one hand, and the emergence of the various forms of national identity and nationalism characteristic of the nineteenth and twentieth centuries, on the other. If the early reading public was the embryo of the nationally imagined community, why did it take nearly three centuries for this embryo to mature?

14   This term is similar to the expression used by Horton and Wohl: in an early and insightful article, they suggested that mass communication gives rise to a new type of social relationship which they call 'para-social interaction'. See Donald Horton and R. Richard Wohl, 'Mass communication and para-social interaction: observations on intimacy at a distance', *Psychiatry*, 19 (1956), pp. 215–29.

15   This is demonstrated in an effective way by Meyrowitz in *No Sense of Place*; see also Thompson, *Ideology and Modern Culture*, ch. 5.

16   See Natalie Zemon Davis, 'Printing and the people', in her *Society and Culture in Early Modern France* (Stanford, Calif.: Stanford University Press, 1975), pp. 189–226; Roger Chartier, 'Figures of the "Other": peasant reading in the Age of Enlightenment', in his *Cultural History: Between Practices and Representations*, trans. Lydia G. Cochrane (Cambridge: Polity Press, 1988), pp. 151–71; and Roger Chartier (ed.), *The Culture of Print: Power and the Uses of Print in Early Modern Europe*, trans. Lydia G. Cochrane (Cambridge: Polity Press, 1989).

17   See David Morley, *Family Television: Cultural Power and Domestic Leisure* (London: Comedia, 1986); Dorothy Hobson, 'Soap operas at work', in Ellen Seiter, Hans Borchers, Gabriele Kreutzner and Eva Maria Warth (eds), *Remote Control: Television Audiences and Cultural Power* (London: Routledge, 1989), pp. 150–67, and 'Women audiences and the workplace', in Mary Ellen Brown (ed.), *Television and Women's Culture: The Politics of the Popular* (London/Newbury Park, Calif.: Sage, 1990).

18   For more extended discussions of this dichotomy, see Habermas, *The Structural Transformation of the Public Sphere*, ch. 1; and Norberto Bobbio, *Democracy and Dictatorship: The Nature and Limits of State Power*, trans. Peter Kennealy (Cambridge: Polity Press, 1989), ch. 1.

19   See Bobbio, *Democracy and Dictatorship*, pp. 17ff, and his *The Future of Democracy: A Defence of the Rules of the Game*, trans. Roger Griffin, ed. Richard Bellamy (Cambridge: Polity Press, 1987), pp. 79ff.

20   See Bobbio, *Democracy and Dictatorship*, p. 19; *The Future of Democracy*, pp. 76–9.

21   See Peter Burke, *The Fabrication of Louis XIV* (New Haven, Conn./London: Yale University Press, 1992); J. H. Elliott, 'Power and propaganda in the Spain of Philip IV', in Sean Wilentz (ed.), *Rites of Power: Symbolism, Ritual, and Politics since the Middle Ages* (Philadelphia: University of Pennsylvania Press, 1985), pp. 145–73.

22   See S. R. F. Price, *Rituals and Power: The Roman Imperial Cult in Asia Minor*

(Cambridge: Cambridge University Press, 1984); Clifford Geertz, 'Centers, kings, and charisma: reflections on the symbolics of power', in his *Local Knowledge: Further Essays in Interpretive Anthropology* (New York: Basic Books, 1983), pp. 121–46.

23 See Habermas, *The Structural Transformation of the Public Sphere*; Alvin W. Gouldner, *The Dialectic of Ideology and Technology: The Origins, Grammar and Future of Ideology* (London: Macmillan, 1976); Richard Sennett, *The Fall of Public Man* (Cambridge: Cambridge University Press, 1974).

24 For a more extended critical discussion of Habermas's argument, see my *Ideology and Modern Culture*, ch. 2; and Craig Calhoun (ed.), *Habermas and the Public Sphere* (Cambridge, Mass: MIT Press, 1992).

25 See Michel Foucault, *Discipline and Punish: The Birth of the Prison*, trans. Alan Sheridan (Harmondsworth, Middlesex: Penguin, 1977), pp. 200ff.

26 In recent years some excellent ethnographic studies have appeared; see esp. Janice A. Radway, *Reading the Romance: Women, Patriarchy and Popular Literature* (Chapel Hill, NC: University of North Carolina Press, 1984); Tamar Liebes and Elihu Katz, *The Export of Meaning: Cross-Cultural Readings of Dallas* (New York and Oxford: Oxford University Press, 1990); and James Lull, *China Turned On: Television, Reform, and Resistance* (London: Routledge, 1991). For discussions of the relevance of ethnographic inquiry to media studies, see James Lull, *Inside Family Viewing: Ethnographic Research on Television's Audiences* (London: Routledge, 1990); and Roger Silverstone, 'Television and everyday life: towards an anthropology of the television audience', in Marjorie Ferguson (ed.), *Public Communication: The New Imperatives* (London/ Newbury Park, Calif.: Sage, 1990), pp. 173–89.

27 Elsewhere I have tried to show that the concepts of culture and ideology can be reformulated in this way; see Thompson, *Ideology and Modern Culture*.

28 These and related themes are pursued in my forthcoming book on social theory and the media.

3

Medium Theory

Joshua Meyrowitz

Most of the questions that engage media researchers and popular observers of the media focus only on one dimension of our media environment: the content of media messages. Typical concerns centre on how people (often children) react to what they are exposed to through various media; how institutional, economic, and political factors influence what is and is not conveyed through media; whether media messages accurately reflect various dimensions of reality; how different audiences interpret the same content differently; and so on. These are all very significant concerns, but content issues do not exhaust the universe of questions that could, and should, be asked about the media.

A handful of scholars – mostly from fields other than communications, sociology, and psychology – have tried to call attention to the potential influences of communication technologies in addition to and apart from the content they convey. I use the singular '*medium* theory' to describe this research tradition in order to differentiate it from most other 'media theory'. Medium theory focuses on the particular characteristics of each individual medium or of each particular type of media. Broadly speaking, medium theorists ask: What are the relatively fixed features of each means of communicating and how do these features make the medium physically, psychologically, and socially different from other media and from face-to-face interaction?

Medium theory examines such variables as the senses that are required to attend to the medium, whether the communication is bi-directional or uni-directional, how quickly messages can be disseminated, whether learning how to encode and decode in the medium is difficult or simple, how many people can attend to the same message at the same moment, and so forth. Medium theorists argue that such variables influence the medium's use and its social, political, and psychological impact.

Medium questions are relevant to at least two social levels: the micro, individual-situation level, and the macro, cultural level. On the micro level, medium questions ask how the choice of one medium over another affects a particular situation or interaction (calling someone on the phone versus writing them a letter, for example). On the macro level, medium questions address the ways in which the addition of a new medium to an existing matrix of media may alter social interactions and social structure in general. The most interesting – and most controversial – medium theory deals with the macro level.

The analyses of the medium theorists are often more difficult to test and apply than the results of studies of media content, but they are of significance because they suggest that media are not simply channels for conveying information between two or more environments, but rather shapers of new social environments themselves.

This essay begins with an overview of the perspectives of a number of the 'first generation' of medium theorists. Their theories are then consolidated into a composite, macro view of the evolution of human civilization. Next, I present an outline of my own 'second-generation' medium theory, which attempts to lower the level of abstraction a few notches by articulating principles for the interaction of media environments and social roles. I conclude with a summary of some of the strengths and weaknesses of medium theory relative to a more traditional analysis of media content and of the social forces that shape the content.

First-generation Medium Theorists

The best known and most controversial medium theorists are two Canadians, Harold Adams Innis and Herbert Marshall McLuhan. Trained as a political economist, Innis adapts the principles of economic monopolies to the study of information monopolies. He argues that one way in which social and political power is wielded is through control over communication media (such as a complex writing system controlled by a special class of priests). Information monopolies can be broken, however, by new media. Innis suggests that the medieval Church's monopoly over religious information, and thereby over salvation, was broken by the printing press. The printing press bypassed the Church's scribes and allowed for the wider availability of the Bible and other religious texts. The same content, the Bible, therefore, had different effects in different media.

Innis argues that elites can more easily control some media than others. A medium that is in short supply or that requires a special encoding or decoding skill has more potential to support the special interests of elite classes because they have more time and resources to exploit it. On the other hand, a medium that is easily accessible to the average person is more likely to help democratize a culture.

Innis also argues that most media of communication have a 'bias' either towards lasting a long time or towards being moved easily across great distances. He claims that the bias of a culture's dominant medium affects the degree of the culture's stability and conservatism as well as the culture's ability to take over and govern a large territory. 'Time biased' media such as stone hieroglyphics, he argues, lead to relatively small, stable societies because stone carvings last a long time and are rarely revised, and their limited mobility makes them poor means of keeping in touch with distant places. In contrast, messages on light, 'space-biased' papyrus allowed the Romans to maintain a large empire with a centralized government that delegated authority to distant provinces. But papyrus also led to more social change and greater instability. The Romans conquered and administered vast territories, but then their empire collapsed when they lost their supply of papyrus from Egypt.

In his densely written *Empire and Communications* and *The Bias of Communication*, Innis rewrites human history as the history of communication technologies.[1] His overview begins with the cradle of civilization in Mesopotamia and Egypt and ends with the British empire and the Nazis.

Among the people Innis influenced was a literary scholar, Herbert Marshall McLuhan. Extending aspects of Innis's perspective, McLuhan's work adds the notion of 'sensory balance'. He analyses each medium as an extension of one or more of the human senses, limbs, or processes. McLuhan suggests that the use of different technologies affects the organization of the human senses and the structure of the culture. He divides history into three major periods: oral, writing/printing, and electronic. Each period, according to McLuhan, is characterized by its own interplay of the senses and therefore by its own forms of thinking and communicating. McLuhan also suggests that each medium requires its own style of behaviour, so that an intense performance that works well on the 'hot' medium of radio might seem very stiff and wooden on the 'cool' medium of television.[2]

Innis and McLuhan stand alone in terms of the breadth of history and culture they attempt to include within their frameworks. Other medium theorists, however, have looked at various segments of the spectrum of past and present media effects. Walter Ong, whose work influenced and was influenced by McLuhan's, has offered wonderfully rich studies of the shift from orality to literacy. Dimensions of this transition have also been explored by J. C. Carothers, Eric Havelock, Jack Goody and Ian Watt, and A. R. Luria.[3] All these scholars argue that literacy and orality foster very different modes of human consciousness. They describe how the spread of literacy affects social organization, the social definition of knowledge, the conception of the individual, and even types of mental illness.

The seemingly less dramatic shift from script to print has been explored in detail by H. L. Chaytor and Elizabeth Eisenstein.[4] Chaytor argues that print significantly changed the oral and scribal worlds by altering literary style, creating a new sense of 'authorship' and intellectual property, fostering the growth of nationalistic feelings, and modifying the psychological interaction of words and thought. Eisenstein echoes many of these themes and presents many cogent analyses and an enormous amount of evidence to support the argument (put forward by Innis and McLuhan) that the printing press revolutionized Western Europe by fostering the Reformation and the growth of modern science.

Walter Ong, Edmund Carpenter, Tony Schwartz, and Daniel Boorstin have looked at the ways in which electronic media have altered thinking patterns and social organization.[5] Carpenter and Schwartz are generally McLuhanesque in content, method, and style, but they add many fresh insights and examples. Ong and Boorstin present more traditional scholarly analyses that support McLuhan's basic arguments but also go beyond them. Ong describes the similarities and differences between the 'primary orality' of preliterate societies and the 'secondary orality' that results from the introduction of electronic media into literate societies. He looks at the spiritual, sensory, and psychological significance of the return of 'the word', as a spoken event, in an electronic form. Boorstin describes how new media 'mass-produce the moment', make experience 'repeatable', and join many other recent technological inventions in 'leveling times and places'. He also compares and contrasts political revolutions with technological revolutions and discusses the impact of new technologies, including electronic media, on our conceptions of history, nationality, and progress.

The History of Civilization from a Medium-Theory Perspective

Each of the medium theorists mentioned above covers different territory, takes a different approach, and reaches somewhat different conclusions. Yet when their arguments and analyses are taken together, a surprisingly consistent and clear image of the interaction of media and culture emerges. Broadly speaking, these theorists' works cohere into a shared image of three phases of civilization matched to three major forms of communicating: the move from traditional oral societies to modern print societies (via a transitional scribal phase), to an electronic global culture.

Traditional oral societies

In oral societies, the preservation of ideas and mores depends upon the living memory of people. A great deal of time and mental energy, therefore, must be spent in memorization and recitation. This form of 'living library' ties people closely to those who live around them. To make memorization possible, ideas are generally put in the form of rhythmic poetry and easily remembered mythic narrative. The oral culture's laws and traditions are conveyed through familiar stories filled with stock phrases and formulaic actions and events.

Oral cultures are 'closed' in two senses. First, since orality requires physical presence, oral cultures have few if any ways of interacting with the thinking of those who do not live with them physically. Second, 'individuality', in the modern sense, is limited. Individual expressions, novel ideas, and complex arguments can find little place in such cultures because they are difficult to remember (even by the persons who come up with them) and almost impossible to pass on to any significant number of others.

Such societies are 'traditional', not only in the sense of comparison with later ones, but also internally. That is, they tend to work hard to conserve what they already have and are. Change is slow because cultural and personal survival depend so heavily on memorizing what is already known and what has already been done and said. Creativity and newness are discouraged as potentially destructive forces.

The closed sphere of the oral community, however, also fosters dimensions of openness and fluidity in terms of social and sensory experience. There are relatively few distinctions in social status and perspective. And the oral world is one of rich involvement with and interplay of all the senses of hearing, sight, smell, taste, and touch.

The transitional scribal phase

Writing begins to break down tribal cohesion and the oral mode of thinking because it offers a way to construct and preserve prose and to encode long strings of connected ideas that would be almost impossible for most people to memorize. The development of writing alters not only dissemination patterns but also the content of what is disseminated. Writing establishes the potential for true 'literature', 'science', and 'philosophy'.

With writing, symbolic communities begin to compete with practical communities. That is, writing allows literate people who live next to each other within the same physical environment to know and experience different things, to have different world views. At the same time, writing permits people who read the same material to feel connected to each other regardless of the physical distance between them. Writing, therefore, both splinters and unites people in new ways.

But, unlike speech and hearing, writing and reading are not 'natural' means of communicating. They require much learning and rote practice, and they have their full effect only when they are learned at a very young age, when the writing system used is easily mastered by large portions of the population, and when written materials are widely available. The impact of writing, therefore, is uneven until the development of the printing press in the fifteenth century, the spread of schooling, and the corresponding growth of literacy from the sixteenth to the nineteenth centuries. Further, the printing press has more impact on Western cultures than on Eastern cultures because many of the written symbol systems used in the East have too many signs to be learned by large portions of the population and are not easily adaptable to the technology of repeatable type.

The rise of modern print culture

The printing press and the relatively wide availability of printed materials further undermine the importance of the 'local community' in several ways. First, print divides people into separate communication systems. The poor and illiterate remain wholly dependent on oral communication, while the upper classes and growing middle class increasingly withdraw (both literally and metaphorically) to their libraries. For the literate, there is a retreat from the web of community life and extended kinship ties and a move toward greater isolation of the nuclear family.

While the wholly oral nature of community life once bound people into similar experiences and knowledge, reading and writing separate people into different informational worlds. The literate now read and write about things the illiterate cannot hear, speak, or remember, and different readers and writers develop different 'viewpoints' and 'perspectives'.

At the same time as printing creates smaller units of interaction at the expense of the oral community, it also bypasses the local community in the creation of *larger* political, spiritual, and intellectual units. The ability to 'see' on a printed page what were once only spoken folk languages, for example, fosters a sense of unity among all those who use the same language (not just among those who speak it in the same time and place). Conceptions of 'them vs. us' change. Feudal societies based on face-to-face loyalties and oral oaths begin to give way to nation-states and to nationalism based on a shared printed language. Similarly, religious cohesion no longer depends exclusively on shared rituals with those one can see, hear, and touch. The potential for religious unity across great distances, along with disunity among those in the same place, is fostered by the patterns of sharing holy texts.

In oral societies, words are always *events* – as time-bound as thunder or a scream. Members of an oral culture are enmeshed in the ongoing texture of spoken communication. (Plato – an early booster for writing – wanted to ban the poets from his Republic in order to free citizens from the spell of oral recitation.) But in a print society the word becomes an *object* spatially fixed on a page – that one can stare at and think about. Indeed, literate people often have difficulty thinking of a word without picturing it in written or printed form. Thus ideas move from the world of the aural and temporal to the world of the visual and spatial.

Print, even more than writing, undoes the tribal balance of the senses. The importance of the simultaneous aural surround yields to the dominance of the sequential sense of sight ('seeing it in black on white', 'following your line of thought', 'developing your point of view'). In the circular world of hearing, a person is always at the centre of whatever he or she is experiencing. But the visual, typographic person is, in a sense, always on the edge, an observer, who has time to think before reacting. A listener interrupts a speaker with a response, but a reader must let a writer have his or her 'say' before drafting a reply.

The break from intense, ongoing aural involvement distances people from sound, touch, and direct response and allows people to become more introspective and more individualistic. 'Rationality', which comes to be highly valued, resembles the form of printed type: step-by-step abstract reasoning along a continuous line of uninterrupted thought. From the simultaneous world of sound, literate cultures move toward a one-thing-at-a-time and a one-thing-after-another world. The isolation of stimuli fosters cause-and-effect thinking. Literate thinking diminishes the view of life as a repeating sequence of natural cycles and promotes the view of constant linear change and improvement.

Changes in thinking patterns are echoed by changes in physical settings: habitats evolve, over time, from villages and towns with winding paths to linear streets in grid-like cities. Production of goods moves to the assembly *line*. Modern classrooms are built with chairs bolted to the floors in rows just as letters are fixed on a page. The new physical settings generally discourage informal oral conversation. In short, the mental and physical worlds shift in structure from circles to lines, from the round world of sound to the linear form of typography.

The production of multiple copies of exactly the same text creates new conceptions of literary style, fame, authorship, and intellectual property. The ability to share the same knowledge across wide areas and the continual possibility of adding to, modifying, and correcting texts – without losing parts of them through mistakes in scribal copying – also fosters a

new form of incremental growth of knowledge. In both oral and manuscript cultures, the key intellectual process was one of *preservation*. But with
the printing of multiple copies of exactly the same text, there is a new
'safety in numbers' that allows the intellectual challenge to become one of
discovery and change.

While scholars in a scribal culture spent much of their intellectual
careers as in-depth commentators on the relatively few manuscripts
available to them, scholars in a print culture shift to comparing and
contrasting a wide spectrum of related literature and to contributing their
own original work to the wide and rapidly widening stream of ideas.

In these ways, the printing press fosters the rapid growth of scientific
inquiry and the rejection of traditional authority. In sixteenth-century
Europe, for example, the ready availability of copies of holy texts in
native tongues weakens the monopoly over salvation held by the Church
and supports the Reformation, and the sudden spurt of cumulative
knowledge fuels the Scientific Revolution and the spread of mechanical
production.

Global electronic culture

Ironically, print culture comes to its full power just as the seeds of its
destruction are planted. The late nineteenth century sees the drive toward
universal literacy, but during the same years the first electronic media
begin to be widely used: the telegraph and the telephone herald the future
age of radio, television, and beyond. The use of electronic communication, like other media, takes time to develop and ripen before having
dramatic, visible impact on social structure in the mid-twentieth century.

Electronic media bring back a key aspect of oral societies: simultaneity
of action, perception, and reaction. Sensory experience again becomes a
prime form of communicating. Yet the orality of electronic media is far
different from the orality of the past. Unlike spoken communication,
electronic communication is not subject to the physical limitations of time
or space. Electronic messages can be preserved, and they can be experienced simultaneously by large numbers of people regardless of their
physical locations.

Once again, the boundary line between 'them' and 'us' shifts, but the
result is more diffuse and less predictable. The sense of 'us' is no longer
formed solely by face-to-face oral solidarity or by the sharing of similar
texts. Electronic media bypass traditional 'literary circles', group associations, and national boundaries and give us a new world view by
thrusting us among people who have not read what we have read, have
not shared our territory, and may not even speak our language.

While print allows for new ways of sharing knowledge, and

industrialization enables the wide scale sharing of *products*, electronic media tend to foster new types of shared *experience*.

New forms of concrete sensory experience compete with abstract print knowledge. And the word returns in its old form – as an event rather than as an object. But the scale of sharing is far different. Electronic media are like extensions of our sensory apparatus that reach around the planet. Electronic sensors return us to seemingly 'direct' encounters, but on a global scale.

As a result of the widespread use of electronic media, there is a greater sense of personal involvement with those who would otherwise be strangers – or enemies. The seemingly direct experience of distant events by average citizens fosters a decline in print-supported notions of delegated authority, weakening the power of political parties, unions and government bureaucracies. The sharing of experience across nations dilutes the power of the nation state.

While written and printed words emphasize ideas, most electronic media emphasize feeling, appearance, mood. There is a decline in the salience of the straight line – in thinking, in literary narrative, in human-made spaces and organizations. There is a retreat from distant analysis and a dive into emotional and sensory involvement. The major questions are no longer 'Is it true?' 'Is it false?' Instead we more often ask, 'How does it look?' 'How does it feel?'

Information-system Theory: An Example of Second-generation Medium Theory

One dimension that is missing from the first generation of medium theory is a detailed attempt to link this theoretical perspective with analyses of everyday social interaction. My own medium-theory work involves a reformulation of role theory that can address the influence of media. There is room here only to sketch my model in its broadest outlines. Further, although the theory functions on both the micro and the macro level, I will focus here on the macro level in order to work towards a summary sketch of changes that can act as a sort of template to fit over the phases of civilization described above.

Roles as information networks

I argue that everyday behaviour is susceptible to change by new media of communication because social roles are inextricably tied into social communication. Social identity does not rest in people, but in a network of social relations. When social networks are altered, social identities will change. In any given social period, roles are shaped as much by *patterns* of access to social information as by the *content* of information. That is, different cultures and different historical periods are characterized by different role structures not only because of 'who knows what', but also because of 'who knows what about whom' and 'who knows what *compared to whom*'.

Patterns of access to social information are linked to patterns of access to social situations. People of the same status in society generally have access to the same or similar situations and information. People of different social status usually have access to different information and experience. Put differently, distinctions in behaviour, identity, and status are created and supported by separating people into different informational worlds. Patients are kept out of hospital staff meetings, customers stay out of restaurant kitchens, the officers' club is off limits to enlisted personnel, students are usually excluded from faculty meetings. If such distinctions could not be maintained, then the distinctions in identity and behaviour would also begin to blur. Of course, greater and lesser social differentiation is not brought about by a single act of inclusion or exclusion, but by the cumulative contribution of many prior different or similar experiences for different people.

In general, *the more situations and participants are segregated, the greater differentiation in status and behaviour.* Conversely, *the more situations and participants overlap, the less social differentiation in status and behaviour.* Situation segregation supports differences among people of different status by exposing different people to different experiences, by isolating the contexts for one social role from those of another, and by allowing for increased access to what Erving Goffman calls a 'back region': a private 'backstage area' for preparing for, and relaxing from, performances for 'the other'. The more backstage time and space social performers have, the more formal and distinct the onstage role performance can be.

Situations as information-systems

Although 'situations' are usually thought of in terms of physical locations, I argue that they are in fact 'information-systems'. That is, we often think of a social setting as being a *place* because the physical barriers of walls and distance once largely defined the boundaries of inclusion and exclusion in the communication processes occurring there. But *media* also play a role in defining the boundaries of social situations. In a literate culture, for example, an advice book for parents functions as an isolated 'place' for adult communication that cannot be 'overheard' by young, illiterate children. Conversely, the presence of a television camera can transform a 'private' adult conversation into one that is accessible to children (as happens daily with TV talk shows).

Roles should therefore be thought of as fluid information-networks that are susceptible to restructuring through changes in information-flow patterns, such as those brought on by changes in media use. Different media enhance and reduce the amount of shared experience for different people. Media also alter the extent to which we have a private, backstage area where we can relax from and rehearse for our onstage roles. In general, *media that segregate access to social situations will work to segregate roles; media that blur access to social situations will foster less distinct roles.*

The role triad

The impact of information access patterns becomes clearer when we look at how virtually all social roles can be described in terms of an information-network-sensitive triad of social roles:

Group Identity / Socialization / Hierarchy

Group Identity entails roles of affiliation or 'being' (such as male vs. female; professional vs. hard-hat; lawyer vs. doctor). Socialization involves roles of transition or 'becoming' (such as child to adult; medical student to doctor; immigrant to citizen; husband to father). Hierarchy describes roles of authority (such as political leader vs. voter; company president vs. company secretary; officers vs. enlisted personnel).

In everyday reality, the categories are not mutually exclusive. Most of us function in all three simultaneously: identified with a number of groups, at various stages of socialization into new roles, and at some particular rank or ranks within one or more hierarchies. Further, many roles have elements of more than one category. Being a child, for example, involves the issue of socialization, yet the relatively greater power and authority of adults make childhood an issue of hierarchy as well.

At the same time, each category has distinct elements: Group Identity allows for 'separate but equal' relationships, where members of different groups need not necessarily stand in any particular hierarchical or developmental relationship (doctors and lawyers, for example). Socialization is unlike group identity and hierarchy in that it involves expected development into the reference role (while doctors do not become lawyers, and men do not usually become women, all surviving children become adults). And roles of hierarchy depend on a 'separate but *un*equal' dimension that must appear to rest on inherent superior qualities.

Each role category describes a myriad of roles, but is also represented by a quintessential example, a role that is shared by everyone in the society:

Group Identity – Male vs. Female.
We are each either male or female.

Socialization – Child to Adult.
We all move from childhood to adulthood.

Hierarchy – Political Leaders and Average Citizens.
We all participate in this relationship of political power.

Informational Characteristics of the Role Triad

Virtually every aspect of every social role can be described in terms of group identity, socialization, and/or hierarchy. Each of these role categories, in turn, can be described in terms of set patterns of access to social information.

Group identity depends upon *shared, but secret* information – that is, information and experience must be shared among group members but remain inaccessible to 'outsiders'. Traditional distinctions between social groups, therefore, are supported by separating people into different informational spheres where they have different experiences, develop different world views, become somewhat mysterious to each other, and where they can 'privately' rehearse for roles of interaction with members of other groups.   Socialization involves *staggered access* to the situations and information of the new role or 'destination group'. Every stage of socialization into a new role involves both exposure to, and restriction from, social information. We tell sixth graders things we keep hidden from fifth graders, for example, and we continue to keep hidden from sixth graders things we will tell them as seventh graders.

Hierarchy rests upon *non-reciprocal* access to information, including tight control over performance, and mystification surrounding the need for control. Status is maintained by secrecy and by non-secret information going 'through channels', that is, passing from higher status to lower status individuals rather than the other way around or in no particular pattern.

Changes in the role triad

Changes in the number and type of social information-systems do not obliterate group identity, socialization, and hierarchy, but they change the specific form that each type of role takes in a given social period. The greater the number of distinct information-systems, the greater the number of distinct group identities, stages of socialization, and ranks of hierarchy. The more information-systems interlock, the more group identities, stages of socialization, and ranks of hierarchy blur. If, for example, we always taught fifth, sixth, and seventh graders in the same classroom, we would find it difficult to establish three distinct social identities for the children.

A medium-theory approach to role change suggests that different media are like different types of rooms – rooms that include and exclude people in different ways. The introduction of new media into a culture restructures the social world in the same way as building or removing walls may either isolate people into different groups or unite them into the same environment. Media that segregate situations will foster segregated behavioural patterns. Media that integrate situations will foster integrated behavioural patterns.

As I have detailed elsewhere, print media and electronic media differ along a number of dimensions that interact with the structure of social information networks.[6] In general, print media tend to segregate what people of different ages, sexes, and statuses know relative to each other and about each other, while electronic media, particularly television, tend to integrate the experience and knowledge of different people. Further, television's focus on personal appearance, gesture, and emotion demystifies many roles and emphasizes what is common to all humans. And television and other electronic media are especially potent transformers of roles since electronic media alter the once taken-for-granted relationship between physical place and social place, between *where* one is and what one experiences.

My medium-theory analysis of social roles yields a view of three phases of Group Identity, Socialization, and Hierarchy that is consistent with but adds another dimension to the three phases of culture outlined by the first-generation medium theorists.

Three Phases of Social Roles

Oral conceptions of Group Identity, Socialization, and Hierarchy

In oral societies, most of the distinctions that exist in group identities, socialization stages, and hierarchal roles are spatially rooted and supported.[7] Separate huts and activities support separate information-systems and therefore separate roles.

The importance of separate spheres in maintaining social differentiation is made more evident by the relative lack of role distinctions in nomadic oral societies. In nomadic hunter and gatherer societies, the difficulty of maintaining many separate places, or information-systems, for different people tends to involve everyone in everyone else's business. The lack of boundaries leads to relatively egalitarian male/female, child/adult, and leader/follower roles.[8]

Although men and women have some division of labour in hunter and gatherer societies, it is not as sharp as in agricultural and industrial societies, and doing the work of the opposite sex is not considered shameful or unusual. Because nomadic men cannot separate the public sphere from the domestic one, they cannot establish aura and distance. Women are involved in public decisions, and they play an important role in supporting the family. Men participate in childcare, and both men and women are expected to be gentle, mild-mannered, and non-competitive. The lack of a separate sphere for the nuclear family often leads to community involvement in family disputes.

Through the openness of nomadic life, children are included in most adult activities and are not sharply segregated by age or sex. Play and work often take place in the same sphere and involve similar activities. Sex play among children and adolescents is common. Obedience to adults is emphasized less than self-reliance, and physical punishment of children is rare.

Because leaders in nomadic societies cannot get away from those they lead, leaders cannot horde information or project a public image sharply different from their private behaviours. Leadership, therefore, is often more of a burden than a privilege. Leaders gain authority by setting the best example, by working harder than everyone else, by sharing more than others. Moreover, since there are no distinct spheres to which one can move as one changes status, nomads have few large-scale or long-term initiation rites.

But much of this changes when nomads settle down. Once they attach themselves to particular places, their social spheres begin to segregate. Household privacy leads to new forms of social differentiation. Women's responsibility for birth and lactation isolates them at home and starts to separate their everyday experience from that of men, who are more involved in a newly developed public sphere. Work becomes more clearly sex-typed and the socialization experiences of boys and girls become much more dissimilar. Spatial segregation also supports the development of a rudimentary hierarchy.

Even in sedentary agricultural societies, however, there is a limit to role segregation. The communication networks of the society remain oral; and, while some segregation is possible, separating what different members of the society know into *many* different oral networks is difficult. In oral societies, isolating children into year-by-year categories, for example, is generally impossible. The more typical distinctions are simply between children and adults, with a single significant rite of passage from childhood to adulthood (especially for boys). These rites are often called 'puberty rites', but they rarely coincide with individual physiological puberty.[9] They are, in fact, information-network rites, in which a whole group of children is given access to the locations and secrets of adults, whose dress and roles they then assume. Similarly, while separate spheres for men and women support some gender distinctions in knowledge, experience, behaviour, and dress, there is rarely a complex system of division of labour or a splintering of society into many different group identities. Unlike modern societies, there are not many stages or levels of differences among people, and rites of passage are significant but minimal in number.

Literate forms of Group Identity, Socialization, and Hierarchy

In the transitional scribal phase, society develops a split personality. In the Middle Ages, for example, the elites of the nobility and the Church use a monopoly on literacy to foster a starkly hierarchical system, marked by dramatic differences in dress, language, and activity between the literate elites and the illiterate masses. But within the continuing oral societies of village life far fewer distinctions exist.

In pre-print Western Europe, for example, children of illiterate families are treated as 'little adults'. Once past infancy, children dress like adults, work beside adults, go to war with adults, drink in taverns with adults, and sleep in the same beds as adults. What few schools exist (primarily to train clerics) are not segregated by ages. Children are not shielded from birth or death, and they often witness and engage in sex play. Conversely, adults are childlike by modern standards, enjoying games and stories that literate societies associate with children.[10]

Similarly, in pre-print Western Europe men and women share many rights and responsibilities. Women have the right to participate in municipal affairs; to sit on, and testify before, courts; to substitute for incapacitated husbands; and to inherit, as widows, the legal prerogatives of their dead husbands.[11] Peasant dress for men and women is very similar.

But the spread of print supports compartmentalization and special-ization. The new emphasis on reading as a source of wisdom and religious salvation widens the gap between those who can read and those who cannot. Further, distinctions in reading abilities come to be seen as tied to 'natural' differences in rank and identity.

The young and illiterate are excluded from all printed communication, and come to seem very 'innocent'. Both 'childhood' and 'adulthood' are invented in Western culture in the sixteenth century, and their spread follows the spread of schooling.[12] All-age roles, behaviours, and dress begin to splinter into separate spheres for people of different ages and reading abilities. Children are increasingly isolated from adults and from children a year or two younger or older. Many topics come to seem unfit for children's ears and eyes.

Classrooms that mix the ages gradually fall into disfavour, and the age-graded school comes to be seen as the natural means of education. The schools develop a convenient monopoly. They depart from education in oral societies in that they control both knowledge and the skill (reading) that is required to attain it. Every grade of schooling involves revelation of some new information and continued secrecy surrounding other information.

The different levels of reading complexity offer a seemingly natural means of segmenting information – and people. All fields begin to develop 'introductory' texts that must be read before one can go on to 'advanced' texts. Identities splinter into a multitude of separate spheres based on distinct specialties and mastery of field-specific stages of literacy. The new grading of texts serves as a barrier to straying from one field into another. Crossing into a new field demands that one must bear the embarrassment of starting again as a novice and slowly climbing a new ladder of printed knowledge. This contrasts markedly with the oral and scribal approach, which is inherently interdisciplinary and non-graded.

As printing spreads, women are told that only men need to become literate, and men use restricted literacy to enhance their positions relative to women. The earliest feminist movement in Western culture in the sixteenth and seventeenth centuries involves a failed attempt by women to maintain old rights.[13] Women come to be seen as part adult, part child. Elizabethan males express doubts over whether a woman could be considered as a reasoning creature and whether she has a soul.[14] Women are increasingly isolated in the domestic sphere and are increasingly thought to be too weak, irrational, and emotional to deal with activities in the male realm. As late as 1865, doctors warn officials of Vassar, a new college for women, that attempting to educate a woman as if she were a man is dangerous.[15] For many years, women are confined to a primarily oral subculture within a literate, male-dominated society. Moreover, minimally literate women are given the responsibility of caring for the increasingly dependent illiterate children.

Unlike oral societies with oral vows of allegiance, leadership in print societies is organized from a distance and is based on inaccessibility, delegated authority, and tight control over public image. Machiavelli's *The Prince* – written at the start of the print age – is an early 'political public-relations manual'. Training and etiquette manuals are published for people of both sexes and different ages. Indeed, every category of age, sex, and class begins to be increasingly isolated from the information and experience of others.

The development of bounded nation-states with centralized leadership is paralleled on a lower level by the isolation of the nuclear family from the extended community of kin and neighbours. The spread of literacy, with its emphasis on hierarchy and sequence, supports a linear chain of command, from God-the-Father, through a strong national leader, to a father who is a god to his wife and children.

Separate information-systems foster distinct uses of separate places, with increasingly distinct rules of access to them and distinctions in appropriate behaviour within them. People pass from role to role many times a day and change status through various rites of passage (matriculation, graduation, promotion, marriage, etc.) dozens of times in a lifetime.

Birth, death, mental illness, and celebrations are increasingly removed from the home and put into isolated institutions. The membranes around the hospital, prison, military barracks, factory, and school thicken over several centuries.[16]

The unity and continuity of a print society is far different from the unity of an oral society. The oral society's unity is a 'homogeneous solidarity' that relies on people acting, thinking, and feeling in relatively similar ways. Unity in a print society, however, depends on heterogeneity. The whole world begins to be seen as a machine with distinct parts, distinct types of people, that fit together to make it work. Print society depends on division of labour, separation of social spheres, segmentation of identities by class, occupation, sex, and so forth. People are increasingly separated into distinct places in order to 'homogenize them into groups' – groups with single identities: 'students', 'workers', 'prisoners', 'mentally ill'. The people in these groups are each seen as interchangeable parts. And the distinct identities are subsumed under the larger system of internally consistent, linearly connected, and hierarchically arranged units.[17]

Print leads to an emphasis on stages, levels, and ranks. The world comes to seem naturally layered and segmented. There is a place for everything, and everything is to be in its place. Those who remain illiterate, however, remain at the bottom or outside of this system. They continue to maintain many of the features of oral societies. Ironically, as late as the nineteenth century, the labour of illiterate children helps to feed the growth of a special subculture for the innocent children of the literate classes: publishers hire lower-class children to hand-tint the engravings in the growing number of books for middle-class children.[18]

Electronic conceptions of Group Identity, Socialization, and Hierarchy

Electronic media begin to be widely used even as the impact of print leads to heightened attempts to isolate social spheres. The 'child savers' of the late nineteenth century try to extend the isolation of the children's sphere to the lower classes. A woman's place is to be in the home. The isolation of rich from poor, men from women, young from old intensifies, and 'institutions' become more fully isolated spheres for handling each aspect of social life.

But electronic media begin to reverse the trend. The telephone, radio, and television make the boundaries of all social spheres more permeable. One can now 'witness' events without being physically present; one can communicate 'directly' with others without meeting in the same place. As a result, physical structures no longer fully mould social identity. The walls of the family home, for example, no longer wholly isolate the home from the outside community. Family members at home now have access to others and others have access to them. Now, *where* one is has less to do with who one is.

The social information available to the ghetto family now more closely resembles the information available to the middle-class family. Information available to women now more closely resembles information available to men. Formerly distinct groups share more information about society and about each other – information that once distinguished 'insiders' from 'outsiders'. As a result, traditional group bonds are weakened and traditional distinctions among groups become partially blurred. This leads to a pressure to integrate roles and rights even when no clear mechanisms for doing so exist.

The explosion of clashing cultures comes in the mid- to late 1960s, when the first generation to watch television before entering school (the temple of literacy) comes of age. This generation rejects traditional distinctions in roles for young and old, for men and women, and for authorities vs. average citizens. The integration of information networks leads to a demand to integrate physical locations through the civil rights movement, the women's movement, and the children's liberation movement. The tense confrontations of 'The Sixties' become more muted, not when the drive for such integration subsides, but as the 'revolutionary' values and behaviours of the 1960s spread throughout the culture.[19]

The membranes around institutions are thinning. Hospital and prison visiting hours and rights, for example, are expanding, and children are being allowed to visit institutions more freely. Fathers and children, once excluded from births of babies, are now included in what is called the 'family birthing process'. There is a decline in male-only clubs, adult-only restaurants, and dress-specific events and locations.[20]

We still live in and interact in segregated physical locales. But television and other electronic media have broken the age-old connection between *where* we are and what we know and experience. Children may still be sheltered at home, but television now takes them across the globe before parents give them permission to cross the street. Through television, women – once isolated in the domestic sphere – have been exposed to places and activities men used to tell them they should know nothing about. And while few of us actually travel to see our leaders in the flesh, television now shows us our politicians close up – stammering and stumbling in living colour. Television blurs the line between public and private by bringing the public sphere into the home, and by emphasizing the personal and emotional dimensions of public actions through its intimate close-ups of human faces.

Television has lifted many of the old veils of secrecy between children and adults, men and women, and politicians and average citizens. By blurring 'who knows what about whom' and 'who knows what compared to whom', television has fostered the blurring of social identities, social-ization stages, and ranks of hierarchy. The electronic society is char-acterized by more adultlike children and more childlike adults; more career-oriented women and more family-oriented men; and by leaders who act more like the 'person next door', just as average citizens demand to have more of a say in local, national, and international affairs.

As we move forward, our society also spirals backwards. The middle and upper classes are moving towards the behaviours once associated with the illiterate lower classes. Premarital sex, high illegitimacy rates, 'shacking up', and drug use spread upward through all levels of society. As recently as the early 1970s, differences in teenage sexuality could still be predicted accurately on the basis of race, socio-economic status, reli-gion, and residence. But many of these distinctions have largely dis-appeared.[21] These changes violate the print industrial society's belief in 'Progress'. Yet they support the view that we are retreating from 'literate forms' and returning to 'oral forms' of behaviour.

The relatively shared information environment fostered by electronic media does not lead to identical behaviours or attitudes. Far from it. While the world is more homogenized on the macro, societal level, the experience on the micro, personal level is the opposite: the individual's world becomes more heterogeneous, a world filled with more variety, more choices. Just as traditional differences among people of different ages, sexes, status, families, neighbourhoods, and nationalities are blur-ring, people of the same age, sex, status, families, neighbourhoods, and nationalities are becoming less similar to each other.

While the print social order segregated people in their 'special spheres' in order to homogenize individuals into interchangeable elements of a larger social machine, the electronic society integrates all groups into a common sphere with a new recognition of the special needs and idio-syncrasies of individuals. What people share is not identical behaviour, but a common set of options.

But sharing of options is too weak a bond to hold people together. Metaphors aside, one cannot consider the whole country or world as one's 'neighbourhood' or 'village'. Another outcome of the homogenization of information networks, therefore, is the development of many new, more superficial, more shifting groupings that form against the now relatively unified backdrop of common information. People traditionally united and divided into groups that corresponded primarily to social class, ethnicity, race, education type and level, religion, occupation, and neighbourhood. But current groupings also develop on the basis of wearing similar clothes, participating in similar sports, listening to the same type of music, or attending the same class.

Nations evolved from feudal systems of local alliances when local membranes and arteries of communication were superseded by national ones. Now, new arteries and membranes are bypassing nations and fostering the rise of a system of quickly changing, neo-feudal ties and alliances on a global scale. Here, too, there is both unification on the macro level and fragmentation on the micro level. Old boundary lines fade in significance as distinct European countries plan to join into a single economic unit and as once taken-for-granted differences between East and West blur. But new boundary lines are created as earlier unions – Soviet, Yugoslav, Czech/Slovak – splinter.

The above is merely a rough sketch of a medium-theory analysis of role changes. I have explored other aspects of this information-system approach to social behaviour elsewhere.[22] Moreover, this analysis of role change is only one example of second-generation medium theory. Other scholars have expanded this perspective in other ways. Susan Sontag has written about the pervasive role of photography in our culture. Edward Wachtel has explored the impact of technology on art and perception. Paul Levinson has written about technology as an agent of cognitive development and about the impact of computer networks and electronic text. Neil Postman has explored the epistemology of television compared with print. Sherry Turkle and Judith Perrolle have written about the ways in which computers affect what we know, how we behave, and the ways we think about ourselves. Susan Drucker has analysed how the televising of trials dramatically alters the way they are experienced by the culture. Shoshana Zuboff has studied the role of the 'smart machine' in redefining work and power. Ethan Katsh has written about the ways in which electronic media have transformed the legal system. Gary Gumpert and Susan Drucker have explored the ways in which communication technologies alter the nature and the use of public space. Roderick Hart has analysed how television has changed the way politics is conducted and perceived. Medium theory has also played a key role in Alvin Toffler's and James Burke's theories of social change.[23]

Relative Strengths and Limits of Medium Theory

Unlike content research, the 'effects' that medium theorists look for are generally difficult to demonstrate through 'social-scientific' methods. The recreation of a pre-electronic 'print culture' for observation or experimental manipulation, for example, is virtually impossible. And surveys are not particularly useful in medium theory since the point is often to examine types of structural changes and sources of influence that are out of the awareness of most people. There have been some significant attempts to test aspects of medium theory experimentally and descriptively.[24] For the most part, however, medium theory, especially macro-level medium theory, relies heavily on argument, historical analysis, and large-scale pattern identification. Although the best studies weigh evidence carefully and search for disconfirming as well as confirming examples, most medium theory is not supported by systematic quantitative analyses. For some people, this makes medium theory much more exciting and interesting than traditional content analysis; to others, it makes medium theory frustrating and 'unscientific'.

Just as traditional content approaches tend to obscure important differences among media, medium approaches tend to overlook the significance of content. Generally, medium research is most helpful when looking at broad structural patterns over a long period of time. But medium theory is not terribly useful in short-term analysis of how to use a communication technology and whether and how to regulate it. A parent who is angry about the violent and advertising-saturated programmes his or her children see will find cold comfort in a medium perspective that argues that TV in general weakens the print-supported sphere of innocent childhood and returns us to a world where, to control what children know, parents must either censor their own experience or isolate themselves from their children. Similarly, a woman faced with a daily stream of often demeaning gender images on television may have difficulty focusing on the encouraging medium-theory argument that television, more than print, includes women in many all-male spheres of the culture. Rather than leaving such situations at the medium-theory level, we also need to look at the institutional and economic forces that shape media content. And, if we want to change the current media systems, we need to look at the available political options for doing so.

Medium theorists' focus on the characteristics of media has tended to lead to another weakness. Most medium theory begins with the invention and use of a medium and has tended to ignore the institutions that have important political and economic stakes in the development of some technologies over others. A political and economic system that is interested in stimulating consumption of goods and ideology, for example, is likely to foster the development of uni-directional mass communication technologies such as broadcast radio and television. Other technologies or similar technologies used differently – such as ham radio or interactive community television – may receive much less support and encouragement. Medium theory has also tended to ignore vast cultural differences that mute and alter the development, use, and perception of various communication technologies.

Although the response is inadequate, some medium theorists would probably counter that those who have focused on the roles of powerful political and economic institutions and on the influence of culture almost always ignore the ways in which the 'chosen' technologies have social consequences apart from those planned and often alter those very institutions and cultures that develop them.

Another common attack on medium theory is that, as a wholly 'deterministic' perspective, it ignores free will and is disproved by the many exceptions to its broad claims. Part of this critique may stem from the fact that medium theorists, in exploring a process that has been largely ignored by mainstream media researchers, have tended to sketch very broad patterns of social change and have not been especially careful in stating qualifications. Certainly, the most useful way to look at medium theory is to think of it not as deterministic, but as a model that deals in general tendencies. Medium theorists suggest that each medium invites, allows, encourages, fosters some human actions while discouraging others. This perspective is no more deterministic than widely accepted analyses of how the paths of rivers and other geographical features have shaped general patterns of human settlement and exchange. Unlike medium theory, such analyses are rarely dismissed as deterministic and are not usually thought of as being disproved by exceptions to the general patterns. Like medium theory, such analyses do not claim to predict precise outcomes (sharing a waterway may lead societies to peaceful trade or to war), but they do argue for a general structural prediction (sharing a waterway is more likely to lead to interaction than being on either side of an imposing mountain range). Indeed, since medium theory deals with human-made 'rivers' and 'mountains', it is inherently less deterministic than analyses of the impact of geographical features. Ultimately, the greatest loss of freedom and control results from ignoring the ways in which the communication pathways and barriers we shape tend to reshape us.

The relative strengths and weaknesses of content and medium perspectives are often most visible when we look to the past. Neither approach in isolation, for example, would have told us the full story of the impact of the spread of printing in the sixteenth and seventeenth centuries. A content/institutional approach probably would have led researchers to conclude that books had two major influences: (1) the fostering of religion (most early books were religious texts); and (2) the further empowering of central monarchical and religious authorities (who controlled most of what was printed). Yet most analysts would now agree that in the long term the printing press fostered the opposite: the weakening of religion with the growth of science and the decline of monarchs with the development of constitutional systems.

With respect to these long-term consequences, medium theory clearly wins. But one cannot discount the implications of content control over those people who actually lived through the initial years of printing. The medium-theory analysis of the long-term tendencies of printing would give little comfort to the family of William Carter who, after printing a pro-Catholic pamphlet in Protestant-dominated England in 1584, was promptly hanged. Similarly, our current information environment is choked by the way television content is controlled – regardless of the 'inherent characteristics' of the medium.

While examples from several centuries ago may be clearer and less controversial than those of the last few years, recent events such as 'People Power' in the Philippines, the Tienanmen Square protests in China, the revolutions in Eastern Europe, and the dissolution of the Soviet Union also offer insight into the relative strengths and weaknesses of content and medium approaches.

Conventional wisdom claims that most of these events were not predicted by 'the experts'. Yet, while it is certainly true that those who have focused on the traditional institutional/content approach could not anticipate such dramatic shifts within cultures where the media content was so tightly controlled, medium theorists have long predicted just such changes.[25]

Electronic media's inherent disregard for physical boundaries made it difficult for these countries to restrict their citizens' access to many aspects of Western culture. This gave these populations awareness of what they did not have, as well as awareness of global awareness. Television allowed them to protest not simply for the government forces that faced them in the streets but for the global television audience. And the rapid feedback of electronic technology allowed them to be encouraged by the ongoing global response (televised globally as well as transmitted through telephones and fax machines). The heightened global consciousness of heightened global consciousness encouraged each Eastern European country to wait its turn to enter the global television arena. These events were not simply reported on television; in many ways, they happened in, on, through, and because of television.[26]

Medium theory alone, however, cannot explain why the 'stories' we were told about the Philippines and Eastern Europe were still highly selective or why 'global television' does not look to all countries equally. The content of the US coverage of Philippine people power, for example, tended to embrace the century-old narrative of US 'benevolence' towards the Philippines, while largely ignoring the sordid aspects of the United States' 'pacification' of the islands and the backing of the Marcos dictatorship.[27] Similarly, while massive TV news coverage was given to the overthrow of Soviet-backed regimes in Eastern Europe, almost no attention was given to the simultaneous dramatic push for democracy in Latin America, where voters in Brazil and Chile – whose populations exceed that of all Eastern Europe – held their first free presidential elections since the United States encouraged brutal military coups in 1964 and 1973 respectively.[28]

The medium-theory view of the unique features of global electronic media gives us tremendous insight into the power and potential of our new technologies. But the content/institutional perspective allows us to observe how the selective use and foci of the global spotlight intersect with issues of power, ideology, economics, and journalistic conventions. We need to study all these things if we are to understand our media world.

Ultimately, medium theory is most helpful when it is used not to supplant content concerns but to add another dimension to our understanding of the media environment. What is needed is a better integration of medium theory with other perspectives.[29]

Notes

The author wishes to thank Edward Wachtel for his useful comments and suggestions.

1   See Harold A. Innis, *The Bias of Communication* (Toronto: University of Toronto Press, 1964); and *Empire and Communications* (Toronto: University of Toronto Press, 1972).

2   See e.g. Marshall McLuhan, *The Gutenberg Galaxy: The Making of Typographic Man* (Toronto: University of Toronto Press, 1962), and *Understanding Media: The Extensions of Man* (New York: McGraw-Hill, 1964).

3   J. C. Carothers, 'Culture, psychiatry, and the written word', *Psychiatry*, 22 (1959), pp. 307–20; Jack Goody and Ian Watt, 'The consequences of literacy', *Comparative Studies in Society and History*, 5 (1963), pp. 304–45; Eric A. Havelock, *Preface to Plato* (Cambridge, Mass.: Harvard University Press, 1963); A. R. Luria, *Cognitive Development: Its Cultural and Social Foundations*, trans. Martin Lopez-Morillas and Lynn Solotaroff, ed. Michael Cole (Cambridge, Mass.: Harvard University Press, 1976); Walter J. Ong, *Ramus, Method, and the Decay of Dialogue* (Cambridge, Mass.: Harvard University Press, 1958); Walter J. Ong, *The Presence of the Word: Some Prolegomena*

for Cultural and Religious History (New Haven, Conn.: Yale University Press, 1967); Walter J. Ong, *Rhetoric, Romance and Culture* (Ithaca, NY: Cornell University Press, 1971); Walter J. Ong, *Orality and Literacy: The Technologizing of the Word* (Ithaca, NY: Cornell University Press, 1982). For a collection of case studies on the effects of literacy in traditional societies, see Jack Goody, (ed.), *Literacy in Traditional Societies* (Cambridge: Cambridge University Press, 1968).

4   H. J. Chaytor, *From Script to Print: An Introduction to Medieval Vernacular Literature* (1945; rpt. London: Sidgwick & Jackson, 1966); Elizabeth L. Eisenstein, *The Printing Press as an Agent of Change: Communication and Cultural Transformations in Early-Modern Europe*, vols I and II (New York/Cambridge: Cambridge University Press, 1979).

5   Daniel J. Boorstin, *The Americans: The Democratic Experience* (New York: Random House, 1973), pp. 307–410; Daniel J. Boorstin, *The Republic of Technology: Reflections on our Future Community* (New York: Harper & Row, 1978); Edmund Carpenter, *Oh, What a Blow that Phantom Gave Me!* (New York: Holt, Rinehart & Winston, 1973); Edmund Carpenter and Ken Heyman, *They Became What They Beheld* (New York: Outerbridge & Dienstfrey/Ballantine, 1970); Tony Schwartz, *The Responsive Chord* (Garden City, NY: Anchor, 1974); Tony Schwartz, *Media: The Second God* (Garden City, NY: Anchor, 1983); Walter J. Ong, *The Presence of the Word*, pp. 17–110, 259–62, 287–324; Ong, *Interfaces of the Word: Studies in the Evolution of Consciousness and Culture* (Ithaca, NY: Cornell University Press, 1977), pp. 82–91, 305–41; Ong, *Orality and Literacy*, pp. 79–81, 135–8; Tony Schwartz, *The Responsive Chord* (Garden City, NY: Anchor, 1974).

6   Joshua Meyrowitz, *No Sense of Place: The Impact of Electronic Media on Social Behavior* (New York: Oxford University Press, 1985), pp. 69–125.

7   The references within this section are to anthropological and historical sources that document each particular role behaviour described. The overall argument presented in this section – that these behaviours fall into a pattern linked to different dominant forms of communication – is my own and is not necessarily one with which the cited authors would agree.

8   The claims about roles in hunter and gatherer societies in the next few paragraphs are culled from Charlotte G. O'Kelly, *Women and Men in Society* (New York: Van Nostrand, 1980); Patricia Draper, '!Kung women: contrasts in sexual egalitarianism in foraging and sedentary contexts', in Rayna R. Reiter (ed.), *Toward an Anthropology of Women* (New York: Monthly Review Press, 1975), pp. 77–109; Jane C. Goodale, *Tiwi Wives: A Study of the Women of Melville Island, North Australia* (Seattle: University of Washington Press, 1971); Lorna Marshall, *The !Kung of Nyae Nyae* (Cambridge, Mass.: Harvard University Press, 1976); Colin M. Turnbull, *The Forest People* (New York: Simon & Schuster), 1961; Ernestine Friedl, *Women and Men: An Anthropological View* (New York: Holt, Rinehart & Winston, 1975). For an analysis of how our own society now resembles some features of nomadic societies, see my *No Sense of Place*, pp. 315–17.

9   Arnold van Gennep, *The Rites of Passage*, trans. Monika B. Vizedom and

Gabrielle L. Caffee (Chicago: University of Chicago Press, 1960).

10 Philippe Ariès, *Centuries of Childhood: A Social History of Family Life*, trans. Robert Baldick (New York: Vintage, 1962).

11 David Hunt, *Parents and Children in History: The Psychology of Family Life in Early Modern France* (New York: Basic Books, 1970).

12 Ariès, *Centuries of Childhood*; Lawrence Stone, *The Family, Sex, and Marriage in England, 1500–1800* (New York: Harper & Row, 1977). See also, Meyrowitz, *No Sense of Place*, pp. 258–65, for an analysis of the many historical hints to the role of literacy in the development of 'childhood'.

13 Anne Oakley, *Sex, Gender and Society* (New York: Harper & Row, 1972).

14 Stone, *The Family, Sex, and Marriage in England, 1500–1800*, p. 196.

15 Sheila M. Rothman, *Women's Proper Place: A History of Changing Ideals and Practices, 1870 to the Present* (New York: Basic Books, 1978), pp. 26ff.

16 Michel Foucault, *Discipline and Punish: The Birth of the Prison*, trans. Alan Sheridan (New York: Pantheon, 1977).

17 Ibid.

18 John C. Sommerville, *The Rise and Fall of Childhood* (Beverly Hills, Calif.: Sage, 1982), pp. 145 and 160.

19 For documentation of this trend, see Meyrowitz, *No Sense of Place*, pp. 140–3.

20 For a detailing and analysis of all these trends, see Meyrowitz, *No Sense of Place*.

21 Alan Guttmacher Institute, *Teenage Pregnancy: The Problem that Hasn't Gone Away* (New York: Guttmacher Institute, 1981), p. 9.

22 Meyrowitz, *No Sense of Place*; Meyrowitz, 'Media as social contexts', in Ralph Rosnow and Marianthi Georgoudi (eds), *Contextualism and Understanding in Behavioral Science: Implications for Research and Theory*, (New York: Praeger, 1986), pp. 229–50; Meyrowitz, 'The generalized elsewhere', *Critical Studies in Mass Communication*, 6:3 (Sept. 1989), pp. 326–34; Meyrowitz, 'Using contextual analysis to bridge the study of mediated and unmediated behavior', in Brent D. Ruben and Leah A. Lievrouw (eds), *Mediation, Information, and Communication: Information and Behavior*, vol. 3, (New Brunswick, NJ: Transaction Press, 1990), pp. 67–94; Meyrowitz, 'Three worlds of strangers: boundary shifts and changes in "them" vs. "us"', *Annals of the Association of American Geographers*, 80:1 (Mar. 1990), pp. 129–31; Meyrowitz, 'Redefining the situation: extending dramaturgy into a theory of social change and media effects', in Stephen Riggins (ed.), *Beyond Goffman: Studies on Communication, Institution, and Social Interaction* (New York: Mouton de Gruyter, 1990), pp. 65–97.

23 Susan Sontag, *On Photography* (New York: Farrar, Straus & Giroux, 1977); Edward Wachtel, 'The influence of the window on Western art and vision', *The Structurist*, 17/18 (1977/1978), pp. 4–10; Edward Wachtel and Casey Man Kong Lum, 'The influence of Chinese script on painting and poetry', *Et cetera*, 48:3 (Fall 1991), pp. 275–91; Paul Levinson, *Mind at Large: Knowing in the Technological Age* (Greenwich, Conn.: JAI Press, 1988); Levinson, *Electronic Chronicles: Columns of the Changes in our Time* (Tallahassee,

Fla.: Anamnesis Press, 1992); Neil Postman, *Amusing Ourselves to Death: Public Discourse in the Age of Show Business* (New York: Penguin, 1985); Sherry Turkle, *The Second Self: Computers and the Human Spirit* (New York: Simon & Schuster, 1984); Judith A. Perrolle, *Computers and Social Change: Information. Property, and Power* (Belmont, Calif.: Wadsworth Publishing, 1987); Susan J. Drucker, 'The televised mediated trial: formal and substantive characteristics', *Communication Quarterly*, 37:4 (Fall 1989), pp. 305–18; Shoshana Zuboff, *In the Age of the Smart Machine: The Future of Work and Power* (New York: Basic Books, 1984); M. Ethan Katsh, *The Electronic Media and the Transformation of Law* (New York: Oxford University Press, 1989); Gary Gumpert and Susan J. Drucker, 'From the Agora to the electronic shopping mall', *Critical Studies in Mass Communication*, 9:2 (1992) pp. 186–200; Roderick Hart, *Watching Politics: How Television Makes Us Feel* (New York: Oxford University Press, forthcoming); Alvin Toffler, *Future Shock* (New York: Random House, 1970); Alvin Toffler, *The Third Wave* (New York: Morrow, 1980); Toffler, *Powershift: Knowledge, Wealth, and Violence at the Edge of the 21st Century* (New York: Bantam Books, 1990); James Burke, *Connections* (Boston: Little, Brown, 1978).

24   See e.g. Stanley Milgram, 'The image freezing machine', in *The Individual in a Social World: Essays and Experiments* (Reading, Mass.: Addison-Wesley, 1977), pp. 339–50; Michael Pfau, 'A channel approach to television influence', *Journal of Broadcasting & Electronic Media*, 34:2 (Spring 1990), pp. 195–214; Michael Pfau and Jong Geun Kang, 'The relationship between media use patterns and the nature of media and message factors in the process of influence', *Southern Communication Journal* (forthcoming); Doris A. Graber, *Processing the News: How People Tame the Information Tide*, 2nd edn (New York: Longman, 1988), pp. 166–74. Turkle and Zuboff's work, cited in note 23, is rich in participant observation, but their real contributions are in their interpretation and analysis.

25   More than two decades before the 'surprise' fall of communism, for example, Marshall McLuhan and Quentin Fiore wrote in *War and Peace in the Global Village* (New York: Simon & Schuster, 1968), p. 5, that communism was a thing of the past and that electronic media would 'turn on' the Soviet Union. Here, as elsewhere, McLuhan also wrote of the splintering of nation-states and of 'retribalization'. Similarly, in the mid-1980s, I described how electronic media were limiting the significance of the physical boundaries 'marked by walls, doors, and barbed wire, and enforced by laws, guards, and trained dogs' (*No Sense of Place*, p. 117).

26   For a further discussion of this issue see Joshua Meyrowitz, 'The power of television news', *The World & I*, 7:6, (June 1992), pp. 453–73, and Deirdre Boden, 'Reinventing the global village: communication and the revolutions of 1989', (unpublished paper).

27   For an excellent history of the US's early role in the Philippines and of the distortions in the US press concerning it, see Leon Wolff, *Little Brown Brother: How the United States Purchased and Pacified the Philippine Islands at the Century's Turn* (Garden City, NY: Doubleday, 1961). For an analysis of the

US's 20-year alliance with the Marcos dictatorship, see Raymond Bonner, *Waltzing with a Dictator: The Marcoses and the Making of American Policy* (New York: Times Books, 1987).

28   For an analysis of this general coverage pattern, but with a focus on print media, see Lawrence Wechsler, 'The media's one and only freedom story', *Columbia Journalism Review* (Mar./Apr. 1990), pp. 25–31.

29   As I have argued elsewhere, content approaches and medium approaches should be combined with at least one other approach, media 'grammar' studies, in order to explore the media environment more fully. See Joshua Meyrowitz, 'The questionable reality of media', in John Brockman (ed.), *Ways of Knowing: The Reality Club 3* (New York: Prentice-Hall, 1991), pp. 141–60; Meyrowitz, 'Images of media: hidden ferment – and harmony – in the field', *Journal of Communication*, 43:3 (Summer 1993), pp. 55–66.

4

A Recursive Theory of
Communication

Klaus Krippendorff

Introduction

This is an essay in human communication. It *contains* 'communication', *mentions* and is, hence, *about* communication, but, what is important here yet often overlooked in other essays, it also *is* communication to its readers. This exemplifies that no statement, no essay and no theory can say anything *about* communication without also *being* communication to someone. Among the scientific discourses, this is an unusual fact – fact in the sense of having been made or realized – and I suggest it is constitutive of communication scholarship that its discourse is included in what it is about and, therefore, cannot escape the self-reference this entails. If I had to formulate a first axiom for communication research I would say that to be acceptable,

Human communication theory must also be about itself.

Although this seems obvious, I understand that many writers on the subject do not recognize this axiom and talk about communication as if their own use of language had nothing to do with communication. I suspect the reason for this omission lies neither in bad intentions nor in an inability to understand this phenomenon, but in the unquestioned commitment to certain ontological assumptions and vocabularies that in effect prevent these scholars from facing *themselves* in their own constructions.

For much of the history of science, self-reference and the paradoxes it entails have been treated like an oddity of logic and a source for amusement at dinner-table conversations among intellectuals. Indeed, whether or not Epimenides the Cretan lied when he claimed 'all Cretans are liars' left much of the world around him unchanged. Bertrand Russell was the first, I believe, to recognize the seriousness of such paradoxes.[1] However, instead of coping with their 'vicious circularities', he invented *the theory of logical types* in order to completely ban self-reference – and its relatives, reflexivity and circularity – from scientific discourse. I contend that this ghost still haunts scientific theory construction, and if self-reference indeed is a defining feature of communication scholarship, it hurts the understanding of human communication especially.

This essay seeks to resurrect self-reference in understanding human communication. To succeed, it has to find an antidote to the Russellian Ghost. I believe this can be found in a *recursive conception for human communication* and in conceiving social scientific inquiries into communication as being accomplished *in* human communication. This is a project that Margaret Mead initiated by suggesting that cybernetics be applied to itself; that Heinz von Foerster defined as a shift in the focus of attention from what is observed to the process of observing; that Lars Lofgren understood as a search for a type-free logic or autology; that Ernst von Glasersfeld sought to realize in his radical constructivism; that Malcolm Ashmore and colleagues pursued in the name of a reflexive sociology; and that Anthony Giddens recently acknowledged in the reflexivity of socially knowledgeable agents.[2]

The reflexivity that needs to be pursued will, I am convinced, usher radical changes in understanding human communication and attendant social phenomena. However, all I can do here is take a few steps: one is towards a recursive theory for human communication; and the second is to explore how an established social theory looks in comparison.

Towards a recursive theory, I will add two propositions for understanding of communication to the above and articulate a few of its corollaries. By 'theory' I do not mean one that can be fed into a computer to yield valid predictions about events *outside* its embodiment. Social theories arise, as all theories do, *within* a social fabric, constitutively involving human beings capable of inventing and articulating them. But social theories, in contrast to natural scientific ones, may also re-enter their social fabric and become *embodied in* the very practices of knowledgeable human agents. Thus a (social) theory for human communication has to acknowledge the understanding that practitioners of communication have of it; provide spaces for their individual participation; and inform those involved about the joint consequences of their practices. I am saying 'theory *for* . . .' to indicate this enabling quality. 'Theory *of* . . .' would limit it to a representation.

As the established theory, I will take parts of Giddens's recent work.[3] Giddens does not claim to be a communication theorist, nor is he concerned with epistemology, so taking his conceptions as an example might seem unfair. However, since he takes knowledge and human agency as his primary focus and, unlike most social scientists, builds reflexivity right into the centre of his social theory, I will conclude this essay by showing the space a fully reflexive social theory of communication can offer the inquiring scientist and the practising communicants.

The Centrality of Understanding

To guide the argument towards a recursive theory for human communication let me suggest my second proposition:

> *Everything said is communicated*
> *to someone understanding it as such.*

The explicit self-reference in this proposition, the 'as such' pointing back to 'everything said', is important here. It locates saying things and communication *within* someone's understanding. Substantially, the proposition asserts that anything is what it is because someone understands it that way; that the judgement of whether something is real or true always is someone's judgement; and that communicating things cannot exist without someone's cognitive participation. Theories of communication may be written on a piece of paper but they exist only in someone's under-

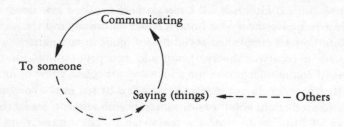

Figure 4.1 Someone's understanding

standing. This proposition might be depicted as in figure 4.1. By 'saying', I am not restricting communication to spoken communication; obviously one can *say* things in pictures or communicate in gestures or by touch, involving no language at all. Neither am I suggesting that 'saying' must originate in other speakers. Although conversation with others is prototypical of human communication, speakers too must understand their speech and monitor their own practices. Humberto Maturana's formula 'everything said is said by an observer' focuses attention on humans as being both speakers *and* observers.[4] My proposition merely adds *human understanding as constitutive* of what (if anything) is being said.

The proposition could be seen as reformulating Watzlawick, Beavin, and Jackson's admirably simple first axiom of communication: 'One cannot not communicate.'[5] This suggests that all features of human behaviour, sounds and silences, the mailing and the not mailing of a letter are meaningful (which I would qualify by adding 'to someone'), that even a deliberate effort not to engage in communication reveals itself as such, and hence communicates something. This axiom admits the powerlessness of speakers or actors to control the meanings their (discursive or non-discursive) practices have for others, but gives these others no credit in determining what this means to them. In contrast, my proposition is stated from the position of a listener or observer who always controls his/her understanding within the constraints of his/her cognitive abilities. Indeed, Watzlawick and colleagues' axiom necessarily fails when communication is directed to or withdrawn from someone unwilling or incapable of understanding what is taking place in terms of communication.

My second proposition is intended to overcome the Cartesian dualism which manifests itself in the distinction between what something *really* or *materially* is, a text for example, and its *subjective interpretation* or subject-dependent meaning. This counters any suggestion that one can *see* a text prior to *seeing it as such* and then explain it as a cause of one's perceptions or interpretations, as if the dualism implied in this distinction resided outside of an observer's metaphysics. Whatever gives rise to the awareness of something being said and communicated, the causes of one's experiences, must be located *within* one's horizon of understanding.

This inaccessibility to understanding of its external causes does not mean that understanding could not be extended to embrace something heretofore unknown. For example, TV viewers see sharply contoured and moving images on their screens. Yet a magnifying glass applied to the screen will reveal independently flickering but otherwise stationary dots of light. The correlation between the two views may be suggestive of what a magnifying glass does relative to how perception works, but any explanation of this correlation links two kinds of experiences, not an objective (pre-experiential or observer-independent) cause of one. *There is no escape from one's understanding.*

Nor does it mean that understanding is wholly subjective and free of circumstantial constraints. For example, Giddens describes 'knowledgeable agents' as continuously monitoring what they do, turning certain consequences of their actions into information which potentially challenges and revises the knowledge that directs their future actions.[6] This describes a reflexive loop which is so constituted as to remain viable. It is guided by knowledge that is in turn constrained by the re-entering in this knowledge of the practical consequences of the agent's actions as they

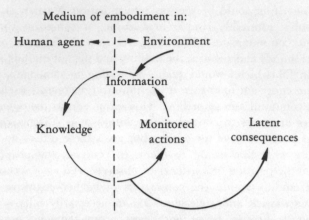

Figure 4.2 Giddens's construction of a knowledgeable agent

have passed through his/her environment. Figure 4.2 depicts an abstract
version of my reading of Giddens's construction.

In constructing knowledgeable agents this way, Giddens maintains a
position outside his agents. In figure 4.2 this is indicated in the epistemological status assigned to 'latent': what remains unintended and unseen
for the otherwise knowledgeable agent becomes the consequences of that
agent's being and acting for the observing sociologist. My proposition
implies that the latter takes place in an observer's (Giddens's) understanding and that this too is a construction involving social subjects, their
monitored environment, and its unfolding into latent consequences of
their actions. To capture this, figure 4.3 embeds an observed subject's

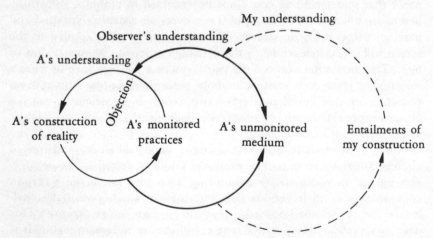

Figure 4.3 An observer's construction of someone's understanding in the medium of the
observer's own understanding

understanding in the understanding of its observer, such that each involves both a construction of reality (knowledge) and the practices that derive from it.

Herein understanding is constituted in a reflexive loop, in the unfolding of one's reality construction into one's practices and their re-entry into the very constructions from which they were derived. What enter a reflexive loop are not physical stimuli, things, or messages as seen by an external observer, but challenges to or constraints on someone's understanding. I will call these 'objections' from the medium of a loop's embodiment. *Objections* 'say no' to someone's construction of reality when the expectations that derive from a construction are incommensurable with the experiences resulting from one's actions. A medium, by definition, provides the background of one's reflective monitoring and hence is outside the horizon of that person's understanding. It includes what an outsider may conceptualize as latent consequences; as the work of the unconscious or other biological phenomena; and as the co-presence of extra-individual events. A reflexive loop is always 'meaning-tight', 'informationally closed', or 'hermeneutically impenetrable'. This suggests a major difficulty in conceptualizing communication among reflexive practitioners in which their understanding is constitutively involved.

Note that my proposition does not use 'understanding' representationally. Comprehension is always *of* something and invokes the norm of a privileged observer external to a reflexive loop, such as the correct interpretation of a text or the accurate decoding of an encoded message – wherein the Russellian Ghost is again evident. In contrast, understanding simply *is*. I assume that its norm is set by the knower himself: the comfort of seeing oneself involved with something said or experienced; the confidence in the viability in practising one's constructions of reality; the certainty of continued participation in a community of others, etc. This understanding should not be confused with the one in Alfred Schutz's phenomenology, which is entirely subjective and not embedded in a reflexive loop constitutively involving an unknown medium.[7] Thus the assertion 'I understand (you)' can hardly mean comprehending what someone else had in mind when saying something, but might be taken as indicating a sense of coherence or closure of one's state of knowing and as a signal marking the readiness to proceed in a conversation. This is similar to Wittgenstein's notion of understanding a sequence of numbers, expressed in the exclamation 'now I can go on'.[8] Conversely, lacking understanding almost invariably signals a state of not being in touch with another, or a strangeness that ethnographers after Martin Heidegger have called 'breakdown'.[9] In a technical context this is referred to as 'perturbation' or, as I call it, 'objection.'

Ultimately, my proposition claims humans to be *cognitively autonomous*.

In support of this claim I submit that:

1 *Nobody can be forced to understand* something as intended, as it exists or as it should be from someone else's perspective.
2 *Nobody can directly observe or access someone else's understanding* (its inference from observed practices, both discursive and non-discursive is always one's own).
3 The reflexive circle involving the repeated construction, decomposition, and re-construction of realities, the continuous enacting of these constructions into practices, the re-entering of the consequences of such practices into the very reality that justified them initially is *dedicated to preserve human understanding* by criteria internal to the process.
4 Understanding is *never finished*, even in the absence of objections from an environment. The process *directs itself*.

For me, understanding can neither be abstracted out of the medium of its embodiment as logical positivists routinely do, nor can it be reduced to an individual's biology and/or environment, as behaviourists insist upon. Only by reference to the medium of its embodiment can one see how *objections* (perturbations or breakdowns) limit the space within which understanding is arbitrary and free. Fatal accidents and suicides exemplify the fact that individuals have the cognitive autonomy to construct realities whose practices can become biologically non-viable. Under such extreme conditions understanding destroys itself via its embodiment. It follows that the persistence of one's understanding in time indicates not a state of adaptation to an environment, but rather that one's constructions of reality as invented and practised have stayed within what its unknowable medium of embodiment afforded. Thus cognitive autonomy can reach beyond the biological autopoiesis that embodies it, but in the long run *understanding cannot violate its own embodiment*.

A Recursive Construction for Communication (theory)

In view of the foregoing, I cannot write about communication without reminding myself that I am also practising communication at the same time, that communication cannot reside entirely outside or independent of my understanding, and that my cognitive autonomy grants me considerable freedom in constructing other fellow beings as participants in the process. Particularly, I cannot subscribe to notions of communication whose practices are predicated on denying others, readers or partners in communication, the kind of cognitive abilities the preceding proposition claims. This brings me to my third proposition:

Human communication constitutes itself
in the recursive unfolding of communication constructions,
held by participants (including of each other),
into intertwining practices that these participants can
recognize and explain in terms of being in communication.

This proposition locates constructions of reality and individual practices (that is of communicating and saying things) in some participant's understanding. But it goes beyond the second proposition by asserting that communication arises in the *concurrent unfolding* of communication constructions, simultaneously held by its participants, into intertwining communication practices. Each reflexive loop, each individual's understanding here becomes potentially challenged by the consequences of other participants' practices. These practices could be said to be in co-ordination when the joint practices no longer challenge or object to each other's unfolding reality constructions, when they are viable relative to each other, or when understanding 'resonates.' Figure 4.3 can be expanded as follows to depict this part of the proposition.

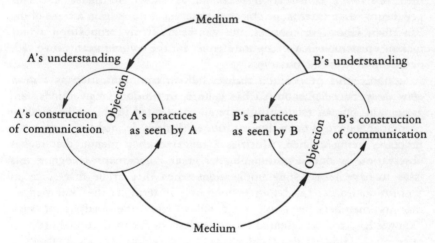

Figure 4.4   An observer's construction of communication between others

Figure 4.4 fundamentally differs from diagrams commonly used by communication researchers who investigate what A says to B, what B says to A, and how the whole sequence develops. Such researchers take their own understanding as the only understanding that matters. Their research does not make allowance for others' understanding and thus only inquires into their own. My second proposition suggests that an external observer might well explain what challenges or objects to the reflexive loop involving someone else, but that this observer's description cannot enter as such into the understanding of the observed. Consequently, figure 4.4 does not suggest that whatever A hears himself as saying, A's practices, corresponds to what B hears A as saying. Both communicants have their own understanding, generate their own ideas about what they hear the other saying, provided it remains viable in the presence of the other's practices. The constructions of communication that do emerge in such a process must accommodate the objections they pose for each other – through their continuous unfolding in intertwining practices. Coordination simply is intertwining as understood by those involved.

While figure 4.4 seems superficially fair to both communicants, the diagram demonstrates how ignoring my first proposition necessarily privileges the vantage point of an external observer or reader. Indeed, the figure indicates no problem in describing what A and B (mean to) say to each other – and enables a viewer to assess, for example, their cognitive sharing, their misunderstanding, the accuracy of transmission. But all of these privilege that outside observer's norms, while denying the observed communicants the like ability to access each other's meanings, and also their observer's construction of them, as shown in figure 4.4 This privileging of an external or objective observer is once again a trace of the Russellian Ghost. In contrast, the symmetry in my proposition avoids making epistemological exceptions, either for the communicants involved, or for their scientific observers.

Secondly, this proposition realizes human communication as a *social phenomenon*. Social phenomena like culture, institutions, conventions, language, and human relationships are all constituted in the understanding participants have of them. By 'constituted' I mean defined from *within* the processes being defined, which is a reflexive phenomenon that makes observation by outsiders difficult. Berger and Luckmann recognize this issue to have far-reaching implications when they argue that since an 'institutional order can be understood only in terms of the "knowledge" that its members have of it, it follows that the analysis of such "knowledge" will be essential for an analysis of the institutional order in question'.[10] Giddens also acknowledges this by giving 'knowledgeability' a defining role in his construction of social agents.[11] But neither has an answer to the question of how such knowledge can enter social processes, much less processes of human communication.

My third proposition does not merely echo the importance of such knowledge in understanding human communication, it spells out a *recursive form* that incorporates into this understanding the very understanding communicants have of communication. My proposition thus no longer conceptualizes those involved in communication as observers of social events outside of themselves (a position into which the viewer of figure 4.4 is thrust) but as co-creators of the very social phenomenon of communication in which they participate. This is an important deviation from traditional conceptions of communication as the sending and receiving of mutually known messages, symbols, or meanings, of social phenomena as shared, and of facts as objective and observer-independent, decided by someone outside the phenomenon in question. To avoid objections/breakdowns in the reflexive monitoring of one's part in the intertwining communication practices, it becomes natural:

1   that one invent others in one's own construction of reality;
2   that these invented others are equally able to understand the unfolding of their own reality constructions into their own practices and to monitor them in their own terms;
3   and that these others can understand the co-ordination that arises in terms of their respective conceptions of communication.

Figure 4.5 depicts an individual's (A's) *minimum* understanding of his or her communicative involvement with another (B) – *minimum* in the sense

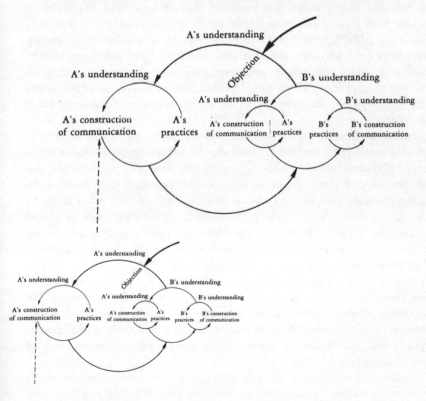

Figure 4.5   A's (minimum) construction of communication

that the embedding of constructions into each other may have greater recursive depth.

In this figure, communication does not appear as a variable to be entered into an equation. As a social phenomenon, it is constituted in a reflexive practitioner's understanding. Nor does communication require mutually shared knowledge.[12] Rather, it is depicted here as a construction that constitutively involves one's own and others' understanding, including these others' understanding of their own and their others' understanding, etc., which comes back to one's self but from these others' perspectives. Individual differences in understanding communication are considered natural rather than deviant from some outsider's theoretically motivated norm.

This conception for communication is a recursive one, applicable to itself. Appropriately, figure 4.5 includes at least one reference to itself. 'A's construction of communication' on the left side of the diagram refers to the diagram as a whole, rendering the whole as its own part. In practice, such a recursive conception for communication is *fractal*-like extendable – without involving the Russellian Ghost. Naturally, a diagram with greater recursive depth would exhibit many more such self-references. Although this may seem unsettling to readers with strong preferences for linearities, the difficulty may stem from not being able to envision a space in which apparent part-to-whole relations become recursive constructions of unities. The two dimensionality of paper seems to be an awkward medium to depict a recursive construction of communication.

Communication researchers who consider their interaction with subjects as a social phenomenon, as they should, can recognize in figure 4.5 a theory of themselves that can be recursively extended to embrace the understanding of those whose communication practices they theorize. In practice, though, people are not able to keep track of very many levels of recursion at the same time (see a review of R. D. Laing's work by David and Dorothy Miell).[13] However, the realities of such cognitive limitations should not serve as an excuse for altogether ignoring recursive accounts of social phenomena, as many social scientists do.

For example, a candidate for political office who knows what voters think about her – and what they know about how she thinks of them – is likely to be a better communicant than one who merely knows how many know her. Understanding human communication as a social phenomenon requires adequate recursive depth at least equal to the understanding of those communicated with.

Thirdly, *language* is constitutively involved in any recursive construction for communication. This is not to deny the possibility of non-linguistic phenomena entering processes of communication. For example, consider human communication with pets. Pet owners often create elaborate constructions of what their pets can understand, usually including their pets' ability to understand their own intentions in talking to them. Aetiologists are likely to dismiss the attribution of this ability as mere anthropomorphic projections. However, as long as such constructions of communication remain viable in the practices they inform, the owners' accounts of how they communicate with their pets has to be respected as an explanation of what they do and experience. The therapeutic value of practising such constructions is unquestioned. The fact that humans, including aetiologists, do not have the faintest evidence of how non-human animals see their world (notwithstanding Uexkuell's gedanken-experiments[14]) gives pet owners considerable liberties to invent one for their pets without expecting expressions of dissent. This disparity demonstrates the central role of language in human communication. Pet owners can explain to each other – as the propositions imply – their constructions, including those of their pets' reality; pets cannot.

It is too easy to equate communication simply with language use and thereby exclude practices grounded in what Michael Polanyi (1969) calls 'tacit knowledge', what Giddens describes as 'practical consciousness' and what Mark Johnson analyses in terms of 'non-propositional meanings'.[15] It is not sufficient to rely on such otherwise agreeable metaphors as in Heidegger's saying that: 'language is the house of Being' (or the house we live in).[16] The fact that human communicants (even pet owners) can be held socially accountable for their actions,[17] and can offer verbal explanations, clarifications, justifications, even whole theories of their realities, undoubtedly demonstrates that language is part of the very construction of communication that unfolds into social practices. Here communication can be said to be *constructed in language* while being practised (see my first proposition) and thus involves not only the coordination of practices (as in communication with pets) but also the coordination of that co-ordination.

While I cannot get too deeply into the many roles languages can play in communication, I want to emphasize three implications:

1 Language cannot be regarded as being *about a world outside* its speakers, as representative of objective facts, or as a conveyor of information. Since everything said must be understood as such, meanings always reflect a speaker's cognition, feelings, experiences, intentions, and constructions of reality. Tropes such as substitutions, categorizations, metonymies, and metaphors, which do not play important roles in conceptions of language as a medium of representation, are seen here as indispensable windows into a speaker's or writer's process of re-ception, re-cognition and re-construction of realities.

2 By the same token, language cannot be considered *shared* in the

sense that some linguistic forms (as identified by an external observer such as a linguist) have the same meanings for all speakers of that language. This does not prevent language from being used as a medium of coordination of communication practices. Austin's *performatives* or Searle's *speech acts* (for example, declarations, promises, questions, apologies, greetings) may not express much about a speaker's cognition but they do create what they assert and commit participants to particular communication practices. Gregory Bateson's message 'this is play' shows that language provides speakers with the ability to coordinate how they shift from one socially constructed context to another.[18] Coordination surely is a more appropriate explanation of the use of language than sharing.

3   Language use is not *governed by abstract rules* but by speakers' discursive competence – which may include the understanding of some such rules and their histories. Rules of language are invented to account for various aspects of human speech: in the linguistic tradition, primarily for the generation of well-formed sentences; in the speech-communication tradition, for the evolving relationships among speakers, etc. But such rules are also stated in language, are communicated among the users of that language, and may hence become constituted in the very language used in human communication. Thus rules cannot be separated from the language they are assumed to describe. Here, language is no longer a medium of coordination of something else but it coordinates itself in the understanding of its rule-knowledgeable users. The foregoing three points suggest that language is a prerequisite of understanding communication as a social phenomenon, hence 'everything said ...'.

Fourthly, my third proposition neither *preconceives a particular theory of communication* nor does it require participants in the process to agree on one. By not specifying from the outside or in advance of an encounter with others what communication is or how it should be understood by those involved – whether as conveying knowledge, reproducing pattern, maintaining relationships, exerting influence and control, negotiating meanings, cooperating in the consensual pursuit of goals, etc. – this proposition provides no more than a recursive *frame whose space can be filled* by any construction participants happen to bring to it or develop in the process of communicating with each other. It provides a scaffold that invites practitioners to invent and try out their own constructions relative to each other. And it invites scientists not only to observe but also to listen and respond to accounts offered in communication. The open yet formal nature of this recursive theory *for* communication might be alien to traditional social scientists accustomed to formulating disembodied theories *of* communication that predict or control observations, without realizing their own hermeneutic participation in what is always a social process as well.

As stated, the propositions are neither true nor false in the representational sense. I do believe that humans, at least I, could accept living with mutual respect in the spaces this recursive theory provides – and the ability to live in this space would speak for its social viability. For inquiring scientists, one methodological implication is that it offers conceptual spaces in which observed forms of communication can be explored relative to those that do not occur in practice. For the theorized, it provides spaces for participation and respecting each other's contributions in the social construction of theories concerning them. One could say that the propositions 'socialize' communication theory construction but without ideology or idealism – for they can potentially embrace markedly unequal but *mutually acceptable* forms of interaction such as human communication with pets, or where one participant claims privileges as a superior scientific observer and the other willingly accepts the inferior role.

Fifth, and finally, knowledgeable human agents have the ability to move within the virtual space of their known. Specifically, this entails the ability:

1   *to position* themselves in their own constructions of reality which, in the case of communication, must include (a population of) other human beings;
2   *to move* their position into their constructed others' constructions of reality; and
3   to *see or understand themselves through these others' eyes.*

This goes far beyond recommending, for example, that a politician should keep his or her voters 'in mind' although this is where the awareness of human communication starts. The proposition takes knowers as part of their known – and communication as involving others with similar capabilities to construct themselves, other fellow beings, their knowledge, their perceptions, and their motivations. Without the ability to construct others, communication would be reduced to a monologue, to a performance for an audience, or to the mere 'production' of messages as mass communication is often and inadequately described. Without the understanding of others, the intertwining of practices would not be explainable and society would reduce to a mechanism. Without the ability to appreciate the often astounding differences in others' understanding, empathy and love could not arise and creativity would be stifled by norms imposed from the outside. Without the ability to explore the constructions others have of themselves, one would not be able to understand oneself. Also, one would not be able to pull oneself out of one's cognitive traps whose nature can be realized only from another's perspective,[19] which in my view is a fundamental requirement of all *emancipatory pursuits*. My recursive theory for communication supports this possibility.

To be clear, there is no way of escaping one's horizon of understanding. This is what positivists have tried to do only to find themselves entangled in epistemological contradictions and struggles for authority. Neither is it possible to enter someone else's understanding and assess commonalities and differences between them. This is what many popular theories of communication-as-sharing assume. To make sense out of one's own practices of living with others and to sustain one's own understanding while respecting the cognitive autonomy of others, recursive constructions of reality inevitably suggest themselves. Such constructions are inconsistent with the idea of a single *uni-verse* and instead support a *multi-verse of radically distributed but coordinated constructions* of reality continuously unfolding themselves into the *mutually non-challenging* practices of cognitively autonomous beings. To me, communication is nothing less than an effort to understand such an unfolding.

Communication in Giddens's Society

Any social theory, if accepted by social practitioners, will have social consequences commensurate with what it claims to be about. A sociological theory should address this reflexivity and I take this to be Anthony Giddens's primary aim.[20]

I read Giddens's *Constitution of Society* to be wholly in agreement with my recursive theory for communication in two respects: first, in his construction of humans as knowledgeable agents; and secondly, in his inclusion of the observing social scientist within his conception of society. Both locate reflexivity at the centre of social theory construction.

According to Giddens, humans demonstrate their *knowledgeability* in two ways: first, in their ability to monitor their actions, receiving information about the consequences of their actions, adjusting their knowledge accordingly, and having reasons of their own for being so engaged; secondly, in their ability, if asked, to account for the nature of their actions and elaborate (or lie) discursively upon their reasons for them. Giddens terms these two abilities *practical* and *discursive* consciousness, respectively.

Giddens is unique among sociological theorists in *including social scientists* into his theoretical concerns and granting them, as well as the social actors they describe, similar reflexive capabilities. Accordingly, social actors are able to engage each other discursively about their practices, much as sociologists do with their professional peers. They can also construct their own social theories within their domain of experiences and thus become sociologists, on the level of their discursive consciousness;

and methodological specialists, on the level of their practical consciousness.

Since Giddens is not a communication theorist, it would be unfair to criticize his work from a perspective alien to his. However, because knowledge plays such an important role in his constructions, issues of interest to communication scholars are implicated almost everywhere. It is therefore instructive to see how Giddens conceptualizes communication and wonder whether recursive constructions could add to his programme. In this effort, it would be equally counter-productive to cite disconfirming evidence or to raise questions of validity – for this would bring me back to the very competitive and objective stance I tried to leave behind by proposing a recursive theory for communication and other social phenomena. The following, therefore, are merely intended to ascertain the spaces that these conceptualizations provide for social scientists to explore and for social practitioners to occupy.

I shall limit my comments to five intersecting issues between Giddens's sociological framework and communication theory: (1) positioning oneself and Giddens's double hermeneutic; (2) taking the linguistic turn seriously; (3) acknowledging one's cognitive involvement; (4) communicating communication; and (5) considering ethical consequences of constructing social theories.

Positioning oneself and Giddens's double hermeneutic.   While Giddens grants all humans a measure of knowledgeability and reflexivity, he conceives the sociological project as a collective effort by social scientists to observe, describe, and theorize the social practices of actors and the structures that emerge as a consequence of these practices. Social scientists, he observes, enter a social situation already conceptualized by its human constituents and must therefore invent second-order concepts that account for the knowledge and conceptions ordinary actors already bring to a situation. According to Giddens, a sociological language capable of second-order conceptions is thus necessarily more abstract and has the logical status of a meta-language (a term fundamental to Russell's theory of logical types) relative to the language that actors use to express their knowledge to each other. Categorizing the separate reflexive monitoring by each, Giddens calls the process by which social scientists let their theoretical knowledge guide their inquiries into how ordinary actors let their practical knowledge guide their social lives a 'double hermeneutic'.[21]

In writing about sociology, Giddens describes himself as a *metasociologist* – and this builds the Russellian Ghost solidly into his sociological project. This tradition of seeing observers and observed as operating on different logical levels leads Giddens to take what Hilary Putnam calls a 'God's eye view' of reality.[22] And in reproducing this rather asymmetrical

relation *to* his sociological object *into* his sociological theory, the double
hermeneutic that sociologists are asked to recognize comes to subsume the
(single-hermeneutic) reflexive practices of ordinary social agents. For
Giddens, sociological theories are abstract, expansive, and potentially
valid. In contrast, actors' theories are practical, limited in scope, and often
based on apparently credible, yet fallible beliefs. In spite of the
acknowledgement that both are reflexively involved with their world, the
Russellian Ghost makes the actors being theorized into logical 'flat-
landers',[23] and condemns them to occupy a restricted space subordinate
to that of their sociological observers – who, in turn, are missing some of
the dimensions only meta-sociologists are free to explore.

Theories that set social scientists and social practitioners apart on *logical*
grounds are prone to *(re)produce inequalities in social practices* as well. For
example, readers of a sociological literature that arose under such asymmetrical conditions undoubtedly learn to think with its categories and
conceptions, talk in its terms, and become accustomed to assuming the
logically superior positions *vis-à-vis* the subject matter this literature brings
forth for them. When practical situations present themselves in which this
literature is relevant, there is then a good chance that the knowledgeability
of such readers unfolds into talking in abstract and general sociological
categories (stereotypes) and down to those whom this literature casts in
the role of the logically inferior observed.

This need not be so. The Russellian Ghost which equates objectivity
with taking logically superior positions relative to and external to a subject
matter can be dethroned:

1 I think, by carrying the reflexivity Giddens's knowledgeable agents
   already have into the *interaction* between them, viewing them as
   recursively involved with each other, as cognitively autonomous
   communicants, as substantially unequal but engaged in a mutual
   inquiring process;
2 by recognizing that the very process of social scientific inquiry is a
   social one in the sense that it is constituted in the knowledge theorists,
   theorized, and users of scientific knowledge have of each other;
3 and by allowing those affected by an inquiry *to participate* in the
   construction of theories concerning them, which means that neither
   can assume a position on top of a hierarchy of logical levels that
   subsumes everything and everyone else.

In a recursive theory for communication, individuals are *invited* to include
themselves in their own knowledge and are able to take different positions
within the realities they construct. I would hope that social scientists, who
ought to have better sense than ordinary communicants of the social

entailments their constructions have, will avoid taking 'God's eye views' of the worlds of others. This would open the possibility for two-way communication with those whose realities they seek to understand.

Taking the linguistic turn seriously. Giddens acknowledges the 'linguistic turn' the social sciences have been taking but also reminds us of the contributions of both hermeneutical and ethnomethodological traditions. The lesson I draw from these is that the language we use is not quite as unproblematic and transparent as commonly assumed. It means becoming cognizant of the Russellian Ghost which leads us to think about thinking by using one language to talk about another language – which encourages unawareness of our languaging. The linguistic transparency that follows is characterized as the awareness of writing *about a subject matter* without the equal ability to acknowledge that this writing takes place *within a language* as well. My first proposition suggests that these two phenomena – content and languaging – should not be separated, at least not in writing about communication. For the same reasons, sociological writing should not be separated from the social phenomenon I claim it is.

I mentioned the god-like position the Russellian Ghost encourages scientists to assume *vis-à-vis* their (construction of) reality. Such a view undoubtedly is encouraged by an academic writing style that consists of *positionless* (impersonal and objective) statements of facts which readers can only reject in rare defiance of the scientific authority that establishes itself in this style. How something is said, what its saying assumes, and the role the discourse plays within one's already formed constructions of a social reality can be as important as what is said. An impersonal and detached use of language invites and *legitimizes authorities* that are detached from that which they are called to adjudicate. Theories written in this manner can nourish hierarchical forms of social organization and the oppression they entail can become severely restrictive of communicative practices. Besides writing, there are other modes of doing social science (such as conversing, negotiating, interviewing, exemplifying, performing, advocating, organizing), which may bring forth other social realities worth exploring.

In sum, I am suggesting that we as social scientists should be aware of the social nature of the processes of inquiry as well as the consequences of communicating findings and theories and, therefore, should not treat our own language as if it did not matter. This would mean applying the reflexivity recognized in others to our own discursive practices, admitting our conceptual struggle with the subject matter we are trying to bring forth through writing, realizing our own entanglement in the language we are using, and creating spaces that enable those that might be affected by our inquiries to participate in as equal a fashion as possible.

Acknowledging one's cognitive involvement. In my reading of Giddens, mutual knowledge combines the idea of common knowledge (A knows X; B knows X) and knowledge of each other (A knows B and himself; B knows A and herself) and becomes the stock of knowledge social actors must share (both A and B then share knowledge of X, and of each other). In this conception, knowledge requires reference to a common ground, a territory populated by social actors and social structures, a social maze for people to move around in, the 'factual evidence and theoretical understanding' of which serves social scientists as a criterion for 'validating' the accounts social actors give for what they do and why they do it. The assumption of *a common social universe* or of *one* reality for all is further evidence in Giddens's definition of mutual knowledge as that which is 'shared by lay actors and sociological observers'; and that which provides 'the necessary condition of gaining access to valid descriptions of social activity'.[24]

With this in mind, Giddens writes about sociology, about the discursive effort of sociologists to account for and clarify what a social uni-verse is like, and about social practitioners whose theories refer to the same social uni-verse they all populate – as if his own cognitive involvement in the subject matter, his own professional commitment, interest, and social position, and his own experiences in society had nothing to do with it. In fact, when he uses the word 'understanding' it usually seems to have the sense of a general consensus within a particular scholarship, during a certain period or concerning a particular phenomenon, mostly excluding his own. Apparently, the notion of mutual knowledge encourages sociological theorists to hide their own cognitive creativity behind the construction of a disowned yet privileged generalized other's knowledge. This renders an understanding of that theorist's cognitive involvement either taboo, irrelevant, or not at variance with what everyone else ideally understands.

The logical force of my second proposition leads to the contrary conclusion: all writing is bound to stay within a writer's horizon of understanding; and there can be no escape into the real world or into someone else's understanding outside one's own. As social scientists, we need to learn to interpret what we say and write as being not about mutual knowledge, nor about a world that exists outside of ourselves, but about our own construction of objects, people, and society, and our own understanding. Giddens writes neither about sociology nor about society. He can do no more than express his understanding of them. We have to admit our own cognitive involvement in the phenomena we claim to write about and assume ownership of our constructions.

I understand the need for a knowledge-based concept by which the connectivity of people within of society can be explained. I also agree with

Giddens's observation that the possibility of mutual knowledge and a common social universe to which it refers is tacitly assumed in the everyday life of ordinary practitioners as a matter of common sense. The motivation for such a single uni-verse view needs further explorations. However, I see no reason to adopt a model of knowing that is incommensurate with the thesis of humans as reflexive social practitioners. In Giddens's non-reflexive model, knowledge is mutual by virtue of it being *about* a joint social universe in which everyone resides and to which everyone has access, at least in principle. In his reflexive model, knowledge appropriately resides *within* a reflexive loop that couples cognitively autonomous beings to their environment and is no more than what shows its beholder, in Giddens's words, 'how to"go on" in forms of life'.[25] Giddens seems to resolve the conflict between the two models by allowing the non-reflexive model to govern the interpersonal, discursive, and social domain.

This is unfortunate or perhaps even self-serving because it privileges, as already remarked, the construction of one reality by social scientists over that of alternative realities. I suggest that it is this tenaciously held belief in a single social universe, in which the social sciences concur with everyday life, that brings forth such socially value-laden concepts as errors, biases, distortions, misunderstandings, false consciousness or invalidities which the social sciences then call upon themselves to criticize and correct. This kind of sociological theorizing virtually creates the kind of social phenomena it attends to. Indeed, social actors may have very good reasons to construct their social worlds very differently from each other and from their scientific observers. In contrast, a recursive theory for communication could not be called upon to judge but to understand these differences and to ascertain what would happen if they were to interact.

A recursive theory of social phenomena, including of human communication, preserves the reflexivity which Giddens needs as a building block for sociology – without banishing the variety of human understanding. But note the difference: in the above example, 'X, A and B' is the *shared* object of A's and B's knowing. But in 'A knowing B's knowing . . .' and 'B knowing A's knowing . . .', knowledge is not shared and hence not mutual either, but its practical social consequences *intertwine*. I believe that this intertwining or coordination of practices is a good entry point for understanding social phenomena constituted in the understanding participants have of it. But this becomes an issue of communication.

Communicating communication.   As I said, Giddens theorizes communication only indirectly and the two notions of communication he seems to pursue may well be a logical corollary of his double hermeneutic. I will review these and add my reading of his work as the manifestation of a third.

A good entry to his first notion can be found where he takes a historical perspective: 'a self-evident feature of traditional society . . . [is that] all contacts between members of different communities or societies, no matter how far-flung, involve contexts of co-presence. A letter may arrive from an absent other . . . has to be taken physically from one place to another.'[26] He argues that modern communication makes co-presence no longer a requirement of social interaction. Herein, communication appears as a technology of transportation, a substitution for co-presence, whose working is describable in terms of the theory of coding from one system of signification to another.[27] Giddens is not alone in playing out transportation metaphors, even where mediating technologies are not an issue. Most communication scholars speak just as freely about the communication of meanings, making knowledge available, transmitting information, conveying messages – as if meanings, knowledge, information, or contents came in the form of thing-like entities, tokens of discursive consciousness, or signs whose social qualities remain invariant during processes of dissemination and are equally accessible to all. Indeed, the vocabulary of everyday English encourages such constructions. In Giddens's case, this also connects with his notion of mutual knowledge as a common stock from which social actors must draw.[28]

To be fair, this overly simplistic notion of communication as selecting from a common repertoire and conveying entities contained therein to someone else does have a place in institutionally stable or conventionally regulated circumstances where innovation or multiple realities are discouraged. Examples include the flow of commands through a military hierarchy; the use of traffic signs as enforced by law; and the choice of words from a standard English dictionary. Commands, traffic signs, and single words are learned in advance of their use. But their use is governed by institutionalized (and sometimes discursively available) rules or codes of conduct that in effect coordinate, control, or time the reproduction of institutionally appropriate behaviours. We certainly do not communicate by responding to isolated tokens or signs – as monkeys do. The examples show, however, that we are quite capable of understanding and complying with rules or codes of conduct that reduce us, temporarily in certain circumstances, to machine-like respondents.

However, practising a transportation conception of communication (in the social sciences and in everyday life) has at least three social consequences:

1   It does not explain the communication processes that take place prior to compliance with such rules, and thus obscures the understanding of

alternative and more embracing forms of human communication. The deliberate concealment of such knowledge can be viewed as a cause of oppression.

2 It invites authorities external to this process capable of arbitrating disputes about what is to be taken as mutual, valid or legitimate.[29]

3 It confines the spaces within which communicants are allowed to be knowledgeable and to construct alternative ways of living with each other.

Giddens advances a second, and somewhat less restricted, notion of communication in his account of the effects social-scientific knowledge has on social action. He writes: "Discoveries" of social science, if they are at all interesting, cannot remain discoveries for long; the more illuminating they are, in fact, the more likely they are to be incorporated into actions and thereby become familiar principles of social life.'[30] In such situations, Giddens argues, '[t]he social scientist is a communicator, introducing frames of meanings associated with certain context of social life to those in others.' He views Erving Goffman's work as exemplary of social inquiry that turns 'tacit forms of mutual knowledge, whereby practical activities are ordered' into discursive accounts that 'draw on the same sources of descriptions (mutual knowledge) as novelists'[31] . . . do.

I do not think that either of Giddens's two notions of communication apply to himself. Giddens is certainly not just explaining and reproducing his (scholarly) practices excepting his use of standard English in much the same way as he claims his knowledgeable actors do – in which he contradicts his *first* notion of communication. Nor is he merely analysing the tacit practices of social actors, or critically evaluating their discursive accounts against empirical evidence – which would render his *second* notion inapplicable to him. For me, Giddens is *creating a narrative*, taking stretches from various literatures, particularly sociological ones, and weaving them into a *novel story* which does make sense to both of us but not necessarily in the same way. I see this as a *third* notion of communication.

I would not be interested in his narrative:

1 if it merely reproduced or authenticated what I already know;
2 if it did not make sense to me (irrespective of his own understanding);
3 if I could not find a space in which to move around, taking on some positions he takes with respect to other writers;
4 if it did not invite me to construct and enter into a new social reality that has relevance to my life outside this reading.

Such a reading makes Giddens not a theorist of how sociology works, but an innovator who enables me to construct a way of seeing sociology and society and engage in conversations with colleagues familiar with the text. This is what I mean by coordination.

Anyone who takes a discursive account like mine into consideration while writing is, *ipso facto*, involved in a recursive notion of communication. Under these conditions, a transportation notion of communication, coupled with the idea of drawing from a stock of mutual knowledge and comprehending the items selected for what they are, seems very naive and limiting. Acknowledging communicants' accounts of communication avoids the three above mentioned consequences of the transportation notions. It means:

1   not ignoring the history of the emerging coordination which is part of a recursive understanding of communication;
2   not presupposing that understanding and knowledge can be shared, common or mutual – and thereby questioning authorities and attendant oppression;
3   not imposing standards for the kind of communication constructions people may develop, demanding merely that they be viable in conversation relative to each other.

Giddens's second notion of communication needs to recognize that sociological theorists and social practitioners – like political scientists and politicians or communication researchers and journalists – are surely different, but not necessarily superior to one another.

I suggest that the third notion of communication, which I have added to Giddens's two, occurs in many spheres of social life, not merely in reading scientific writing. For example, second-order conceptualizations, to use Giddens's term, emerge even in ordinary conversations wherein one participant can bring forth in others a way of seeing which they could not come upon by themselves. Good therapists make a profession out of this skill. Social accountability works in much the same way. Unfortunately, the social sciences tend to limit issues of social accountability to questions of validity and thereby avoid the need to take responsibilities for their 'findings'. With this third notion of communication, social inquiry would have to be conducted like a good conversation, rather than a demeaning and deceptive process.

Considering ethical consequences. Giddens is clearly concerned with the validity of sociological theories when he separates 'credibility criteria' that social actors use to evaluate their reasons for actions from 'validity criteria [as] criteria of factual evidence and theoretical understanding employed by the social sciences in the assessment of reasons as good reasons . . . [and] . . . in terms of knowledge either simply unavailable to lay agents or construed by them in a fashion different from that formulated in the meta-languages of the social theory.' He justifies the privileging of sociological reality constructions at the expense of those held by social practitioners by explicitly valuing 'the internal critique' of theories and findings 'generated by social science . . . which . . . [are] substantially constitutive of what social science is'.[32]

Giddens also observes that the social-scientific critique of false beliefs, bad reasons, and invalid social theories constitute *interventions* into these same social practices. However, if a social-scientific theory, which is accepted as valid relative to its empirical domain, becomes the source of critique and transforms this very domain, then such a theory also effects its own validity. This calls into question the epistemology in which these disembodied validity criteria are formulated and the methodology that seeks to apply them. For me, this is observing Giddens's double her-meneutic in action. Ostensibly to maintain validity, social scientific cri-tique becomes part of a reflexive loop but on shifting grounds. It involves social scientists and practitioners in a recursive struggle that ends up reinforcing scientific representationalism, grants scientists the privilege of a 'God's eye view' of the social realities of other fellow humans, and keeps the institution of social science alive while the social realities are being (unwittingly) transformed and (re)constructed. The single-minded search for validity seems to *blind* social scientists from realizing the *constructed* nature of social reality and *their own recursive involvement* in it.

Cognitive autonomy – the individual ability to make sense, to achieve new understandings, to construct new theories, and to create new realities – is something which poets, inventors, and politicians have always known first-hand but scientists have consistently denied. When cognitive auton-omy enters what a social theory seeks to explain – and a recursive theory for communication is at the core of such phenomena – *ethical criteria must be applied to social theory constructions* in preference to *validity* criteria. Consider Giddens's example of concepts like capital, investment, market, and industry which entered the discourse in economics in the eighteenth and early nineteenth centuries and have now become a reality of modern life.[33] Consider the example of Karl Marx's theories, invented to describe early capitalist society and to extrapolate from the course of its develop-ment. These theories were taken as approximations to the truth, but have served as social inventions that have shaped the world, fed numerous revolutions, changed the boundaries of countries, and advanced the very capitalism whose doom it predicted. On a minor scale consider the example of Erving Goffman's book *The Presentation of Self in Everyday Life* (1959), which was widely read and led to, among other things, architects designing places of business for people to better perform for others;

clothing boutiques with little stages, restaurants with dramatic entrance ways, theatrical department stores, etc.[34]

In much the same way, Giddens is more than a mere accountant of what sociologists do. He is creating and reconstructing a sociological theory in which some social scientists hope to find a better place for themselves and a novel way of describing people they communicate with in the course of their inquiries. Like all sociologists, at least in part, he invents social reality while claiming to describe it. We can no longer hide behind the validity of our theories; we must take *social responsibilities* for what they do bring forth.

Let me propose to treat all theories as *social inventions* that intervene with, transform, create, or maintain the realities we experience. As such, scientific efforts should be guided, not by criteria of validity or of correspondence to a reality that needs to be constructed for this purpose, but by ethical consideration of the reality that scientific theories are able to bring forth. Social theories differ from theories in the natural sciences in that they must constitute themselves in the understanding humans have of them, and they must prove themselves *viable in the communicative practices they engender*. Given the social nature of social theory, the ethical considerations I advocate cannot be cast in terms of abstract principles or rational foundations – which only create new and potentially oppressive institutions – but in terms of communicative processes that coordinate the different lives of cognitively able people. *Social theories must be liveable*.

The virtue of my recursive theory for human communication is that it is also a theory for understanding others' theories for human communication – and provides individuals living with them ample space for constructing social realities that encourage respect for the cognitive autonomy of others. I for one enjoy exploring the spaces it provides and the opportunities it opens for relating to others. This may be the most that social scientists can encourage and enact in their own social practices.

Anthony Giddens's work does not give us much help in understanding human communication. However, his concept of *knowledgeable social agents* could serve as a bridge between sociological and communication literatures.

Notes

1 Alfred North Whitehead and Bertrand G. Russell, *Principia Mathematica*, 3rd edn (New York: Macmillan, 1958; first publ. 1910).

2 Margaret Mead, 'Cybernetics of cybernetics', in Heinz von Foerster et al. (eds), *Purposive Systems* (New York: Spartan Books, 1968), pp. 1–11; Heinz von Foerster, *Cybernetics of Cybernetics or the Control of Control and the Com-*

munication of Communication (Urbana, Ill.: Biological Computer Laboratory, University of Illinois); Lars Lofgren, 'Autology for second order cybernetics', in *Proceedings of the 10th International Congress on Cybernetics* (Namur: Association International de Cybernetique, 1984), pp. 77–83; Ernst von Glasersfeld, 'An introduction to radical constructivism', in Paul Watzlawick (ed.), *The Invented Reality* (New York: W. W. Norton, 1984), pp. 17–40; Malcolm Ashmore et al., *The Reflexive Thesis: Wrighting Sociology of Scientific Knowledge* (Chicago: University of Chicago Press); Anthony Giddens, *The Constitution of Society: Outline of the Theory of Structuration* (Cambridge: Polity Press, 1984); *Modernity and Self-Identity* (Stanford, Calif.: Stanford University Press).

3   Giddens, *The Constitution of Society; Modernity and Self-Identity*.

4   Humberto R. Maturana, 'Neurophysiology of cognition', in P. Garvin (ed.), *Cognition: A Multiple View* (New York: Spartan Books, 1970), pp. 3–23.

5   Paul Watzlawick, Janet H. Beavin and Don D. Jackson, *Pragmatics of Human Communication* (New York: W. W. Norton, 1967), pp. 48–51.

6   Giddens, *The Constitution of Society*, pp. 2–7.

7   Alfred Schutz, *On Phenomenology and Social Relations: Selected Writings*, ed. H. R. Wagner (Chicago: University of Chicago Press, 1970).

8   Ludwig Wittgenstein, *Philosophical Investigations*, 3rd edn (New York: Macmillan, 1958), 59e.

9   Michael H. Agar, *Speaking of Ethnography* (Beverly Hills, Calif.: Sage, 1986).

10   Peter Berger and Thomas Luckmann, *The Social Construction of Reality* (New York: Doubleday, 1966), p. 65.

11   Giddens, *The Constitution of Society*.

12   Ibid., p. 375.

13   David K. Miell and Dorothy E. Miell, 'Recursiveness in interpersonal cognition', in Charles Antaki and Alan Lewis (eds), *Mental Mirrors: Metacognition in Social Knowledge and Communication* (London: Sage, 1986), pp. 27–40.

14   Jacob von Uexkuell, 'A stroll through the world of animals and men: a picture book of invisible worlds', part 1, in *Instinctive Behavior: The Development of a Modern Concept*, trans. Clair H. Schiller, intro. Karl S. Lashley (New York: International Universities Press, 1957).

15   Michael Polanyi, *Knowing and Being* (Chicago: University of Chicago Press, 1969); Giddens, *The Constitution of Society*; Mark Johnson, *The Body in the Mind: The Bodily Basis of Meaning, Imagination and Reason* (Chicago: University of Chicago Press, 1987).

16   Martin Heidegger, 'Letter on humanism', in William Barrett and Henry D. Aiken (eds), *Philosophy in the Twentieth Century: An Anthology*, vol. 3 (New York: Random House, 1962), p. 271.

17   John Shotter, *Social Accountability and Selfhood* (Oxford: Basil Blackwell, 1984).

18   Gregory Bateson, *Steps to an Ecology of Mind* (New York: Ballantine Books, 1972), pp. 177–93.

19   Klaus Krippendorff, 'The power of communication and the communication

of power: toward an emancipatory theory of communication', *Communication*, 12 (1991), pp. 257–96.

20 Giddens, *The Constitution of Society; Modernity and Self-Identity*.

21 Giddens, *The Constitution of Society*, pp. 248, 374.

22 Hilary Putnam, *Reason, Truth and History* (New York: Cambridge University Press, 1981), pp. 49–74.

23 Edwin A. Abbott, *Flatland: A Romance of Many Dimensions*, 6th edn (New York: Dover, 1952).

24 Giddens, *The Constitution of Society*, p. 375.

25 Ibid.

26 Ibid., p. 143.

27 Ibid., pp. 28–31.

28 Ibid., p. 29.

29 Klaus Krippendorff, 'A heretic communication about communication about communication about reality', in Miriam Campanella (ed.), *Between Rationality and Cognition* (Turin/Geneva: Albert Meynier, 1988), pp. 257–76.

30 Giddens, *The Constitution of Society*, p. 351.

31 Ibid., p. 285.

32 Ibid., p. 339.

33 Ibid., pp. 40–1.

34 Walter T. Anderson, *Reality Isn't What it Used to Be* (New York: Harper Collins, 1990), p. 135.

Part II

Messages, Meanings, Discourse

5

Discourse and Cognition in Society

Teun A. van Dijk

Introduction

This essay analyses some of the relationships between discourse and society. Its major thesis is that such relationships are not direct, but should be framed within a theory of the role of *social cognition* in processes of social, political and cultural reproduction. Thus social representations in our minds (such as socially shared knowledge, beliefs, attitudes and ideologies) are assumed to act as the necessary 'interface' between micro-level interactions and individual text and talk, on the one hand, and societal macro-structures, on the other hand. This assumption goes beyond the classical 'correlational' approaches to the relationships between language and society, for instance in sociolinguistics. At the same time, it provides a necessary extension of work in critical linguistics and discourse analysis about the ways language use or discourse contribute to the reproduction or legitimation of social power. By way of illustration, I shall summarize results of research into the properties of news discourse and its role in the reproduction of racism.

It is generally agreed that an adequate study of the relations between discourse and society presupposes that discourse should be located *in* society, as a form of social practice or as an interaction of social group members (or institutions). This overall inclusion relation, however, remains rather vague and is in need of further specification in order to explain which properties of text and talk typically condition which properties of social, political or cultural structures, and vice versa. The same is true for other relations between discourse and society, for instance if we study discourse as presupposing, embodying, enacting, reflecting or legitimating social and institutional arrangements.

The social nature of these relations is traditionally accounted for in terms of speakers and recipients as social actors playing specific social roles in social contexts. The micro-sociology of interaction, and ethno-methodological approaches in particular, have emphasized the role of interpretation and implicit, socially shared 'methods' for making sense of interaction and the social world.[1] Although this seems to address the importance of social cognition in the production of text and talk, micro-sociology usually limits itself to the 'observable' properties of knowledge and understanding, that is, to the ways that cognitions are 'displayed' for recipients as social members. The further conceptual analysis of the precise mental representations and processes involved are generally left to psychology, if found relevant at all.[2]

In our interdisciplinary framework we take the interface of social cognition seriously, as socially shared mental strategies and representations that monitor the production and interpretation of discourse.[3] Thus, if specific knowledge or other beliefs are said to be presupposed and shared by speech participants, we need to make such knowledge and beliefs explicit in order to be able to specify how such presuppositions affect the structures of discourse. Conversely, the crucial concept of 'understanding' text and talk is not adequately explained by merely examining the observable manifestations of such mental processes. This does *not* mean that cognitive analysis should be limited to individual or universal psychological processes of understanding. On the contrary, in the same way as discursive activities are viewed as social (and historical), many dimensions of cognition should also be studied in this double social perspective, at the level of interaction and at the level of groups, institutions or other social structures. In this sense, my approach points beyond much of current psycholinguistics.

Societal analysis: power, dominance and access

Within this broader framework of critical and multidisciplinary discourse analysis, I will first focus on some crucial properties of societal structures, such as power and access, and then relate these to both discourse and social cognition. The point of this analysis is to show how, through socially shared mental representations, social power is reproduced by its discursive enactment and legitimation.

Ignoring many theoretical complexities, *social power* here is simply defined as a property of intergroup relations in terms of the control exercised by (the members of) one group or institution over the actions of (the members of) another group.[4] Such power is based on access to socially valued resources, such as force, wealth, income, status or knowledge. Besides forms of force or coercive power, such control is usually persuasive: acts of others are indirectly controlled through influencing such mental conditions of action as intentions, plans, knowledge or beliefs. It is at this point where power relates to both discourse and social cognition.[5] For specific groups, social power may be limited to special domains or situations (for example, those of politics, the media or education). Also, power is seldom absolute, as long as other groups retain some measure of freedom of action and mind. Indeed, many forms of power breed resistance, in the form of attempts to exercise counter-power.

Critical discourse analysis is interested in *dominance*, defined here as an abuse of social power abuse, that is, as a deviation from accepted standards or norms of (inter)action, in the interest of the more powerful group, resulting in various forms of social inequality. Racism is a form of dominance exercised by whites (Europeans) over ethnic or racial minority groups, or over non-Europeans generally. Dominance is reproduced by enforcing privileged access to social resources by discrimination. It is also reproduced by legitimating such access through forms of 'mind control' such as manipulation and other methods for seeking acceptance or compliance among the dominated group. More generally, this can be viewed as manufacturing consent and consensus. Again, text and talk play a crucial role in the cognitive processes involved in this reproduction process. Their analysis may provide explicit insight into commonly used but vague notions of 'manipulation'. It is the task of this essay to spell out some of the relationships between the structures and strategies of discourse and the cognitive processes and representations underlying the enactment or legitimation of dominance.

Dominance also involves special *access* to various forms of discourse or communicative events.[6] Dominant groups, or elites can be defined by their special access to a wider variety of public or otherwise influential discourses than less powerful groups. That is, elites have more active and better controlled access to the discourses of politics, the media, scholarship, education or the judiciary. They may determine the time, place, circumstances, presence and role of participants, topics, style and audience of such discourses. Also, as a form of 'topical access', elites are the preferred actors represented in public discourse, for instance in news reports. This means that elites also have more chances to have access to the minds of others, and hence to exercise persuasive power. Less powerful groups have active access only to everyday conversations with family members, friends or colleagues, less controlled access to institutional dialogues (for example, in their interaction with doctors, teachers or civil servants), and largely passive access to public discourses, such as those of the mass media. The *reproduction* of dominance in contemporary society is largely managed by maintaining and legitimating such unequal access patterns to discourse and communication, and thus to the public mind: who is allowed (or obliged) to speak or listen to whom, how, about what, when and where and with what consequences.

Power, dominance, access and reproduction, as well as their enactment or legitimation by text and talk, need analysis both at the *macro* level of overall intergroup relations and institutional control, as well as at the *micro* level of everyday, situated (inter)actions by individuals who, as group members, enact and reproduce group power. This is also true for social cognitions, which may be studied as socially and culturally shared knowledge and beliefs of groups, as well as at the level of their individually variable 'applications' or 'uses' by members in specific situations. Indeed, I hope to show that social cognition and discourse precisely allow us to link these micro- and macro-structures of society.[7]

Social cognition

Processes of reproduction and relations of dominance not only involve text and talk, but also shared representations of the 'social mind' of group members. Unlike much other work on discourse and society, my approach assumes that there are crucial theoretical reasons why such *social cognition* should be analysed as the interface between discourse and society and between individual speech participants and the social groups of which they are members: (1) discourse is actually produced/interpreted by individuals, but they are able to do so only on the basis of socially shared knowledge and beliefs; (2) discourse can only 'affect' social structures through the social minds of discourse participants, and conversely (3) social structures can only 'affect' discourse structures through social cognition. Social cognition entails the system of mental strategies and structures shared by group members, and in particular those involved in the understanding, production or representation of social 'objects', such as situations, interactions, groups and institutions.[8]

Although I cannot discuss in detail the complexities of a theory of the social mind, I can summarize the main concepts of such a theory as it connects to both discourse and society. We generally distinguish between more personal and ad hoc cognitions of specific events (models), and more abstract, socially shared or group-based social representations (knowledge, attitudes, ideologies), both represented in what is usually called Long Term Memory. The strategic operations based on these models, such as perception, discourse production and understanding, take place in Short Term (working) Memory. Without going into detail on these (highly complex) mental strategies, we can identify some basic types of memory representation and then proceed to the role of discourse in their formation and change.[9]

Models. All social perception and action, and hence also the production and interpretation of discourse, are based on mental representations of particular episodes. These event or situation *models*[10] are subjective and unique; they represent the current knowledge and opinions of social actors or individual language users about an episode. Planning an action (or discourse) entails building a model of future activities. During discourse understanding old models about the same episode may be activated and updated (as when we read the news); or new models may be formed (for example, about a particular 'race riot' or about an employer who discriminates against minorities). Besides personal experiences and opinions, models also embody instantiations of social knowledge and attitudes, which precisely allow mutual understanding and communication. Hence models are the crucial cognitive interface between the personal and the social dimensions of discourse.

Context models. A special and very influential type of model is the model discourse participants form, and continuously update, of the present communicative situation. Such *context models* feature representations of the participants themselves, their ongoing actions and speech acts, their goals, plans, the setting (time, place, circumstances) or other relative properties of the context. Context models monitor discourse, telling language users what relevant information in their event models should be expressed in their discourse, and how such discourse should be tailored to the properties of the communicative context (for example, through the use of deictic expressions, presuppositions about the knowledge and roles of participants, etc.).

Social knowledge. Besides the personal and ad hoc knowledge represented in their models of specific events, social members also share more general and abstract knowledge about the world. Knowledge about language, discourse and communication is obviously a crucial precondition for verbal interaction, and may be 'applied' in the context model of a communicative event. Similarly, social members share social knowledge, represented in *scripts*, about stereotypical social episodes, such as shopping or travelling.[11] Such social scripts are formed through inferences from repeatedly shared models. Conversely, they are used to understand new episodes through (partial) instantiations in models of such episodes. For instance, in the understanding of news reports, scripts are continuously activated and applied, in order to understand stories about ethnic events such as the disturbances in Los Angeles in the spring of 1992.

Social attitudes. Our personal opinions, as represented in models about specific events, may be contextually specific, individual instantiations of social opinions. These general opinions may further be organized in structured opinion complexes, which can be denoted with the traditional notion of 'attitude'.[12] The notion of persuasion and its role in the enactment and legitimation of dominance, as discussed above, involves the (trans)formation of these social attitude schemata.[13] Most white people in Europe and North America have attitudes about foreigners, refugees, blacks, immigration and affirmative action, and these will be activated, applied and possibly changed during discourse production or understanding about such other group members and ethnic issues.

Ideologies. Finally, attitudes may in turn be grounded on and organized by ideological frameworks. These provide for coherence and function as the general building blocks and inference mechanisms of attitudes. General norms, values and goals of groups and cultures form the elements from which such ideological frameworks are built. Thus ideologies are the more or less permanent, interest-bound, fundamental social cognitions of a group. Their relationship to discourse and language use is indirect. According to our theory of ideology, they operate through attitudes and models before they become manifest in action or discourse. The complex system of ethnic attitudes that underlie ethnic discrimination is organized by such an ideological framework. Unfortunately, we have as yet no explicit theory that details the internal structures and the strategic uses of such ideological frameworks in the (trans)formation of beliefs.[14]

Strategies. Models, knowledge, attitudes and ideologies are permanently formed, updated and changed by various types of mental operations, such as the basic processes of memory search, retrieval, (de)activation, as well as the more complex mental 'work' involved in interpretation, inference, categorization and evaluation. Unlike the 'fixed' rules of grammar, we assume that these operations are 'strategic'. That is to say, they are on-line and tentative – but also fast, goal-oriented, context-dependent, parallel (operating at several levels) and using different kinds of (often incomplete) information at the same time.[15] Strategic understanding of a news report involves the fast activation of relevant scripts or attitudes. It also entails making (and correcting) guesses about the meaning (or the functions) of a whole text or a whole sentence even when we have only read part of it (for example, the headline or the first words). Other strategic processes include the formation or updating of a mental model related to the meaning of a news report; or the formation of scripts or attitudes from models. All mental operations that define the relations between discourse, cognition and society discussed below have such a strategic nature.

The Discourse–Cognition–Society Link

This brief review of the architecture of the social mind implies that all links between discourse and society are mediated by social cognition. Social structures of dominance can only be reproduced by specific acts on the part of dominant group members, and such acts are themselves controlled by social cognition. Thus elite discourses such as news reports about ethnic affairs influence societal structures of ethnic dominance through socially shared representations of dominant group members about ethnic minority groups and ethnic relations. Along both directions of influence, social cognitions provide the crucial interface. And discourse is in turn essential for the acquisition and change of social cognition.

Knowledge and beliefs about society in general, and about majority–minority group relations in particular, may also be acquired through social perception and the experiences of interaction.[16] Majority group members may directly observe the appearance and 'behaviour' of minority group members, and such experiences may also contribute to more or less biased social representations about minority groups.[17] But appearances and behaviour can only be understood on the basis of social cognitions. It is well known, for instance, that 'racial' differences are social constructions or representations, and not objective, observable facts. This *a fortiori* is also the case for the perceived cultural differences that underlie much modern racism-ethnicism. The same is true for the evaluative, biased interpretation of minority behaviour in terms of stereotypes and prejudices.[18] Moreover, prejudice and discrimination by majority group members do not presuppose direct contacts with or observations of minorities. Indeed, much modern racism can be understood as 'symbolic'.[19] Much of what most majorities know and believe about minorities is acquired through discourse and communication.[20] In sum, any approach to the study of how racism is reproduced must account for shared social representations, but it must also account for discourse as a major means whereby social representations are acquired, shared and confirmed.

In present-day Western societies most of what white people know or believe about ethnic relations is derived from the media – from news, TV programmes, movies, advertising and literature – that is, from discourse being produced by the symbolic elites.[21] These elites in turn acquire much of their ethnic information and beliefs from other media discourse and from political, scholarly and other elite discourses. Their views are acquired only marginally from independent 'observations' or from non-elite sources, such as interviews or eyewitness reports of 'ordinary' white people.[22] Elite discourses are therefore the major source of information and opinions about ethnic affairs. This is also true, indirectly, for the sources of everyday conversation on ethnic affairs, which are also largely based on information from the mass media. It follows that since discriminatory (inter)actions are based on models shaped by social cognitions, and since such models and social cognitions about ethnic affairs are partly derived from (elite) discourse, then elites play a prominent if not 'exemplary' role in the reproduction of racism.

Consequences of Social Representations

If ethnic dominance presupposes socially shared cognition, and if the acquisition of social representations on ethnic affairs largely depends on discourse, then the next question is: how exactly does discourse influence such representations? Instead of talking about vague 'influences' or about unspecified processes of persuasion, we need to spell out the various cognitive strategies that underlie discourse comprehension, processes of inference, and the formation and change of social representations as a result of these processes. Such an account presupposes an analysis of the various structures of discourse that may be specifically effective in the (trans)formation of social representations. Since, conversely, discourse may also express or otherwise 'code for' underlying social representations, such an analysis partly answers the complementary question of how social representations are most effectively expressed in text and talk about ethnic affairs.

There are a vast number of properties of discourse that may have a potential effect on the formation, change or confirmation of social representations. Instead of examining all of these discourse properties, I shall reason 'backwards', highlighting some of the processes involved in social cognition, and then try to predict theoretically which discourse structures are particularly relevant in affecting these processes.[23]

We have seen above that social representations, such as knowledge scripts, attitudes and ideologies, may be derived from event and context models. This happens through processes of abstraction, generalization and decontextualization. Individual knowledge and opinions about particular events are transformed into socially shared scripts about stereotypical episodes and thus into white group attitudes about ethnic minority groups or their prototypical members. Without further discussion of the precise cognitive processes involved, we can assume that the formation of social representations is facilitated by one or more of the following conditions, among others:

1   The resulting social representations can be subsumed by an ideological framework that reflects the interests of the group.

2   There are social representations that have similar contents and structures.
3   The structures of the models are similar to those of the social representations.
4   Members are repeatedly confronted with similar models.
5   The models are consistent with other knowledge and beliefs, that is, they are plausible and hence acceptable.
6   The authors of the discourse (as represented in the context model) are thought to be reliable and credible.

Let us examine these conditions in somewhat more detail by applying them to news reports and models on ethnic events.[24] If it is in the interest of the dominant group that minority group members should have less access to valued social resources, then the attitudes controlled by such a self-serving ideology should feature specific opinions that are consistent with or even conducive to the realization of such a goal. For instance, if competition for scarce resources is represented as being inconsistent with such interests, then competition needs to be avoided, and such an opinion may in turn require the development of the social opinion that large-scale immigration generally enhances competition. Similarly, if unemployment is assumed to be inconsistent with one's interests, and if unemployment is seen to result from immigration, then immigration may be evaluated negatively. If foreigners have already immigrated, then the same valued resource (to get the best possible job) may be 'protected' by finding 'good reasons' why minorities should have less access to such jobs. Such reasons may for instance consist of the ethnic prejudices that minorities are less qualified, that they are lazy, that they do not have the right job mentality, have a different culture and hence are less comfortable to work with, and so on.[25]

In sum, given a specific ideological framework, for instance that of nationalism or ethnocentrism, attitudes are favoured whose opinions support the interests (goals, values) embodied in such a framework. This means that special attention is paid to those models that allow 'self-fulfilling' generalization towards such attitudes. For example, events might be subjectively interpreted to show that, indeed, a specific minority worker was unqualified, did not cooperate, or did not have the required work ethic.[26] Similar relations between models and attitudes may be assumed for many other social domains, such as housing, education, welfare and safety. In other words, prejudiced ethnic attitudes will tend to feature those opinions about ethnic minorities that pertain to the conditions of their equal access to social resources and models are selected or constructed in such a way that such opinions are supported.

When such an attitude has already been developed for groups such as

Turks, Moroccans or Mexicans, it is relatively easy to develop similar ones for other immigrant groups. With the exception of the identity of the main actors, structures and abstract contents of the new attitude can simply be 'copied', whether or not relevant models support such attitudes. This is precisely the characteristic property of prejudices; they are negative attitudes about ethnic minorities that are not supported by models; or, as we shall see below, they are based on biased or insufficient models.

We may also assume that the internal structures and contents of attitudes are easier to derive from models that rather closely resemble them, for instance if the model itself features general opinions (such as 'Minorities are less qualified') or event representations that allow such an opinion as an obvious inference. Indeed, the very inference relations between more general and more specific social opinions that define ethnic attitudes may be expressed in discourse itself as generic statements ('Minorities are less qualified', 'Minorities do not speak our language well', 'Minorities have less education'). Such is typically the case in argumentative discourse. Similarly, specific opinions about minorities, for instance about their assumed lack of competence, are facilitated if they are found to be consistent with other, already present social opinions or knowledge (for example, 'Minorities generally have less education').

Whereas attitude formation is facilitated by specific models, these models themselves also need to meet certain conditions. First of all, they must be found to be subjectively credible. That is, they should in principle not be blatantly inconsistent with other known facts, that is with other models. In cases of inconsistency, special operations of discounting must be applied to make this comparison less compelling. This is indeed what happens in prejudiced understanding of discourse. Credibility may thus be superseded by the 'fit' of a model with respect to a more general attitude. If young black males are assumed to be specifically violent or criminal, then stories that illustrate such attributed properties will be more easily believed than stories that are inconsistent with such an attitude. We may assume that those models are most effective that are both consistent with general attitudes, and feature facts or arguments that experientially buttress the negative opinion about a particular event. The same is true for the credibility of the writer (journalist, newspaper). A liberal quality newspaper reporting negative 'facts' about minorities will be more credible, at least for liberal readers, than an explicitly xenophobic right-wing tabloid.

For similar reasons of generalizability, models must feature actors that have prototypical properties. Thus, in models about crime, drugs, mugging or violence, a young black male is more prototypical than an elderly woman from India, who may in turn be more prototypical for a story about poverty. The same is true for majority actors, who need to be represented in such a way that many whites can identify or sympathize with them. Generally, then, credible ethnic models should clearly mark the difference between (positive) US, and (negative) THEM, feature proto-typical actors, and stereotypical episodes in familiar settings. This facil-itates their comprehensibility, and also enhances their plausibility, acceptability and generalizability. But stereotypical episodes may be so common that they are less remarkable and hence less memorable. For models to serve as the basis for storytelling in processes of informal, conversational sharing, it is necessary that the events are interesting, relevant and remarkable. Besides conditions on mental models, we may also have conditions on stories and more generally conditions on 'effec-tive' discourse.

Discourse structures

From these preferred structures of models and social representations, we can speculate about the properties discourses, such as news reports, should have in order to facilitate credibility, acceptability and the forma-tion of social representations that are consistent with ideologies under-lying the reproduction of racism in society. Theoretically and methodo-logically, however, it should be emphasized that the very complexity of these relationships and conditions does not allow determinacy. News reports that have such preferred structures do not always have such socio-cognitive 'effects'. Rather, such consequences are general and structural. In many communicative contexts they facilitate specific cognitive pro-cessing and hence social functions. Equally crucial are the existing atti-tudes and ideologies of the readers. The same stereotypical news stories may be read 'oppositionally' by some groups of readers, such as mino-rities themselves, whose ideologies do not favour the development of negative prejudices about minorities. On the contrary, their judgement may reflect back on the journalist or the newspaper as indicative of prejudiced reporting.

With this caveat in mind, let us examine some examples of news structures that facilitate the formation of 'preferred' ethnic situation models as specified above.

Topics. The meaning of discourse can be described at two levels: the local (micro) level of word and sentence meanings; and the global (macro) level of topics. Topics, theoretically represented as the propositions that form its semantic macro-structure, embody the most important information of a discourse, and play a vital cognitive role in production and compre-hension. They define the overall (global) coherence that assigns the necessary 'unity' to a text. Topics are sometimes directly expressed in discourse, as is the case with headlines and leads (defining the summary) of news reports. Topics express the most important (highest-level) information of mental models, and are also used by the readers to build such models. In a sense, topics may be seen as subjectively 'defining the situation'; what is topical information in a news report influences the most important information in the readers' model of a news event.

In news about ethnic affairs topics define the ethnic situation and may also manipulate the ways the readers interpret the news event. Thus urban disturbances by young blacks may be defined as a 'race riot' in the main topic (as expressed, for example, in the headline) and focus on irrational violence, instead of defining it as an act of protest, or as a form of resistance. Since deviance and violence of young blacks are stereotypical elements of racist prejudices, such models are relatively easy to generalize or may confirm existing prejudices. Similarly, other important topics in the text may be downgraded (for example, poverty, discrimination, police harassment) while relatively unimportant ones are upgraded – via strategies that are controlled by the ethnic representations of the journalist. Depending upon the social representations of the reader, of course, suggested topics of news reports may well be transformed into different topics: minority readers or white anti-racists may find quite different information important in a given news report and may disregard the persuasive topical structure of the news report.

Models are more easily generalized as social representations when they are repeatedly used, as may be the case for models about minority crime. This does not mean, however, that majority group members do not form prejudiced attitudes on the basis of only one or two experiences. Research on news about ethnic minority news shows that crime is indeed one of the most frequent topics.[27] The same is true for news about immigration, cultural differences and race relations, which are also major topics in everyday conversations and reflect the frequency and the prominence of these topics in the media. Less stereotypical topics, such as the contributions of minorities to the economy, the arts or political organization, are relatively rare. This leads to less well-established and less complete models, which in turn may impair more neutral knowledge and belief formation about minorities.

In sum, special topics may indirectly play a role in the formation of social beliefs about minorities: by their influence in the formation of the (easily retrievable) higher levels of models, as well as by their frequency. Socially speaking, special topics do not merely express the individual models of a reporter, but also the generalized, shared models and social representations of journalists and newspapers as institutions, as well as of their elite sources. This is why frequent ethnic topics often reflect the major interests and concerns of white elites.

Schemata. The global meaning of a discourse, as represented in topics, is usually organized by fixed, conventional categories that form an over-all text schema or superstructure. Just like stories or arguments, news reports in the press also have such a schema, featuring such conventional categories as Summary (Headline + Lead), Main Event, Backgrounds (History + Context), Verbal Reactions and Comments (Evaluation + Expectations).[28] Such a schema also defines the canonical order of the topics and their corresponding text fragments in the news report, although topics in news may be discontinuous: the information organized by a topic may be delivered in various 'instalments', by placing the most important information first and the details last.

Although formal text schemata do not carry meaning as such, the presence, absence or order of specific categories may well be significant and influence the structures of models and hence social representations. We have already seen above that it matters which topics are expressed in the Headline category and which topics are not expressed. Similarly, information in the Background category usually facilitates interpretation of a current news event (expressed in the Main Event category) by providing information about causes or the socio-political context. If a report on minority unemployment does not specify in a Background category that unemployment may also be due to discrimination, then readers may build partial, if not biased, models of minority unemployment events, which in turn may affect their social representations of this issue. This is indeed often the case: news about minorities often lacks a Background category, or only focuses on negative characteristics attributed to minorities, thereby often blaming the victim. Similarly, 'Verbal Reactions' may tend to feature quotes by white officials.

Local Meaning. Whereas topics and news schemata define the global level of news reports, we also need to pay attention to the local meanings of actually expressed words and sentences (propositions) and their immediate relations. One important notion at this level is (local) *coherence.* Subsequent sentences (or rather the propositions they express) are coherent under two conditions: (1) extensionally, when they denote facts whose mental representations are related in the mental model of the text (for example, by relations of cause, condition or time); and (2) intentionally, when a proposition has a specific function relative to another, usually previous, proposition (for example, a specification, generalization, example, contrast). Hence coherence relations as they are expressed in the text tell us something about the structure of news events as represented in the model of the journalist. Coherence relations in news reports may also suggest relations between the facts that do not actually exist. In news about ethnic affairs we may expect, for instance, biased coherence markers that suggest preferred explanations for ethnic issues, such as unemployment. For instance, the use of a clause like 'because of their lower education levels' may suggest that lacking education is the (only or main) cause of unemployment. Thus a news report in a British tabloid emphasized that a white club owner, convicted of discrimination against a black singer, had several times been mugged by black men. Mentioning such a 'psychological cause' may be interpreted as an excuse in this case. As we have seen earlier for the schematic category of Background, such local forms of biased, subjective coherence strategies may influence the structure of models, and hence that of social representations of minorities.[29]

Another prominent property of local meaning is *implicitness*. Models usually embody much more information about an event than speakers or writers would usually express. This is because such information is assumed to be already known by the recipients, or because the information is contextually irrelevant or uninteresting, or because the recipients can infer such information from the information that is expressed. Semantically speaking, discourses are tips of the icebergs of information represented in their underlying models, of which most information remains implicit in the text. For news about ethnic affairs we may predict that precisely that information remains implicit that will reflect positively on minorities and negatively on the majority. The same is true for the *presuppositions* signalled by a news report, which may suggest that some fact is generally known, even if such a fact does not exist. If newspapers, following conservative politicians, claim that 'This tolerant country cannot admit more refugees', then such a statement presupposes that 'our country is tolerant', an opinion that is controversial at best. Suggested implications are a powerful while indirect way of influencing the structures of models.

Events may be described with more or less *details* and at more or less general or specific *levels of representation*. In the news, important, relevant or otherwise newsworthy information is described with more detail and at lower levels of specificity. In line with the predictions formulated above, we may expect more detail and more specifics for those topics that are consistent with stereotypes and prejudices, such as crime, violence, deviance or cultural differences, and less for white prejudice, discrimination and racism, as is indeed the case.

Finally, the functional relations between propositions in discourse may also have a more strategic nature. That is, they may be moves, or local 'steps', in a global discourse and interaction strategy. Characteristic moves in discourse about ethnic affairs are disclaimers, such as Apparent Denial ('We have nothing against the black community, but . . .'), or Apparent Concession ('The Turks have a very rich culture, but . . .'). Such semantic moves on the one hand contribute to the overall strategy of positive self-presentation of the white group and its members, while at the same time preparing a move that has a function in the strategy of negative other-presentation. Such strategic moves may have a strong influence on readers' models of ethnic events, because they allow readers to develop negative opinions about minorities without feeling guilty of racism. The model, thus structured, does not violate the social norms of tolerance.

Style. At the level of word choice, we may also observe *stylistic* uses that have an impact on the formation of opinions in mental models. In the press, the choice of lexical items to describe people, actions or events depends on the opinions, attitudes and ideology of the journalist, as in the familiar pair 'freedom fighter' vs. 'terrorist', for which Reagan's discourses about Nicaragua were a well-known example. Similarly, we may expect, and do indeed find, that although overt abuse of minorities is no longer common in contemporary news reports, at least in the quality press, minority groups, and especially young black males and their actions tend to be described by more negative words (such as 'mobs'). Similarly, minority 'disturbances' will usually be described as a 'riot' in the right-wing press. For anti-racists in Britain, the right-wing tabloid press has an impressive list of terms of abuse, routinely featuring 'mobs of activists', 'snoopers' and the like, but also concoctions such as 'unscrupulous or feather-brained observers', 'rent-a-mob agitators', 'blinkered tyrants', or 'left-wing crazies', among others. The opinions that such lexical items code for are obvious, as are those preferred in the models of the readers. The reverse is true for the news coverage of the police and for (white) 'law-abiding citizens', who tend to be praised or described neutrally, if not as victims of black violence or crime. Again, frequent repetition of such terms may soon confirm the negative opinions they express, and such models may be easily generalized to very negative attitudes about the 'intolerance' of the anti-racist 'brigade'. Conversely, words such as 'racism' will either be totally avoided or at least be put between quotation marks, or will be down-toned to weaker terms such as 'discrimination', 'bigotry', 'xenophobia' or simply 'resentment'.

Syntax. The formal structures of sentences may also be used to express and persuasively convey a biased model of ethnic events. Prominence of news actors or their actions, as well as the perspective of their account in the news, may be coded by word order. For instance, it has often been shown that minority actors tend to be placed in early sentence-topical positions, i.e. as syntactic subject and as semantic agent, if they are engaged in negative actions (for example, 'Black youth involved in rape case'). The converse is true for majority actors. Their negative agency may be played down by leaving it implicit, say in a passive sentence (for example, 'Black youths beaten up by police', or 'Blacks beaten up'), or by nominalizations

('Blacks victims of aggression').[30] Typically, syntax codes for semantic
relations as well as for the perspective or the prominence of specific
relations as represented in underlying journalistic models. Syntactic
structures may thus also subtly influence the representations of ethnic
events in the models of the readers, for instance by emphasizing or de-
emphasizing agency and responsibility for positive or negative actions.

Rhetoric. Of the many other properties of news discourse, we should also
mention those of rhetoric, such as alliteration, metaphor or hyperbole. As
is the case for all formal structures, these do not have direct semantic
interpretations. However, rhetorical structures are used to attract attention, to highlight, to emphasize, or to de-emphasize specific meanings of
discourse. Thus propositions about negative properties of minorities may
be highlighted (and hence be better processed and better recalled) by
rhyme, alliteration, repetition, or hyperbole, as is the case in the British
tabloid press. On the other hand, negative propositions about majority
actors will typically be understated and played down in many rhetorical
ways. Such formal structures invite specific semantic interpretations,
focusing on specific properties of models and stressing the relevance of
specific ethnic opinions represented in such models.

Conclusions

Discourse structures express structures of mental models, which are
related to more permanent social representations such as knowledge,
attitudes and ideologies, which in turn are the shared ways groups and
cultures represent their goals, interests, concerns, structures or institutions. An analysis of the position of discourse 'in' society needs a cognitive
interface. Institutions, social structures, group relations, group member-
ship, power, dominance, at the macro level, as well as structures of
situations and interactions at the micro level of society, can only be
expressed, marked, described, enacted or legitimated in discourse through
their representations in attitudes, scripts and mental models of events.
The same is true for the way discourse affects the social situation, speech
participants, as well as broader social structures.

Analysis, therefore, must always be that of discourse–cognition–
society. In such a triangle of relations, both discourse and cognition are
not merely linguistic or psychological objects, but also inherently social.
Social cognition is acquired, used and changed in social situations, and
discourse is one of the major sources of its development and change. No
social actions or practices, and hence no group relations of power or
dominance, are conceivable without social cognition and discourse.

Although virtually all of the humanities and the social sciences have paid attention to some of the links involved, these have either been studied too superficially or have neglected vital relationships.

In my examples of how racism is reproduced through news discourse, I have highlighted some of the relations between discourse, social cognition and society. Discourse plays a prominent role in the reproduction of racism defined as ethnic group dominance. Ethnic dominance, especially of white elites, may be enacted by limiting and controlling active or passive access to discourse, genres or communicative events. Minority journalists and writers thus have much less access to the media, and hence to news reports, than comparable white groups, elites or institutions. They also have less access to such resources as press offices and press conferences. They tend to be seen as less competent, less reliable and (hence) as less newsworthy. As a consequence, their activities and opinions are less covered, and they are less quoted, which in turn influences the readers' models for ethnic events. These models, then, are necessarily partial, imbalanced and organized by a white group perspective. Thus structures of dominance, as enacted in the routines of news- gathering and news-writing, are represented in the mental models of journalists, which in turn influence the structures and the meanings of news reports.

Detailed discussion of some of the structures of these news reports shows that such structures may in turn lead to preferred mental models of ethnic events. On the whole, such models tend to represent minorities negatively, and the dominant group as positive or neutral. If these models meet a number of other conditions, such as *structural resemblance, plausibility* or *prototypicality*, they may be generalizable to socially shared prejudices, which in turn represent the ideological level of racism. Thus, through these social cognitions, discourses may contribute to the reproduction of racism in society. Structures and strategies of news manipulate model-building of the readers and indirectly manufacture the ethnic consensus. Discourse topics (such as crime, deviance, violence or cultural differences of minority groups) define the ethnic situation, and what information should have a prominent position in mental models. News schemata may further organize such topics in ways that make some events more prominent, and others less prominent, such as negative properties of the majority, primarily intolerance, prejudice and racism. At the level of style, rhetoric and local meanings, negative properties of minorities may be emphasized, in such a way that models easily 'fit' or confirm existing stereotypes or prejudices.

While being able to variously code and enact relations of dominance, or other social structures, through the social minds of group members, discourse may in the same way also reproduce such dominance. It does so by affecting the models and social representations of social members, which

124 *Teun A. van Dijk*

in turn monitor social actions and interactions that 'implement' dominance. At the macro level, discourse thus indirectly conditions the group relations, organizations and institutions that define social structure. Research in the near future should focus on the more subtle and complex of these relationships between discourse, cognition and society.

Notes

1 See e.g. J. M. Atkinson and J. Heritage (eds), *Structures of Social Action* (Cambridge: Cambridge University Press, 1984); D. Boden and D. H. Zimmerman (eds), *Talk and Social Structure: Studies in Ethnomethodology and Conversation Analysis* (Cambridge: Polity Press, 1991).
2 See, however, the early pleas for a cognitive sociology by A. V. Cicourel, e.g. in *Cognitive Sociology* (Harmondsworth, Middx.: Penguin, 1973).
3 T. A. van Dijk, 'Social cognition and discourse', in H. Giles and R. P. Robinson (eds), *Handbook of Social Psychology and Language* (Chichester, Sussex: Wiley, 1990), pp. 163–83.
4 For details see e.g. S. Lukes (ed.), *Power* (Oxford: Blackwell, 1986).
5 T. A. van Dijk, 'Structures of discourse and structures of power', in J. A. Anderson (ed.), *Communication Yearbook 12* (Newbury Park, Calif.: Sage, 1989), pp. 18–59.
6 T. A. van Dijk, 'Discourse, power and access', in D. R. Caldas-Coulthard (ed.), *Critical Discourse Analysis* (London: Routledge, forthcoming).
7 For background, see the contributions to K. Knorr-Cetina and A. V. Cicourel (eds), *Advances in Social Theory and Methodology: Towards an Integration of Micro- and Macrosociologies* (London: Routledge, 1981).
8 For further details and discussion see R. M. Farr and S. Moscovici (eds), *Social Representation* (Cambridge: Cambridge University Press, 1984); R. S. Wyer and T. K. Srull (eds), *Handbook of Social Cognition* (3 vols; Hillsdale, NJ: Erlbaum).
9 For detail see T. A. van Dijk and W. Kintsch, *Strategies of Discourse Comprehension* (New York: Academic Press, 1983).
10 See A. Garnham, *Mental Models as Representations of Discourse and Text* (Horwood: E. Halstead Press, 1987); P. N. Johnson-Laird, *Mental Models* (Cambridge: Cambridge University Press, 1983); T. A. van Dijk, 'Cognitive situation models in discourse processing: the expression of ethnic situation models in prejudiced stories', in J. P. Forgas (ed.), *Language and Social Situations* (New York: Springer, 1985), pp. 61–79; T. S. van Dijk, 'Episodic models in discourse processing', in R. Horowitz and S. J. Samuels (eds), *Comprehending Oral and Written Language* (New York: Academic Press, 1987), pp. 161–96.
11 R. C. Schank and R. P. Abelson, *Scripts, Plans, Goals, and Understanding: An Inquiry into Human Knowledge Structures* (Hillsdale, NJ: Erlbaum, 1977).
12 For a recent social psychological discussion of the attitude concept, see e.g.

J. R Eiser and J. van der Pligt, *Attitudes and Decisions* (London: Routledge, 1988).

13 See van Dijk, 'Social cognition and discourse'; J. C. Turner, *Social Influence* (Milton Keynes, Bucks.: Open University Press, 1991).

14 A different social psychological approach to ideologies is the rhetorical theory proposed by Billig and his associates, see e.g. M. Billig, *Ideology and Social Psychology* (Oxford: Basil Blackwell, 1982); M. Billig, *Ideology and Opinions* (London: Sage, 1991); M. Billig et al., *Ideological Dilemas* (London: Sage, 1988).

15 van Dijk and Kintsch, *Stratagies of Discourse Comprehension*.

16 L. A. Zebrowitz, *Social Perception* (Milton Keynes, Bucks.: Open University Press, 1990).

17 D. L. Hamilton (ed.), *Cognitive Processes in Stereotyping and Intergroup Behavior* (Hillsdale, NJ: Erlbaum, 1981).

18 D. Bar-Tal, C. F. Graumann, A. W. Kruglanski and W. Stroebe (eds), *Stereotyping and Prejudice* (New York: Springer, 1989).

19 J. F. Dovidio and S. L. Gaertner (eds), *Prejudice, Discrimination, and Racism* (New York: Academic Press 1986).

20 See S. Jäger, *Brandsätze*, dissertation, Duisburg, 1992; T. A. van Dijk, *Prejudice in Discourse* (Amsterdam: Benjamins, 1984); T. A. van Dijk, *Communicating Racism* (Newbury Park, Calif.: Sage, 1987); T. A. van Dijk, *Racism and the Press* (London: Routledge, 1991); R. Wodak, P. Nowak, J. Pelikan, H. Gruber, R. De Cillia and R. Mitten, 'Wir sind unschuldige Täter', in *Studien zum antisemitischen Diskurs im Nachkriegsösterreich* (Frankfurt/Main: Suhrkamp, 1990).

21 See e.g. P. Hartmann and C. Husband, *Racism and the Mass Media* (London: Davis-Poynter, 1974); van Dijk, *Racism and the Press*; C. C. Wilson and F. Gutiérrez, *Minorities and the Media* (Beverly Hills, Calif./London: Sage, 1985); Wodak et al., 'Wir sind unschuldige Täter'.

22 T. A. van Dijk, *Elite Discourse and Racism* (Newbury Park, Calif.: Sage, 1993).

23 There is a vast literature in cognitive and social psychology, as well as in interpersonal and mass communication, about the ways speakers influence or persuade their audiences. See e.g. R. N. Bostrom, *Persuasion* (Englewood Cliffs, NJ: Prentice-Hall, 1983); A. H. Eagly and S. Chaiken, 'Cognitive theories of persuasion', in L. Berkowitz (ed.), *Advances in Experimental Social Psychology; Vol 17* (New York: Academic Press, 1984). Our discussion focuses only on a few often neglected aspects of these acts and processes, viz. on the relations between specific structures and specific properties of (social) cognition.

24 For the research results see van Dijk, *Racism and the Press*.

25 For details on such ethnic ideologies and attitudes see e.g. J. P. Fernandez, *Racism and Sexism in Corporate Life* (Lexington, Mass.: Lexington Books, 1981); R. Jenkins, *Racism and Recruitment: Managers, Organizations and Equal Opportunity in the Labour Market* (Cambridge: Cambridge University Press, 1986); van Dijk, *Elite Discourse and Racism*.

26   M. Snyder, 'On the self-perpetuating nature of social stereotypes, in D. L. Hamilton (ed.), *Cognitive Processes in Stereotyping and Intergroup Behavior* (Hillsdale, NJ Erlbaum, 1981), pp. 183–212.

27   van Dijk, *Racism and the Press*.

28   T. A. van Dijk, *News as Discourse* (Hillsdale, NJ: Erlbaum, 1988).

29   For more detailed analysis of examples of similar elite 'explanations' of minority unemployment in the media as well as in political and corporate discourses see: van Dijk, *Elite Discourse and Racism*.

30   See e.g. R. Fowler, B. Hodge, G. Kress and T. Trew, *Language and Control* (London: Routledge, 1979); R. Fowler, *Language in the News: Discourse and Ideology in the Press* (London: Routledge, 1991).

6

Risk Communication and Public Knowledge

William Leiss

Introduction

Professional developments are occurring for us in the field of communication studies at a time when political events around the world are demonstrating once again the centrality of communicative processes in social life. In Europe and elsewhere the mask of legitimacy has been torn from many long-standing political structures, along with the nation-state entities that gave them legal force, all of which have proved to be artificial and obsolete and are crumbling. Social groupings based on what appear to be more solid foundations – a collective identity that is defined most sharply by language and an associated cultural tradition – are reasserting themselves against the artificial political structures in which they had been submerged. Above all what has been revealed in this process is how fraudulent were the superficial tokens of public allegiance offered in the past to those now-discredited political regimes. For those tokens had been extracted in some cases by simple terror; in others, by promises of a rosy future that itself had turned out to be just a massive fraud perpetrated by corrupt elites; in still others, by a fear that the standard of living and economic prosperity citizens were accustomed to would be jeopardized if they were to vote to change the existing political order.

To the extent to which these recent developments represent an authentic expression of the popular will, against the inauthentic public manifestations of the past, they are an immensely hopeful sign. To be sure, there are other forces at work as well, especially the global integration of economic and technological change, which will require new political associations, different from the discredited or obsolete ones, to bind together the linguistically defined communities. And, of course, there are regressive features as well which must be combated, especially the immediate outbreaks of intolerance and hatred among groups with long traditions of ethnic rivalry or the ancient European scourge of anti-Semitism.

Given the nature of these developments, I believe, specialists within the discipline of communication studies may be expected to contribute to understanding them and to resolving the new social problems that have arisen in their wake. I claim no special expertise in these matters and have made these preliminary remarks just to introduce my theme. What I want to do is to refer back to an old paradigm in communication theory, and to show how an awareness of the unique features of communication processes has been helping to form an effective approach to a major public policy issue in North America. The results illustrate for me the vitality of our discipline in the contemporary period.

The Message Transmission Theory

What I have chosen to call the 'message transmission theory' has its origins in 1948 in the famous Lasswell definition of the act of communication:

A convenient way to describe an act of communication is to answer the following questions:

Who
Says What
In Which Channel
To Whom
With What Effect?

The scientific study of the process of communication tends to concentrate upon one or another of these questions. Scholars who study the 'who,' the communicator, look into the factors that initiate and guide the act of communication. We call this subdivision of the field of research *control analysis*. Specialists who focus upon the 'says what' engage in *content analysis*. Those who look primarily at the radio, press, film and other channels of communication are doing *media analysis*. When the principal concern is with the persons reached by the media, we speak of *audience analysis*. If the question is the impact upon audiences, the problem is *effect analysis*.[1]

Like other aspects of the study of communication in the immediately preceding period, this definition arose out of the concern with the nature and effects of propaganda.[2]

An early variant on this theme, and the first account (so far as I know) which gave a diagrammatic representation for the message transmission

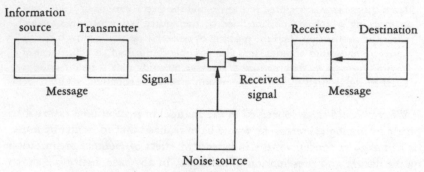

Figure 6.1 The engineering theory of communication
Source: Shannon and Weaver, *Mathematical Theory of Communication*.

theory, appeared a year later in Claude Shannon and Warren Weaver's *The Mathematical Theory of Communication* (see figure 6.1). This version was oriented towards the engineering aspects of communication – in fact, it was Weaver's discursive interpretation of Shannon's mathematical theory – and so it incorporates the additional elements of signal and noise, as well as the transmitting and receiving devices. In addition, it conceives of the channel as either a technological or a natural medium: a wire in the case of telephony, the 'space' in the case of radio; owing to the special characteristics of the medium, there is a new element (a *coding and decoding process*) when the transmitter/receiver turns a message into a signal and vice versa. For Weaver, the theory is applicable to the familiar situation of human face-to-face communication, as well as to all forms of technologically mediated communication: 'When I talk to you, my brain is the information source, yours the destination; my vocal system is the transmitter, and your ear and associated eighth nerve is the receiver.'[3]

Later Weaver extends the engineering analogy further by suggesting that another box, the 'semantic receiver', could be added to the diagram between the engineering receiver and the destination, which 'subjects the message to a second decoding, the demand on this one being that it must match the statistical *semantic characteristics* of the message to the statistical semantic capacities of the totality of receivers, or of that subset of receivers which constitute the audience one wishes to affect'. Curiously, Weaver did not think of a complementary 'semantic transmitter', that is, a second level of encoding interposed between the information source and the engineering transmitter – probably because the elaborate effort of 'repackaging' information, for example in marketing and advertising, was not well understood at the time. But Weaver does mention 'semantic noise', as an adjunct to engineering noise:

From this source is imposed into the signal the perturbations or distortions of meaning which are not intended by the source but which inescapably affect the destination. And the problem of semantic decoding must take this semantic noise into account. It is also possible to think of an adjustment of original message so that the sum of message meaning plus semantic noise is equal to the desired total message meaning at the destination.[4]

If Weaver could have conceived of the channel in institutional rather than purely technological terms, he would have realized that in 'semantic noise' he had a good concept of the independent effect of channel organization on the nature and presentation of messages. In any case, figure 6.2 shows what Weaver's complete version of the message transmission theory would look like if these additions were to be made.

All theories have inherent limitations on their applicability, and the message transmission theory is no exception. The hidden feature of Lasswell's original conception is that it pretends to be a full and complete representation of the act of communication *per se* – that is, of all possible expressions of communicative processes. This is inappropriate. A proviso is required, and indeed is indicated in the name which I have bestowed upon it: the Lasswell definition describes well the elements of the communication act considered as a process for the transmission of messages, especially when they are mediated via a technological channel – as a theory of mediated communication. When we recognize this limitation, however, we can also acknowledge the theory's power and range.[5]

In *Social Communication in Advertising* (1986) my colleagues and I did not refer explicitly to the message transmission theory in our study of advertising, but we might very well have done so, since our treatment of the subject fits nicely into this framework. This is because we approach advertising as both a powerful mode of persuasive communication and as

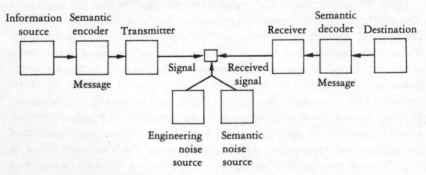

Figure 6.2   The engineering theory (complete)
Source: Shannon and Weaver, *Mathematical Theory of Communication*.

a form of mediated communication – indeed, one which incorporates a threefold process of mediation.[6] One type of mediation occurs between producers and consumers, wherein advertising agencies assist producers in encoding products with symbolic meanings; another, between producers and the media, wherein agencies assist producers in choosing the right 'media mix' (and the media content – advertising content relation) for attaining the strategic objectives of their marketing campaigns; and a third, between media and their audiences, wherein agencies assist both producers and the media in understanding the decoding processes of audiences.

Our study of advertising shows that the message transmission theory is capable of accommodating an approach that gives full recognition to social institutions and their operative capacities. Seen within the framework of a detailed institutional analysis, relations of power and control, manipulation, equity, and so forth are shown to be represented concretely in both what is present and what is absent in message content (in the form of selectivity, bias, stereotyping, dominant values, etc.). Thus one can 'overlay' the institutional analysis on the message transmission model: Combining the complete version of Weaver's engineering model with the threefold structure of mediation in advertising yields the result shown in figure 6.3, which demonstrates how the message transmission theory is capable of being infused, in a structured way, with the 'real', historical content that exists in the development of modern social institutions.

This is not an example I wish to focus on, however, in illustrating the vitality of our discipline that is expressed in the new applications of communication theory. Rather, I want to do this by examining the relatively unfamiliar domain which goes by the name of 'risk communication'. What I intend to show is that a model of communication processes was required in order to make a significant advance in our approach to a

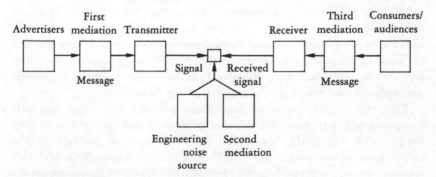

Figure 6.3 An institutional version of the engineering theory: the case of advertising

very important aspect of public policy in all advanced industrial societies today. In this example, too, we will discover that the message transmission theory is capable of representing in a dynamic way a set of contents and relations that have developed in the play of institutional forces in contemporary society.

Risk Communication

Risk communication has been defined as 'any purposeful exchange of information about health or environmental risks between interested parties'.[7] Almost everyone is now aware that natural processes, industrial technologies and consumer preferences all give rise to hazards which threaten human health, non-human species, and the functioning of planetary ecosystems upon which the former depend. An earthquake is an example of a natural hazard; acid rain is a type of ecosystem hazard arising from industrial technology; and cigarette smoking is a kind of voluntary consumer choice which exposes individuals to a wide range of specific health hazards. The chances that any individual or group will suffer adverse consequences of varying severity stemming from exposure to such hazards can be expressed as a measure of the risk we incur in particular situations.[8] Popular demands for better protecting human health and the environment from the impacts of industrial technologies are now a major determinant of public policy in many nations.

The phrase 'risk communication' originated in English usage only in the mid-1980s; it has attained wide recognition in a specialized literature since that time, and is slowly appearing in other European languages, such as German.[9] Over the period of its development there has been a shift in emphasis from the adjective to the noun in this phrase. As it was first conceived, the chief task of risk communication was thought to be learning how to convey, to the relatively unsophisticated members of 'the public', the pure, rational knowledge content inherent in the assessment of risks made by scientific and engineering 'experts'.[10] In this phase the chief obstacle to meaningful risk communication was thought to be the public's inability or unwillingness to grasp the nature and implications of the concept of risk itself and, flowing from this, the public's unrealistic demands for protection from certain types of hazards.

Thus the emphasis was on technically assessed risk itself; the presumption was that, once the rational content of technical risk was conveyed more effectively, the 'irrational' resistance of publics to the calculations of acceptable risk which were derived from technical risk assessments would evaporate. An example that appeared frequently in the literature was that of nuclear power: whereas most 'energy experts' think that the risks attendant upon nuclear energy generation are relatively low, in comparison with many other risks in contemporary society, most members of 'the public' see the matter quite differently, ranking these risks well above most others with which they are familiar. Many experts regard the public view in this case as highly irrational and wrong-headed, and they believe that this view results in incorrect public policy choices – for example, leading to preferences for other types of energy generation which have greater adverse environmental impacts. Such disagreements about the assessment of risk occur in virtually every aspect of our uses of technological innovations: chemicals in agriculture and every type of industry; transportation of hazardous goods; food additives; the siting of waste treatment facilities; energy production and distribution; forest practices; and many others.

It is necessary for us to appreciate just how large are the stakes for society as a whole in this type of controversy. Among other things, what is at stake is the ability of citizens to have substantive input into the decisions that affect their lives. In addition, there are huge costs involved in providing adequate remedies for polluted environments and in protecting us from exposure to various types of hazards. We need to know urgently whether our priorities for environmental protection policies, and for the allocation of public- and private-sector resources to pay the costs of the actions we believe should be undertaken, are based on the best information and reasoning on these matters. For if we make serious mistakes in this regard, the risk we run is that we will have wasted considerable sums of money – money which might have been spent in other ways to control the effects of serious hazards.

But a discussion about risks that was structured as lectures by experts to the public soon showed itself to be a counter-productive exercise. There was massive distrust on both sides: the public saw experts as using the language of risk as a cover for letting industry have a free hand with project developments, and the experts saw many members of the public as using an ignorance of risk assessment as a way of opposing everything that appeared to change established routines of life. Governments, caught in the middle, were unable to facilitate solutions to this impasse.

It was at this point that risk practitioners in the United States, led by Vincent Covello, began to champion a radically different approach to public debates on risk management. They did so by re-framing the issue of risk communication as a problem in communicative theory and practice, rather than in the concept of risk. In other words, they shifted the emphasis from the adjective to the noun in this phrase. Moreover, they chose the message transmission model as a specific way of representing the many problems that had been encountered in the earlier approach; these were now labelled source problems, message problems, channel

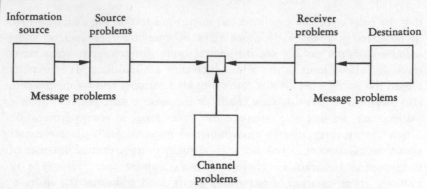

Figure 6.4   Risk communication problems
Source: Adapted from Shannon and Weaver, *Mathematical Theory of Communication*.

problems, and receiver problems.[11] These problems may be mapped onto the simplified version of the engineering theory as shown in figure 6.4.

Source Problems in risk communication include disagreements among experts (resulting in different messages about the same set of conditions); lack of understanding of and information on the concerns, confusions, and values of those members of the public who are most directly affected by specific proposals (for example, the communities in the immediate vicinity of plant sitings); and lack of public credibility for experts attached to certain institutions, such as corporations or governments, when those institutions are perceived as being proponents for industrial developments that are likely to generate incremental risks. Thus 'source problems' are doubts about the accuracy, truthfulness, or completeness of the message which arise from doubts about the impartiality or competence or thoroughness of the experts who are assessing risks.

Message Problems most often result from inadequacies in the established scientific databases relevant to proposed developments (so that key information is not available when decisions are taken); from the irreducible uncertainties that are necessarily a part of the statements of risk in scientific terms (which are always expressed as probabilities); and from the inherent complexities in the concept of risk itself. These types of message problems create difficulties even when there is a predisposition on the part of an agency to do the best possible job in communicating about risk with the public.

For risk experts, *Channel Problems* are almost always thought of in terms of the inadequacies of the mass media in reporting 'objectively' about health and environmental hazards.[12] Bias, sensationalism, and oversimplification are charges laid at the media's door by those who think that both electronic and print journalists do a poor job of reporting about risks. Journalists respond that risk experts often do not willingly tell the whole story, that they sometimes conceal material facts or even disseminate falsehoods, that they do not express themselves clearly, and in general are patronizing in their relations with the public and the press.

Finally, *Receiver Problems* have to do with the ways in which non-expert members of the public assimilate and react to risk situations of all kinds; research in the field of risk perception has been extremely valuable in clarifying this issue. People respond in varied ways to probabilistic situations in everyday life, for example in gambling, and their responses are relevant to the area of technological hazards as well. Many people are overconfident in areas familiar to them, such as driving, and at the same time can be very fearful of risks where they are unfamiliar with the technologies involved. These and many other factors turn out to be decisive elements in assessing how members of the public react to the scientific assessment of risks.[13]

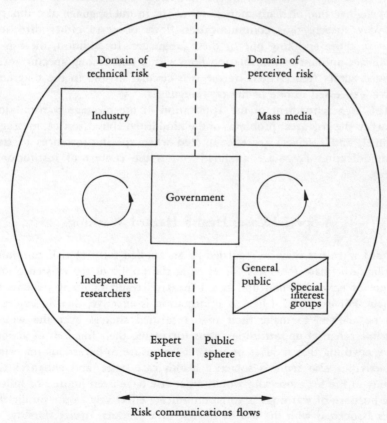

Figure 6.5 The communications processes model of risk communication
Source: Leiss and Krewski, 'Risk communication: theory and practice'.

This reconceptualization of the problem of risk communication enabled its proponents to break down what appeared to be a single, large, and intractable problem (as initially expressed: how scientists could get the public to understand the expert conception of risk) into a structured set of much smaller and potentially manageable issues. The process of reconceptualization was the adaptation of the message transmission theory, as a model of the persuasive communications approach, to the problem of forming social consensus about environmental risk. The 'solution' to the difficulties experienced in the earlier approach to risk communication was to put the emphasis on communication processes themselves.

In an earlier paper Dan Krewski and I presented a general conception of risk communication as it appears from the perspective of communications processes (see figure 6.5).[14] What is implied here is that information exchanges about risks occurring in a public policy context are likely to be expressed either in the 'language' of technical risk (in scientific, engineering, or mathematical terms) or in the language of ordinary, everyday speech; thus communication flows occur in either direction between those speaking one of these languages. In addition, there is a significant amount of information flow within and among specific institutional actors (represented by the two circular arrows in the diagram) that is expressed in one of the two languages.

This is a refinement of the application of the message transmission theory to the risk area; problems of the kind listed above (source, message, channel, and receiver) are encountered when specific instances of risk communication flows are analysed within the context of institutional forces.

A Special Case: Health Hazard Warnings

Hazard warnings may be regarded as an applied form of risk communication. Adequate measures for alerting the public to the existence and nature of environmental and health hazards result in many benefits to society. For example, if hazard information is effective, then individuals can be allowed to make their own informed choices over the widest possible range of opportunities, thus increasing their freedom of action. Also, anything that reduces or prevents exposure to hazardous materials or activities also reduces society's health care costs, and enhances the quality of life for those who would otherwise have been injured or killed. The purpose of warnings is to communicate effectively to the public the risks associated with the use or misuse of a product, device, facility, or type of activity.

By communicating those risks, product manufacturers, government regulators, or facility operators seek to both (1) inform users about the circumstances under which their health and safety might be jeopardized, and (2) advise them as to what actions they can take to reduce their risk. For example, a major effort was launched in Canada in the early 1990s to increase the effectiveness of the hazard warnings required on tobacco product packages, by changing the major design parameters (placement on package, colour contrast, size of warning panel) as well as the wording of the warning texts (the most dramatic of the proposed new warnings being 'Smoking is Addictive').[15] Since tobacco use is, among all 'voluntary' activities, the single greatest source of adverse health impacts in Canadian society, there is a great deal at stake in such exercises in applied risk communication.

In an influential article published in 1980, W. J. McGuire applied the persuasive communications model (what I have called the message transmission theory) to the field of hazard warnings.[16] Experts in the latter field then used this approach to organize the substantial body of knowledge that has accumulated in all aspects of the design, implementation, and evaluation of effectiveness of health hazard warnings. The message transmission theory turned out to be the most useful model for identifying the nature and interrelations of the structural components in the hazard warning process.[17]

Finally, one can see also in a related field of applied communication (which is also very important in contemporary society) – namely, health promotion strategies – that the message transmission theory has been helpful as an analytical tool.[18]

Conclusion

In this essay I have tried to show how a model developed long ago in communication theory has been applied recently in a number of very important arenas of contemporary public policy debate. How to deal with health and environmental protection is one of the most difficult and challenging public policy issues of our time, and one key aspect of that issue is the public understanding of risk assessment and risk management, and the public acceptance of the place of scientific and technical knowledge in the making of decisions about risks. What is evident in the development of this issue is that the policy debates, and indeed some regulatory action on risks, had reached an impasse, owing to public distrust of the form of risk communication where experts preached to the public about the authoritative way in which risk must be evaluated. This impasse was broken with the recognition that the problem at hand was fundamentally a matter of communicative processes. The adoption of the persuasive communication model certainly did not provide a magical solution to problems in risk communication, but in my view it did supply the necessary preconditions for arriving at those solutions. In so doing it demonstrated the vitality of our discipline and the contributions it can make to progressive steps in social policy.

Notes

I wish to thank Professor David Crowley of McGill University for assisting in uncovering the origins of the message transmission theory.

1 Harold D. Lasswell, 'The structure and function of communication in society', in L. Bryson (ed.), *The Communication of Ideas* (New York: Cooper Square Publishers, 1964), p. 37. This volume was first published in 1948.

2 B. L. Smith, H. D. Lasswell, and R. D. Casey, *Propaganda, Communication, and Public Opinion* (Princeton NJ: Princeton University Press).

3 Claude E. Shannon and Warren Weaver, *The Mathematical Theory of Communication* (Urbana: University of Illinois Press, 1949), pp. 7–8. I was introduced to this unusual work by Dallas Smythe, when we were both in Regina, more than 20 years ago.

4 Ibid., p. 26.

5 It seems to me that this power and range is seriously underestimated in the influential text by M. L. DeFleur and S. Ball-Rokeach, *Theories of Mass Communication*, 5th edn (New York/London: Longman, 1989), pp. 189–190. A more credible indicator of just how great that power and range is can be found in a review-article about the literature on persuasive communication, as a part of the larger topic of attitudes and attitude change, by W. J. McGuire. He organized his discussion within the framework of what I have called the message transmission theory, and which he labels 'an input/output analysis of the communication/persuasion process'. The inputs in this matrix are the components of the message system itself (source, message, channel, receiver, target); and the output side is described by McGuire as a succession of 'response steps that the receivers must be induced to take if the communication is to have its intended persuasive impact'. His discussion of the relevant published literature occupies no fewer than 36 pages of single-spaced, double-column text and demonstrates that each of the points of intersection in the matrix has been the subject of many separate studies. See William J. McGuire, 'Attitudes and attitude change', in G. Lindzey and E. Aronson (eds), *Handbook of Social Psychology* vol 2, 3rd edn(New York: Random House, 1985), pp. 233–346.

6 W. Leiss, S. Kline, and S. Jhally, *Social Communication in Advertising*, 2nd edn. (Toronto: Nelson, 1990), fig. 7.2 and pp. 191–3.

7 V. Covello, D. von Winterfeldt, and P. Slovic, 'Risk communication: a review of the literature,' in *RiskAbstracts*, 3 (1986), p. 172.

8 W. Leiss, 'Risks: managing the consequences of innovation', in L. Salter and D. Wolfe (eds), *Managing Technology* (Toronto: Garamond, 1990).

9   The earliest reference in the review article by Covello (see n. 7) is dated 1984. For Germany, see H. Jungermann, R. E. Kasperson, and P. M. Wiedemann (eds), *Themes and Tasks of Risk Communication* (Kernforschungsanlage Julich, 1988).

10 See generally B. Fischoff, P. Slovic, and S. Lichtenstein, ' "The public" vs. "the experts": perceived vs. actual disagreements about risks', in V. Covello et al. (eds), *The Analysis of Actual Versus Perceived Risks* (New York: Plenum Press, 1983), pp. 235–49.

11 V. Covello, D. von Winterfeldt, and P. Slovic, 'Communicating scientific information about health and environmental risks', in J. C. Davies, V. T. Covello, and F. W. Allen (eds), *Risk Communication* (Washington, DC: Conservation Foundation, 1987), pp. 110–12.

12 For a review of this literature see Richard Smith, 'Risk communication and the media: an annotated bibliography', in L. Craig (ed.), *Issues and Challenges in Risk Communication and the Mass Media,* IRR Paper 17 (Institute for Risk Research, University of Waterloo, 1990).

13 The best introduction to this subject is the report prepared by D. Wehrung and I. Vertinsky from the 'Workshop on Risk Perception and Drug Safety Evaluation' (Ottawa: Drugs Directorate, Health Protection Branch, Health and Welfare Canada, March 1990). Fig.3 in this report provides a nice overview of how the many components of risk perception may be integrated with risk communication practices.

14 W. Leiss and D. Krewski, 'Risk communication: theory and practice', in W. Leiss (ed.), *Prospects and Problems in Risk Communication* (Waterloo: University of Waterloo Press, 1989), pp. 99–102.

15 Health Protection Branch, Health and Welfare Canada, 'Proposed amendments to the tobacco products control regulations', *Information Letter*, 776 (1 Mar. 1990), Ottawa.

16 W. J. McGuire, 'The communication-persuasion model and health-risk labeling', in L. A. Morris et al. (eds), *Product Labeling and Health Risks,* Banbury Report 6 (Cold Spring Harbor Laboratory, 1980), pp. 99–122.

17 M. R. Lehto and J. M. Miller, *Warnings,* vol. 1: *Fundamentals, Design, and Evaluation Methodologies* (Ann Arbor, Mich.: Fuller Technical Publications), p. 18 and fig. 2-2.

18 Donna Phillips (University of Calgary), 'Health promotion theories, strategies and models: application to nutrition education,' (paper delivered at the CCA/ACC Annual Conference, Victoria, BC, June 1990).

7

Talk, Text and History:
Conversation Analysis and
Communication Theory

Deirdre Boden

History is made through talk and written as text. This essay examines these intertwining processes of making history; that is, the activity of creating the narratives out of which people interpret the moments and events that sediment into that solid story we call 'history'. The example used will be a short dramatic incident during the Kennedy Administration in 1962. The core empirical materials are a series of telephone calls made between President Kennedy and the Governor of Mississippi during the crisis in which James Meredith was to register as the first black student to attend a traditionally white institution of higher learning in that then deeply segregated state – precipitating what was termed the 'insurrection at Ole Miss'. My general theoretical approach will be ethnomethodological and the empirical findings of conversation analysis will be used to examine the reflexive relations between talk, text and history.

Conversation Analysis and Communication Theory

Until the 1960s, it had not occurred to anyone to study ordinary everyday talk. Linguists took the study of language to be concerned with analysing autonomous linguistic systems of phonetic, syntactic, semantic and overall semiotic structures.[1] Speech specialists were concerned with irregularities and disfluencies in the pathology of spoken language.[2] Communication scholars, for their part, were preoccupied with the transmission and reception of information through designated channels. Everyday discourse was assumed to be idiosyncratic and largely irrelevant to these endeavours. Chomsky confirmed this trend by announcing a new agenda for linguists.[3] It was to take the formal study of language firmly away from empirical analysis and into a realm of theoretical enquiries based on invented and highly unlikely syntactic structures independent of the intense intimacy of everyday human intercourse.

Interested both in the challenge posed by Chomsky and the philosophical pronouncements offered by Wittgenstein,[4] a young scholar at Berkeley began to wrestle with a way of making the discipline of sociology responsive to rigorous observation of social action.[5] Through his own innovative ideas, Harvey Sacks created a new approach to describing and documenting social phenomena which came to be called conversation analysis. In essence, what Sacks proposed was that a genuinely scientific study of human action should be *observational*, that is, it should be able to observe human activities *directly*, with replicable rigour. Audio tape recording was just becoming generally available at that time. Sacks decided to study talk, not as linguistic data, nor in terms of the technical production of speech, but as a fundamentally communicative and *social* phenomenon. His approach was ethological, which is to say that he proposed first to observe and record conversation as a *basis* for developing more formal understandings of regularities. This method was inductive but also obliged observers to stay close to the empirical ground at all times. In this, Sacks was influenced by the work of Harold Garfinkel and the ethnomethodologists who always insisted on bracketing out *a priori* assumptions and hypotheses in the interests of an unmotivated and 'open' view of the world as it happens.[6] The fundamental phenomenon for conversation analysis was to be real people really talking and, one might add, in real time. No substitute or coded summary would do. As a result, audio (and later video) recordings of naturally occurring interaction became the data. These materials are transcribed in a very precise and detailed manner,[7] and always presented within research texts and reports without any coding or schematic overlay, and the actual tapes are always regarded as the primary data.

Over the past thirty years, Sacks's path-breaking angle of analysis has attracted a range of researchers from a variety of academic fields including communications, anthropology, linguistics and sociology. In the past decade especially, publications of conversation analytic studies have grown virtually exponentially, to such an extent that even a superficial review cannot be undertaken here.[8] With the growth of video technology, work has also moved more generally into 'interaction analysis',[9] permitting a wide area of analytic curiosity and research results, especially in professional settings and hi-tech work environments.[10]

142 *Deirdre Boden*

Sequence and Structure

The core of conversation analysis is the exploration of the sequential structures of social action.[11] This focus emerged from the examination of sequences of talk. As Sacks and his colleague, Emanuel Schegloff, began to work with recorded materials in their early research,[12] it became clear that the temporal quality of talk embodied apparently essential sequences of action.[13] These were, moreover, intriguingly paired and the pairs were adjacently organized: a greeting produced a greeting, a question an answer, an invitation an acceptance (or declination), an accusation a denial, a compliment a demurral, a complaint an apology (or disclaimer), and so on. These 'paired objects' or 'adjacency pairs', as they came to be called, appeared to provide a pivotal series of dynamic opportunities linking elements of interaction which, chained together, sequenced both the unfolding talk and the interactional and institutional agendas that everyday interaction embodies. Turn-taking was found to be the basic mechanism of interaction.[14] Through a fine-grained analysis of conversation, adjacent sequences anchor and articulate all manner of talk-based exchanges in ways that are both trans-situational and trans-cultural.[15]

In this essay, I am going to build on the analysis of these sequential structures of talk to propose that sequence and structure are mutually constitutive; consequently, the discoveries of conversation analysis are critically important to *communication* analysis. The cumulative research findings that have grown out of Sacks's initial insights are also of considerable consequences to social theory in general.

What follows is thus not a review of conversation analysis; these are available in excellent number and quality elsewhere.[16] Instead, using materials from the Kennedy study noted earlier, I shall attempt to illustrate the potential linkages between the grounded methods of conversation analysis and the challenges facing communication theorists and researchers today. Central to these are, I believe, the *multiple* channels in which social actors must now function, make decisions, initiate action, and insert themselves and their agendas into the swift flow of modernity. Communication is inherently interactive but is now accomplished through multiple, and often simultaneous, modes. What I hope to show is that both through and despite the many modalities of modern communication, the adjacent and sequential structures of social action shape the world, turn by turn.

This is to suggest that, *through sequences*, people create the contexts of action out of which next actions must be realized. The concrete historical conditions central, for instance, to Marxist theory are located, in this sense, in the immediacy of human action and reaction. How larger historical factors come to bear on immediate events is thus *mediated* through everyday intercourse. As we shall see in the brief presentation that follows, what each person does 'next' contains the seeds of change that so fascinate all students of social life. It is in this way that sequence is at the heart of social theory and research, or should be.

Typically, however, it is historians who have been the students of sequences of human events. For other social scientists, sequence has been regarded as a largely methodological matter as, for instance, in time series analysis or the recent vogue in event history analysis, neither of which has much more than a technical interest in either time or history. My own emphasis will be instead to argue that the sequential properties and consequences of action actually shape history.[17] As people provide accounts of their actions and interpret those of others, they simultaneously and recursively constitute those actions and accounts as narratives of the moment. In the process, local narratives of 'what's happening' become the stories out of which conventional history is written and rewritten.[18] Moreover, the sequential structure of what is happening and people's finely structured accounts of 'onrolling' events are the *stuff*, the very fibres of the historical tapestry.

In this essay, my purpose is to suggest, in a necessarily brief exposition, some of the ways in which talk, text and history are connected.

History in the Making

To treat history as talk (or talk as history) is somewhat provocative. Most history books suggest that important people engage in big actions to create large structures that have huge consequences.[19] Even with recent efforts by historians, anthropologists and sociologists to offer details of the lives of everyday people and important correctives on earlier elite-centred and often Eurocentric versions of various histories, the record of the past still suggests that rather large patterns of key events over long periods of time constitute 'history'. The academic discipline of history itself is, moreover, constructed out of written documents – political treaties, parish records, public testimonies, private diaries. Through careful comparison and multiple sources, historians of each age sift the 'facts' out of the sands of time, put them into sequences, and lay out their logic.

Recently, however, increased availability and improvements in audio, film, video, and now a variety of electronic storage devices for sound and picture have transformed the fundamental process of recording human events. These new 'documents' continue to be treated by historians as quite conventional sources, but it is clear that a new era of historical analysis is opening up, one that is ideally suited to specialists of discourse, semiotic and visual materials. Images of the recent past can now be subjected to quite rigorous analysis.[20] While, to be sure, they do not record 'everything' that happened, nor from every angle, nonetheless the camera's unblinking eye and the sentinel microphone provide startling insight into events which indubitably 'happened', and they capture them *as they happened*. Such real time records, moreover, are unmediated by a secondary interpretation or by the selective blur of remembrance of things past. Indeed, in recent years, amateur as well as professional video and surveillance cameras have had an increasing importance in all manner of *later* interpretive procedures such as legal evidence. For social science research purposes, recordings, whether audio or video, are open to re-examination – in their raw state – by any analyst and thereby build in a kind of replicability never available to earlier interpreters of history. When combined with more established methods of historical analysis such as official documents and personal accounts, the effect can be quite persuasive and, ultimately, theoretically provocative.

The empirical materials I shall be drawing on here are just such a combination of talk and text.[21] The larger study on which this discussion is based comprises a variety of oral and textual materials that trace a chronology of events from January 1961 to October 1962. For my purposes, the key data are a series of twenty telephone calls recorded in the Oval Office of the White House during a four-day period, 29 September to 2 October 1962, for which the original audio recordings are available.[22] These are a series of communications between President Kennedy and Governor Ross Barnett of Mississippi, with additional callers including Attorney General Robert Kennedy and a number of members of the Kennedy Administration talking to key actors in the crisis. In addition, there are audio recordings of approximately seven hours of meetings and informal discussions between President Kennedy, Robert Kennedy and other members of the White House team during the same period, often with the same telephone calls going on in the background. The data also include official White House transcripts of a further twenty telephone calls made between Robert Kennedy and Ross Barnett or his lawyer between 15 and 27 September 1962. Textual materials that also track this crisis include the President's daily log, telegrams, court injunctions, White House memos, Justice Department documents and drafts of a TV speech made to the nation by the President on the night of 30 September 1962, as well as the televised speech itself. As background to the crisis, there are also White House and FBI documents, correspondence between James Meredith and the University of Mississippi, further telegrams to and from the Governor, legal dispositions and Circuit Court rulings, and internal reports from the archives of the US Civil Rights Office on the 'Meredith vs. University of Mississippi' case.[23]

The Insurrection at Ole Miss

The incidents at 'Ole Miss', the oldest campus of the University of Mississippi, started simply enough. On the day after he heard John Fitzgerald Kennedy's inaugural Presidential address in January 1961, a young man in Mississippi took the first step that was to lead to the greatest confrontation between US Federal and southern state governments since the Civil War a hundred years earlier.[24] He heard Kennedy's appeal that 'the torch has been passed to a new generation of Americans' who would 'begin anew' to 'explore what problems unite us instead of laboring those problems which divide us'. James Howard Meredith wrote to the Registrar of the University declaring that he wished to complete his college education at the main campus in Oxford, Mississippi, and asked for application materials. He received a routinely 'warm' bureaucratic response from the Registrar, dated 26 January 1961, expressing pleasure at the knowledge of Meredith's 'interest in becoming a member of our student body'. In his own next letter, 31 January, Meredith replied that he sincerely hoped 'that your attitude toward me as a potential member of your student body reflects the attitude of the school, and that it will not change upon learning that I am not a White applicant'. In his next paragraph, he went on to note his racial origin as being 'an American-Mississippi-Negro citizen', adding that with all the 'changes in our old educational system taking place in our country in this new age, I feel certain this application does not come as a surprise to you'.[25] The university, for its part, was less than enthusiastic and immediately backdated the deadline for Spring admissions to before 25 January, as a first step in avoiding this legally mandated but long avoided change in American education.

With the exception of the following telegram dated 4 February, Meredith was not to have further direct contact with the Registrar until his historic registration twenty months later:

[to] JH MEREDITH, 1129 ST APT 5-D JACKSON MISS FOR YOUR INFOR-MATION AND GUIDANCE IT HAS BEEN FOUND NECESSARY TO DIS-CONTINUE CONSIDERATION OF ALL APPLICATIONS FOR ADMISSION OR REGISTRATION FOR THE SECOND SEMESTER WHICH WERE RECEIVED AFTER JANUARY 25 1961. YOUR APPLICATION WAS RECEIVED SUBSEQUENT TO SUCH DATE AND THUS WE MUST ADVISE YOU NOT TO APPEAR FOR REGISTRATION
ROBERT B. ELLIS REGISTRAR[26]

This was the first in a series of strategies adopted by the university and state officials to create non-racial reasons for not enrolling the young black applicant.

Meredith's own initial action, triggered, at least in part, by the famous Kennedy inaugural address, thus set in motion a complex sequence of delaying tactics and outright alterations of university rules and Mississippi state laws aimed at blocking his admission. These were under-taken initially by university administrators, then by the Trustees of the university, and finally by the Mississippi State Legislature. All were designed to prevent desegregation of the proud institution in a state that is variously described as 'most traditional' or 'most backward' of the former Confederate states, in the light of the 1954 'Brown vs Board of Education' ruling on school desegregation.[27] These actions were coun-tered by an accelerating series of moves by the National Association for the Advancement of Colored People (NAACP) lawyers, the US Depart-ment of Justice, numerous local courts, the Fifth Circuit Court of Appeals in New Orleans and, ultimately, by the US Attorney General and the President himself.

Text and History

James H. Meredith was twenty-seven years old at the time of application to the university, married with one small son. He was then enrolled in political science at Jackson State College in Jackson, Mississippi, an all-negro institution. He was also active in the local NAACP but not a central figure. By February 1961, he had support and legal counsel from the NAACP and was further obliged to seek protection from the US Justice Department. He explained his position to them in a letter dated 7 Feb-ruary 1961:

> Why do I feel you will or should be concerned about me? I have no great desire to protect my hyde [*sic*], but I do hope to see the day when the million Negroes that live in the state of Mississippi will have cause not to fear as they fear today. High ranking officials of this state . . . have made public statements saying that the law enforcement agencies of this state will not be use [*sic*] to enforce laws as proclaimed by the federal courts . . .

In the same week, the Federal Bureau of Investigation (FBI) was already compiling information on Meredith and the situation in Mississippi, detailed in a memo dated 13 February 1961. The memo is headed 'Racial situation, Memphis Division; Attempt of Negro to register at University of Mississippi, Oxford, Mississippi, February 1 1961':

On February 6, 1961, HUGH H. CLEGG, Director of Development, University of Mississippi, and BURNS TATUM, Chief of Campus Police, University of Mississippi, advised an Agent of this office that application for admission to the University of Mississippi had been received from a Negro, J. H. MEREDITH on February 1 1961. These individuals advised at the time that the application of MERIDTH [sic] had been referred by school officials to the office of the Governor ROSS BARNETT, Jackson, Mississippi. Mr. CLEGG further advised that MERIDTH [sic] did not appear on the campus on February 6, 1961, the opening day of registration, and no information has been received by the University indicating that he would appear.

The report goes on to claim that Meredith's application was 'incomplete and inadequate' and had not been received prior to the 25 January deadline for applications. It also notes that Meredith did not, in his application, name five alumni of the university with whom he was acquainted, as required in their standard application. What the memo does not mention is whether the university officials had also advised the FBI that the 25 January deadline had been altered so as to exclude Meredith's application, nor the fact that the above telegram had been sent to discourage him from appearing to register for the same managed reason. Less surprising is that fact that the memo also fails to note any irony in the requirement of providing the names of five alumni of a university that had only ever enrolled white students.[28]

The role of the FBI in relation to such situations and to the NAACP in particular is a part of this narrative that cannot be taken up here. That story is, in turn, intertwined with the history of the civil rights movement during the 1960s, a complex account which is still being unravelled.[29] The Mississippi view of the NAACP and Meredith was often expressed to the FBI by white business organizations such as the Association of Citizens' Councils of Mississippi. The conventional wisdom of white southern policitians, business leaders and the media identified the NAACP as a 'communist' organization in funding and guidance. Meredith's college ambitions were thus defined as a communist plot.

By 31 May 1961, Meredith was forced to file suit against the Board of Trustees, Chancellor, Dean of Liberal Arts College, and Registrar of the University of Mississippi, charging that his admission was being blocked on racial grounds. For over a year, the issue was held in check by legal manoeuvres in the Southern District Court of Mississippi. Then, in June 1962, the University, through state officials, moved to retaliate by initiating criminal proceedings against Meredith for a violation of voter registration law, using this offence as the basis for blocking his admission while continuing to claim that race had no part in their action. Every delaying tactic was used throughout the final months, with complicated legal moves from the District Court to the Court of Appeals and back, and with an eventual intervention by the US Justice Department which led to the reluctant signing of a court order instructing the University to register Meredith in their regular Fall admissions period, in September 1962. That order was signed on 14 September 1962.

For the next ten days, the period of the court order, there was a series of intense telephone calls between Attorney General Robert Kennedy and Governor Ross Barnett, as well as between other members of the Attorney General's office on civil rights and officials in Mississippi. The content and interactional intensity of these calls was to be reflected and magnified in the later calls between President Kennedy himself and the Governor, and for good interactional and organizational reasons (see pp. 157–61, below). The University, in the mean time, refused to obey the court order and on 20 September civil proceedings were instigated against them. For their part, the Mississippi legislature also invented and passed a law that no convicted felon could be admitted to the University; Meredith's trumped-up voter registration charge constituted a felony. On 24 September the Fifth Circuit Court in New Orleans, comprised of judges from all over the South, ruled that the University Board of Trustees had engaged in wilful refusal to comply with the court order. The Board of Trustees themselves, assembled before the court, agreed unanimously to accept and retain Meredith as a student.

The stage was then set for a series of final confrontations to be engaged mainly by the Governor and his own legal staff and state troopers. James Meredith was, by this time, under constant escort of US marshals and was staying with relatives across the Mississippi–Tennessee state line near Memphis, waiting for the closing stages of his own historic college registration process. Working hourly to effect this goal were the US Justice Department and the office of the Attorney General, as well as the NAACP and, in the background, the FBI.

This then is a very brief chronology of the events leading to the insurrection at Ole Miss. It is worth noting that the kinds of documentary evidence presented so far in this discussion comprise a rather conventional historical account, namely correspondence, memos and other records of written exchanges. Typically these relatively decontextualized documents would constitute *all* of a historian's sources, however detailed; documents that for some local reason of accountability came to be produced as routine records, as institutional information or as bureaucratic correspondence or, in the case of the modern period, as oral histories of survivors of events.

Written texts have, of course, long played a central role not just in recording history, but in making it. Until recently, both written language and the production of texts have provided a singularly important durable and thereby stable record. Some writers have suggested that written texts 'freeze' the past, providing ways for societies to use recorded tradition to effect both social control and social change. They have been the basis for writing and revising national and cultural myths. In a classic study, for instance, Innis compares oral and written communication and argues for the power of the latter to create empires.[30] This early work is supported by more recent anthropological investigation that traces the relation between writing – originally for accounting purposes – and the growth of complex civilizations.[31] 'Oral' in this context refers, of course, to traditional, non-literate cultures, and much of this discussion predates the invention of audio and video recording techniques and their routine use in everyday settings.

In the modern era, oral and written texts are dynamic and reflexive in very new ways. In the Kennedy period, the timing and sequential pace of telephone calls, telegrams and face-to-face settings were critical, as we shall see. And, in this last decade of the twentieth century, there is a notable added simultaneity of messages as mobile phones, fax communications and other satellite linkages accelerate social change. In the next sections of this essay, I shall explore the Meredith case in more detail as a way of outlining these essential issues of communication and social action.

Talk and History

The crisis at Ole Miss, as with all human events, was *talked* into being. Most of the talk was initially private: Meredith with his family, friends and NAACP advisers; the discussions of FBI agents and routine chats at the Justice Department; the backroom talk of lawyers and court officials; the surely intense discussions at the University of Mississippi and in the Governor's office in Jackson, Mississippi, during the period outlined above, and so on. Of these, no records remain.[32] It is, though, fortunate for communication researchers, journalists and film-makers, that a number of US Presidential administrations have chosen, apparently independently, to 'bug' the White House. The Roosevelt Library has, for instance, recently discovered quite early recordings of Second World War discussions during 1940. The watershed for such recording activities was, of course, Nixon and the Watergate tapes.[33] In any case, the system installed by the Kennedy administration, while crude by today's sound standards, was to leave an impressive historical account,[34] capturing the creative and often fragmentary quality of decision-making and agenda-setting on the move. Some calls were recorded on dictabelt and transcribed daily by White House secretaries, including key calls made from the Attorney General's office and from the President's phone, and a reel-to-reel tape machine ran intermittently in the Oval Office recording ambient sound (imperfectly, to say the least). The result is a decidedly haunting record of the Kennedy brothers and their team in action.

On 15 September, Attorney General Robert Kennedy began a series of telephone negotiations with Governor Ross Barnett designed to ensure James Meredith's safe and successful registration while maintaining law and order. A central question became *who* would do so. In the interests of space, I shall only summarise the sense of these exchanges and cite very brief examples, as there are no audio recordings remaining of these calls. The exchanges were, however, significant in shaping how the Kennedy team responded to the Governor on the crisis weekend, and vice versa, and thus analytically relevant in this discussion of *sequenced* interactions and their reflexive tying to so-called 'larger' events.

During this same time, there were several attempts to register Meredith, once at the Oxford campus and once in Jackson, the state capital, at the insistence of the Governor. Each was met with outright refusal of the Registrar to register Meredith, and with the Governor reading a standard statement to him, his lawyers and the assembled national media as state troopers blocked the entrances. The calls between Robert Kennedy and Ross Barnett embed and embody both the tension of these events and the shifting legal conditions under which both were operating – particularly as the University Board of Trustees was ordered by the New Orleans Court of Appeals to register Meredith peacefully and effectively, and without further wilful delay.

Without a lengthy excursion into US constitutional law, it is important to stress that the balance between Federal authority and states' rights is a delicate one, to say the least. Between North and South these issues were still more fraught. Moreover, in those early days of the civil rights movement, emotions were running high on both sides. The Kennedy election had been a barely won affair and the cooperation of the southern Democrats was important yet fragile. The reputation of the Kennedy brothers was, moreover, also none too solid among civil rights activists and the NAACP. They were held to be more concerned with politics than justice. In Mississippi, Ross Barnett was determined not to be a governor presiding over the end of a cherished southern way of life. It is these biographical, political and historical elements that are made relevant in fine laminations of the historical narrative as the negotiated order unfolds.

Early in their phone exchanges, on 15 September for example, as they discuss the need for safety during Meredith's first attempt to register, Kennedy and Barnett defer to each other's sensibilities and shared interests:

RFK-1

RFK	I thought we should discuss some of the details of how to work this thing out with this fellow coming in on Thursday.
Barnett	I will cooperate in any way I can. You will recall our conversation immediately prior to-
RFK →	I think the first extremely important point that we are both interested in is that there will be no violence, no disturbance, that he is protected-
Barnett →	I promise you, sir, that there will be no violence. The people do not want to get involved in violence, strife and I have urged them not to do so and I do not anticipate any trouble.
RFK	Governor, we have heard reports from various sources that the people of Mississippi are aroused – that there might be violence when he comes in and or in one or two days after.
Barnett	Mr Kennedy, I do not anticipate violence, you know, I am opposed to violence.

At this early stage, RFK's proposal to work out details meets with immediate cooperation. In conversation analytic terms, the alignment is sequentially placed in that Kennedy's proposal of 'how to work this thing out' is matched adjacently by Barnett with a promise of cooperation. Similarly, Kennedy's recommendation that there be no violence is matched by Barnett immediately and in identical words (arrows).[35] As we will see shortly, such quick conversation collusion is not guaranteed.

After several unsuccessful attempts to register Meredith (escorted by US marshals), and quite a few phone calls, Robert Kennedy and his team learn of the Board of Trustees' acceptance of the New Orleans Court of Appeals ruling on 24 September. Kennedy calls the Governor that evening:[36]

RFK-2 OPENING OF CALL:

RFK	I expect that you probably have heard the decision of the Court and the agreement of the Board of Trustees to register Meredith down in New Orleans.
Barnett →	Did they agree to that?
RFK	Unanimously.
Barnett →	All of them? That's really shocking to me.

Given this setback for the Governor, Kennedy presses his own advantage:

RFK-2 (CONTINUED)

| RFK | They agreed to do it by 2 o'clock tomorrow. |
| Barnett → | By 2:00? |

RFK	I think they have to report back to the Court by 4 o'clock.
Barnett →	Did the trustees actually sign anything?
RFK	They all got up in Court and agreed and then they polled the absent one and they agreed to pass a resolution-
Barnett →	They told the Court that?
RFK	That's correct.
Barnett	I'm surprised at that really. They were so firm about it two days ago. They changed their minds mighty quick.
RFK	The Court's decision was unanimous that they should do this.
Barnett →	Did they do this under any threat that the Court would fine them?
RFK	No, they asked the Court what they wanted them to do and the Court told them and they said they would do it. They met and agreed unanimously they would take this step . . .

This was a genuine setback for the Mississippi cause and, after some discussion about what action the Governor would now take, Robert Kennedy sums up the legal situation as it has evolved. This kind of formulation and re-formulation is typical of all talk,[37] and critical to the continuous updating shared understanding demands.[38] Notice throughout these brief examples that the Governor's turns are now mostly taking the form of questions (arrows), clarification requests with a good deal of apparent incredulity built into them. Cooperation no longer marks these exchanges, and the questions are, at best, lateral moves:

RFK-2 (CLOSING OF CALL):

RFK	Can I run though this situation with you briefly . . . [summary] Now it has gone before the Court of Appeals and they declared unanimously with one absentee that Meredith should be registered at the University of Mississippi. They said- they- the Board of Trustees and the president- they announced that they would arrange for the registration of Mr Meredith.
Barnett →	They said that?
RFK	The registrar got up in Court and said he would register Meredith. You've got now that the federal courts have acted-
Barnett →	Ellis? The regular registrar?
RFK	I don't know. I imagine it was he . . .

Kennedy had announced the decision of the Court of Appeals at the opening of his call and 'the agreement of the Board of Trustees to register Meredith'; Barnett's only response was a question: 'Did they agree to that?' As he summarizes, Kennedy again notes the agreement of the Board to 'arrange for the registration of Mr. Meredith', to which Barnett's continuing response is a recycled question: 'they said that?' Kennedy's attempts at getting the Governor to cooperate are faltering, and the process is embedded in and created through the talk. The Attorney General's patience has also been sorely tested by these repetitious and increasingly uncooperative exchanges, and the tension is clearly audible in the audio tape recordings of their later exchanges. The pace of events is also quickening, and by the weekend of 29/30 September the Kennedy team is determined to move ahead with registering Meredith within the mandate of the federal court order.

'This is the President'

Early on the afternoon of Saturday, 29 September, in the Oval Office of the White House, President Kennedy and his team held an informal meeting about the crisis. It was to be the first of many meetings that were to become a continuous crisis session lasting into the early hours of 1 October. In addition to the President, at this stage in the afternoon, there was Robert Kennedy, with Burke Marshall, his Assistant Attorney General for Civil Rights, and a number of other advisers. They were, as is so typical of organizational actors the world over, rehearsing their actions and *how they would look afterwards*. This essentially ethnomethodological process of retrospective–prospective analysis is at the heart of the ways in which the structure of talk itself organizes experience and creates the ongoing contexts of the accounts actors provide for their actions.[39] The President was planning to call the Governor – for the first time – and they were discussing how he should handle the call:

JFK-1 MEETING:[40]

1	Adviser?		. . . a third uh- uh *crit*ical point (.)
2			I guess is- uh- will- what if the
3			governor chooses, in effect, to call out
4			the guards before *you* do? And- again
5			if he- uh *says* you're challenging him on
6			keeping law and order, and (.) uh he
7			said 'Arright, I'll keep law and order'?
8			For one thing, he'll tell you if you'd
9			ca::ll off Meredith why there won't be
10			any disturbance.
11			(0.2)
12	JFK		I can't call off Meredith for *that*.
13	Adviser?		NO! No. I agree with you,
14	JFK	→	(I don't have) the *power* to call off

15		Meredith.
16	Adviser?	But (0.3) he- he'll *put* that in the
17		conversation that *you're* the one inciting
18		the trou::ble.
19	JFK	Already said that.
20	Adviser?	But (0.3) u:::h- the other point is: do you
21		want him to call the guard? If he says:
22		'Well, I could keep law and order, I guess,
23		if I call out the guard'
24		(0.4)
25·		Uh- you hafta thi::nk of whether he might
26		pre-empt you (.) on that.
27	JFK	Well, let him do it. Let him *do* it.
28	RFK	I don't mind that.
29	JFK	(No?)
30	Adviser?	You can always *fede*ralize the guard . . . .

Note the especially *mediated* quality of power in this extract. James
Meredith had set in motion a sequence of events that no one, not even the
President, had control over. One clear area of their struggle is, as noted
above, over *who* will maintain law and order in Oxford, Mississippi. This
issue goes to the heart of tensions between federal and state authority.
Through his earlier phone calls with Robert Kennedy, Governor Barnett
has eschewed any kind of violence while promising nothing specific to
prevent it. As the final moments of court-ordered registration approach,
the locus of power is shifting *technically* to the federal level, but the *practice*
of power is another far more local matter. In his earlier interactions with
the Attorney General, the Governor has placed blame for all this trouble
on those who would impose the federal court ruling, hence the President's
quick 'already said that' in response to the advice that Barnett may blame
him for inciting the trouble. This recursive quality of talk-as-action is
central to this crisis and to the constitution of society.[41] The power of
interaction and its sequentially unfolding properties holds these men in a
temporal pattern. The talk matters because guns, troops and the rule of
law by force are only a last resort – especially in a democracy. In the mean
time, positioning the federal government's obligation to support a private
citizen's intent to register at a public university *within* the logic of local
agendas and capacities is the goal. At the end of the above extract, we see
both Kennedys agreeing, at *this* stage, that Barnett's eventual use of the
National Guard would be acceptable.

Within minutes, the President is placing his call to Barnett:

JFK-2 – FIRST PHONE CALL:

1	JFK	Hello?
2	Operator	Arright.

3	JFK	Hello? Hello *Gov'*nor?
4	Barnett	Arright, yes.
5	JFK	How are you?
6	Barnett	Is this =
7	JFK	= This is the *President* uh-
8	Barnett	Oh! Well (0.2) Mr *Pres'*dent (glad t'ta::lk)
9	JFK	Well, I'm glad to talk to *you*, Governor. I'm
10		con*cern*ed about- uh- this situ*a*tion uh- down
11		as I know uh-
12	Barnett	*Oh* I should *say* I *am* concerned about it, Mr
13		President. It's- it's- it's a *horr'*ble
14		situation.
15	JFK	Well now, here's my *prob*lem-
16	Barnett	(Well, I-)
17	JFK	Governor.
18	Barnett	Ye:::s,
19	JFK	This- uh- listen, I didn't uh put him *in* the
20		university, but on the other hand, under the
21		Constitution
22	Barnett	(Uh-huh)
23	JFK	I have to carry ou::t the orders of the-
24		carry that *order ou::t* and I don't- I get-
25		uh- I don't want to do that in any way that
26		causes uh- *dif*ficulties to *you::* or to
27		anyone else?
28	Barnett	(Uh-huh)
29	JFK	But I've gotta do it. Now I'd like your help
30		in *doing* that,
31	→	(2.9)
32	Barnett	Ye::::s,
33	→	(1.4)
34	Barnett	Well,
35	→	(0.8)
36	Barnett	Uh- Have you talked with uh- Attorney General
37		this *morn*ing?
38		(0.2)
39	JFK	Yeah, I *talk*ed to him and uh- in fact, I just
40		me::t with him for 'bout an hour an' we went
41		*over* the situation.
42	Barnett	Uh, did he and Mr Watkins have a talk this
43		morning? Tom Watkins the lawyer from Jackson,
44		or not?
45		(0.2)
46	JFK	Uh, *yes*, he talked to Tom Watkins (.) he told
47		me . . . .

While much can be analysed in this opening section, I want to narrow attention to matters of cooperation and shared responsibility. We will find that these are located *first* within the structure of the talk itself, and then within institutional obligations extended in time and space.

After a routine opening sequence,[42] the President 'self-identifies' with 'This is the President' (line 7), which Barnett acknowledges as a change from Robert to John Kennedy ('Oh!' at line 8),[43] and there is a brief exchange of pleasantries (lines 8–9). The President, again in classical manner, introduces the reason for his call which provides an interactional platform on which he can build his larger topic while reflexively aligning himself with the Governor. He expresses (lines 9–11) his concern about 'this situation' and, with notable delicacy, invites the Governor's comment by cutting off his remarks mid-stream with 'as I know uh-.' The Governor matches the mood of this concern emphatically but characterizes the situation as 'horrible' (line 13). In conversational analytic terms, an assessment of this description is expectable, since the Governor has upgraded the President's original formulation. The President instead expressly ignores the Governor's idea of the way things are, and uses a typical topic transition marker, 'Well now . . . ' to shift to *his* version of the problem. He then uses a framing device: 'listen' (line 19) and begins to lay out his position (lines 19–30).

There is much (much) more that could be analysed here, but let me note again only a few key features for the purposes of the present discussion. One is the way in which President Kennedy builds on the 'preservable' past[44] of this situation, namely he summarizes the historical and legal issues that have brought them to this impasse, all in one complex turn at talk. He wants, he says, to carry out the constitutionally mandated court order with as little difficulty as possible to the Governor or to anyone else, but (line 29) he is determined to do so. He then solicits the Governor's help in doing so (lines 29–30). The silences (arrows) are what I want to focus on now.

They constitute, in a few seconds, *all* of the Governor's agenda and, we may say, the reluctance of the American South over this new phase of history.[45] Silences, in the formal analysis of everyday conversation, rarely exceed 1 second between speaker turns.[46] Longer pauses *regularly*, which is to say predictably, signal 'trouble' in the talk, which is to say that the silence *projects* a problem upcoming in the stream of interaction.[47] The pause at line 31 is such a pause, as are the two that follow. Moreover, the Governor's 'yes' (line 32) is uttered *very* slowly, more slowly than any southern dialect style might suggest, and is by no means 'affirmative' in a semantic sense. His subsequent pause + 'well' (lines 33–4) initiates a remarkable topic change, 'remarkable', that is to say, in analytic terms. Whereas the President (at line 15 above) is *continuing* his own topic (of concern about the situation), the Governor is here shifting the grounds of discussion quite disruptively. Cohesion of both turns and topic is basic to all conversation. The Governor's topic shift at line 36, asking the President if he has spoken to the Attorney General and *ignoring* in the adjacent and appropriate slot everything the President has said, violates expectations of contiguity in topic and cohesion in 'next positioned' conversational objects.[48] The silences are, in a way, the 'invisible' yet decidedly hearable devices through which the Governor achieves this departure from both the stated first topic of the call and from what most social scientists would assume is the prerogative of power: namely the President's ability to set the conversational agenda.

The Governor uses the *structural procedures of turn-taking* to subvert conventional notions of Presidential power in four distinct and sequential phases: (1) through the positioning and gradual reduction in length of pauses (i.e. 2.9 seconds, 1.4, 0.8); (2) by using the pauses to signal 'trouble', especially the first pause which is very long for a telephone call *and* the first pause of this particular call; (3) by explicitly ignoring the adjacency organization of requests, namely that they are 'first' elements of a two-part sequence: request + compliance/rejection[49]; and (4) by using 'well' + 'uh' to shift to a completely different topic without any apology for doing so.[50] The latter is a typical device for constructing a disagreement, however, making the Governor's move all the more effective. Note that, at this stage of their first negotiation, the President accepts this topic shift after a brief pause (lines 39–41) although he recycles his interest in the 'situation'. But he is unable, at least for the duration of this call, to elicit a commitment from the Governor:

JFK-2 (LATER IN SAME CALL):

1	JFK	All right. (0.3) Well, now let me =
2	Barnett	= Uh you =
3	JFK	= let me say thi::s, uh-
4	Barnett	know what I'm u::p against, Mr *Pre::s*'dent,
5		I took an oa::th, you know? to *abide* by the
6		laws of *this* state,
7	JFK	That's right.
8	Barnett	And *our* constitution here and the Constitution
9		of the *United* States. I'm- I- I'm on the
10		*spo::t* here, you know?
11		(0.2)
12	JFK	Well (.) now you've got ⌈uh-⌉
13	Barnett	⌊I- ⌋ I've taken an
14		oath to do that (0.2) and you *kno::w* what
15		*our* laws are with reference to
16		(0.4)
17	JFK	Yes, I understand that.

18	Barnett	And, uh-
19	JFK	Well now we've got ⌈the-⌉
20	Barnett	⌊we⌋ we have a statute
21		that was enacted a couple of weeks ago stating
22		positively that no one who had been convicted
23		of a crime- or, uh- whether the *crim*inal action
24		pending against them would not be *eli*gible for
25		*any* of the institutions of higher learning.
26		And uh *that's* our law and it s- seemed like
27		Court of Appeal didn't pay any *atten*tion to
28		that?
29	JFK	Right.
30		(0.2)
31		Well, of course-
32	Barnett	And-
33	JFK	The *problem* is- is, Governor, that uh- I got
34		*my* responsibility just like you have you::rs,
35	Barnett	Well, that's *true*. I-
36	JFK	and my responsibility, of course, is to the =
37	Barnett	= I *rea*lize that and I appre::ciate that *so*
38		*much*.
39	JFK	Well now here's the thing uh Governor, I will
40		uh- the Attorney *Gen*'ral can talk to- uh-
41	→	Mr Watkins tomorrow. What I want- would
42	→	*like* to do is to try to work this out in an
43	→	amicable way. We don't want a lot of people
44		down here getting hurt =
45	Barnett	= Oh, that's right.

In fact, at lines 39–41 of this extract near the end of the call, he seems to accept the Governor's definition of the situation, but he ends by recycling his own initial hope, of both cooperation and lack of violence. Note especially his shift (lines 41–2) from 'what I want' to 'would *like* to do . . .' (arrows) and the Governor, consistent with earlier promises to Robert Kennedy, quickly agrees to not wanting 'a lot of people down here getting hurt' (lines 44–5). After this minimal agreement, they close out the call promising to talk later.

Much happens in the next 24–30 hours that cannot be detailed here: more phone calls between Robert Kennedy and the Governor's attorney, more meetings in Washington (and, no doubt, in many locations in Mississippi), contingency plans to federalize troops, a football game in Mississippi at which the Governor makes an inflamatory speech, and a whole Sunday of intense communications.

From a distance, the White House team tracked the unfolding crisis, discussing the action of their own US marshals on the Oxford campus. By

Sunday, 30 September both President Kennedy and his brother made further attempts to control the local situation by getting the Governor to cooperate; bringing a federalized National Guard across state lines (from Tennessee) was the least desirable solution to the rapidly degenerating situation.

By evening, about 9:00 p.m. Washington time, the President's team was located in the Cabinet Room as TV crews were setting up equipment in the Oval Office in preparation for his nationwide speech at 10:00 p.m. They had several open phone lines to the Mississippi campus and were receiving reports from their own people who had flown into Oxford the night before. It was an hour before dark in Mississippi. Meredith had also been flown in secretly that afternoon and was being hidden in one of the dorms. Students of Ole Miss were returning from a football game played the previous day in Jackson. The mood in Mississippi and elsewhere in the South was ugly and the campus was also filling with strangers, armed and looking for trouble. In Washington, a discussion was under way as to the newly sworn marshals' ability to handle the growing crowd without firing (and with the Governor holding back his own state troopers several blocks away from the campus):

JFK-3 CABINET ROOM:

1	RFK		If- if they get [tear]gas, it's not really
2			a =
3	JFK		= problem?
4	RFK		= problem because they're gonna get the- uh-
5	O'Brien		= the support?
6	Marshall		Unle- unless the- uh- the Bureau [FBI]-
7			See, the Bureau says- uh- *says* that there-
8			there are people moving *in*.
9	RFK		From outside?
10	Marshall		Yeah. I think they've been coming-
11	(?)		Is that just a coupla hours ago?
12	Marshall		And they- they might be armed.
13	JFK	→	You see, once *one* fellow starts firing,
14			everybody starts firing. That's what
15			con*cerns* me.
16	RFK		*Yeah.*

Several bystanders and a number of state troopers had already been injured. Sporadic firing has occurred and it is unclear what the Governor will actually do to maintain order. In the rapidly changing conditions, real-time assessments, interpretations and estimates – however incomplete and imperfect – were critical. The worst sort of scenario was unfolding in Oxford and darkness was approaching as the President and Governor spoke for a third time:

JFK-4 – SECOND PHONECALL:

```
 1  JFK              Y'see we don'- we got an hour t'go:::
 2                   that's not u:h- we- we may not ha::ve
 3                   an hour ┌what with this┐
 4  Barnett                 └Uh- this man ┘ this man has
 5                   jus' died
 6  JFK              Did he die?
 7  Barnett          Yes ┌sir ┐
 8  JFK                  └Whi┘ch one? State Police?
 9  Barnett          That's the State Police
10  JFK         →    Yea:h, well, you see we gotta get order up
11                   there an' that's what we thou::::ght we
12                   ┌were gonna┐ ha:ve =
13  Barnett          └Mistuh   ┘        = Pre::s'dent PLEA::SE
14                   why don't you uh- can't you give an order
15                   up there to remo::ve Mer'┌dith
16  JFK                                       └HOW┘ CAN I
17                   REMO::VE HIM GOVernor when there's a-
18                   a ri::ot in the street an' he may step out
19                   of that building an' something ha::ppen
20                   to him? I can't remove him under tho::se
21                   conditions.
22                              (1.0)
23  Barnett          ┌┌U::::h-┐
24  JFK              └└Y'go-  ┘
25                   Let's get o::rder ┌up there an' then we
26  Barnett                            └but- but- but we can-
27  JFK              can do something ┌about Meredith┐
28  Barnett                           └we can       ┘
29                   sur::rou::nd it with plenty 'v offi::cials
30  JFK              Well we've got to get somebuddy up there
31                   now to get order, and stop the firing and
32                   shooting. Then we- you and I will ta::lk on
33                   the phone about Meredith
34                              (0.2)
35                   ┌┌But firs'┐ we gotta get order
36  Barnett          └└A::rright┘ I'll- I'll ca:ll an tell 'em to
37                   get every- every official they ca::n?
```

As they discuss the situation, the Governor receives news that an injured state trooper has died. Note Kennedy's reaction (line 10), which is notably absent of any conventional regrets although an assessment of the news would be predictable in that turn slot. Instead, he presses the Governor to take control. Barnett continues the position indicated earlier which is that the President is responsible for bringing Meredith in and for the trouble: 'Mister President PLEASE why don't you uh- can't you give an order up there to remove Meredith' (lines 13–15). Exasperated, Kennedy raises his voice (lines 16–17) to point out that Meredith might get injured if he were moved, and recycles his plea for law and order.

After this call, JFK reports the exchange to RFK and the assembled group in the White House:

JFK-5 CABINET ROOM:

1	JFK		He wants us to move w- to move him. And I
2			said 'Well, we can't move him if the
3			situation's like this.' And he says 'Well,
4			we'll take care of the situation if you
5			move him.'
6	RFK	→	I *can't* get him ou::t! How'm I gonna get
7			him out?
8	JFK		That's what I said to him. Now- now, the
9			pro::blem is- if he can get law and order
10			resto::red (0.3) okay, we'll move him outa
11			there if he can get order restored.
12	RFK		I don't see how we can- uh-

This time it is the Attorney General who protests; in legal and organizational terms, law and order in the nation is *his* responsibility. This final extract highlights the embeddedness of all action and accounts as the *retelling* of exchanges serves again to rehearse retrospectively–prospectively how current events will look later. It also serves critically to provide the continuous updating of shared knowledge essential both to sense-making and decision-taking. About an hour after these exchanges, the President broadcast to the nation on national television but by then there was a full-scale riot in Oxford. During the night, the Kennedy team coordinated the move of further US marshals and National Guard troops stationed 75 miles away from Oxford, near Memphis.

James Meredith was registered at the University of Mississippi the next morning, in relative calm and under tight security. The Oxford campus was strewn with debris and burnt-out cars. Four hundred US marshals from around the country were staked out across the campus and in the local community. In addition, National Guard units from Tennessee had arrived in erratic waves during the early hours of the morning of 1 October, and were continuing to arrive. The Mississippi National Guard had also been belatedly federalized. Two people were dead, the local state trooper and a reporter, Paul Guihard, a correspondent of Agence France-Presse, and 60 to 70 people injured including 25 US marshals. By the end of week, there were 3,000 assorted federal troops in Oxford and Meredith was attending classes under constant guard.[51] He completed his degree at Ole Miss in September 1963.[52]

Talk, Text and Narrative

In this essay, I have woven texts and talk into a narrative. It is not the only story to be told of those events in Mississippi 30 years ago, but it is one that traces the momentary quality of history in the making. The analysis on which this descriptive account is built was originally based only on the final weekend of telephone calls, and on the available audio recordings. As a conversation analyst, my interest had been in having a *series* of telephone calls in sequence with which to examine a number of technical issues in talk.[53] As I examined the tense turn-taking in this collection, the temporal sequencing of talk and event demanded attention. Without any other knowledge of this particular weekend, much was available by simply examining the talk in an unmotivated way. The 'tension' was built into the *timing* of the turn-taking, the distance between the men not only ideological but verbal and *produced* through their interactional asynchrony. The theoretical consequences of *talking* the American presidency and the early civil rights movement into being seemed worth pursuing. The spatio-temporal anchoring of action in talk also became clearly relevant to what 'talk' as a self-organizing yet highly structured activity might be, on the one hand, and what history-as-it-happens might look like, on the other.

As I worked backwards and examined the historical record, the hunch proved valid. Theodore Sorenson, who was present at the White House during much of that fraught weekend and witness to a number of the interaction calls detailed above, confirmed the importance of the telephone calls,[54] as did other accounts of the crisis. The telephone calls and the open telephone lines to the Oxford campus were, in fact, the *only* link between the White House and the crisis.[55] More significantly, they were the only real-time means of communication between the key actors in the drama, with the exception of Meredith, who was kept in seclusion for his own safety.[56]

The incident at Ole Miss highlights a unique feature of modernity, a phenomenon Giddens has dubbed 'action at a distance',[57] namely our ability to make things happen not only in our own immediate environment but far away, in relation not only to people we know but to people whom we may never have met – often instantly, even more frequently simultaneously with other interacting forces. Presence and absence have taken on a new and sometimes fraught connection, a profoundly reflexive quality. While Goffman's 'interaction order'[58] remains the primordial site of human sociability, as many conversation analysts have variously insisted, intense and quite intimate interaction is possible and even routine over vast distances. The result is an instant world anchored through the sorts of sequential properties first discovered by Harvey Sacks and his early collaborators but now taking on global scale and consequences.

Social action of all kinds is a finely structured affair.[59] To track a crisis under conditions of late modernity requires real-time interactional skills as well as real-time technology. It is talk, not technology, that can draw people together or drive them apart. It can create a kind of conversational collusion that structures next moments and shapes next events. Or, equally intensely, it can escalate misunderstanding and create conversational asynchrony and a lack of mutual alignment both in talk and in the actions talk shapes. Typically, talk ties activities together, providing the social cohesion that makes them possible in the first place. It is in this sense that talk makes history. Through its sequential structure and *structuring* properties, talk provides the bedrock of all social life.

Notes

1 In 1916 the Swiss philologist Ferdinand de Saussure had proposed the distinction between *langue* as an independent language system and *parole* as spoken discourse. In his classic work *Course in General Linguistics*, ed. C. Bally and A. Sechabaye (London: Collins, 1974), he set out to seperate speech/speaking, as a heterogeneous activity, from the rigorous autonomy of an independent system of signs. Language, according to Saussure, 'is a product that is passively assimilated by the individual' (p. 14).

2 See e.g. D. S. Boomer and A. T. Dittmann, 'Hesitation pauses and juncture pauses in speech', *Language and Speech*, 5 (1962).

3 N. Chomsky, *Syntactic Structures* (The Hague: Mouton, 1957).

4 L. Wittgenstein, *Philosophical Investigations* (Oxford: Blackwell, 1958).

5 For a definitive discussion of Harvey Sacks's intellectual development, see Schlegloff's Introduction to the recently, and belatedly, issued compendium of Sacks's lectures: *Harvey Sacks: Lectures on Conversation*, vols 1 and 2, ed. G. Jefferson (Oxford: Blackwell, 1992).

6 See H. Garfinkel, *Studies in Ethnomethodology* (Englewood Cliffs, NJ: Prentice-Hall, 1967), his classic work; for the best extant discussion of Garfinkel's work, see J. Heritage, 'A change in state token and aspects of its sequential placement', in J. M. Atkinson and J. Heritage (eds), *Structures of Social Action* (Cambridge: Cambridge University Press, 1984); see also D. Boden, 'People are talking: conversation analysis and symbolic interaction', in H. S. Becker and M. McCall (eds), *Symbolic Interaction and Cultural Studies* (Chicago: University of Chicago Press, 1990). The theoretical 'indifference' with which ethnomethodologists examine social phenomena is discussed in detail in H. Garfinkel and H. Sacks, 'On formal structures of practical action', in

J. C. McKinney and E. A. Tiryakian (eds), *Theoretical Sociology* (New York: Appleton Century Crofts, 1970), pp. 338–66.

7   These techniques have been developed by Gail Jefferson over the years; they constitute a way of capturing for the eye what was heard by the ear, using a variety of conventions based on a standard keyboard. The transcripts in this essay have been simplified considerably to aid presentation:

A: Ye⌐s, two. ⌉
B: ⌊Oh goo:⌋d.

Brackets indicate the point at which simultaneous speech starts and ends.

A: ⌈⌈How–
B: ⌊⌊When did you hear?

Utterances starting simultaneoulsy are indicated by double brackets.

A: Hello =
B: = Hi.

When there is no audible gap between one utterance and the next, equal signs are used.

(0.8)

Numbers in brackets indicate elapsed time in tenths of a second.

(.)

A dot in parentheses indicates a slight gap, typically less than one-tenth of a second.

A: *Right.* HOW MUCH?

Italics indicate emphasis in delivery; capital letters indicate that a word or phrase is louder than the surrounding talk.

A: So : : :

Colons indicate that the immediately preceding syllable is prolonged or 'stretched'; the number of colons denote, approximately, the duration.

For a fuller summary of transcription conventions see e.g. J. M. Atkinson and J. Heritage (eds), *Structures of Social Action* (Cambridge: Cambridge University Press, 1984); G. Button and J. Lee, *Talk and Social Organization* (Clevedon, Avon, UK: Multilingual Matters, 1987); D. Boden and D. H. Zimmerman (eds), *Talk and Social Structure: Studies in Ethnomethodology and Conversation Analysis* (Cambridge: Polity Press, 1991); P. Drew and J. Heritage, *Talk at Work* Cambridge: Cambridge University Press, 1993).

8   Early and now classic articles include H. Sacks, 'On sociological description', *Berkeley Journal of Sociology*, 8 (1963), pp 1–16; E. A. Schlegloff, 'Sequencing in conversational openings', *American Anthropologist*, 70 (1968), 1075–95; E. A. Schlegloff and H. Sacks, 'Opening up closings', *Semiotica*, 7 (1973), pp. 289–327; G. Jefferson, 'A case of precision timing in ordinary conversation: overlapped tag-positioned address terms in closing sequences', *Semiotica*, 9 (1973), pp. 47–96, and 'Error correction as an interactional resource', *Language in Society*, 2 (1974), pp. 181–99; H. Sacks, E. A. Schlegloff and G. Jefferson, 'A simplest systematics for the organization of turn-taking for conversation', *Language*, 50 (1974), pp. 696–735. Recent collections containing key work include G. Psathas, *Everyday Language* (New York: Irvington, 1979); Atkinson and Heritage, *Structures of Social Action*;

Button and Lee, *Talk and Social Organization*; Boden and Zimmerman, *Talk and Social Structure*; Drew and Heritage, *Talk at Work*. The reader is also referred to the extensive bibliography of J. Coulter, *Ethnomethodological Sociology* (London: Edward Elgar, 1990), which contains over 1,200 listings of work in ethnomethodology and conversation analysis.

9   See e.g. G. Jordan and A. Henderson, 'Interaction analysis: foundations and practice', unpublished MS, n.d., Xerox, Palo Alto, Calif., Research Center and Institute for Research on Learning.

10 These include a growing range of work on 'institutional talk', e.g. J. M. Atkinson and P. Drew, *Order in Court: The Organization of Verbal Interaction in Judicial Settings* (London: Macmillan, 1979); G. Jefferson and J. Lee, 'The rejection of advice: managing the problematic convergence of a "trouble-telling" and a "service encounter" ', *Journal of Pragmatics*, 55 (1981), pp. 399–422; R. M. Frankel, 'From sentence to sequence: understanding the medical encounter through micro-interactional analysis', *Discourse Processes*, 7 (1984), pp. 135–70; J. M. Atkinson, *Our Master's Voices: The Language and Body Language of Politics* (London: Methuen, 1984); D. W. Maynard, *Inside Plea Bargaining* (New York: Plenum Press, 1984); D. H. Zimmerman, 'Talk and its occasion: the case of calling the police', in D. Schiffrin (ed.), *Meaning, Form and Use in Context* (Washington, DC: Georgetown University Press, 1984), pp. 210–28; C. Heath, *Body Movement and Speech in Medical Interaction* (Cambridge: Cambridge University Press, 1986); M. Whalen and D. Zimmerman, 'Sequential and institutional contexts in calls for help', *Social Psychology Quarterly*, 50 (1987), pp. 172–85; S. Clayman, 'The production of punctuality: social interaction, temporal organization, and social structure', *American Journal of Sociology*, 95 (1989), pp. 659–91; Giolo Fele, *L'insorgere del conflitto: uno studio sull'organizzazione sociale del disaccordo nella conversazione* (Milan: FrancoAngeli, 1991); A. Garcia, 'Dispute resolution without disputing: how the interactional organization of mediation hearings minimizes argument', *American Sociological Review*, 56 (1991), pp. 818–35. For an illuminating discussion of talk in institutional settings, see J. Heritage and D. Greatbatch, 'On the institutional character of institutional talk: the case of news interviews', in Boden and Zimmerman, *Talk and Social Structure*, pp. 93–137; Drew and Heritage, *Talk at Work*. There has also been work in organizational settings more generally, e.g. R. J. Anderson, J. A. Hughes and W. W. Sharrock, *Working for Profit: The Social Organization of Calculation in an Entrepreneurial Firm* (Aldershot, Hants, UK: Avebury, 1987); and D. Boden, *The Business of Talk: Organizations in Action* (Cambridge: Polity Press, 1994); also a variety of video-based analyses in hi-tech work settings, e.g. L. Suchman, *Plans and Situated Actions: The Problem of Human/Machine Communication* (Cambridge: Cambridge University Press, 1987).

11 See Atkinson and Heritage, *Structures of Social Action*.

12 e.g. Schlegloff, 'Sequencing in conversational openings'.

13 In an especially ethnomethodological vein, see H. Garfinkel, M. Lynch and E. Livingston, 'The work of a discovering science construed from materials

from the optically discovered pulsar', *Philosophy of the Social Sciences*, 11 (1981), pp. 131–58.

14   Sacks, Schlegloff and Jefferson, 'A simplest systematics'; see also T. P. Wilson, J. Wiemann and D. H. Zimmerman, 'Models of turn-taking in conversational interaction', *Journal of Language and Social Psychology*, 15 (1984), pp. 159–83.

15   See D. Boden, 'This is the President: issues of identity and identification in telephone calls', paper presented at the Annual Meeting of the Pacific Sociological Association, Albuquerque, New Mexico, 1985.

16   See n. 9 above; see also J. Heritage, 'Recent developments in conversation analysis', *Sociolinguistics*, 15 (1985), pp. 1–19; J. Heritage, S. Clayman and D. H. Zimmerman, 'Discourse and message analysis: the micro-structure of mass media messages', in R. P. Hawkins, J. M. Wiemann and S. Pingree (eds), *Advancing Communication Science: Merging Mass and Interpersonal Processes* (Newbury Park, Calif.: Sage, 1988), pp. 77–109; D. Zimmerman, 'On conversation: the conversation analytic perspective', in J. A. Anderson (ed.), *Communications Yearbook 11* Newbury Park, Calif.: Sage, 1988), pp. 406–32; Boden. 'People are talking'; D. W. Maynard and S. Clayman, 'The diversity of ethnomethodology', *Annual Review of Sociology*, 71 (1991), pp. 385–418.

17   For interesting discussions of these matters from the perspective of historical sociologists, see e.g. A. Abbott, 'Conceptions of time and events in social science methods: causal and narrative approaches', *Historical Methods*, 23 (1990), pp. 140–50; L. J. Griffin, 'Narrative, event-structure analysis, and causal interpretation in historical sociology', *American Journal of Sociology*, 98 (1993), pp. 1094–133.

18   For an insightful recent discussion on the relevance of history, narratives and social theory, see F. Inglis, *Media Theory: An Introduction* (Oxford: Basil Blackwell, 1990), pp. 4–5.

19   e.g. C. Tilly, *Big Structures, Large Processes, Huge Comparisons* (New York: Russell Sage Foundation, 1984).

20   In the US, for instance, all the Presidential Libraries since Roosevelt archive audio and video materials. There are also excellent media archives, e.g. the network television news archive at Vanderbilt University.

21   I shall not be concerned here with the post-structuralist notion that everything is a text; talk is talk and text comprises written materials in which 'talk' has become transformed into a documentary record. As an ethnomethodologist, I take 'discourse' similarly to be a practical matter accomplished in and through the actions of everyday actors. They may, to be sure, use a variety of linguistic forms but these too must be realized in concrete settings of action.

22   These and a limited number of other audio recordings made in the Oval Office of the White House during the Kennedy administration are available to researchers at the Kennedy Presidential Library in Boston, which also holds a large collection of other audio-visual materials of the Kennedy era.

23   Many of the written documents are archived as the 'Papers of Burke Marshall' at the Kennedy Presidential Library in Boston. Burke Marshall

was Assistant Attorney General for Civil Rights during the Kennedy Administration and, indeed, throughout much of the 1960s. He was a central figure at the White House during the weekend in question.

24 See e.g. T. Brooks, *Walls Come Tumbling Down: History of the Civil Rights Movement, 1940–1970* (Englewood Cliffs, NJ: Prentice-Hall, 1977).

25 Letter from James H. Meredith to Robert B. Ellis, Office of the Registrar, University of Mississippi, Oxford, dated 31 January 1961; Archives of the Kennedy Presidential Library, Papers of Burke Marshall.

26 Western Union telegram dated 4 February 1961, 2.05 p.m.; Archives of Meredith vs. University of Mississippi case, Kennedy Presidential Library.

27 e.g. S. Tucker, *Mississippi from Within* (New York: Arco Publishing, 1965).

28 This irony was not, of course, lost on Meredith himself who, in his letter of 31 January to the Registrar (cited above), notes that he 'will not be able to furnish [them] with the names of six University Alumni because I am a Negro and all the graduates of the school are White . . . [e]xcept for [this] requirement . . . my application is complete.'

29 See e.g. L. A. Sobel (ed.), *Civil Rights, 1960–1966* (New York: Facts on File, 1967); Brooks, *Walls Come Tumbling Down*.

30 H. A. Innis, *The Bias of Communication* (Toronto: University of Toronto Press, 1951): cf. A. Cicourel, 'Text and discourse', *Annual Review of Anthropology*, 14 (1985), pp. 159–85; W. Chafe and D. Tannen, 'The relation between written and spoken language', *Annual Review of Anthropology*, 16 (1987), pp. 383–407.

31 See e.g. J. Goody, *The Logic of Writing and the Organization of Society* (New York: Cambridge University Press, 1986).

32 Today, 30 years later, the general use of audio cassette tape recorders and amateur video equipment has opened a new era of analysis when both institutions, e.g. the Watergate tapes, and individuals, e.g. the Rodney King video that led to violent riots in Los Angeles, can precipitate massive social change through these new routine 'extensions of modernity' to borrow from M. McLuhan, *Understanding the Media: The Extensions of Man* (New York: McGraw-Hill, 1964).

33 See H. Molotch and D. Boden, 'Talking social structure: discourse, dominance and the Watergate hearings', *American Sociological Review*, 50 (1985), pp. 273–388.

34 In addition to the Mississippi crisis tapes, the Kennedy Presidential Library also has available and archived limited tapes on the Cuban Missiles crisis, a long series of meetings related to 1963 tax cut discussions and a number of other rather minor topics.

35 Since these are White House transcripts and there is no way to check their accuracy, not too much should be made of this but, as will be seen, in later researcher-transcribed tapes similar patterns can be seen in initial cooperation that gives way to reluctance.

36 This call is logged at 9.50 p.m. Washington time. In 1962 the time difference between Washington and Mississippi was two hours.

37 See e.g. J. Heritage and D. R. Watson, 'Formulations as conversational

objects', in G. Psathas (ed.), *Everyday Language: Studies in Ethnomethodology* (New York: Irvington, 1979), pp. 123–62.

38 See J. Heritage, *Garfinkel and Ethnomethodology* (Cambridge: Polity Press, 1984).

39 See Garfinkel, *Studies in Ethnomethodology*; also J. Heritage, 'Accounts in action', in P. Abell and G. N. Gilbert (eds), *Accounts and Action* (Aldershot, Hants, UK: Gower, 1983).

40 This meeting occurs about 1.20–1.40 p.m. on Saturday, 29 September 1962. From this point on, the transcripts are based on my own analysis of audio tapes. See n. 7 above on transcription conventions used in conversation analysis. The extracts presented here have been greatly simplified for presentation purposes.

41 The issue of recursivity is central to Giddens's theory of structuration, e.g. in A. Giddens, *The Constitution of Society: Outline of the Theory of Structuration* (Cambridge: Polity Press, 1984), but it is also a central feature of ethnomethodological notions of the local, practical, sequential and serial constitution of social order; see e.g. Garfinkel, *Studies in Ethnomethodology*, pp. 35–53; and D. H. Zimmerman and D. Boden, 'Structure-in-action', in Boden and Zimmerman, *Talk and Social Structure*, pp. 11–19.

42 See Schlegloff, 'Sequencing in conversational openings'.

43 On the marking of changes in participants' state of knowledge with 'oh', see Heritage, 'A change in state token and aspects of its sequential placement'.

44 For a primary discussion on the ways in which offering a 'reason for calling' builds on a 'preservable feature' of earlier interactions, see Sacks, *Harvey Sacks: Lectures on Conversation*, pp. 773–6.

45 This claim is admittedly fairly sweeping without recourse to an entire analytic framework in which to justify it. On the basis simply of members' knowledge, it has much to support it, however: I have played the *tape* of this telephone call to audiences throughout the United States (including the deep South) and overseas. The silence at line 31 never fails to be immediately marked by audiences, even non-native speakers. This is, after all, the President of the United States speaking; the silence and what follows is noted by both professional and lay listeners. They have, I think, little doubt about what is at stake in this highly structured strip of talk.

46 G. Jefferson, 'Preliminary notes on a possible metric which provides for a "standard maximum" silence of approximately one second in conversation', in D. Roger and P. Bull (eds), *Conversation: An Interdisciplinary Perspective* (Clevedon, Avon, UK: Multilingual Matters, 1989), pp. 156–97.

47 J. Davidson, 'Subsequent versions of invitations, offers, requests, and proposals dealing with potential or actual rejection', in Atkinson and Heritage, *Structures of Social Action*, pp. 102–28.

48 See e.g. G. Jefferson, 'On stepwise transition from talk about a trouble to inappropriately next-positioned matters', in Atkinson and Heritage, *Structures of Social Action*, pp. 191–222; H. Sacks, 'On the preference for agreement and contiguity in sequences in conversation', in G. Button and

J. R. E. Lee (eds), *Talk and Social Organization* (Clevedon, Avon, UK: Multilingual Matters, 1987), pp. 54–69.

49 e.g. first-pair part: I'd like to get your help in doing that / second-pair part: Sure (or, Gosh, I wish I could but . . .).

50 In more cooperative talk, indeed even in tense situations, speakers usually mark their 'disjunctive' talk with objects like 'on a completely different topic . . .' or 'Oh, that reminds me . . .' or similar explicit announcement of transition. Otherwise, topics shift 'stepwise' and shade one into another (Jefferson, 'On stepwise transition').

51 Civil Rights Archives 1962, 'Meredith and the University of Mississippi: Riot in Oxford (Miss.), pp. 110–11; Kennedy Presidential Library.

52 J. H. Meredith, *Three Years at Mississippi* (Bloomington, Ind.: Indiana University Press, 1966).

53 See e.g. D. Boden, 'This is the President: issues of identity and indentification in telephone calls', paper presented at the Annual Meeting of the Pacific Sociological Association, Albuquerque, New Mexico, 1985.

54 See T. Sorenson, *Kennedy* (New York: Harper & Row, 1965).

55 e.g. D. C. Lord, *John F. Kennedy: The Politics of Confrontation and Conciliation* (Woodbury, NY: Barron's Educational Services, 1977).

56 Interestingly, Meredith's own account of the fateful weekend published in 1966 (*Three Years at Mississippi*) is very brief, which is hardly surprising, given the very narrow window through which he was able to observe events.

57 A. Giddens, *The Consequences of Modernity* (Stanford, Calif.: Stanford University Press, 1990).

58 E. Goffman, 'The interaction order', *American Sociological Review*, 48 (1983), pp. 1–17.

59 See also W. Sharrock and G. Button, 'The social actor: social action in real time', in G. Button (ed.), *Ethnomethodology and the Human Sciences* (Cambridge: Cambridge University Press, 1990), pp. 137–76; see also D. Boden, 'Temporal frames: time, talk and organization', unpublished MS, Department of Sociology, Lancaster University, n.d.

Part III

Contingency, Reflexivity, Postmodernity

8

The Mode of Information and Postmodernity

Mark Poster

A post-structuralist approach to communication theory analyses the way electronically mediated communication (what I call 'the mode of information') both challenges and reinforces systems of domination that are emerging in a postmodern society and culture.[1] My general thesis is that the mode of information enacts a radical reconfiguration of language, one which constitutes subjects outside the pattern of the rational, autonomous individual. This familiar modern subject is displaced by the mode of information in favour of one that is multiplied, disseminated, and decentred, continuously interpellated as an unstable identity. At the level of culture, this instability poses both dangers and challenges which, if they become part of a political movement, or are connected with the politics of feminism, ethnic/racial minorities, gay and lesbian positions, may lead to a fundamental challenge to modern social institutions and structures.

Communication theory needs to account for electronically mediated communication and by doing so take its proper place of importance in general social theory. This importance has not generally been recognized by the great theorists of modern society who emphasized action (labour) and institutions (bureaucracy) over language and communication. Marx and Weber, for example, fall clearly within this tendency. Yet their theories reflect the dominant communicational mode of their time, even though they failed fully to take it into account. They were heirs of the eighteenth century Enlightenment, an intellectual tradition that was profoundly rooted in print culture. The Enlightenment theory of the autonomous rational individual derived much sustenance and reinforcement from the practice of reading the printed page.[2] Hegel struck such a chord when he referred to newspaper reading as 'the morning prayer of modern man'. The spatial materiality of print – the linear display of sentences, the stability of the word on the page, the orderly, systematic spacing of black letters on a white background – enable readers to distance themselves from authors. These features of print promote an ideology of the critical individual, reading and thinking in isolation, outside the network of political and religious dependencies. In an opposite, but yet complementary way, print culture, by the materiality of the word on the page as compared with the evanescence of the word in oral culture, promotes the authority of the author, the intellectual and the theorist. This double movement engenders the reader as critic and the author as authority, an apparent opposition or contradiction but actually an oscillation of dominance characteristic of communication in modern society.

In the case of both the reader and the author print culture constitutes the individual as a subject, as transcendent to objects, as stable and fixed in identity, in short, as a grounded essence. And this feature of print culture is homologous with the figure of the subject in modern institutions – the capitalist market with its possessive individuals, the legal system with its 'reasonable man', representative democracy with its secret ballots and presumption of individual self-interest, bureaucracy with its instrumental rationality, the factory with its Taylorite system, the educational system with its individualized examinations and records. In response to these developments, Marx theorized the emancipation of rational individuality through the class struggle and Weber regretted the fixing of instrumental rationality in unchangeable social organizations. Both presumed a configuration of the subject which was a product of print culture and both viewed modernity as the final instantiation of that social individual. However, both missed the role of communications in the process of constituting such subjects and both understood the process of subject constitution only in part. Marx realized that individuals change in different modes of production, but posited man as a 'species being' that communism would fully actualize, one that looks very much like the Enlightenment's autonomous rational agent. Weber allowed four types of subjects (value rational, instrumental rational, emotional and traditional), understood them as in some sense historically produced, but saw modernity as inscribing only one, the instrumental rational. For both, history ended with the appearance of the autonomous rational agent as subject, as fixed essence.

The emergence of the mode of information, with its electronically mediated systems of communication, changes the way we think about the subject and promises to alter as well the shape of society. Electronic culture promotes the individual as an unstable identity, as a continuous process of multiple identity formation, and raises the question of a social form beyond the modern, the possibility of a postmodern society.³ Electronic culture promotes theories (such as post-structuralism) that focus on the role of language in the process of the constitution of subjects. These theories undermine views of the reader and author as stable points of criticism and authority respectively. When print mediates the theorist's understanding of the subject, language is understood as representational, as an arbitrary system of signs, invoked by a thinker in order to point to objects. As long as this regime is in place, the subject remains a stable point, fixed in space and time. Figures that upset such an understanding of the subject – women, children, non-Europeans – are placed in the position of being Other, of not being taken seriously into account. When electronic communication is a factor in the theorist's understanding of the subject, language is understood as performative, rhetorical, as an active figuring and positioning of the subject. With the spread of this regime of communication, the subject can only be understood as partially stable, as repeatedly reconfigured at different points of time and space, as non-self-identical and therefore as always partly Other.

Electronic communications, like print, place a distance between the addressor and the addressee; they accentuate the feature of language that permits a gap between the speaker and the listener. This gap is often understood by proponents of modern print-oriented theory as efficiency. From smoke signals to communication satellites, the principle is the same: extend the human voice. Just as tools may heighten the powers of the muscles in the production of goods, they may amplify the larynx, allowing speech at a distance. Theories that view communication technology purely as a question of efficiency unduly discourage new questions that arise from electronic communication, placing them within the older paradigms generated to theorize oral and print culture. When electronic communication is seen as simply allowing greater spatial and temporal extension, the analyst reconfirms the figure of the autonomous rational individual and reinstates the stability of the subject.

In terms of politics oral communication, from the point of view of print culture, binds the individual in relations of political domination. When communication is restricted to speech (and manuscript as its simple extension), individuals are easily restrained in ties of dependence. By enlarging the gap mentioned above as inherent in language, print allows a distance to intervene between speaker and listener and this gap permits the individual to think, coolly to judge the words of the other without his or her overbearing presence – or so advocates of print culture contend.

Theorists of print culture interpret the gap as enhancing the powers of reason and permitting individual autonomy. In other words, they link the gap in language to the subject as centred in reason. The ideological force of modern Enlightenment communication theory derives in good part from this move, a move that incorporates print technology within modern social theory. But the stability of this move is always partial, always threatened. For the gap instantiated by print could be turned against modern theory: it could be appropriated by excluded groups such as workers, women and non-Europeans to promote their ends; it could be turned into cultural resistance as in avant-garde art movements since the Romantic period.[4] Nineteenth-century jeremiads against the dangers of reading novels are indications that the inducement to fantasy was one appropriation of the gap that resisted its Enlightenment containment. As early as Rousseau's *Emile*, Sophie falls in love with Emile because he resembles a character in a novel she had read. Love was mediated by the gap inscribed in print.

Electronic culture permits a different interpretation of the gap. The tremendous extension of the space between speaker and listener in the mode of information upsets the confinement of the gap to the self-identical subject. The combination of enormous distances with temporal immediacy produced by electronic communications both removes the speaker from the listener and brings them together. These opposing tendencies – opposite from the point of view of print culture – reconfigures the position of the individual so drastically that the figure of the self, fixed in time and space, capable of exercising cognitive control over surrounding objects, may no longer be sustained. Language no longer represents a reality, no longer is a neutral tool to enhance the subject's instrumental rationality: language becomes or better reconfigures reality. And by doing so the subject is interpellated through language and cannot easily escape recognition of that interpellation. Electronic communication systematically removes the fixed points, the grounds, the foundations that were essential to modern theory. I shall illustrate these transformations of cultural and social life by diverse examples of electronically mediated communication: the TV ad, the database and computer writing. And I shall explore these examples from the post-structuralist perspectives of Jean Baudrillard, Michel Foucault and Jacques Derrida.

In the register of humanist morality, TV ads are manipulative, deceptive and repugnant; they solicit consumer decisions on 'irrational' grounds and encourage a 'quick-fix' drug mentality as a false solution to life's problems. In the register of marketing, TV ads are evaluated in relation to their ability 'to create effective demand' for the product. In the register of democratic politics, TV ads undermine the independent thinking of the electorate, diminishing its ability to distinguish truth from falsity, the real and the imaginary, and passifying it into a state of indifference. In the register of Marxist social criticism, TV ads stimulate false needs that detract from the revolutionary purpose of the working class and serve only to pump up an economy that is beyond the control of the producers. Each of these perspectives contains a degree of validity but none approaches the crucial issue of the role of TV ads in contemporary culture, none reveals the altered language structure of the ads, and, most importantly, none draws attention to the relation of language to culture in the constitution of new subject positions, that is, new places in the network of social communication. I contend that TV ads exploit electronic mediation so as to inscribe a new technology of power, one whose political effects need to be assessed in relation to the possible emergence of a postmodern society.

Like monologues, print and radio, TV ads are nominally unidirectional communications: the sender addresses the receiver. Yet all communications enable responses, feedbacks, replies, however delayed. Monologues are subject to interventions, print to reports or to conversations, radio to telephone call-ins. But each of these communication technologies is enunciated as unidirectional. The TV ad, unlike the other examples, easily combines images, sounds and writing. It displays moving, aural narratives of everyday reality, at times with great verisimilitude. Because they control the context, the background, as well as the text of the narrative, TV ads contain special powers. The 'reality' they represent can be 'hyperreal', editing in contents not normally found together in 'reality'. Voice-overs, as another example, inject a superego-like authority in the ad. With great flexibility the ad constructs a mini-reality in which things are set in juxtapositions that violate the rules of the everyday. In particular, TV ads associate meanings, connotations and moods that are inappropriate in reality, subject to objections in dialogic communications, but effective at the level of desire, the unconscious, the imaginary. TV ads constitute a language system that leaves out the referent, the symbolic and the real, working instead with chains of signifiers (words) and signifieds (mental images). The referent, the symbolic and the real are absent and only come into play if the viewer buys the product.

The meaning structure of the TV ad, strictly keeping itself to the levels of signifiers, meanings and images, powerfully invites the viewer to identify with the commodity. The ad stimulates not an object choice, a cognitive decision, a rational evaluation, but works at other linguistic levels to produce the effects of incorporation and attachment between the viewer and the product. The viewer is the absent hero or heroine of the ad. The viewer is solicited to displace him or herself into the ad and become one with the meanings associated with the product. In its monologue, in its construction of context and its association of non-connected meanings, the TV ad inscribes a new pattern of communication into the culture, one repeated *ad infinitum*, one extended to politics, religion and every conceivable aspect of social life.

Through these communications, the realist linguistic paradigm is shaken. The TV ad works with simulacra, with inventions and with imaginings. The modernist print-oriented communications associated with education, capitalism/socialism, bureaucracy and representative democracy – identities centred in Weber's instrumental reason – are displaced in favour of a postmodernist, electronic-oriented communication in which identity is destabilized and fragmented. This is accomplished not in the highly ritualized collective action of religion or other community function, but in the privacy, informality and isolation of the home. And it is accomplished not at special moments of the calender, but every day and for long hours. The population places itself in communication situations in which the TV ad is the norm of language construction, and the effects on the construction of subject positions are no doubt profound.

Jean Baudrillard, in *Consumer Society, The System of Objects* and *Toward a Critique of the Political Economy of the Sign*, began the line of thinking about contemporary culture which I am pursuing in relation to TV ads as part of the mode of information.[5] Baudrillard broke with the realist paradigms of social science at first by combining Roland Barthes's semiology with the neo-Marxism of Henri Lefebvre. In the late 1960s and early 1970s, he attempted to move social critique from the level of action to that of language. He began to look at consumer culture not as a process of Veblenesque mimesis, of 'keeping up with the Joneses' of conformist behaviour, but as a peculiar restructuring of signs. Structuralist linguists had shown that meaning was a result of relations of difference between words. The key to language was not so much a connection between a word and a thing but an arbitrary designation that depended on a differential mark. Language for them was composed of binary oppositions of signifiers – I/you; black/white, and so forth – whose ability to have meaning hinged on the stable relation between the terms or what they termed the 'structure'. Language was theorized as a vast machine for generating such differential relations. But in order to grasp this the theorist needed to shift his or her point of view away from the individual as a subject who produced and received meaning to language as an objective system of relations. In other words language became intelligible only from the standpoint of its structure; language then constituted the subject, not the reverse.

For Baudrillard the structuralists were too formalist, restricting themselves too closely to linguistic signs. He shifted the object of analysis to daily life, taking society itself as the field for interpretation. Consumer activity would then be seen as a circulation of signs in the structuralist sense. The commodity is thus extracted from the domain of economic theory or moral commentary and viewed as a complex code. The key to consumerism is not an irrational tendency to conspicuous display but the insertion of individuals into a communication relation in which they receive messages in the form of commodities. The consumer is not 'irrational' and the object is not a 'utility'. Between the poles of object and intention is the advertisement which disrupts the normal set of differential relations of signs. The ad presupposes language not as a reference to a 'real' but as an arbitrary connection of signifiers. It simply rearranges those signifiers, violating their 'normal' references. The aim of the ad is to associate a chain of signifiers in a narrative of a desirable lifestyle: Pepsi = youth = sexiness = popularity = fun, for example.

The status of the ad as a linguistic and cultural phenomenon, Baudrillard argued in the 1980s, is that of a simulacrum, a copy that has no original, has no objective referent. For him today's culture increasingly is composed of these simulacra which taken together compose a new order of reality which he terms 'the hyperreal'. Culture consists of constructed realities, Disneylands, which are more real than the real they are supposed to refer back to. But in the end there is no reference back since once social life is presented as a theme park in one place, its constructed element emerges and tends to dominate over its presence as a fixed, natural order. Society becomes a collage of theme parks which one enters at will (and for a price). Baudrillard totalizes his view of the hyperreal, dismissing other modernist perspectives on politics and the economy as without value. By contextualizing his understanding of consumer culture in relation to the mode of information, by connecting it with specific communication technologies, I hope to extract the critical impulse of his position without acceding to his monolithic vision.

Computerized databases are another form of electronically mediated communication that have been studied from various perspectives. Liberal writers have rightly been concerned that the vast store of data accumulated in this form and its relative ease of transfer poses a threat to the privacy of the individual. With so much information about individuals now digitalized in databases, one's life becomes an open book for those who have access to the right computers. Agencies of all kinds – military, police, governmental, corporate – continuously gather data to be exchanged from one computer to another while the individuals to whom the data refer have little control over this flow or, in many cases, knowledge of its existence. In the eyes of liberals, society is indeed nearing the nightmare of 1984, only a few years behind Orwell's schedule. Marxists for their part have shown how databases are a new form of information as commodity, one which has largely passed into the control of the largest corporations. Increasingly society becomes divided into the information rich and the information poor. Existing class divisions on a national and even a global scale are reinforced and further sedimented by the technology of computerized information. As the economy relies more and more upon information, access to databases is not at all a trivial matter. The fate of companies, even nations, hinges upon the timely procurement of information. In comparison with feudal regimes, capitalist societies once prided themselves on establishing the free flow of information, thinking of this feature of modernity as a touchstone of freedom. The digitization of information in the form of databases acts to facilitate its instantaneous, global availability, so the restraint of commodification flies in the face of the advance of the technology.

While these perspectives are valuable for a full understanding of the database as a communication technology, they neglect a fundamental aspect of the phenomenon: its ability to constitute and multiply the identity of the individual and thereby to promote his/her control. The social model implicit in the above positions is one of individuals/groups confronting institutions and social forces in a relation of struggle, contest and opposition. At the most general level, liberals and Marxists assume a world of discrete, stable entities. Hence the notion of privacy, for example, with its sense of a micro-world in which individuals are sequestered from others and about which no one has knowledge without the explicit agreement of those individuals. Without such privacy, liberals contend, resistance to the state is impossible because privacy is a sort of small cloud within which critical reason may safely function, the space of independent thought, distant from the influence of the phenomenal, perceptual world of the senses. Liberals value urbanism precisely for its tendency to lose the individual in the anonymity of the crowd in contrast with the rural village in which everyone knows everything about everyone else. The city, for them, is the locus of freedom, paradoxically because its density of population is an obscuring mask behind which the atomized individual may secure independent thought.

The contemporary urban quotidian strips the mask away. Individual actions now leave trails of digitized information which are regularly accumulated in computer databases and, at the speed of light or sound, transmitted back and forth between computers. Previously anonymous actions like paying for a dinner, borrowing a book from a library, renting a videotape from a rental store, subscribing to a magazine, making a long distance telephone call – all by interacting with perfect strangers – now is wrapped in a clothing of information traces which are gathered and arranged into profiles, forming more and more detailed portraits of individuals. This postmodern daily life is not one of discrete individuals, hidden behind shields of anonymity in market interactions with strangers; nor is it a return to the village of familiar faces.[6] Instead it combines features of both without the advantages of either. In the credit card payment for dinner, the waiter is a stranger but the computer which receives the information 'knows' the customer very well. Urban life now consists of face to face interactions with strangers coupled by electronically mediated interactions with machines 'familiar' with us. The lines dividing individual from individual and individual from institution are consistently crossed by computer databases, cancelling privacy as a model of action or even as an issue.

Information flows today double the action of individuals and subvert theoretical models which presuppose either privacy or the class struggle. Society is now a double movement: one, of individuals and institutions; another, of information flows. A recent television drama, for example, depicted the fine grained level of current information retrieval. A murderer attempted to secure his alibi by leaving a message on the answering machine of the person he murdered, falsifying the time of the call. But he did so from his cellular car phone so that the police were able to find out the actual time of the call because all such calls are logged by the cellular phone company. The murderer took into account one aspect of the mode of information (answering machines) but forgot another, the traces left in databases by calls from car phones.

Databases are inherently limited and restricted structures of information. Unlike the subtlety of narratives, they rely upon severe restrictions of inputs. In database programs only certain marks may be made in certain 'fields' or areas. For instance, if after the name of the individual, a 'field' for magazine subscriptions follows, normally one cannot fill this field with the name of the magazine, but only by a code for certain groups of magazines. Thus the *New Republic* might be coded as 'l' for liberal and the *Guardian* as 'r' for radical. If video rentals are included in the database, *Deep Throat* and *Last Tango in Paris* might both be coded as 'X'. Such simplification of data, one might complain, drastically distorts particular experience, but it also vastly facilitates the speed with which information may be retrieved. In this way, databases configure reality, make composites of individual experience that could be characterized as caricatures. By contrast, databases may also include graphics, that is to say pictures or copies of fingerprints, for example. Information about individuals then becomes much more complex. The important consideration, however, is not the question of verisimilitude: would any individual be pleased by the accuracy of the information portrait contained in a database? But rather that databases constitute additional identities for individuals, identities which – in the interactions between computers and between institutions which rely upon them, on the one hand, and individuals on the other – take the place of those individuals. When a computer search is done for John Smith, the output from the machine is, from the point of view of the receiving computer or institution, John Smith himself. Just as actions in daily life are doubled by information traces, so identities are multiplied in the interactions of computer databases.

The theoretical problem of accounting for the social impact of databases is best assisted by the work of Michel Foucault. This is so in three senses: first, Foucault theorized power in relation to a specific social formation, the Panopticon, which has direct application to databases; secondly, Foucault theorized the relation between social phenomena and the subject that is relevant to the case of databases; and thirdly, Foucault theorized the relation between discourse and practice, ideas and action, attitudes and behaviour in a way that permits the understanding of databases outside the limitations of the paradigms of liberal and Marxist theory.

In *Discipline and Punish* Foucault uses the term Panopticon to designate the control mechanism in prisons by which a guard, stationed in a central tower, could observe the inmates, arranged in cells around the tower with windows facing in towards the tower, without himself being seen by them.[7] Panopticon, literally 'all-seeing', denotes a form of power which attempts to orient the prisoners towards the authority system of the prison as a step in their reformation or normalization. For the process of reform, the Panopticon is a part of a broader set of mechanisms which included a minutely regulated schedule, a file-keeping system on each prisoner, and so forth. What interests Foucault in the system of discipline is not only its micrological detail but also its 'positive' inscription of power. Unlike the central government which uses power as a 'negative' principle of preventing or denying certain activities, the Panopticon shapes and moulds the behaviour of the criminals, producing, in a sense, a new person, the prison inmate. The key to the mechanism of discipline is the continuous, systematic, unobserved surveillance of a population. The criminal is coerced to follow a plan and to be aware that the slightest deviation on his part from the plan would be observed and would have consequences for him. Through the workings of the Panopticon, a norm is imposed on a population, on its practices and its attitudes, a norm that is a result not of the imposition of someone else's will, as in feudalism, but rather of an anonymous authority that is seemingly omnipresent. In the Panopticon Foucault locates a system of power at the level of the everyday as opposed to the level of the state which combines discourses and practices to instantiate the social character of the inmate. As a general feature of society, the Panopticon is an example of what Foucault calls a 'technology of power' or a 'microphysics of power'.

In a second way Foucault's theory of the Panopticon applies to databases. As a positive instantiation of power, the Panopticon constitutes the individual criminal as an inmate. The discourse/practice of discipline produces the behaviours and attitudes of the prison population, regardless of the degree to which the prisoners resist or subvert that imposition. Their identity becomes that of an inmate however enthusiastic they may or may not have been about such a fate. By the same token, databases in the super-Panopticon constitute identities for each individual and they do so regardless of whether the individual is even aware of it. Individuals are 'known' to computer databases, have distinct 'personalities' for them and in relation to which the computer 'treats' them in programmed ways. These identities also serve as a basis for the communication between computers, communications that occur routinely and without the knowledge of the 'real person'. Such identities are hardly innocent since they may seriously affect the individual's life, serving as the basis for a denial of credit, or an FBI investigation, or the termination of social assistance, or the denial of employment or residence. In each case the individual is acted upon in relation to his or her identity as it is constituted in the database. Simply because this identity has no intimate connection with the internal consciousness of the individual, with his or her self-defined attributes, in no way minimizes its force or effectiveness. With the dissemination of databases, a communication technology pervades the social space and multiplies the identity of individuals, regardless of their will, intention, feeling or cognition.

In order fully to comprehend the significance of the constitution of identities by databases, one must appreciate the epistemological break Foucault enacts with the commonplace sense of the distinction between action and language, behaviour and intention, a distinction that is one of the hallmarks of modern social theory. In relation to the social import of databases, Marxists, for example, concern themselves with the use made of databases by the state and the corporations. They criticize the way these organizations use databases to enhance their control and power over subordinate classes. In their work they maintain a clear distinction between institutions and individuals, action and knowledge, behaviour and information. The state is a force external to individuals, an institution whose power increases by dint of the tool of databases. The vast information at the state's disposal constitutes another link in the chain of oppression. By contrast Foucault focuses on the way power is both action and knowledge and the way power implicates the individual. He looks for the connections between phenomena which others see as discrete oppositions. The science of criminology for him is simply another element in the mechanism of discipline, not a privileged locus of truth outside the play of power. Similarly the individual's identity is not outside power but constituted by its operations, linked to it inextricably. The super-Panopticon then emerges not as an imposition or restraint upon the individual but rather as part of the individual's identity. Foucault's ability is to specify the relation that a Panopticon inmate derives from his post-structuralist rejection of the separation of mind and body, language and action, ideology and institution in favour of their mutual imbrication. My analysis of databases, following Foucault, moves to a model of communication in which the level of the subject is not cut off from practice, the body, power, institutions.

Databases, I argue, operate as a super-Panopticon. Like the prison, databases work continuously, systematically and surreptitiously, accumulating information about individuals and composing it into profiles. Unlike the Panopticon, the 'inmates' need not be housed in any architecture; they need only proceed with their regular daily life. The super-Panopticon is thereby more unobtrusive than its forebear, yet it is no less efficient at its task of normalization. Each characteristic of an individual's profile in a database is easily distinguished for unusual qualities, from credit ratings and overdue book notices to excessive traffic violations. Another advantage of the newer power mechanism over the older one is its facility of communications, or transport of information. Computers easily exchange databases, the information in one being accessible to others. Instantaneously, across the globe, information from databases flows in cyberspace to keep tabs on people. Databases 'survey' us without the eyes of any prison guard and they do so more accurately and thoroughly than any human being. A major impact of the super-Panopticon is that the distinction between public and private loses its force since it depended on an individual's space of invisibility, of opaqueness to the state and the corporations. Yet these characteristics are cancelled by databases because whereever one is and whatever one is doing, traces are left behind, traces that are transformed into information for the grist of computers.

Electronic writing is the third example of the mode of information as a communication technology. It covers a wide variety of writing practices, including word processing and hypertext,[8] electronic mail and message services and computer conferencing. In each case the computer mediates the relation of author and reader, altering the basic conditions of the enunciation and reception of meaning.[9] Electronic writing continues the tendency begun with handwriting and print: it permits the removal of the author from the text, increases the distance, both spatial and temporal, of author from the reader and augments the problem of the interpretation of texts. Compared with speech, writing is a way of storing language, fixing it so that it can be read by those not directly intended by the author. Writing thus promotes the transmission of culture from generation to generation, the transformation of cultural works into monuments and the elevation of authors into authorities. Writing also fosters the development of critical thinking on the part of the reader: with words stabilized on the page, the reader can reflect upon them, go back to earlier passages and re-examine links of argument, and accomplish all of this in isolation without the presence of the author or the community exerting any pressure on the act of interpretation. Printing is often credited with shaping the autonomous rational individual, a condition of modern democracy. Electronic writing furthers all these features of handwriting and print simply because it is a far more efficient system of storage. Compared with print, digitized writing requires less time to copy and less space to store.

But electronic writing also subverts the culture of print.[10] In the case of word processing, the ease of altering digital writing, the immateriality of signs on the screen compared with ink on the page, shifts the text out of a register of fixity and into one of volatility. Also digital texts lend themselves to multiple authorship. Files may be exchanged between people in several ways, each person working on the text, with the result, in its spatial configuration on a screen or printed on paper, of hiding any trace of signature. In addition, hypertext programs encourage the reader to treat the text as a field or network of signs in which to create his or her own linkages, linkages which may become part of the text and which other readers may follow or change at their will. These programs permit searches for words or phrases throughout a text or group of texts which may be added to the text or saved. The result is a new text which brings terms together that were not so associated by the author. The reader has substituted her own hierarchy of terms for that of the author. With electronic writing the distinction between author and reader collapses and a new form of text emerges that may challenge canonicity of works, even the boundaries of disciplines.

Computer message services establish a form of communication that also subverts the culture of handwriting and print. There are several forms of these electronic 'post offices'. In the case of electronic mail, the individual has an 'address' on a computer and anyone who knows it may send a message or letter to it from his or her own computer. In another instance, certain computers serve as 'bulletin boards' which allow many individuals to browse through messages and leave their own. These 'electronic cafés' encourage strangers, individuals who have never met face to face, to communicate to one another. Strangers here exchange messages without the extraneous presence of the body or the voice, only signs passing from one to another. What is more, these bulletin boards use pseudonyms or handles: individuals do not use their own names and may easily disguise any of their attributes, such as gender or ethnicity. As a form of writing, the message services foster not the autonomous, rational stable individual but the playful, imaginative multiple self. In countries that have experimented extensively with message services, such as France, they have proved enormously popular.[11] People seem to enjoy a communication technology in which they invent themselves in the process of exchanging signs.

Another form of communication made possible by computer writing is computer conferencing.[12] In this instance, digital writing substitutes not for print but for face-to-face meetings and oral communications. Computer conferences eliminate the need for gathering people in one place at one time. There exists now an alternative to synchronous meeting or community as we know it. A central computer reserves an area for the conference. Individuals, using their personal computers hooked up to telephones, call that computer and read the presentations and comments of others, responding as they see fit. Studies of computer conferences reveal that the gain is not simply efficiency: new qualities of community relations develop in this cyberspace. Without the cues of body language, status, force of personality, gender, clothing style – all present in face-to-face situations – conversation changes in character. Interventions are less conventional, less deferential, as social authority is cancelled through computer writing. Criteria for effective responses change to typing speed and terse expression. Some analysts argue that computer conferencing creates conditions for a form of democracy more vibrant and animated by unorthodox thought than the colonial town meeting.[13] While this form of computer writing may never fully replace traditional community, it offers an alternative to synchronous meeting that meliorates the increasing isolation of the information age.

The theory of deconstruction of Jacques Derrida anticipates in many ways changes brought about by computer writing. He counters the traditional theory of writing as fixity of meaning, monumentality, the authority of the author by focusing on the material aspect of signs inscribed on pages. He argues that such inscription leaves language open to multiple meaning, that the spacing of traces differs and displaces meaning away from the author, that the linear form of the book, with its order of pagination, its margins, its diacritical markings, its chapters and paragraphs, imposes a hierarchy that the reader may subvert by taking it as a text, a stream of marks whose contradictions and impasses are open to a close reading. Western thought relies upon printed writing to support the author's stable meaning, to insist that the book signifies only what the author intended. This 'logocentrism', as Derrida terms it, works by exclusions, supplements and marginalizations which may be reintroduced in a subversive reading. Books establish oppositions of terms, binaries in which one term is subordinate to the other and often absent from text. In the American Declaration of Independence the phrase 'All men are created equal' omits women and suppresses the question of race, even as it inscribes these groups as inferior. Deconstruction attempts to destabilize the march of univocal meaning in written texts by unlocking the logic of difference that it hides.

Derrida's interpretive gesture is similar to my understanding of electronic writing. Both deconstruction and electronic writing understand the volatility of written language, its instability and uncertain authorship.

Both see language as affecting a destabilization of the subject, a dispersal of the individual, a fracturing of the illusion of unity and fixity of the self. Derrida, however, understands these qualities of writing as applying to all of its forms and he differentiates only partially between handwriting, print and digital writing.[14] Deconstruction, then, is Derrida's interpretation of writing in all its forms. By contrast my effort is to distinguish between print and electronic forms of writing, to assess the significance of the difference enacted by a new communication technology. Derrida's strategy removes the task of interpretation from the context of contemporary changes in culture and society, repeating the gesture of earlier thinkers by producing a discourse as a reinterpretation. Ultimately, then, the force of deconstruction returns to see Derrida as a Western philosopher, defeating his own effort to subvert that position. Nonetheless the corpus of Derrida's writing provides powerful analytic tools to criticize the cultural and ideological patterns that have accompanied print writing. In that way and to a certain extent, deconstruction permits the reading of texts in a manner that suits electronic writing.

In the examples of TV ads, databases and computer writing, post-structuralist perspectives permit a comprehension of the linguistic features of new communication technologies and relate these to the cultural problem of the constitution of the subject. In particular they enable us to see the way electronically mediated communication promotes a new configuration of the subject that may be termed postmodern in the sense that it is structurally different from that of the modern era. Research on the mode of information has barely begun and much remains to extend these analyses to communication technologies not even mentioned here. I want now to raise some epistemological and political issues concerning the use of post-structuralist theory in the field of communication studies and point to additional areas for further research.

The theory of mode of information intersects with critical social theory's recognition of the stalled dialectic. As the Frankfurt School recognized long ago, in the course of the twentieth century, working-class movements have become attenuated, have been abated or have disappeared altogether, interrupting or permanently suspending the dialectic of the class struggle. The critical social theory of the Frankfurt School and more generally Western Marxism interpreted this situation as the deleterious effect of mass culture on the proletariat. However, these theorists do not adequately conceptualize the role of electronically mediated communications in the cultural integration of the working class into modern society. A good part of their difficulty stems from a theoretical model that does not account, with regard to the phenomena of mass culture, for the constitution of the subject through language, more specifically through the language patterns of the mode of information. The theoretical tendency of

Western Marxism has been to approach the question of a politically stabilized modernity from orientations themselves far too rooted in modernity and its communication technologies. Like modern thinkers since Descartes, they attempt to establish an atemporal or universal foundation for theory which usually takes the form of some definition of the human.

The grounding of theory in the human tends to dehistoricize one's position, making it invulnerable to temporal contingency but also to render it blind to its dependence on that contingency. In the twentieth century, for example, communication has been dramatically altered by electronic technologies, a situation, as I argue above, that urges social theorists to look anew at many of their fundamental assumptions. The widespread dissemination of radio, telephone, film, television, computer-enhanced communication such as electronic mail and computer conferencing, telex and fax machines, satellite communication systems changes not only communication but basic features of social life. Whatever *theoretical* priority one wishes to place on the question of communication, when recent *historical* developments are taken into account, it must move from the periphery to the centre of social science. But this means that the problem of communication theory begins with a recognition of necessary self-reflexivity, of the dependence of knowledge on its context. It requires from the outset a frank acknowledgement of contingency: the 'truth' of communication theory is registered in relation to historical change and is in no sense 'absolute', offering no vantage point from which one can claim a purchase on universality. A continuing issue for communication theory, then, is to sustain this sense of contingency, to develop strategies to avoid at every level and turn becoming grounded, stabilized, founded, established in the Truth. Communication theory must produce a new kind of truth, one not linked to the modernist goal of universality.

Because communication theory is so obviously and directly responding to the world with its unpredictable shifts and turns, the temptation is strong for theorists, at the epistemological level, to flee that world, to reduce that contingency, to find some stable ground upon which to secure a firm knowledge. Norbert Wiener's 'cybernetic' theory of communication, to take one example, turned for a ground to mathematics, the traditional locus of pure theory, a theory that appears at least not to depend in any way on the vagaries of human time.[15] Communication knowledge for him becomes a precisely determinable ratio of information to noise. But an important lesson learned from the impact on social theory of the shift to electronically mediated communication is that theory must avoid the pretence that it is independent of the world, protect itself at every point against slipping into the assumption that it is somehow constructed on a foundation of self-generated certainty. The first principle of communication theory in the age of electronic technology, then, is that there is no first principle, only a recognition of an outside of theory, an Other to theory, a world that motivates theory.

The requirement that theoretical categories have built into them a certain contingency or self-limitation faces an equal difficulty from an opposite side, the side of history. The danger here is that history, once invoked to forestall abstract theorizing, itself becomes a stable, dogmatic ground. In this case the context provides the foundation for theory: a presumed certainty or closure within the context of theory 'guarantees' its truth. The pertinent example in this case is Marxist writing on communications which takes the mode of production as a fixed horizon, focusing on questions that refer back to it (such as what is the effect of the corporate structure on the information age and vice versa) and omitting or repressing questions that do not appear to relate to the class structure. History in this perspective is already a given and the new ingredient, in this case electronic communication, poses no new questions, merely reinforces old ones. For communication theory, the turn to history must sustain a sense of an open field, not a closed totality, a sensitivity to the new, not a confirmation of the already given.

Post-structuralist interpretive strategies are germane to communication theory because they attempt to confront both of these theoretical dilemmas. They make problematic both the authorial position of the theorist and the categories he/she develops. By focusing on language and stressing the instability of meaning in language, post-structuralist theory undermines the effort to dissolve communication into a 'real' of action or into a universal definition of the human. At the same time it calls into question versions of the relation of theory and history/context that present the latter as a closed or totalized field that serves to turn theory into ideology, into a discourse whose assumptions are disavowed or made invisible.[16] For these reasons post-structuralist theory opens the field of electronically mediated communication in a way that locates its internal complexity and its relation to culture. It enables one to see what is new in the dissemination and emplacement of these technologies.

Post-structuralist theory is often accused of its own kind of totalization, linguistic reductionism. It is charged with never going beyond the text, of depoliticizing social action, of theorizing only an endless play of discourse analysis. While the practice of some post-structuralists may lend itself to this accusation, my effort, in theorizing the mode of information, has been to counteract the textualist tendency by linking post-structuralist theory with social change, by connecting it with electronic communication technology, by 'applying' its methods to the arena of everyday life, by insisting on communications as presenting a historical context which justifies the move to an emphasis on language. The 'linguistic turn' of post-structuralism is apposite not only for its ability to critique modernist theory but because of changes in the socio-historical field. By the same token, I relate post-structuralist theory to the mode of information to underline the contingency of that theory, not to provide it with a false stability, a solid foundation in history. The political implications of the resort to post-structuralism, then, must be viewed in this light.

Post-structuralist theory invalidates modernist political positions, those that rely upon a view of humanity as in need of emancipation from forms of external oppression.[17] These views presuppose man as centred in rational autonomy but as prevented from attaining this centre by institutions that block its realization: arbitrary government, religious intolerance, private appropriation of the means of production. However, the focus on language rejects this position because language already configures the individual. Only after the individual has been constituted as centred in rational autonomy by Enlightenment discourse does it appear that monarchy, institutional religion and capitalism are external fetters to freedom. If language is seen as already implicating the individual, then the question of emancipation changes its character. The question becomes one of understanding the positioning of the individual in the given language pattern and the relative change of altering that pattern, rather than one of a search for an absolute, universal beyond the given order, one that would somehow allow an already defined human creature to emerge as if from its tutelage, or chains.

Contemporary society contains modernist institutions and discourses which privilege certain configurations of the subject, those that support autonomous rationality, and subordinate others (women, ethnic minorities, etc.). But contemporary society also contains 'postmodernist' institutions and discourses, such as electronically mediated communications, which support new configurations of the subject. To the extent that it is now appropriate to raise the issue of the restrictions of modernist forms of subject constitution, electronic communication, understood in a post-structuralist sense, provides a basis for critique. This does not mean that every emission from such communication technology is automatically revolutionary; by far the preponderance of these communications work to solidify existing society and culture. But there is a way of understanding their impact that reveals its potential for structural change. In other words, there is a secular trend emanating from electronic communication that undermines the stability of the figure of the rational autonomous individual. Hence the outcry against these forms of communication, the warnings of their dangers by those adhering to modernist political positions.

The other tendency that amplifies the post-structuralist understanding of the political impact of electronic communication is the spread of protest movements from outside the modernist paradigm, certain feminist and ethnic positions, certain aspects of gay and lesbian politics, certain kinds of ecological and anti-nuclear concerns. To the extent that the politics of these groups challenges the privilege of the rational individual as the universal ground of human identity (the Western tradition), they affect changes that are parallel with those of electronic communication. The operation of hegemonic ideology is effective to the extent that it is unrecognized. When everyone assumes that human beings have a nature, centred in reason, that is violated by institutional chains, then those chains are exposed but that ideology is confirmed. Electronic communication and the social movements mentioned above sometimes tend to put modernist ideology into question thereby changing the terms of political discussion. When this is effective, as in the effort to abandon the required teaching of Western civilization as the exclusive introduction to culture, modernists of all stripes, from the Marxist Eugene Genovese to the conservative Lynn Chaney, recognize only a threat to freedom. To those not completely under the spell of this ideology, its operations become manifest and hence dissolved: 'man' cannot mean Western man, rationality is not the final ground of human experience.

Electronically mediated communication opens the prospect of understanding the subject as constituted in historically concrete configurations of discourse and practice. It clears the way to seeing the self as multiple, changeable, fragmented, in short as making a project of its own constitution. In turn such a prospect challenges all those discourses and practices that would restrict this process, would fix and stabilize identity, whether these be fascist ones which rely on essentialist theories of race, liberal ones which rely on reason, or socialist ones which rely on labour. A post-structuralist understanding of new communication technologies raises the possibility of a postmodern culture and society that threatens authority as the definition of reality by the author.

Notes

1 Mark Poster, *The Mode of Information* (Chicago: University of Chicago Press, 1990).
2 Elizabeth Eisenstein, *The Printing Press as an Agent of Change: Communications and Cultural Transformations in Early Modern Europe* (Cambridge/New York: Cambridge University Press, 1979).
3 Jean-François Lyotard, *Inhuman*, trans. Geoff Bennington and Rachel Bowlby (Cambridge: Polity Press, 1991).

4 J. Hillis Miller, 'The work of cultural criticism in the age of digital reproduction', in *Illustration* (Cambridge, Mass.: Harvard University Press,
   1992).
5 Jean Baudrillard, *Selected Writings*, ed. Mark Poster, trans. Jacques Mourrain
   (Stanford, Calif.: Stanford University Press, 1988).
6 Joshua Meyrowitz, *No Sense of Place: The Impact of Electronic Media on Social
   Behavior* (New York: Oxford University Press, 1985).
7 Michel Foucault, *Discipline and Punish: The Birth of the Prison*, trans. Alan
   Sheridan (New York: Pantheon, 1977).
8 Michael Heim, *Electric Language: A Philosophical Study of Word Processing* (New
   Haven, Conn.: Yale University Press, 1987); George Landow, *Hypertext: The
   Convergence of Contemporary Critical Theory and Technology* (Baltimore: Johns
   Hopkins University Press, 1992).
9 Jay Bolter, *Writing Space: The Computer, Hypertext, and the History of Writing*
   (Hillsdale, NJ: Erlbaum, 1991).
10 Richard Lanham, 'The electronic word: literary study and the digital revolution', *New Literary History*, 20 (1989), pp. 265–90.
11 Marie Marchand, *La Grande Aventure du Minitel* (Paris: Larousse, 1987).
12 Andrew Feenberg, 'Computer conferencing and the humanities', *Instructional
   Science*, 16 (1987), pp. 169–86.
13 Starr Roxanne Hiltz and Murray Turoff, *The Network Nation: Human Communication via Computer* (London: Addison-Wesley, 1978).
14 Jacques Derrida, *Postcard: From Socrates to Freud and Beyond*, trans. Alan Bass
   (Chicago: University of Chicago Press, 1987).
15 Norbert Wiener, *The Human Use of Human Beings* (New York: Anchor,
   1954).
16 Louis Althusser, 'Ideology and ideological state apparatuses', in *Lenin and
   Philosophy and Other Essays*, trans. Ben Brewster (London: New Left Books,
   1971).
17 John Hinkson, 'Marxism, postmodernism and politics today', *Arena*, 94
   (1991), pp. 138–66.

9

In the Realm of Uncertainty:
The Global Village and Capitalist
Postmodernity

Ien Ang

Speaking about the present condition of the world, or 'today', has become a thoroughly messy and capricious matter. The collapse of official communism in Eastern Europe and the subsequent ending of the Cold War, the Gulf War, the gradual decline of American hegemony, the rise of Japan to world economic might, the spread of the Aids virus, and the environmental crisis are only some of the major historical events which signal a reshuffling of geopolitical relations whose eventual outcomes remain deeply uncertain. Indeed, as Immanuel Wallerstein has noted, the capitalist world-system is in mutation now; we have arrived 'in the true realm of uncertainty'.[1]

I cannot dissociate myself from this condition of uncertainty. Indeed, what I would like to do here is take this uncertainty on board – not only as to the state of the world 'today' but also regarding the current state (and status) of 'theory', let alone 'communication theory'. The very idea of a book on 'communication theory today' assumes that such an entity exists or should exist (despite its undoubtable internal plurality and diversity), that it can be proposed and formulated, and that it matters. But this assumption cannot go unquestioned. 'Communication' is, and should be, a crucial site of critical intellectual reflection on cultural relations, although the very notion of 'communication' itself, encompassing such a mixed bag of events and processes, is hardly specific enough to be used as a starting point for theorizing the complicated entanglements between peoples, powers and cultures in the world 'today'.

At any rate, what I will try to explicate here is that if we are to

understand Wallerstein's true realm of uncertainty, we have to go beyond
the concerns of communication theory, however defined. This is because
the very idea of communication, neccessarily predicated on reduction if
not elimination of uncertainty, marginalizes uncertainty as a positive
force, and a necessary and inevitable condition in contemporary culture,
the condition of *capitalist postmodernity*.

One of the most popular metaphors used to describe this condition has
been McLuhan's 'global village'. However, this very popularity tends to
foreclose a closer engagement with exactly what it means when we say that
today's world is a 'global village'. Often the unwarranted (but reassuring)
assumption is made that the creation of the 'global village' implies the
progressive homogenization – through successful communication – of the
world as a whole.[2] However, as George Marcus has noted, the fact 'that
the globe generally and intimately is becoming more integrated . . .
paradoxically is not leading to an easily comprehensible totality, but to an
increasing diversity of connections among phenomena once thought disparate and worlds apart.'[3] In other words, the global village, as the site of
the culture of capitalist postmodernity, is a thoroughly paradoxical place,
unified yet multiple, totalized yet deeply unstable, closed and open-ended
at the same time. I will propose here a theorization of capitalist postmodernity as a chaotic system, where uncertainty is a built-in feature.

I

Communication theory has traditionally used metaphors of transport and
flow to define its object. In the resulting transmission models of communication, as James Carey has remarked, 'communication is [seen as] a
process whereby messages are transmitted and distributed in space for the
control of distance and people.'[4] In putting it this way, Carey foregrounds
the deeply political nature of theoretical models. In Carey's words,
'(m)odels of communication are . . . not merely representations of communication but representations *for* communication: templates that guide,
unavailing or not, concrete human interaction'.[5] In historical and economic terms, the instances of human interaction Carey refers to pertain
primarily to the geographical expansion of modern capitalism, with its
voracious need to conquer ever more extensive and ever more distant
markets. Such was the context for the creation and spread of a spatially
biased system of communication, epitomized by the parallel growth of the
railroad and the telegraph in the nineteenth century, which privileged
speed and efficiency in the traversing of space. Spatial integration was the
result of the deployment of these space-binding communication technologies, first at the level of the nation, then extending over increasingly large
parts of the globe. Following the Canadian theorist Harold Innis, Carey

describes modern capitalist culture as a 'space-binding culture': 'a culture whose predominant interest was in space – land as real estate, voyage, discovery, movement, expansion, empire, control'.[6] In this respect, McLuhan's 'global village', a world turned into a single community through the annihilation of space in time, represents nothing other than (the fantasy of) the universal culmination of capitalist modernity. In short, what I want to establish here is the intimate interconnection between the transmission paradigm of communication, the instalment of high communication systems, and the logic of capitalist expansion.

But the control effected by communication-as-transmission does not only pertain to the conquest of markets for the benefit of economic gain; it is also a control over people. In social terms, then, communication-as-transmission has generally implied a concern with social order and social management; hence, for example, the long-standing interest in communication research, particularly in the United States, in the 'effects' of messages: persuasion, attitude change, behavioural modification. What is implicit in this social-psychological bias in communication research is an (unstated) desire for a disciplined population and therefore a belief in the possibility of an ordered and stable 'society'. In this sense, communication research evolved as a branch of functionalist sociology, for which the question of social integration (e.g. through the dissemination of a 'central value system' throughout the entire social fabric) is the main concern. The effects tradition was a specification of this concern in relation to the media: are the media (dys)functional for social integration? This concern did not remain restricted to the population within a society; it has also been envisaged beyond the societies that make up the core of modern capitalism, as in the information diffusion theories of Third World 'development' and 'modernization' of the fifties and sixties, where mass communication processes were thought to play a vital role. Here, the making of the 'global village' can be rewritten as the transformation, or domestication, of non-Western Others in the name of capitalist modernity, the civilization which was presumed to be the universal destiny of humankind: global spatial integration is equated with global social and cultural integration.

It should be clear that in theoretical terms transmission models of communication inherently privilege the position of the Sender as legitimate source and originator of meaning and action, the centre from which both spatial and social/cultural integration is effectuated. Communication is deemed successful if and when the intentions of the Sender, packaged in the Message, arrive unscathed at the Receiver, sorting the intended effects. But the hegemony of such linear and transparent conceptions of communication has been severely eroded in the last few decades. This erosion was simultaneously an epistemological and a political one. A telling case is

Everett Rogers's declaration, in 1976, of the 'passing' of the 'dominant paradigm' of the diffusion model of development. As author of *The Diffusion of Innovations* in 1962,[7] Rogers had to submit almost fifteen years later that the model's weakness lay precisely in its emphasis on linearity of effect, in its reliance on hierarchy of status and expertise, and on rational (and presumably benevolent) manipulation from above.[8]

Not coincidentally, the same period saw the ascendancy of alternative, critical accounts of development, often framed within theories of cultural imperialism and dependency. The rise of such accounts can be understood in the light of the growing force of anti-systemic, new social movements in the West which have challenged the unquestioned hegemony of capitalist modernity's 'central value system', as well as the increasing desire for self-determination in post-colonial, developing nations. As John Tomlinson has argued, 'the various critiques of cultural imperialism could be thought of as (in some cases inchoate) protests against the spread of (capitalist) modernity.' However, Tomlinson continues, 'these protests are often formulated in an inappropriate language of domination, a language of cultural imposition which draws its imagery from the age of high imperialism and colonialism.'[9] I would add here that this inappropriate language is symptomatic of the fact that most theories of cultural imperialism remain firmly couched within transmission models of communication. Indeed, the pronounced emphasis within the notion of cultural imperialism on the dimension of power operating in the relation between Sender and Receiver importantly exposes the illusion of neutrality of the transmission paradigm. But because it conceptualizes the relation in terms of more or less straightforward and deliberate imposition of dominant culture and ideology, it reproduces the mechanical linearity of the transmission model. Such a vision is not only theoretically but also historically inadequate: in a world-system where capitalism is no longer sustained through the coercive submission of colonized peoples (as in nineteenth-century high imperialism) but through the liberal institutions of democracy and the sovereign nation-state, equation of power with imposition simply will not do. The problem, rather, is to explain how capitalist modernity 'imposes' itself in a context of formal 'freedom' and 'independence'. In other words, how are power relations organized in a global village where everybody is free and yet bounded? In order to grasp the ramifications of this question we need to develop new theoretical tools.

For the moment, I would like to stress how the transmission paradigm was not just an internal, academic affair.[10] Rather, it ran parallel with developments in the 'real' world, where the spread of modern capitalism from core to periphery was very much undergirded by the increasingly global deployment of ever more sophisticated space-binding media. These have led not to the creation of an ordered global village, but to the multiplication of points of conflict, antagonism, and contradiction. Never has this been clearer than in today's new world (dis)order, Wallerstein's 'true realm of uncertainty'. In short, the crisis of the transmission paradigm takes the shape here of a deep uncertainty about the *effectiveness* of the Sender's power to control. In this context, it should surprise no one that the transmission paradigm was particularly pervasive in communication theory during the high period of American hegemony as the superpower within the modern capitalist world. Neither is it surprising that the crisis of the paradigm erupted when that hegemony started to display cracks and fissures.

Within communication theory, this crisis has led to a proliferation of *semiotic* models of communication, which foreground the ongoing construction of meaning as central to communicative practices. What such models reject is the assumption of transparency of meaning which underlies the idea of communication as transmission; instead, communication is now conceived as a social practice of meaning production, circulation, and exchange. James Carey's rich and important work epitomizes this shift: Carey adopts such a semiotic model in his formulation of a *ritual* view of communication, which he defines as 'the production of a coherent world that is then presumed, for all practical purposes, to exist'.[11] From this perspective, communication should be examined as 'a process by which reality is constituted, maintained, and transformed',[12] the site of 'symbolic production of reality'.[13] In Carey's view, this social reality is a 'ritual order' made up by 'the sharing of aesthetic experience, religious ideas, personal values and sentiments, and intellectual notions' through which a 'common culture' is shaped.[14]

The gist of Carey's theoretical argument is that communication *is* culture. Without communication, no culture, no meaningful social reality. However, there are problems with Carey's emphasis on ritual *order* and *common* culture, inasmuch as it evokes the suggestion that such an order of common meanings and meaningfulness can and should be securely created. Carey's proposal to build 'a model of and for communication of some restorative value in reshaping our common culture'[15] stems from a genuine critique of the instrumentalist values of capitalist modernity, but his longing for *re*storing and *re*shaping cultural sharing suggests a nostalgia for a past sense of 'community', for a local-bound, limited, and harmonious *Gemeinschaft*. But it is difficult to see how such a (global?) common culture can be created in the ever-expanding and extremely differentiated social reality constructed by capitalist modernity. To put it differently, Carey's concern with the time-binding functions of communication – its role as social cement through the construction of community and commonality of meanings – seems ironically to perpetuate the concern with social integration which is implicit in the transmission paradigm. Carey's position implies that a global village which is integrated in both spatial and social/cultural terms, can and should be brought about, not through the dissemination of pre-given meanings from Sender to Receiver, but by enhancing rituals of mutual conversation and dialogue. In this sense, he unwittingly reproduces the assumption of capitalist modernity as a universal civilization, at least potentially. The (democratic) promotion of communication-as-ritual is the recipe for it.[16]

Carey, then, privileges in his model the *success*, both theoretically and politically, of communication-as-ritual. In so doing, he tends to collapse communication and culture, as the title of his book, *Communication as Culture*, suggests. For Carey, communication studies and cultural studies are one and the same thing. In this sense, Carey's solution to the crisis of the transmission paradigm is a conservative one in that it ends up securing 'communication', and thus communication theory, as privileged theoretical object for cultural studies.

I would suggest, however, that it is the *failure* of communication that we should emphasize if we are to understand contemporary culture. That is to say, what needs to be stressed is the fundamental *uncertainty* that necessarily goes with the process of constructing a meaningful order, the fact that communicative practices do not necessarily arrive at common meanings at all. This is to take seriously the radical implications of semiotics as a theoretical starting point: if meaning is never given and natural but always constructed and arbitrary, then it makes no sense to prioritize meaningfulness over meaninglessness. Or, to put it in the terminology of communication theory: a radically semiotic perspective ultimately subverts the concern with (successful) communication by foregrounding the idea of 'no necessary correspondence' between the Sender's and the Receiver's meanings. That is to say, not success, but failure to communicate should be considered 'normal' in a cultural universe where commonality of meaning cannot be taken for granted.

If meaning is not an inherent property of the message, then the Sender is no longer the sole creator of meaning. If the Sender's intended message does not 'get across', this is not a 'failure in communications' resulting from unfortunate 'noise' or the Receiver's misinterpretation or misunderstanding, but because the Receiver's active participation in the construction of meaning doesn't take place in the same ritual order as the Sender's. Even when there is some correspondence in meanings constructed on both sides, such correspondence is not natural but is itself constructed, the product of a particular articulation, through the imposition of limits and constraints on the openness of semiosis in the form of 'preferred readings', between the moments of 'encoding' and 'decoding'.[17] That is to say, it is precisely the existence, if any, of correspondence and commonality of meaning, not its absence, which needs to be accounted

for. Jean Baudrillard has stated the import of this inversion quite pro-
vocatively: 'meaning . . . is only an ambiguous and inconsequential
accident, an effect due to ideal convergence of a perspective space at any
given moment (History, Power, etc.) and which, moreover, has only ever
really concerned a tiny fraction and superficial layer of our "societies".'[18]

What we have here is a complete inversion of the preoccupations of
communication theory, of meaningful human interaction as the basis for
the social – or, for that matter, for the global village. As I will try to show
below, this theoretical inversion, which is one of the fundamental tenets of
post-structuralist theorizing, allows us to understand the global village not
as a representation of a finished, universalized capitalist modernity
characterized by certainty of order and meaning, but as a totalized yet
fundamentally dispersed world-system of capitalist postmodernity characterized by radical uncertainty, radical indeterminacy of meaning.

II

Such a move is not merely a theoreticist game, but is essential if we are to
develop a critical theorizing of the new world (dis)order. Let me clarify
this by briefly looking at the presumptions at work in the recent debate
around the 'new revisionism' in mass communication research.[19] This
'new revisionism', I should say at the outset, is a myth, presumably born
out of a rather conservative wish to retain 'mass communication' as a
separate field of study, on the one hand, and a misrecognition of the
radical potential of the idea of the indeterminacy of meaning on the other.
I think it is important to counter some of this myth's assertions in order to
clarify precisely what that radical potential involves. What should be
resisted, I think, is the theoretical and political closure which the myth of
the new revisionism imposes on our understanding of what 'mass communication' means in today's world.

According to James Curran, who proposed the term 'new revisionism'
in what communication scholars used to call 'audience research' has
fundamentally transformed what he calls 'the radical tradition' of mass
communication scholarship. This transformation is exemplified, says
Curran, in the well known ethnographic studies of media audiences by
authors working within critical cultural studies such as David Morley,
Janice Radway and myself.[20] As Curran would have it, these studies revise
the classic radical stance, which was informed by a (neo)Marxist pessi-
mism towards the all-powerful role of the mass media as transmitters of
dominant ideology (and which also undergirds most theories of cultural
imperialism). Instead, since audiences are now conceived as active producers of meaning and produce a diversity of readings, that role of the
media has been considerably diminished, to the point that there might be

no dominant ideology at all. Curran claims that 'radical researchers' now stress 'audience autonomy' and have implicitly concluded 'that the media [have] only limited influence'.[21] In this sense, Curran concludes, previously radical critics have presumably moved towards a more moderate, pluralist position, so that 'the critical tradition in media research has imploded in response to internal debate'.[22] But this is an utterly mistaken conclusion. Curran could reach it only by adopting a narrow conceptualization of power, as if evidence of diversity in readings of media texts could be equated with audience freedom and independence from media power! In other words, while the semiotic notion that meaning is constructed rather than given is now recognized, Curran retains the mechanical, distributional notion of power of the transmission paradigm. This, however, is a truncated rendering of the radical scope of indeterminacy of meaning, made possible by objectifying 'communication', 'media' and 'audience', lifting them out of their larger social and historical context.

If anything, Curran's rendering of 'the new audience research' indicates that merely replacing a transmission model with a semiotic model of communication is not enough. The problem with communication models in general is that they describe the world in terms of closed circuits of senders, messages and receivers. That the unidirectionality of such circuits is complicated by feedback loops, processes of exchange and interaction, or intermediary moments of meaning construction makes the circuit no less closed: there is no 'outside' to the communication event. As a result, it becomes impossible to think about the relation of power and meaning in more multidimensional terms, and to recognize the operation of multiple forms of power at different points in the system of social networks in which both 'senders' (media) and 'receivers' (audiences) are complexly located and produce meanings. Instead, power becomes a fixed entity which simply changes hands from senders to receivers and vice versa. And since critical scholars now acknowledge that audiences are not passive absorbers of 'dominant ideology' transmitted by the media but actively produce their own meanings as a result of the predispositions they bring to texts, a paradigmatic consensus can now be declared, again according to Curran, which favours the liberal pluralist idea that there 'are no dominant discourses, merely a semiotic democracy of pluralist voices'.[23] Here again, another invocation of a unified and integrated global village, now as a space in which power is so evenly diffused that everybody is happily living ever after in a harmonious plurality of juxtaposed meanings and identities.[24]

This is what I mean by the closure imposed by Curran's misappropriation of 'the new audience research'. It is a closure which expels any sense of uncertainty, with no place for unresolved ambiguity and contradiction. It is also a closure which revels in a confidence of having repudiated any notion of cultural imperialism, any idea of unequal power relationships between 'core' and 'periphery' in the global village. To be sure, certain tendencies within critical work on audiences have facilitated this misappropriation, precisely for their lack of clarity about the theoretical status of this work. Thus John Fiske's (in)famous celebration of the semiotic power of audiences to create their own meanings and pleasures has been widely interpreted as a confirmation of the liberal pluralist paradise.[25] What is more, Fiske's excessive romanticism and populism has been severely criticized *within* critical cultural studies for its connivance in free market ideologies of consumer sovereignty.[26] What is important to note here, however, are not so much the apologetic political consequences of Fiske's position, but the theoretical underpinnings of his discourse, particularly his theory of the relationship of power and meaning.

For example, in *Television Culture* Fiske describes the relation between television and its audiences as an antagonism between 'top–down power' opposed by 'bottom–up power'.[27] The latter is predominantly a semiotic power operating within a more or less autonomous cultural economy, to be differentiated from the economic power held by the 'top', for example the executives of the television industries, operating within the financial economy. Fiske is right in wanting to differentiate between these two forms of power – indeed, I would argue that it is precisely by making this kind of theoretical differentiation that we can begin to overcome the simplistic, one-dimensional concepts of power inherent in the transmission paradigm (and reproduced by Curran). The problem, however, is that, Fiske tends to exaggerate the strength of the semiotic democracy by seeing the struggle as a 'two-way force' in which the partners are implicitly considered separate but equal. Again, this rosy conclusion could only be arrived at by isolating the communication between television and its audiences from the broader contexts in which both are shaped. Fiske's radical inclination is thus contained by his holding on to the familiar topography of communication: the sender's sphere (production and distribution) is opposed by the receiver's sphere (reception and consumption). Again, a closed circuit, despite the struggle taking place within it. Again, theoretical closure, systemic certainty. In this sense, Curran's liberal pluralism and Fiske's more radical pluralism tend to collude. In emphasizing this apparent collusion Curran has rushed towards the conclusion that the 'new revisionism' has led critical cultural studies to abandon its 'radical' concerns. This, however, sadly miscomprehends the current state of affairs in critical theorizing.

In the last two decades or so, a transformation in the theorization of power has taken place in critical theory – largely through post-Althusserian elaborations of Gramsci's notion of hegemony and

Foucault's concept of power/knowledge. This has occurred not because it no longer believes in domination but because, in the words of Mark Poster, 'it is faced with the formidable task of unveiling structures of domination when no one is dominating, nothing is being dominated and no ground exists for a principle of liberation from domination.'[28] This, of course, is another way of evoking the contradictory condition of 'free-yet-boundedness' which I noted earlier as characteristic of living in the global village. In this context, John Tomlinson's suggestion that the notion of cultural imperialism should be replaced by the much less determinist (but no less determining) one of 'globalization' is particularly relevant:

> the idea of imperialism contains, at least, the notion of a purposeful project: the intended spread of a social system from one centre of power across the globe. The idea of 'globalization' suggests interconnection and inter-dependency of all global areas which happens in a far less purposeful way. It happens as the result of economic and cultural practices which do not, of themselves, aim at global integration, but which nonetheless produce it. More importantly, the effects of globalization are to weaken the cultural coherence of all individual nation-states, including the economically power-ful ones – the 'imperialist powers' of a previous era.[29]

In other words, critical theory has changed because the structure of the global capitalist order has changed. What it has to come to terms with is not the certainty of (and wholesale opposition to) the spread of a culturally coherent capitalist modernity, but the uncertainty brought about by the disturbing incoherence of a globalized capitalist postmodernity, and the mixture of resistance and complicity occurring within it. The critical import of audience ethnography, placed within the larger theoretical project of critical cultural studies, should be seen in this context as docu-menting how the bottom–top micro-powers of audience activity are both complicit with and resistive to the dominant, macro-forces within capit-alist postmodernity. It has nothing to do with the complacency of Curran's liberal pluralism; on the contrary, it radicalizes the 'radical concerns' of critical theorizing. To elaborate on this point, we need to do away with any notion of the closed circuit of communication, and embrace fully the primacy of the indeterminacy of meaning which, I would argue, is essential for understanding how and why capitalist postmodernity is a 'true realm of uncertainty'.

III

I can begin to explain this by taking issue with the simplistic idea that existence of diversity is evidence of freedom from power and domination. That is to say, variation – for example in audience readings and pleasures

– is not the result of autonomy and independence, as the liberal pluralists would have it, but emerges out of the inescapably overdetermined nature of any particular instance of subjective meaning production. The latter is traversed by a multiplicity of power relations, the specifics of which cannot be known ahead of time precisely because their articulations are always irreducibly context-bound. They are not determined by fixed predispositions but take shape within the dynamic and contradictory goings-on of everyday life and of history.[30] In this sense, the existence of different readings is by no means the evidence of 'limited' power. On the contrary, it merely points to the operation and intersection of a whole range of power relations at any one time, going far beyond linear 'influence' or 'effect'. This is one way in which the idea of indeterminacy of meaning can be concretely qualified: indeterminacy is not grounded in freedom from (external) determinations, but is the consequence of too many, unpredictable 'over-determinations'.

The point I want to make about the liberal pluralist account of variation and difference is that it implicitly assumes a closed universe of readings, making up a contained diversity of audience groupings with definite identities, equivalent to the liberal pluralist conception of electoral politics where voters are distributed over a fixed repertoire of parties. It is in this sense that liberal pluralist discourse conjoins the marketing discourse of market segmentation (where consumers are neatly divided up and categorized in a grid of self-contained demographic or psychographic 'segments'), which is not so surprising given that both discourses are two sides of the coin of 'democratic capitalism'. This conception of diversity presupposes that 'society' is a finite totality, a 'unity in diversity' or, more precisely, a unity of a diversity of meanings and identities. This concept of social totality is conceived as 'the structure upon which its partial elements and processes are founded', that is to say, as 'an underlying principle of intelligibility of the social order'.[31] In this sense, difference and diversity refer to the structured partition of that unitary order – say, the imaginary global village – into fixed parts, such as identifiable readings and audience groupings (to be uncovered by 'audience research').

The idea of indeterminacy of meaning, however, enables us to put forward a much more radical theorization of difference and diversity, one that does away with any notion of an essence of social order, a 'society' which grounds the empirical variations expressed at the surface of social life. Not order, but chaos is the starting point. Variation does not come about as a result of the division of a given social entity into a fixed range of meaningful identities, but represents the infinite play of differences which makes all identities and all meanings precarious and unstable. Any relative fixation of those identities and meanings is not the expression of a structural predetermination within a social order. On the contrary, it is the (temporary and provisional) outcome of, in Ernesto Laclau's words, the attempt to limit the infinite play of differences in the site of the social, to domesticate the potential infinitude of semiosis corroborated by the principle of indeterminacy of meaning, to embrace it within the finitude of an order, a social totality which can be called a 'society'. From this perspective, this ordered social totality is no longer a pre-given structure which establishes the limits within which diverse meanings and identities are constituted. Rather, since the social is the site of potentially infinite semiosis, it always *exceeds* the limits of any attempt to constitute 'society', to demarcate its boundaries, which is the reason why a 'society' can accomplish only a partial closure, a partial fixing of meanings and identities, a partial imposition of order in the face of chaos.[32] That is, any containment of variation and difference within a limited universe of diversity is always-already the product of a determinate ordering by a structuring, hegemonizing power, not, as the functionalist discourse of liberal pluralism would have it, evidence of a lack of order, absence of power. In this sense, the question to ask about the complex relation between media and audiences is not why there is not more homogeneity, but why there is not more heterogeneity.

To illuminate how this altered notion of difference effectively subverts the closure of liberal pluralist discourse, let me briefly summarize the argument I have put forward in *Desperately Seeking the Audience*,[33] also because the more general theoretical implications of that argument were not made very explicit in that book. I have discussed the way in which the development of the practice of 'audience measurement', foundational as it is for the economic and institutional structuration of the commercial television industry, has been led by a progressive sophistication of measurement methods and technologies, aimed at the ever more detailed and accurate determination of size and demographic composition of the audience at any particular moment, for any particular programme or channel. The latest device currently being tested in this respect is the so-called 'passive people meter', a kind of computerized eye roaming people's living-rooms in order to catch their gaze whenever it is directed to the TV screen. The industry's hope is that this technology will deliver ratings statistics that can tell the television companies exactly who is watching what at any split second of the day. However, this very search for the perfect measurement method, which I have characterized as desperate, is based on the implicit assumption that there is such a thing as an 'audience' as a finite totality, made up of subdivisions or segments whose identities can be synchronically and diachronically 'fixed'. I have suggested that this assumption is a fiction, but a *necessary* fiction for a television industry which increasingly experiences the audience as volatile and fickle. It is a hegemonic, empowering fiction which is positively constructed as true by the creation of simulations of order in the ranks of the audience in the form of ratings statistics and other market research profiles.

The paradox of the passive people meter, however, is that it is propelled by a desire to produce a fully precise representation, a completely accurate map of the social world of actual audience practices. This progressive rapprochement of representational strategies and the social, I suggest, is bound ultimately to reveal chaos rather than order. That is to say, it will turn out that the universe of television viewing practices can only be represented as an ordered totality by imposing (discursive) closure on it, because these infinite, contradictory, dispersed and dynamic everyday practices will always be in excess of any constructed totality, no matter how 'accurate'. In attempting to determine the identity of this universe we will, as Laclau puts it, 'find nothing else but the kaleidoscopic movement of differences',[34] which will probably only result in further, more insistent, and more desperate attempts to map it.

In concrete, historically specific terms, the chaos I am referring to relates to the enormous proliferation of possible television viewing practices in the last few decades, possibilities which have been created by the expansion of the television industries in capitalist modernity in the first place. From transnational 24-hour satellite channels (for example CNN and MTV) to a myriad of local or regional cable channels dishing up unmanageable volumes of specialized programming, from video recorders and remote control devices (which have encouraged 'zipping' and 'zapping') to TVs watched in 'uncommon' places (laundries, campsites, airports and so on), and above all, the very ubiquitousness of television which makes it bleed into every corner of day-to-day social life – all this can surely only make for an endless, unruly and uncontrollable play of differences in social practices related to television viewing: continuous social differentiation bordering on chaos. It is this chaos which the functionalist discourse of liberal pluralism cannot account for, and which the functionalist rationality of audience measurement technology is designed to suppress and tame in the form of a statistical order. But it is precisely this chaos which I suggest we need to take into consideration in understanding the logic of power relations in capitalist postmodernity. Capitalist postmodernity may have constructed a spatially integrated global village, but at the same time it encourages social *dis*integration.

IV

But it is important to theorize 'chaos' properly. Often, chaos is associated with loss of control, lack of order. Such a conception of chaos – or, in our context, the infinitude of the social, infinite semiosis – leads to a romanticized view of the practices of everyday life (such as audience practices) as always evading the structures – institutional, ideological – imposed upon them – as the site of resistance *per se*. This, of course, is the position taken up by Fiske. But such a position is informed by a negative theory of chaos: chaos as lack.

It is instructive here to draw comparisons with the emergence of chaos theory in the physical sciences. To begin with, Katherine Hayles, author of *Chaos Bound*, has given a fortuitous example of how chaos can be acknowledged as a positive force in our experience as media consumers: 'Every time we keep a TV or radio going in the background, even though we are not really listening to it, we are acting out a behavior that helps to reinforce and deepen the attitudes that underwrite a positive view of chaos.'[35] This positive view of chaos implies the transvaluation of chaos as having primacy over order. However, Hayles continues, chaos theory does not oppose chaos to order; rather, it sees chaos as 'the engine that drives a system toward a more complex kind of order'.[36] This is not dissimilar to Laclau's idea of how 'society', or for that matter 'audience' (as a functional sub-totality within 'society') is created out of the attempt to put an order to the (chaotic) infinitude of the social. In this sense, 'society' (or 'audience') is, in Hayles's terms, a chaotic system, or a complex kind of order, an order whose ultimate suture is impossible because it is a system born out of the precarious structuration of chaos. If chaos is ultimately impossible to domesticate it is because it is, as chaos theory would have it, 'an inexhaustible ocean of information' rather than a lack, 'a void signifying absence'.[37] The more chaotic a system is, the more information it contains, and the more complex the order established out of it. In other words, what characterizes chaotic systems – and by extension, social systems – is not so much that they are poor in order, but rich in information.[38] This formulation illuminates why the passive people meter is likely to be counter-productive (in creating order in the audience measurement field). It is because it will elicit *too much*, not too little information. Too much information will only lessen the possibility of constructing the (simulated) orderliness of the 'audience', therefore threatening to foreground the return of the repressed: chaos.

Chaos theory is in fact one more example of the recognition that we live in a 'true realm of uncertainty'. Hayles rightly associates the emergence of chaos theory in the physical sciences with the increasing importance of post-structuralist and postmodern theory in the humanities and the social sciences, not least in cultural studies. As Hayles puts it, 'different disciplines are drawn to similar problems because the concerns underlying them are highly charged within a prevailing cultural context'.[40] This context, we can add, is precisely the context of capitalist postmodernity. It is in capitalist postmodernity that the presence of chaos constantly lurking behind any institution of order has become a systemic force. Capitalist postmodernity, in other words, is a truly chaotic system.

What then is the historical specificity of this system, and how can we theorize the structural uncertainty engendered by and within it? It is illuminating here to reinvoke the demise of the transmission paradigm of communication theory, as it finds its parallel, at the level of the social, in the demise of the paradigm of the modern. The modern paradigm was predicated, as I have said earlier, upon the assumption that modernity, under the aegis of the expansion of capitalism, is a universal destination for the whole world. In this view, history is conceived as a linear development in which the modern is designated as the most advanced endpoint – literally the End of History – towards which the less modern, those termed 'traditional' or 'less developed', must and will of necessity evolve. The postmodern paradigm, however, has shattered the certainty of this universalizing evolutionary discourse. It challenges the assumptions of modern discourse by questioning the binary oppositioning of the modern/ Western/present/sender/self and pre-modern/non-Western/past/receiver/ other. The modern and the Western do not necessarily coincide, and the present has many different, complex and contradictory faces, projecting many different, uncertain futures. It is this overdetermined, convoluted and contradictory heterogeneity of the present – characterized by a multiplicity of coeval, overlapping and conflicting cultural self/other relationships[40] – which is foregrounded in postmodernity.

It is important to be precise about the character of this heterogeneity of the present, and it is here that the notion of chaos, as outlined above, and the force of the infinitude of the social takes effect. This heterogeneity of the present does not just refer to the juxtaposed coexistence of a liberal plurality of distinct cultures and societies (which could be said to have existed to a certain extent before the Europeans imposed capitalism on the rest of the world). In postmodernity, heterogeneity is not based on foundational essences, but is a contingent articulation of the fluid and moving play of differences in which 'cultures' and 'societies', tumbled as they are into endless interconnections (to paraphrase Clifford Geertz),[41] constantly construct, reconstruct and deconstruct themselves. Any identity of a 'culture', a 'society', and any other social entity ('nation', 'ethnicity', 'gender', 'audience', 'the people', and so on) is merely the unstable articulation of constantly changing positionalities, a precarious positivity formed out of a temporary fixation of meaning within the capitalist world-system. Paradoxically, heterogeneity arises precisely as a result of the hegemonizing, globalizing, integrating forces of the modern capitalist order. It is for this reason that the system, the totalizing system of global capitalism in which we are all trapped, is nevertheless a profoundly unstable one, whose closure can never be completed.

Crucially, however, this postmodern heterogeneity is not *just* the consequence of the excessive flux of the social which produces a surplus of meaning that the system is unable to master, that is, put in order. To assert this would be tantamount to making a romantic metaphysical statement. What is historically particular about postmodernity's 'true realm of uncertainty' is the system's ambiguous stance to the infinitude of the social itself: as much as it wants to control it, it also depends on exploiting it. It is in the very nature of capitalism, particularly consumption capitalism, to inscribe excess in its very mode of (re)production.

The dynamic of perpetual change is of course characteristic of capitalism *per se*, not just consumption capitalism. But what distinguishes the latter is the way in which perpetual *cultural* (de)construction, perpetual (de)construction of meanings and identities, through for example the fashion system and planned obsolescence, has become the linchpin of the economy. That is to say, the culture of consumerism is founded on the idea that constant transformation of identities (through consumption) is pleasurable and meaningful. This exploitation of the pleasure principle implies that consumption capitalism is, as Jon Stratton has remarked, based on an excess of desire: 'in contrast with earlier, production-oriented capitalism, which catered to given, and thus *limited*, needs and demands, consumption capitalism relies on providing for socially produced, and therefore in principle *limitless*, needs and wants.'[42] This occurs not only at the level of consumption where the consumer is constructed as always 'wanting'; in postmodern culture the post-structuralist dictum that subjects do not have fixed identities but are always in process of being (re)constructed and (re)defined is not just a theoretical axiom, but has become a generalized cultural principle. The historical institutionalization of excess of desire in the culture of capitalist postmodernity (most directly through the discourses of advertising and marketing) exploits the fundamental excessiveness of the social in the creation of an escalating, and ultimately uncontrollable, proliferation of difference and identity, or identities-in-difference. Excess of desire opens up the cultural space for the formulation and proliferation of unpredictable needs and wants – that is, meanings and identities – not all of which can be absorbed and incorporated in the postmodern order of the capitalist world-system.[43] In other words, at the heart of capitalist postmodernity is an extreme contradiction: on the one hand, its very operation depends on encouraging infinite semiosis; but on the other hand, like every systemic order, it cannot let infinite semiosis go totally unchecked.

So, the capitalist world-system today is not a single, undifferentiated, all encompassing whole, but a fractured one, in which forces of order and incorporation (for example those of globalization, unification and 'Westernization'; thus containment of 'information') are always undercut (though not necessarily subverted) by forces of chaos and fragmentation (such as localization, diversification and 'indigenization'; thus proliferation of 'information'). In this world-system there are still dominant forces, although there is never a guarantee in advance that their attempts to impose order will be successful: think only of the current failure to create a 'new world order'. Nor does relative failure to impose order mean that the dominant are any less powerful; on the contrary, it only means that the effectivity of their resources and forms of exercise of power is uncertain. Stronger still, it is precisely because of this uncertainty that order is consciously conceived as a task, a problem, an obsession; a matter of design, management, engineering, and policy.[44] In this sense, the very insecurity of order in capitalist postmodernity – contradictorily based as it is on both fixing and unfixing meanings and identities, both the delimitation and the instrumental expansion of the social – only encourages the dominant to step up feverishly both the intensity and the range of their ordering practices. But the work will never be done: in the capitalist world-system the moment of absolute order will never come. Even worse, precisely because global capitalism becomes ever more totalizing, the task of order-making will become ever more grandiose and complex, the suturing of the fragments of the system into a totality ever more unfinishable: Sisyphean labour. As Zygmunt Bauman puts it, 'Problems are created by problem-solving, new areas of chaos are generated by ordering activity.'[45] For one thing, this is how we can interpret the ceaseless search for better measurement methods and technologies in the ratings industry, or the frantic, neverending quest for new advertising and marketing strategies to capture the elusive consumer.

But if the forces of order are continuously deployed without ever achieving complete order, then the forces of chaos are also continuously impinging on the system without ever resulting in total chaos. Instead, capitalist postmodernity is an orderly disorder, or disorderly order, whose hegemony rests on the setting of structural limits, themselves precarious, to the possibilities of random excess. It is within these limits that 'resistance' to the dominant takes place (except in the rare situations of 'revolutions' which are temporary moments of limitlessness). In Wallerstein's words:

Universalism [of capitalist modernity] is a 'gift' of the powerful to the weak which confronts the latter with a double bind: to refuse the gift is to lose; to accept the gift is to lose. The only plausible reaction of the weak is neither to refuse nor to accept, or both to refuse and to accept – in short, the path of the seemingly irrational zigzags (both cultural and political) of the weak that has characterized most of nineteenth- and especially twentieth-century history.[46]

In other words, the negotiations and resistances of the subordinate, confined as they are *within* the boundaries of the system, unsettle (but do not destroy) those boundaries.

It is convenient at this point to return to John Fiske and to recontextualize his celebration of the bottom–up power that television audiences evince in the construction of their own meanings and pleasures. To be fair to Fiske, his writings are much more complex than some simplified reiterations would have us believe. In no way is he simply an apologist for liberal pluralism. On the contrary, he derives his relative optimism from his analysis of (mainly US) commercial television as 'the prime site where the dominant have to recognize the insecurity of their power, and where they have to encourage cultural difference with all the threat to their own position that this implies'.[47] However, what Fiske tends to overestimate (and romanticize) is precisely that threat. This threat simply makes the task of the television industries to retain their dominance more complicated and expensive, just as the dispersion and proliferation of viewing practices makes the task of audience measurement more complicated and expensive – and therefore more wasteful, more nasty, more aggressive. Furthermore, the encouragement of cultural difference is, as I have argued above, part and parcel of the system of capitalist postmodernity itself. In this sense, it would be mistaken to see the acting out of difference unambiguously as an act of resistance; what needs to be emphasized, rather, is that the desire to be different can be simultaneously complicit with and defiant to the institutionalization of excess of desire in capitalist postmodernity. At most, the resistive element in popular practices is, as Michel de Certeau has suggested in *The Practice of Everyday Life*, a matter of 'escaping without leaving'.[48]

Meaghan Morris has criticized the fact that the idea of what she terms 'excess of process over structure' has led to 'a cultural studies that celebrates 'resistance' as a programmed feature of capitalist culture', and to 'a theoretical myth of the Evasive Everyday'.[49] And indeed, such a celebration can easily take place when the acts of 'evasive everydayness' are taken at face value, in the context, say, of closed circuits of communication (where departure from 'preferred readings' can be straightforwardly read as 'evasion' and this in turn heroized as 'resistance'). However, if we place these acts in the more global and historical context of the chaotic system of capitalist postmodernity, then their 'political' status becomes much more ambivalent. Then we have to take into account their meaning in a system which already incorporates a celebration of limitless flux within its ordering principle. What is built-in in the culture of capitalist postmodernity is not 'resistance', but uncertainty, ambiguity, the chaos that emanates from the institutionalization of infinite semiosis. This is how I want to specify 'the true realm of uncertainty' of the 'global village'.

It should be clear, finally, that the unstable multiplicity of the system no longer makes it possible, as modern discourse would have it, to tell a single, total story about the world 'today'. As Jon Stratton has put it, in the postmodern episteme 'there is no fixed site of truth, no absolute presence; there are just multiple representations, an infinite number of rewritings'.[50] Theorizing in the postmodern context has given up on the search for totalizing and universalizing forms of knowledge and truth. Put more positively, if there is no position from which a fixed and absolute truth (i.e. a Grand Theory) can be put forward, then we can only strive for the construction of 'partial truths', to use James Clifford's term.[51] Critical theorizing, then, always has to imply an acknowledgement of its own open-endedness, its own partiality in its inevitable drive towards narrative closure, in its attempts to impose order on the stories it tells. At the very least, a critical understanding of what it means to live in the true realm of uncertainty that is capitalist postmodernity must take on board a positive uncertainty about its own 'communicative' effect, its own attempts to construct meaningful discourse in which the chaos of the world 'today' is rendered in 'sceptical, if not paranoid assessment'.[52] Or in the words of Laclau: 'Utopia is the essence of any communication and social practice.'[53]

Notes

I would like to thank Jon Stratton for his comments on earlier drafts of this essay.

1 Immanuel Wallerstein, *Geopolitics and Geoculture* (Cambridge: Cambridge University Press, 1991), p. 1.
2 This sense of reassurance (and thus of certainty) applies to both the proponents and the opponents of the 'global village'.
3 George Marcus, 'Past, present and emergent identities: requirements for ethnographies of late twentieth century modernity worldwide,' in Scott Lash and Jonathan Friedman (eds), *Modernity and Identity* (Oxford: Blackwell, 1992), p. 321.
4 James Carey, *Communication as Culture* (Boston: Unwin Hyman, 1989), p. 15.
5 Ibid., p. 32.
6 Ibid., p. 160.
7 Everett M. Rogers, *The Diffusion of Innovations* (Glencoe, Ill.: Free Press, 1962).
8 Everett M. Rogers, 'Communication and development: the passing of a dominant paradigm', *Communication Research*, 3 (1976), pp. 213–40.
9 John Tomlinson, *Cultural Imperialism* (London: Pinter, 1991), pp. 173.
10 As is well known, the passing of the dominant paradigm has been widely felt

within the discipline as a 'ferment in the field', as documented in the special issue of the *Journal of Communication*, 33: 3 (1983).

11   Carey, *Communication as Culture* p. 85.

12   Ibid., p. 84.

13   Ibid., p. 23.

14   Ibid., pp. 34–5.

15   Ibid., p. 35.

16   In this respect, Carey aligns himself with the liberal pragmatism of John Dewey and Richard Rorty. It should be noted that the scope of Carey's 'Great Community' never seems to become thoroughly global: his 'we' remains firmly within the boundaries of the United States of America.

17   Stuart Hall, 'Encoding/Decoding', in S. Hall et al., *Culture, Media, Language* (London: Hutchinson, 1980), pp. 128–38.

18   Jean Baudrillard, *In the Shadow of the Silent Majorities* (New York: Semiotext(e), 1983), p. 11.

19   James Curran, 'The new revisionism in mass communication research: a reappraisal', *European Journal of Communication*, 5: 2–3 (1990), 135–64. See also e.g. Philip Schlesinger, *Media, State and Nation* (London: Sage, 1991), pp. 148–9. For a retort complementary to mine, see David Morley, Introduction in his *Television, Audiences, and Cultural Studies* (London: Routledge, 1992).

20   David Morley, *The 'Nationwide' Audience*. (London: BFL, 1982) and *Family Television* (London: Comedia, 1986); Janice Radway, *Reading the Romance* (Chapel Hill: University of North Carolina Press, 1984); Ien Ang, *Watching Dallas* (London: Methuen, 1985).

21   Curran, 'The new revisionism', pp. 145–6.

22   Introduction, in James Curran and Michael Gurevitch (eds.), *Mass Media and Society* (London: Edward Arnold, 1991), p. 8.

23   Curran, 'The new revisionism', p. 151.

24   The best-known exemplar of such a liberal pluralist inflection of the 'new audience research' is Tamar Liebes and Elihu Katz, *The Export of Meaning* (New York: Oxford University Press, 1991).

25   e.g. Curran, 'The new revisionism', p. 140.

26   e.g. Meaghan Morris, 'Banality in cultural studies', in Patricia Mellencamp (ed.), *Logics of Television* (Bloomington/Indianapolis: Indiana University Press, 1990), pp. 14–43.

27   John Fiske, *Television Culture* (London: Methuen, 1987), e.g. p. 314.

28   Mark Poster, Introduction, in Jean Baudrillard *Selected Writings* (Stanford, Calif.: Stanford University Press, 1988), p. 6.

29   John Tomlinson, *Cultural Imperialism* (London: Pinter, 1991), p. 175.

30   For a further elaboration of this point see: Ien Ang and Joke Hermes, 'Gender and/in media consumption', in James Curran and Michael Gurevitch (eds), *Mass Media and Society* (London: Edward Arnold, 1991), pp. 307–28; and Ien Ang, 'Ethnography and radical contextualism in audience studies', in Lawrence Grossberg, James Hay and Ellen Wartella (eds),

Towards a Comprehensive Theory of the Audience? (Boulder, Colo.: Westview Press, forthcoming).

31 Ernesto Laclau, *New Reflections on the Revolution of our Time* London: Verso, 1991), pp. 90–1.

32 This exposition draws heavily on Laclau's concise essay 'The impossibility of society', in his *New Reflections*.

33 Ien Ang, *Desperately Seeking the Audience* (London: Routledge, 1991).

34 Laclau, *New Reflections* p. 92.

35 N. Katherine Hayles, *Chaos Bound* (Ithaca, NY: Cornell University Press, 1990), p. 7.

36 Ibid., p. 23.

37 Ibid., p. 8.

38 Ibid., p. 6.

39 Ibid., p. xi.

40 For a further elaboration of the concept of coevalness in contemporary global culture, see Johannes Fabian, *Time and the Other* (New York: Columbia University Press, 1983).

41 Clifford Geertz, *Work and Lives* (Chicago: University of Chicago Press, 1988), p. 147.

42 Jon Stratton, *Writing Sites: A Genealogy of the Postmodern World* (New York: Harvester Wheatsheaf, 1990), pp. 297–8.

43 See e.g. Akbar S. Ahmed, *Postmodernism and Islam* (London: Routledge, 1992).

44 Zygmunt Bauman, *Modernity and Ambivalence* (Cambridge: Polity Press, 1991), p. 6.

45 Ibid., p. 14.

46 Wallerstein, *Geopolitics and Geoculture*, p. 217.

47 Fiske, *Television Culture*, p. 326.

48 Michel de Certeau, *The Practice of Everyday Life*, trans. Steven Rendall (Berkeley, Calif.: University of California Press, 1984).

49 Meaghan Morris, 'On the beach', in Lawrence Grossberg, Cary Nelson and Paula Treichler (eds), *Cultural Studies* (New York: Routledge, 1992), pp. 464–5.

50 Stratton, *Writing Sites*, p. 287.

51 James Clifford, 'Introduction: partial truths', in James Clifford and George E. Marcus (eds), *Writing Culture* (Berkeley, Calif.: University of California Press, 1986), pp. 1–26.

52 Meaghan Morris, 'Things to do with shopping centres', in Susan Sheridan (ed.), *Grafts* (London: Verso, 1988), p. 197.

53 Laclau, *New Reflections*, p. 93.

10

By Whose Authority?
Accounting for Taste in
Contemporary Popular Culture

James M. Collins

Over the course of the past decade, the study of popular culture has changed in a number of fundamental ways, yet popular culture, as a critical object posited by most studies, remains remarkably similar to what it was before, in the dark ages of media analysis, when the monstrous Culture Industry, armed with hypodermic needles, roamed the vast wasteland searching for vidiot victims who were helpless outside the walls of the University, Good Taste, and Real Art. All sorts of paradigmatic shifts have occurred within popular culture *theory*, yet the basic mythology appears to be harder to kill than any mythical beast it invents. Most of the attempts to account for the recent technological changes in the production, distribution, and reception of popular culture have done little more than rename the monster 'Postmodernism', and offer the same scenario, but in the form of a pernicious video game in which all the principals and attendant audience are mere simulacra. And, while ethnographic analysis has provided invaluable insight into how global villagers make meanings, they remain imperilled by the same all-devouring monster, helpless unless protected by the magic shield of Subcultural Affiliation.

If the study of popular culture is going to escape from the clutches of its own mythology, it must recognize that its critical object has changed and cannot be adequately accounted for by recycled truisms of the mass culture critique, most of which originated in the later nineteenth century. That popular culture may have changed in form, substance, and function over the course of the past century is not always apparent in most popular culture theory – the titles, genres, and delivery systems may change, but its 'essence' remains the same. Changing the theoretical frameworks is of course the first step towards recognizing the shifting significance of the category of popular culture, but recent changes too often seem to depend more on evolution of critical paradigms within the academy (for example the shift from post-structuralism to cultural studies) and less on the development of 'the popular'.

This is not to suggest that 'the popular' is possessed of some sort of ontological status, or that we should abandon theory and get down to the 'real stuff' of popular texts. On the contrary, popular culture will always be a matter of differential definition, based on a wide range of critical, social, and institutional distinctions that are entirely contingent upon historical circumstances. Whenever academics 'frame' popular culture, that framing is inevitably contingent upon the state of the academy as a discursive formation, but the tendency to essentialize popular culture, founded on the implicit belief that it is always the same beast, but new critical languages give us better insight into its behaviour, is the result of a major failure of popular culture theory – the inability to recognize that popular culture is itself an amalgamation of discursive formations that are likewise contingent, and therefore, by necessity, constantly changing as well.

Escaping the antiquated mythology of popular culture theory means not just envisioning or mapping the terrain that is popular culture differently than before, but also recognizing the extent to which popular culture in its various incarnations maps and remaps its *own* terrain, that popular texts do not simply contribute to chaotic, media-saturated cultural landscapes, but are also engaged in mastering an array of signs, absorbing and refashioning that array into new forms of textuality and, just as importantly, new forms of mass entertainment. By this point we have a much better sense of how audiences use popular texts, yet our understanding of *how popular texts use popular culture* remains remarkably underdeveloped.

In order to ameliorate this uneven development, I will focus on two interconnected issues: *rearticulation* and *authority*. The various forms of rearticulation – the ways in which antecedent texts, genres, icons, and images are refashioned in contemporary 'art' and 'entertainment' – need to be discussed in tandem with 'authority' because they destabilize not just notions of origin and provenance, but also the position from which critics can evaluate the popular. The reworking of signs already invested with significance in order to change their cultural resonances is in and of itself a way of claiming cultural authority, which is especially unsettling since it troubles the evaluative significance of specific signs as well as the ways in which value and meaning are specified. While rearticulation was initially written off by cultural critics in the early eighties as mere 'recycling' that exemplified that was wrong with postmodern culture, the diverse forms of rearticulation have become too inflected with conflicting ideological agendas for them to be categorized as the rotten fruits of postmodernism. An increasing amount of critical attention has been focused on the ways that individual subjects negotiate or manipulate the semiotic excess of day to-day life, but the examination of that negotiation process must be tied to a reconsideration of how popular texts are also negotiating that same array of signs in ways that cannot be appreciated according to mythology of the mass culture critique.

I have argued elsewhere that in order to counteract the Baudrillardian conception of the individual as hopeless vidiot wandering aimlessly in the hyperreal, shattered by the bombardment of signs, we must delineate the various strategies of bricolage employed by individual subjects;[1] rather than formulating an elaborate post mortem on subjectivity, we would be better served by adapting the approach Carlo Ginzburg develops in *The Cheese and the Worms*,[2] when he chronicles the range of works available to Menocchio out of which Menocchio then constructs his own cosmogony. Adjusting for differences in semiotic environments, however, involves more than simply positing a techno-Menocchio armed with a remote control, VCR, and CD player – it should involve a concomitant re-examination of how contemporary forms of bricolage manipulate not 'raw' materials, but highly mediated, thoroughly rearticulated messages. If, as Umberto Eco has argued,[3] much of the media we now encounter is media about media – media squared – we need to conceive of the bricolage of techno-Menocchio as *bricolage squared*, a piecing together of texts drawn from an endless array, which are already negotiations of that same array, negotiations motivated by different exigencies, legitimated by competing standards of cultural capital. Focusing on both types of bricolage in tandem, then, is not merely a matter of giving 'equal time' to both sides of the communication exchange. Rather, it is a matter of recognizing that entire contexts for such exchanges have been radically altered by the proliferation of signs and by the proliferation of strategies used to absorb them, strategies that destabilize traditional distinctions between encoding and decoding, and who or what has the 'authority' to do either.

Sampling the Array: Rearticulation and Evaluation

That rearticulation of one sort or another, either as simple appropriation and recycling, or as more radical hijacking of signs for more explicit ideological purposes, has become an all-pervasive feature of postmodern cultural production is by now common knowledge. Highly self-reflexive forms of intertextual referencing are ubiquitous throughout popular music, television, film, comic books, fashion and interior design.[4] Nor is it restricted to 'high' or 'middlebrow' popular culture. Robert Altman's indictment of contemporary Hollywood in *The Player* (1991) may be built on intertextual quotation, but so too is Penelope Spheeris's *Wayne's World* (1991), targeted for much lower and much younger brows, but nevertheless depends on endless self-reflexive quotations as the major organizing principle of the narrative. While there are, of course, any number of significant differences between the two films and their respective attitudes towards the culture industry, both films – one the darling of critics and art houses, the other the favourite of teens and pre-teens everywhere – feature sophisticated references to their own status as commodities, both reflecting quite explicitly on the nature of film financing, their respective positions in regard to antecedent classics and contemporaneous rivals in the marketplace, and the conditions of their eventual circulation and reception.

The already legendary opening of *The Player*, an eight minute tracking shot modelled on the opening shot of *Touch of Evil*, features explicit references to Welles's film, *The Graduate* (and its proposed sequel as outlined by Buck Henry, screen writer for the original), *The Manchurian Candidate*, *Rope*, etc., all exemplifying the degraded nature of contemporary Hollywood film-making, so obsessed with financial return that only sequels and mindless combinations of the familiar are possible. *Wayne's World* begins with the evil television promoter, played by Rob Lowe, watching *Wayne's World* on a local-access channel, in bed with his nymphet of the moment, a scene paralleling all too explicitly the *mise en scène* of Lowe's own infamous bedroom tapes that made him a tabloid cover boy for weeks on end. Just as Altman's film is situated squarely within Hollywood film culture, unthinkable outside of it, *Wayne's World* can exist only within and across the television-tabloid-rock music culture that forms the very fabric of the film's universe. Altman's movie people refer directly to the materiality of the film medium as they discuss the value of extended tracking shots *vis-à-vis* the cut-happy MTV-influenced film-making, while they themselves happen to be in an extended tracking shot. In *Wayne's World,* we first see Wayne and Garth through the television in the motel bedroom as the woman channel hops with the remote control, then through television camera monitors. The materiality of television's artifice is foregrounded explicitly through the flashing graphics superimposed on the image that describe, utterly redundantly, what we see – 'Unnecessary Close-Up,' 'Get-a-Load-of-This-Guy Cam', etc.

The primacy of this referencing, the fact that these films, one a quintessential critical hit, the other, just as definitely a box-office hit, are both so self-consciously grounded in rearticulation suggests that the self-reflexivity that was once considered a marker of high art, because it reflected a high degree of sophistication on the part of both artist and eventual audience,[5] is now constitutive of all popular entertainment that depends upon a high degree of *media literacy*, which should inevitably force a rethinking of the category of 'sophistication' *vis-à-vis* hierarchies of taste and evaluation. As producer Lorne Michaels says of *Wayne's World's* relentless quotation of film, television, and rock intertexts, 'We live in a time when nothing will ever go away again. [Everything is] on a channel somewhere. All cultural references are, to a ten-year-old, perfectly familiar.'[6]

The ability to access both 'high and low' and to recombine them at will, according to newly invented aesthetic hierarchies, is epitomized by a recent episode of a CBS network television series, *Northern Exposure*, in which the origins of the town that serves as a home base for the action are envisioned in an hour-long flashback, told to the current residents by one of the first settlers. The frame itself is noteworthy in two ways: first, it represents the desire to invent a history for a television series, a narrative form which has been, as John Ellis correctly argued,[7] based on collective amnesia on that part of all characters. The invention of not only a history, but a veritable 'foundation myth' is emblematic of the programme's desire to frame itself differently from other television programmes by giving itself a point of origin, a set of invented traditions that places *Northern Exposure* closer to a nineteenth-century novel than the usual prime-time drama. Second, and especially significant, is the setting for the transmission of the tale – literally, a tale told by a wise old man, with everyone grouped around a fire, invoking an even earlier tradition of oral storytelling. His story details the settling of Cecily, Alaska, when it was still part of the Western frontier. This transitional period is envisioned alternately, but simultaneously, as Western and Early Modernism. The town had been nothing but a mudhole overrun with varmints, until two ultra-civilized women, Rosalind and Cecily, arrive and begin to transform the city into an artist's colony. Before long, the saloon becomes a *salon*, featuring public readings of the work of Stein, Yeats, and Rilke, dance performances by Cecily conceived in the style of Isadora Duncan, and the occasional *tableau vivant*. The synthesis of Western and Early Modernism is actualized with the arrival of Franz Kafka, who is suffering from 'chronic writer's block', but as a 'devotee of horse opera novels, he hoped the Alaskan frontier might inspire him'. In the final confrontation between outlaws and Modernists, Cecily is killed, but the former are defeated, the townsfolk completely won over by the pure aestheticism advocated by Rosalind and Cecily.

In this episode, a history is invented to serve as the antecedent of the town, but the nature of that history provides a kind of ad hoc legitimacy for *Northern Exposure*'s own eclecticism as an entity that is part popular narrative, part self-reflexive deconstruction of all the prerequisites for 'old-

fashioned' storytelling, evidenced most obviously by the occasional rup-
tures in the diegetic world of the story, when actors suddenly walk out of
character, or in the dream sequences of the town's resident film-maker, Ed
(for example, Steven Spielberg and George Lucas suddenly appear as
themselves at an Academy Award ceremony when Ed is given a Life
Achievement Award), or in overt references to *Twin Peaks*, *St Elsewhere*,
and other television series, which occur in virtually every episode. The use
of Kafka exemplifies the refunctioning of authority, as the category of
Early Modernist Artist, synonymous with rarefied sensibility, the agony of
creativity, etc., is itself rearticulated in terms of the Western frontier. This
reworking of Kafka and the myth of the Modernist Artist reflects a total
denial of the Modernist artistic hierarchy, in which the avant-garde is so
clearly superior to mere popular culture that it maintains a cordon
sanitaire to ensure against contamination. The complete interpenetration
of these categories suggests a rearticulation that goes beyond Kafka and
the Western to the very hierarchies that assigned them their specific
positions based on the same gold standard of cultural value.

The proliferation of different standards of evaluation that both shape
and legitimate divergent types of rearticulation leads not to the dis-
appearance of critical distinctions, but rather to their intensification as
they circulate within the same cultural arenas. In his seminal study on the
creation of 'high culture' in nineteenth-century Boston, Paul DiMaggio
argues that 'Not until two distinct organizational forms – the private or
semi-private, non-profit cultural institution and the commercial popular-
culture industry – took shape, did the high/popular culture dichotomy
emerge in its modern form.[8] According to DiMaggio,

> before 1850, there were few efforts to make such distinction, the Philhar-
> monic Society giving classical concerts as well as backing popular singers of
> the day. One typical performance included a bit of Italian opera, a devo-
> tional song . . . a piece by Verdi, 'Bluebell of Scotland', and 'The origin of
> Common Nails', recited by Mr. Bernard, a comedian . . . The visual arts
> were also organized on a largely commercial basis in this era. Museums
> were modeled on Barnum's, fine art was interspersed among such curios-
> ities as bearded women and mutant animals, and popular entertainments
> were offered for the price of admission to a clientele that included working
> people as well as the upper middle class . . . By 1910, high and popular
> culture were encountered far less frequently in the same settings.[9]

What DiMaggio refers to as the 'sacralization of art' was institutionalized
through the differentiation of programme, site, and audience, a process
motivated by entrepreneurship, but also 'classification' and 'framing',
which he sees as concurrent projects undertaken by the Boston Brahmins.
But in the 1990s, this sort of differentiation can no longer 'hold' for

entire societies, since 'authority' in the sense of artistic creation *and* as a matter of critical distinction, are both so *dispersed*. The dispersal of authority and the concomitant shifts in classification and framing have led once again to radical changes in programme, location, and audience that virtually reverse the distinctions that Boston's mandarin class laboured so hard to enforce. One could cite innumerable examples of the destabilization or rewriting of those distinctions, but an especially representative instance should suffice here as an illustration.

In the summer of 1992, I attended the San Francisco Opera Rossini Festival, drawn there by a performance of *Guillaume Tell*, the first complete performance in the original French since the nineteenth century. The event was given the requisite fanfare and publicity, as opera devotees and critics from around the world converged on the city for this once-in-a-lifetime event. The overture was conducted in dazzling fashion by Donald Runnicles, complete with flashing eyes and floating hair, and the audience leapt to their feet in a thunderous ovation. At this moment, the cultural distinctions that were classified and framed by the Boston Brahmins a century ago seemed firmly in place. Yet, just the day before in Symphony Hall, literally across the street from the Opera House, the San Francisco Symphony had also played the William Tell Overture, in a somewhat different mode. The guest conductor was Bobby McFerrin, a well-known performance artist who has recorded with Laurie Anderson, perhaps better known as a pop singer whose *Don't Worry, Be Happy* was a smash-hit record, now enjoying a career as a serious classical musician who has just released another smash-hit album recorded with cellist Yo Yo Ma, entitled *Hush* (Sony, 1992), featuring his own compositions, a bit of Bach, some nursery songs, pieces by Rachmaninoff, Vivaldi, Rimsky Korsakov and a comical interlude in which an imaginary stuffed-shirt announcer introduces a musette by Bach, only to have McFerrin burst into Jimi Hendrix's *Purple Haze* 'by mistake'. The programme that night in San Francisco at Symphony Hall was similarly mixed, McFerrin conducting a Beethoven symphony 'straight' to great applause, and then giving the Rossini overture the same treatment, at least until the final subject (the 'Lone Ranger' theme) began, at which point the members of the orchestra leapt to their feet, put down their instruments, and played the rest of the overture on 'mouth' in McFerrin's signature style – 'brrump, brrump, brrump bump bump, brrump, brrump, brrump bump bump . . .' – which was also met with a delirious ovation.

The key point here is that the virtual simultaneity of these two performances of the same Rossini masterpiece suggests not that we are witnessing a wholesale return to the early nineteenth century, but rather another phase in the history of art and entertainment that is just as distinctive as the two previous phases described so succinctly by DiMaggio.

What distinguishes the current phase is the dispersal of cultural authority, in terms of creation and evaluation, as individual authors and standards of authority both circulate in ever wider orbits, but intersect in unpredictable ways, or at least unpredicted by traditional media theory. McFerrin's ability to move in and out of the worlds of Top Forty Radio, the musical avant-garde, and symphony orchestras depends on his ability as an author to gain authority in each realm, which would be impossible if different standards of cultural capital were not in circulation at the same time. McFerrin plays William Tell on mouth as a master entertainer, but as a consummate musician he has been commissioned to write an opera for the San Francisco Opera. The either/or distinctions DiMaggio describes are no longer uniformly operative in regard to programme, location, and audience because of the rearticulation, at the most fundamental level, of 'authority' itself in each case.

The mixture of the popular and the classical in the postmodern period is not simply a return to critical standards of the pre-/early modern period; the current relationship between the two takes the form that it does precisely because it comes *after* the modern period in which either/or distinctions were secured by an evaluative hierarchy founded on their separation. The popular entertainments that sat alongside classical masterpieces in the museums, music halls, and theatres of the first half of the nineteenth century did not have to justify their presence there, but in the second half of the twentieth century the popular must provide its own justification, its own built-in evaluative standards, because even if the unitary hierarchy of taste no longer holds dominion over all cultural production, it continues to exercise vestigial force, since it is so ingrained within specific institutions.

The Popularization of Auteurism, or Ted Turner Meets Goethe

This rewriting of the criteria of aesthetic evaluation is nowhere more obvious than in contemporary film-making, where the category of the auteur has undergone profound changes since its emergence in the French film criticism immediately after the Second World War. In a series of influential essays, Alexandre Astruc, François Truffaut, Jean-Luc Godard, and others developed a criterion for distinguishing film artistry from mere anonymous entertainment, based on the ability of certain auteur directors to establish and maintain a consistent personal vision. As such, auteurism grounded its own critical activity on borrowed criteria, developed by critics of the legitimate arts over a century before. The Romantic ideology of artistic creation as pure invention by the singular genius had, by the

1950s, already been institutionalized for decades in the worlds of literature, art, and music, and was used as a common coin of exchange by
academics and auctioneers alike. The legitimation of 'the cinema'
depended on the appropriation of this ideology and, not so coincidentally,
the institutionalization of film study within the academy was in large
measure a very successful reclassification and 'reframing' of the medium
by auteurist professors. By the mid-sixties, auteurism had become the
basis of a *critical* authority that was itself entirely dependent upon *creative*
authority in the most unambiguous, Romantic sense of the term – genius
as source and guarantee of value. As such, it served as a model for film
criticism and film-making, the latter exemplified by the emergence of the
'film school generation' of American directors, and the institutionalization
of the *autoren* film that became a rallying cry for the German New Wave.

In the 1980s, auteurism underwent significant reclassification as it
began to circulate in different contexts. Pushed out of the centre ring of
film study within the academy by different forms of ideological analysis
that decentred the auteur as source of a film's meanings, it became a staple
of popular film criticism and, not surprisingly, a staple of the film business. Timothy Corrigan's analysis of the development of brand name
auteurism and its impact on film financing details the factors involved in
this evolution:

> If in conjunction with this so-called international art cinema of the sixties
> and seventies, the auteur had been absorbed as a phantom presence within
> the text, he or she has rematerialized in the eighties and nineties as a
> commercial performance of the business of being an auteur . . . Here the
> auteur can be described according to the conditions of a cultural and
> commercial intersubjectivity, a social interaction distinct from an inten-
> tional causality or textual transcendence.[10]

For Corrigan, Coppola exemplifies this shift because he has exploited the
myth of the Romantic artist so successfully that he now is just as well
known as a 'Romantic entrepreneur'.[11] The interconnectedness of these
two personas that Corrigan attributes to Coppola is summed up in virtual
epigrammatic form by Coppola himself in a recent interview in *Details*, an
American fashion magazine covering the *Dracula* phenomenon.[12] When
asked who his heroes were, he responded, 'Heroes I divide into living and
dead. Living: Ted Turner. Dead: Goethe.' The juxtaposition here of
Media Baron and Romantic Poet embodies Coppola's desire to stake his
own authority on two forms of capital – financial and cultural – which,
though formerly considered mutually exclusive, now intermingle in
increasingly convoluted ways that complicate the determination of the
value of any given text, since that value can no longer be fixed in reference
to one shared standard.

Corrigan's analysis of the commerce of auteurs and the auteurs of commerce is effective in describing how the material conditions of authority factor into film financing, but the persistence of a vestigial Romantic auteurism in the popular evaluation of film remains a crucial determining factor that often operates in contradistinction to that economy. The schizophrenic attitude of the American popular press towards the film industry is a case in point. Apparently, only two types of films are 'newsworthy' beyond the confines of the columns of film reviewers – the mega blockbuster and the 'independent film' of the moment. While the release of most blockbusters is now treated more often than not as a media phenomenon, the fetishizing of the independent auteur has become a phenomenon unto itself. The Sunday edition of the *New York Times* has become a weekly testimonial to the co-presence of two standards of cultural value. The 'Arts and Leisure' section now features, on a regular basis, multiple full page ads for the opening of blockbusters, alongside major feature articles on new independent directors (possessing vision, but little financial backing) who, despite all odds, produce film art. In 1992, for example, the *Times* profiled Stacy Cochran (*My New Gun*), Anthony Drazan (*Zebrahead*), Quentin Tarantino (*Reservoir Dogs*) and Hal Hartley (*Simple Men*). The title of the article devoted to Hartley sums up the paper's criteria quite neatly: 'This Director's Wish List Doesn't Include Hollywood',[13] as does the primary featured quotation: 'Hal Hartley, who made the droll *Simple Men*, is hardly Cecil B. DeMille. And he never wants to be.' The opposition of the *Times* critics' criteria vs 'The Industry's' is even more clearcut in a later article on all of the Independents of the Week. Entitled 'Is a Cinematic New Wave Cresting?' (paired on the front page of this section with an article on the current television season, entitled 'Still Trapped in the Vast Wasteland'),[14] the story features a nearly full-page box containing individual photos of 'Who's Who among the Hot New Filmmakers', with vital data alongside each photo. The text that accompanies each picture lists newest film, name, age, background, and mentor – but also, tellingly, two more categories: 'Why the major studio may have turned down his/her film': and 'Why it deserves notice' (read: why it deserves our notice and, of course, yours).

The persistence of this vestigial Romantic auteurism that serves as a virtually axiomatic justification for a film's status is not restricted to the *Times* or other publications with claims to cultural prestige. Hal Hartley was also the subject of a major article in *Gentleman's Quarterly* (entitled 'The Vision Thing: Hal Hartley's movies are like no one else's – and we mean that in the best possible way'),[15] and the 27 November 1992 issue of *Entertainment Weekly* features a massive black X, with Spike Lee's face superimposed on its side, the title reading, 'The Mind Behind X – How

Spike Lee Willed *Malcolm X* to the Screen'. Lee was also show-cased on NBC's prime-time documentary *The New Hollywood* (21 March 1990), the conclusion of which exemplifies the extent to which Romantic auteurism has become ensconced in American film culture in the broadest sense of the term. After devoting the last section of the programme to the return of vertical integration (in which the major studios are once again attempting to gain control over film exhibition by buying up cinemas) and the impact of the conglomeratization of Hollywood, the anchorman Tom Brokaw, not normally considered a devotee of film art, brings the programme to a close with this final thought:

> Movies and Big Business. They've always been two of the most prominent symbols of America, and they've always been able to live together compatibly. But now there's a danger that one will completely dominate the other, that the bottom line will suffocate the story line, that accountants, not artists will have the final cut. Of course, a lot of people will get rich in the process – studio executives and those stars, producers, and directors who can move people through the box offices at ever higher prices. But what about you? What about the audiences who buy the tickets? Well, if you don't like what you see, you can always go elsewhere, right? Not necessarily. If these big companies have complete control, there will be fewer opportunities for *the unique vision* (italics mine), for the smaller film. In fact, someday these movie marquees could not only hold the title of the picture, but a subtitle: Take It or Leave It.

That Brokaw, speaking as a high profile representative of another conglomerate (NBC, owned by General Electric) should express such auteurist sentiments in his obvious prejudice in favour of brave outsiders is indicative of how ensconced the Romantic ideology of artistic creation has become, how the authority of authority remains an unquestioned value within the television exposé.

A recent instalment of CBS Sports 'This is the NFL' suggests that the institutionalization of auteurism has itself become subject to parody. In a segment entitled 'Highbrow Highlights', viewers were given an idea of how different cinematic auteurs would bend football to their personal vision. The announcer begins, 'Now it's time for the highest of the highbrows. Federico Fellini is the great Italian director who made *La Dolce Vita*. He blurs reality and dream, and he's famous for his grotesque and decadent characters. So here's football a la Fellini: *La Dolce Sporta*.' After screening a segment of highlights edited in Fellini-esque style, the announcer returns to introduce another instalment. 'A different style of moviemaking belonged to the legendary film pioneer, Sergei Eisenstein. Now, in his silent movies he believed that any two images edited together can create meaning. You could place seemingly unrelated images in collision with each other. Sounds like the right guy for a football movie. "Ten Plays that Shook the World".'

The opposition between artistry and box office represents the collision, however, of only two major economies of evaluation. The release of Coppola's *Bram Stoker's Dracula* has been met with the requisite auteurist reviews and feature stories about its financial success, of the film's record-breaking first weekend. Some, like a cover in the *San Francisco Examiner*'s Sunday *Image* magazine manage to situate Coppola and his film within an artistic and commercial context, alternating between the two virtually from paragraph to paragraph. This Thanksgiving issue on 'Holiday Cheer' focuses on the different ways Bay Area celebrities spend their Thanksgiving holidays, but Coppola is featured on the cover, toasting the season and the camera with a glass of his own proprietary red wine, Rubicon. The article comments at length on the luxuriousness of his Napa Valley estate and his recently acquired, meticulously restored Cord, 'the dream car of the 30s'. In the midst of this appreciation of Coppola's good life, auteurism rears its heroic head. While arguing with one of this guests, Fred Fuchs, from American Zoetrope, about what the studio might do to his film, we are told:

> He's afraid the unaltered film will be used and thus Dracula will not be exactly what he has labored two years to produce. At the picnic table, Coppola suddenly jumps to his feet, denouncing what he calls bureaucrats. He walks to a space between the tables and makes a brief, angry speech. He repeats his charges about bureaucrats, refers to his 30 years experience as a filmmaker. Amateurism is making inroads, he says. Firmly, he tells the assembled picnickers that nothing is to be sent out of the estate unless he personally – and no one else – signs off on it.[16]

But this film has been evaluated in reference to other criteria that recontextualize it even as it was being released. The November issue of *Vogue* begins its coverage of the movie with a spread of glamour shots of Winona Ryder in various incarnations, including a homage to the Audrey Hepburn of *Breakfast at Tiffany*'s vintage.[17] These photos are followed by black and white shots of Gary Oldham (who plays Dracula) and Ryder 'in character', looking very Gothic, followed by a short essay by hot new outsider novelist Mary Gaitskill, in which she attempts to explain the timeless appeal of the vampire story. Here the status or value of the film is measured in reference to the star appeal of Ryder, who is given credit for initiating the project ('Winona Ryder not only stars in *Bram Stoker's Dracula*, she made it happen'), and in reference to the literary star appeal of Gaitskill, whose artistic credentials as a novelist give her authority to explain the significance of mere mass entertainment.

The accumulation of these divergent reframings are not just a matter of 'encrustations', in Bennett's sense of the term,[18] that mediate our relationship to the film. The various 'activations' of Bond that Bennett details so impressively are primarily a matter of diachronic evolution, not synchronic conflicts that frame the same text in divergent ways simultaneously. These articles that cover the *Dracula* phenomenon ask their readers to value the film as a star vehicle by Hollywood's newest vamp, as a narrative spectacle that somehow speaks directly to our unconscious desires, as the newest creation by a visionary auteur. If we add the film's intertextual quotations, *Dracula*'s own authority as a work of art is grounded in its historical significance as the inheritor of the great cinematic tradition of Lumière, Murnau, and Griffith, and as the most 'faithful' adaptation of Stoker's novel (a point Coppola insists upon), it also claims literary value through its respect for the book.

A Pedagogy of Partiality

This simultaneity does indeed affect, as Corrigan argues, the inter-subjectivity of the auteur, but it also has a far-reaching impact on the *intra*-subjectivity of individual readers, viewers, and listeners as they make their own evaluations in reference to this array, composed not just of signs, but also evaluative strategies that are advocated with such urgency. Insisting on the polysemic nature of popular texts is now commonplace within contemporary theory, but our understanding of the multi-accentuality of signs in postmodern cultures can only be fully appreciated if we realize that the majority of texts are not only polysemic, but *polyvalued*. One of the most productive recent developments in popular culture theory is the burgeoning interest in exploring the multiplicity of meanings that texts may generate, but the chief limitation of this work is the tendency to separate signification from evaluation. Barbara Herrnstein Smith elucidates this point effectively:

> The study of literary evaluation has been, as we might say, 'neglected', but that the entire problematic of value and evaluation has been evaded and explicitly exiled by the literary academy. It is clear, for example, that there has been no broad and sustained investigation of literary evaluation that could compare to the constant and recently intensified attention devoted to every aspect of literary interpretation. The past decades have witnessed an extraordinary proliferation of theories, approaches, movements, and entire disciplines focused on interpretive criticism, among them (to recite a familiar litany) New Criticism, structuralism, psychoanalytic decon-structionism, reader response criticism, reception aesthetics, speech-act theory. At the same time, however, aside from a number of scattered and secondary essays by theorists and critics who are usually otherwise occupied,

no one in particular has been concerned with questions of literary value and evaluation, and such questions regularly go begging . . .[17]

The use of Bakhtin's concept of heteroglossia has become increasingly fashionable in cultural theory,[20] but that heteroglossia is not merely a matter of semiotic richness – the collision of conflicting languages (conceived as distinct verbal ideological perspectives) that affects the formation of all utterances is due directly to the inseparability of those languages from the mechanisms of evaluation. This critical blind spot is understandable, but problematic nevertheless. Understandable because of the determination of contemporary media scholars to bracket evaluation in favour of a more descriptive ethnographic approach, thereby avoiding the traditional evaluative approach to popular culture that leads inevitably to its dismissal by the intellectual class. This bracketing, however, becomes problematic when it fails to recognize the extremely evaluative nature of all decoding, that critical discrimination is not restricted to the academy, that 'taste' may now be considered an antiquated, counter-productive category for cultural analysis, but it remains a vital component of day-to-day life in cultures where 'taste-making' in various guises is the primary goal of both the education industry and the culture industry. Media scholars, then, in bracketing the issue of taste in order to discuss popular culture, fail to appreciate the inseparability of taste from the actual experience of popular texts and in the process begin to make popular culture what it never is – a play of encoding and decoding strategies devoid of the evaluative energy that dynamizes both.

Accounting for taste in ways that avoid the traditional prejudices of the intellectual class that has perpetuated the marginalization of popular culture, yet still acknowledges the primacy of evaluation and, most importantly, the multiplication of its agencies and authorities should be one of our most pressing pedagogical imperatives if we, as teachers of popular culture, hope to identify with a greater degree of specificity than ever before, how popular culture 'works'. The increased emphasis on audience research advocated so successfully by British Culturalists has led to a more nuanced understanding of how meanings are produced and therefore could be productively expanded in reference to interplay between interpretation and evaluation. But, as I have argued elsewhere, the culturalist approach, in celebrating the heterogeneity of decoding (due to differences in race, class, occupation) has tended to homogenize the encoding of popular texts, which precludes the possibility of under-standing the complexity of taste formation in postmodern cultures. 'Cultural studies' has effectively laid to rest the assumptions of traditional auteur theory by placing such a high degree of emphasis on decoding of texts, but in so doing the category of the author has not been so much recast as reversed. The culturalist attribution of a high degree of agency to the common folk in the creation of meaning has, despite its many positive dimensions, replaced traditional auteurism with receiver auteurism, in which the individual viewer becomes the Romantic outsider possessed of a unique, consistent vision. The basis for that uniqueness may be sub-cultural affiliation rather than personal genius, but the consistency of that vision, now valorized as a guarantee of coherent identity that is set in opposition to the culture industry, is remarkably similar to traditional auteurist inclinations to pose artist against 'the Industry'. There is no sense of how the dispersal of authority occurs, not just in reference to the intersubjective nature of meaning production, but also intra-subjectively in the sense that the individual viewer's 'vision' is not necessarily unitary either, but rather a matter of selection and alternation among different evaluative criteria. Just as the auteur's vision was supposed to remain distinct, superseding all circumstances as a transcendent vision unto itself, individual viewers will allegedly decode in the same way, regardless of text, because internal unity is fixed by social determinations. In either case, a theory of the unified subject remains firmly in place. More recent postmodern theories of the subject conceive the subject as a kind of nexus or intersection of overlapping but not coterminous identities, providing a crucial third alternative to the simplistic, binary oppositions between unified subject and schizophrenic non-subject.[21] If identity formation is a matter of negotiation of discontinuous positions, evaluative decisions depend on the interfacing of the range of identities within the same individual and the range of evaluative economies within the same culture. The determination of value of a given text for individual readers, viewers, and listeners or, more precisely, the selection of which evaluative economy to employ, is ultimately a matter of *partiality*, both in the sense of personal preference and in the sense of incompleteness.

That the partial rather than totality should become the basis for cultural analysis is a common theme in postmodern theory, so a thorough dis-cussion of its permutations is beyond the scope of this essay, but I should like at least to adumbrate the potential uses of partiality in a pedagogical context, especially in regard to teaching popular culture. In their book entitled *Postmodern Education*, Stanley Aronowitz and Henry Giroux argue for the development of a 'border pedagogy' that would reject the tran-scendentalist, universalist dimensions of Enlightenment thinking that served as the basis for modern educational theory. This border pedagogy would pose alternative forms of knowing based on historical contingency by emphasizing cultural specificity and partiality. 'Partiality becomes, in this case, the basis for recognizing limits built into all discourses and necessitates taking a critical view of authority. Within this discourse, students must engage knowledge as border crossers, as people moving in and out of borders constructed around coordinates of difference and power. Border pedagogy decenters as it remaps'.[22] They make a compelling case for this border pedagogy, demonstrating how what they call 'knowledge from the margins', specifically knowledge of marginalized subcultures, can be used very effectively to contest conservative notions of cultural literacy and canonicity.[23] Radical pedagogy has thus far been very effective in arguing for the value of marginal cultures, but what borders do we have to cross in order to recognize the variability of all cultural value?

Giroux argues convincingly that border between the academy and popular culture must be crossed in order to broaden our understanding of what constitutes cultural practice, but the distinction between the canonic and the popular depends on a number of parallel borders that have been maintained since the inception of the academy. One of the most carefully guarded borders, and one that must indeed be crossed if we are to understand the formation of cultural value in all its complexity, is the idea that the academy is or should be the sole guardian of the criteria used to determine 'genuine' cultural value. Janice Radway poses a number of very useful rhetorical questions to this end:

> Can criticism and pedagogy be organized on another model that might lead to newer, more broadly based forms of social articulation? If we didn't valorize distinction, discrimination, and work so confidently in our day-to-day practice, would consumption, entertainment, and pleasure look so suspect? If they didn't, would we better be able to recognize and to act upon our identity with those who have no qualms about indulging in the polymorphous pleasures of the ear, the gaze, the body? Would a less patriarchal discourse prompt us to raise questions of cultural authority more openly by enabling us to avoid demonizing any and all groups in favor of independent, self-regulating individuals represented most prominently and conveniently by our rational selves?[24]

While Radway's questions point up the viability of other pleasures not accounted for by traditional Enlightenment education, but that nevertheless factor into the formation of our cultural identities, the binary opposition she implies in opposing the hyper-rational to the polymorphous still accepts the dichotomy between high art and mass culture, in which the former is based on discrimination, the latter on undifferentiated appetite.

The other forms of experience Radway refers to here are indeed valid objects of knowledge, but evaluation, discrimination, and distinction are as much a part of popular culture as they are of high art – they may be formulated in other sites, according to different criteria, but the need to make evaluative distinctions appears to be intensifying. The crux of the matter here is that the determination of cultural value is not reducible to one economy or logic. Recognizing the partiality of evaluation, the variability of discrimination, the contingency of taste may inevitably lead to standard criticism of all postmodern theory, in that the emphasis on the local, the micro-narrative is its greatest virtue, but also its greatest limitation because it can never move beyond the local. But a postmodern pedagogy that can circulate through the array of authorities and evaluative criteria should be able to resolve the micro-narrative/master narrative dilemma by delivering a sense of the 'big picture' through an amalgamation of specific pictures of particular sites, yielding an *aggregate* knowledge of cultural evaluation in all its simultaneous discontinuity. A postmodern pedagogy that is dedicated to developing and transmitting aggregate knowledge rather than streamlined totalities also involves a concomitant shift in emphasis regarding the ultimate goals of cultural theory, a shift in priorities that makes a master theory of cultural production a less pressing concern than a pragmatics of instruction that focuses on the ways we are all partial to things.

Notes

1 See Jim Collins, *Uncommon Cultures: Popular Culture and Post-Modernism* (New York: Routledge, 1989).
2 Carlo Ginzburg, *The Cheese and the Worms: The Cosmos of a Sixteenth-Century Miller* (New York: Penguin, 1982).
3 Umberto Eco, 'The multiplication of the media', in *Travels in Hyperreality* (New York: Harcourt Brace Jovanovic, 1986), pp. 145–50.
4 Jim Collins, 'Batman: the movie, narrative: the hyperconscious', in William Uricchio and Roberta Pearson (eds), *The Many Lives of the Batman* (New York: Routledge, 1991).
5 See Jane Feuer, 'The MTM style', in Jane Feuer, Paul Kerr, and Tise Vahimagi (eds) *MTM: Quality Television* (London: BFI, 1984), pp. 197–231; Hilary Radner, 'Quality television and feminine narcissism: the shrew and the covergirl', *Genders*, 8 (Summer 1990), pp. 110–28.
6 John Leland, 'Wayne's World', *Newsweek*, 2 March 1992.
7 John Ellis, 'Broadcast TV narration', in *Visible Fictions* (London: Routledge, 1982), pp. 145–59.
8 Paul DiMaggio, 'Cultural entrepreneurship in nineteenth-century Boston', in Chandra Mukerji and Michael Schudson (eds), *Rethinking Popular Culture* (Berkeley, Calif.: University of California Press, 1991), pp. 374–97.
9 Ibid., pp. 375–6.
10 Timothy Corrigan, *Cinema without Walls* (London: Routledge, 1992), p. 114.
11 Ibid., p. 108.
12 Lance Loud, 'Francis Coppola goes for the jugular in Bram Stoker's Dracula', *Details* (Dec. 1992), pp. 141–2.
13 Ellen Paul, 'This director's wish list doesn't include Hollywood', *New York Times*, 11 Oct. 1992, Sec. 2, pp. 11ff.

14   Janet Maslin, 'Is a cinematic new wave cresting?', *New York Times*, 13 Dec. 1992, Sec. 2, pp. 1ff.

15   Martin Kihn, 'The vision thing', *GQ*, 63: 10 (Oct. 1992), pp. 166–70.

16   Jim Wood, 'A taste of the holidays', *San Francisco Examiner Image*, 22 Nov. 1992, pp. 12–14.

17   Dario Scardapane, 'Winsome Winona', *Vogue* (Nov. 1992), pp. 294ff.

18   Tony Bennett, 'The Bond phenomenon,' *Southern Review*, 16: 2 (July 1983), pp. 195–225.

19   Barbara Herrnstein Smith, 'Contingencies of value,' in Robert von Hallberg (ed.) *Canons* (Chicago: University of Chicago Press, 1983), p. 5.

20   See Mikhail Bakhtin, *The Dialogic Imagination*, ed. Michael Holquist (Austin: University of Texas Press, 1981).

21   See Chantal Mouffe, 'Radical democracy: modern or postmodern?', in Andrew Ross (ed.) *Universal Abandon* (Minneapolis: University of Minnesota Press, 1988), pp. 31–45.

22   Stanley Aronowitz and Henry Giroux, *Postmodern Education* (Minneapolis: University of Minnesota Press, 1991), p. 119.

23   For a related criticism see Ava Preacher Collins, 'Intellectuals, power, and quality television,' *Cultural Studies*, 7:1, forthcoming.

24   Janice Radway, 'Mail-order culture and its critics: the Book of the Month Club, commodification and consumption, and the problem of cultural authority', in Lawrence Grossberg, Cary Nelson, Paula Treichler (eds) *Cultural Studies*, (New York: Routledge, 1992), pp. 526ff.

Part IV

Communication and Public Interests

11

Mass Communication and the Public Interest: Towards Social Theory for Media Structure and Performance

Denis McQuail

Media–Society Relations: Conflict and Change

The belief that public communication and the welfare of society are intimately connected is as old as politics, although the nature of the connection is open to diverse and opposed interpretations and it finds different forms of expression. One manifestation is the body of normative ideas which has accumulated within the field of study of mass communication. It is this which provides the subject matter of this essay.

The divergence of views referred to is partly due to inevitable differences of perspective between rulers and ruled in most societies, but it also derives from the widening range of services which the mass media (the main institutionalized form of public communication) are called upon, or choose, to provide. We can also find a difference of perspective on the proper role of media in society, between those inside the media and those outside. Not surprisingly, beliefs in these matters differ from place to place (usually nation to nation) according to tradition, culture and circumstances. They also change over time, as media and society change, leaving behind once seemingly settled concepts of press–society relationships. Between them, persistent divergences of view and accelerating change lend to this essay a provisional and relative character.

A Bias against Normative Theory

The *status* of normative media theory is very uncertain and contested in the growing field of 'communication science', for other reasons as well. An aspiring new social science is reluctant to become enmeshed in matters of ideology, politics, law or ethics. There has been a tendency to take the media institution and its way of working as an empirical given and proceed from there, leaving normative or ethical matters to other specialists; in this way, the stance of value-neutrality is best upheld. Such theory is also thought to risk being too subjective, politicized, ideological and generally 'unscientific'. A 'liberal' bias in the Anglo-American tradition which has been very influential in defining the field of study of mass media has also tended to delegitimate most principles of would-be media social theory aside from that of freedom of communication defined as lack of legal, government or public interference – essentially the principle enshrined in the First Amendment to the US constitution.[1] It is often thought best to deal with normative issues in a descriptive way under such headings as 'communication policy', 'media law' or 'professional ethics', which allows some distancing from value judgements. The result has been a marginalization of the subject of social theory of the media and a widespread reluctance on the part of 'scientists' to generalize about the proper role of mass media in society – what they *ought* to be doing. Of course, there is no shortage of social critics and polemicists who are ready to step in, but what they generally do is to pass judgement rather than formulate or clarify the standards of judgement. What generally passes for 'mass communication theory' seems to exist, therefore, in a wider theoretical and normative vacuum, which is socially and historically decontextualized, aside from largely unexplicated assumptions about the naturalness of liberal pluralist arrangements in a capitalist economy. This state of affairs is unsatisfactory at a time of considerable change and reconstruction of media institutions, when normative questions need to be faced. This essay is concerned with the expectations from 'society' (the organized political community) concerning the mass media and the implications for how these media should (or could) legitimately be organized and conduct themselves.

The Origins of 'Press Theory': Mid-century Liberal Consensus

The main origins of such theory as we have for public communication (defined by Ferguson as 'those processes of information and cultural exchange between media institutions, products and publics which are socially shared, widely available and communal in character'[2]) lie in the roles frequently attributed to the newspaper press in the rise of 'modern' society (capitalist, industrialized, ruled by democratically elected governments). From the seventeenth century onwards, in Europe and its colonies, the newspaper (or similar print publications) was widely seen as either a tool for political liberation and social/economic progress, or a threat to established orders of power (often both at the same time). This perception of the part played by the press in society has understandably left an enduring stamp on questions of the rights and duties of the press itself and on the attitude of civil authorities in relation to the press.

While the press in most places most of the time was engaged in activities other than advancing and protecting the liberty of citizens, the primacy allotted to its liberating role (and its claims to freedom), especially in the Anglo-American tradition and under the influence of the press itself, obscured as well as downgraded ideas about its many other tasks and effects in society. Hanno Hardt has, nevertheless, reminded us that a century ago much more varied perceptions of the role of the press in society (in this case, Germany) were current.[3] The functions attributed included those of 'binding society together'; giving leadership to the public; helping to establish the 'public sphere'; providing for the exchange of ideas between leaders and masses; meeting needs for information; providing a means for group expression; providing society with a mirror of itself; being an instrument of change; acting as the conscience of society. Some such ideas were picked up in early communication theory, especially those which related to social integration, under the influence of Robert Park and the Chicago School.[4]

When modern communication science was being 'invented', about fifty years ago, the development of press theory was greatly influenced by various accidents of circumstance and history. The 'commercialization' of the press, especially in Britain and the USA, had been made possible by a greatly increased potential for mass production and distribution, financially aided by mass advertising. This development was, in turn, associated by critics of the press with sensationalism, scandal-mongering and falling informational standards. The growth of press empires, often with real or assumed right-wing political leanings, provided another dimension of critique. All around the pre-war world, in Germany, Japan and the Soviet Union, authoritarian regimes were also seen to be using the press and other media for purposes of political exploitation and control. The earlier optimistic and democratic visions conjured by the spread of literacy and the potential abundance of information and culture became clouded.

The press was one of the institutions whose reconstruction after the Second World War owed a certain amount to the Anglo-American liberal

model: Significant in this process was the outcome of the privately
financed but publicly influential 'Commission on the Freedom of the
Press'.[5] When it reported in 1947, the Commission not only reaffirmed
the principle of freedom but added to it the notion of 'social responsibility', which the press was called upon to accept, in recognition of its
essential role in political and social life.[6] The report also specified the
main standards which a responsible press should observe. This meant,
first of all, providing a 'full, truthful, comprehensive and intelligent
account of the day's events in a context which gives them meaning'.
Secondly, the press should serve as a 'forum for the exchange of comment
and criticism' and be 'common carriers of the public expression'. Thirdly,
the press should give a 'representative picture of constituent groups in
society' and also present and clarify the 'goals and values of society'. The
report criticized 'sensationalism' and the mixing of news with editorial
opinion. In general, the report supported the concept of an unbiased,
informative and independent press institution. Social responsibility
should be reached by self- control, not government intervention, although
in the last resort even that might be justifiable.

The message about desirable performance was not so far out of line
with leading professional and editorial aspirations within the American
press, of the kind that were already incorporated in codes of ethics and
editorial prospectuses and the influence of the report may have been more
on press theory than on practice. Certainly it stimulated several statements
of media theory, of which the most remembered and cited was the work of
Fred Siebert and colleagues, under the heading *Four Theories of the Press*.[7]
This book suggested that media systems around the world could be
classified according to four main types of theory. One was that of a
socially responsible press, as described. Of the other three, the first was
labelled 'authoritarian' theory, and emphasized the subjugation of the
press to state control, as in the monarchic system from which early
American colonists had tried to escape or as in contemporary totalitarian
(and some developing country) regimes. Another was the 'libertarian'
theory which referred to the idea that the press should be a 'free marketplace of ideas' in which the best would be recognized and the worst
fail. The unfettered laws of supply and demand would provide a self-
righting mechanism against abuse. Even so, it seemed to the Commission
on the Press that libertarian theory was not fully adequate to the
requirements of a modern democracy. The fourth variant was the 'Soviet'
theory of the media which assigned them a role as collective agitator,
propagandist and educator in the building of communism. However, this
was not seen as likely to appeal to free societies.

Dispensing with 'Theories of the Press'

The 'Four Theories of the Press' have often been invoked as a framework of discussion, sometimes modified by additions or subtractions. The present author added two more – 'development' theory and 'democratic participant', to take account of other realities and other models.[8] Merrill argued that there were really only two fundamental kinds of theory of state–press relations, authoritarian or libertarian.[9] Hachten (1981) added the concepts of 'revolutionary', 'developmental' and 'Western' to two of the original four (communist and authoritarian).[10] Altschull said there were basically three models – 'market', 'Marxist' and 'advancing', corresponding to the division into three 'worlds' – First, Second and Third.[11] In his view, each kind of system, in different ways, ensured that media were responsive to their paymasters and each had somewhat different versions of what might constitute freedom and responsibility. More recently, Picard distinguished, within the category of 'Western' models, a distinctive 'social democratic' version of press theory which, in contrast to 'social responsibility' and 'libertarian' (free market) theory, provides legitimation for public intervention, or even for collective ownership, so as to ensure true independence from vested interests, access and diversity of opinion.[12]

The attempt to formulate consistent 'theories' of the press is, nevertheless, bound to break down, for reasons other than the underlying differences of interest and political ideology present in any society. The frameworks offered have generally derived from a simple and outdated notion of 'the press', which provides (mainly political) news and information and have failed to come to terms with the great diversity of mass media types and services and with changing technology and times. There is, for instance, little of relevance in any of the variants of theory named which might realistically be applied to the cinema, or the music industry, or the video market, or even a good deal of sport, fiction and entertainment on television, thus to much of what the media are doing most of the time. It is unsatisfactory to leave all this entirely outside the scope of social-normative thinking. In fact, these are often the aspects of media performance that have been especially the subject of normative discourse, without much benefit of theory of the kind described.

The four or so 'theories' are also formulated in very general terms and do not describe or underlie any actual media system (except, perhaps, in the case of the Soviet model, which has largely been abandoned). Most national media institutions and practices and most relations between state and media display a mixture of several elements: libertarian, 'responsible' and authoritarian. The framework of theory was formulated largely from an American perspective, taking little note, for example, of the distinctive features of public service broadcasting as found in Western Europe. Despite their uncertain future, these institutions have contributed a great deal to notions of media responsibility and accountability. In most countries, in any case, the media do not constitute any single 'system', with a single purpose or philosophy, but are composed of many separate, overlapping elements with appropriate differences of normative expectation or actual regulation.

Media Change: New Theory for New Times?

Quite apart from the relative decline of print, and the rise of electronic, media there are other changes under way in the media landscape which undermine the validity of any unitary, holistic or even consistent framework of norms which applies to a particular national 'media system'. The media are proliferating in their technical and institutional forms as much as in the volume of content produced and disseminated. This 'abundance', whatever its substance, defies any attempt to grapple with it in a comprehensive way. We can never do more than focus on a small part or sample of the reality of media practice. The more media channels there are, the less easy it is to judge what counts as an indispensable service and what the respective roles of different media in society might be.

An additional dimension of media proliferation has been the phenomenon of 'convergence' between media, referring to the fading of the once clear boundaries between print, broadcast and telecommunication-based media which provided the basis for different kinds and degrees of public regulation.[13] The original technological basis for the distinction is rapidly disappearing as electronic transmission becomes capable of delivering all forms of communication – print, voice, film, text, music. While this seems to open the way to more consistent policies and to a similarity of norms for performance across media, in practice this has not been the outcome, nor is it likely to occur as long as media vary in their communicative functions. Some media forms and activities will, for instance, continue to claim more freedom to operate than others, on grounds of their political, artistic or scientific significance, while others will be subject to limitations for social or cultural reasons.

The media are not only proliferating, but are also becoming rapidly more transnational – in ownership, financing, organization, production, distribution, content, reception and even in regulation. This trend reduces the distinctiveness of media experience in any country and makes the application of a normative framework to one particular *national* media system less relevant. There is, *de facto*, less sovereignty over media operations and perceived problems and solutions extend over an area wider than the nation state. Internationalization also raises new normative issues or highlights older ones: especially matters to do with diversity, access and cultural 'integrity' and 'identity'.[14] The gap between issues of national and of international structure and performance is narrowed, since one overlaps with the other.

A related trend is that of the growing conglomeration and formation of large multi-media enterprises which not only cross national boundaries but also lead to vertical (between stages and factors in the production process) and horizontal (between different types of media and different types of business) concentration.[15] It is common to see lists of the top ten world media businesses, whose possessions and company structures are of bewildering complexity. Worldwide conglomeration leads to fears of loss of creative independence and of cultural diversity. It may make it more difficult for a society to choose and implement a media policy of its own.

Often the trends described, which stem mainly from business and technology, have been accompanied by a loss of any clear national consensus about what to expect from the media in their public role. There has also been a general decline of public regulation of media and an increased role for the market in shaping the media.[16] This is most observable in Europe, West and East, formerly the home of strict regulation of electronic media and careful protection of newspapers. The trend is only partly a result of greater 'commercialization', since it also reflects a general decline in normative certainties and an increase in libertarian thinking. Even so, the challenge to the very foundations of European public service broadcasting systems has led indirectly to more conscious thought about the rationale of public intervention and support.[17] The growth of the media as an industry has also been accompanied by greater professionalization, expanded media education and new, albeit less legalistic, forms of accountability. Taken together these changes imply an increasing centrality of media, and have stimulated thought about the role of media in society, even if the forms of accountability have also changed.

Retaining the Concept of a 'Public Interest'

The proposed framework of normative principles for media structure and performance which follows is still based on the presumption that the media are widely expected to serve the 'public interest' or 'general welfare', whether by design or not. This means, in practice, that mass media are not the same as any other business or service industry, but often carry out some tasks which contribute to the wider and longer term benefit of society as a whole, especially in cultural and political matters, over and above their own ostensible organizational goals.[18] For this reason, the media can legitimately be held accountable for what they do, or fail to do, even against their own free choice. This presumption is sometimes invited by the media themselves when they claim, however selectively or conditionally, to exercise a significant public role and expect some rights or privileges as a result. Although this view has its opponents on libertarian political and economic grounds, it also has good credentials, and in modern times it has been acted on in many democratic societies, sometimes leading to public intervention of various kinds (legal or economic).

An assumption of potential media accountability to society does not entail the view that there is a single known form which the media should take, or that some particular goals or effects are more 'in the public interest' than others. It does not imply, either, that the media can legitimately be obliged to conform to some version of the 'popular will' or to carry out some particular mission, as determined by politicians. It is simply to say that in democratic societies there are likely to be grounds on which an argued claim can be made, by reference to some widely held values and according to specific circumstances, that media should do or should not do some particular thing, for reasons of wider or longer term benefit to the society.[19]

Although the general concept of the public interest has been slippery and controversial, without the possibility of making a guiding assumption of this kind about the public task of the media there is little point in bothering with social-normative principles. Once the assumption is made, however, it becomes useful, even necessary, to have some ordered version, however provisional, of the relevant performance criteria. The problem, however, is to move from the notion of a public interest in general to its interpretation in terms of particular media realities.

In keeping with the provisional character of the public-interest notion, the criteria for assessing the media which are proposed below are not universal. The countries from whose experience they derive (mainly North American and West European) happen to share some characteristics: they are politically pluralistic, predominantly capitalist and often have mixed media institutions. The structure and operation of the media in most of these countries have often been hotly debated and public control of media has been applied or advocated on grounds of the 'public interest', as have deregulation and the further extension of the free market. This has led to wide-ranging inquiry and debate. In general, the limits of action, if not of debate and advocacy, have been set by the status quo of property ownership and the guidelines of electoral democracy. Within these limits, a quite diverse set of expectations from, or on behalf of, 'society' have been articulated in different forms. Expression of these expectations has provided the materials for the framework offered below, even if the wealth of source material cannot possibly be acknowledged. The rather diverse set of principles making up this framework may be the nearest we can get to a body of social theory for the media. In the nature of things, no definitive version can be offered and there is a continuing process of evolution and change at work.

The Main Issues Leading to a Social Theory of the Media

The type of media theory under discussion has, for the reasons given, been actively forged in the course of changes in media and society, often in a context of great political controversy and debate. Principles of media operation have been invoked, developed and changed in these processes. These principles can best be introduced by summarizing the main issues on which controversy has centred, as follows.

1   The earliest challenge to the new industrialized media order of the twentieth century concerned the danger to democracy and freedom contained in the *concentrations of power in the hands of press 'barons'*, especially in the USA and Britain, but later in the British commonwealth and in continental Europe, following the waves of economic concentration of the 1960s. The North American phenomenon of 'one-newspaper cities' and the formation of large 'chains' provoked a fear of *monopolies*, with reduced freedom and independence of news and views.[20] In general, press concentration also threatened the balanced representation of opposed political views, especially where media proprietors belonged, by definition, to the propertied classes. If nothing else, concentration seemed to spell a loss of political choice for the reader, reduced opportunities for access to media channels and, generally, reduced media diversity.[21]

2   A long-standing theme of debate, although a less politically sensitive one, which has surfaced in many discussions of the social role of the press, concerned *the general quality of the news* about events of the day and of the world as supplied to the average citizen, who depends on the media in order to reach informed choices and judgements. The press was often accused of sensationalism and superficiality, of omission and inaccuracy and even falsification and lying. One common theme of criticism has been the failure to cover international news in a comprehensive and balanced way.[22] The UNESCO Media Declaration of 1978 underlined the responsibilities of the press to resist warlike, nationalist and racist propaganda.[23] While television, under public scrutiny, promised higher standards of news journalism, the proliferation of channels has led to new fears of sensationalism and lowered informational quality.

3   Perhaps the oldest and most controversial issue of all is that of *the relationship of media to the security and authority of the state*. The media are

often thought to have a responsibility not to undermine the social order in any fundamental or violent way. While the issue might appear to be settled by constitutional guarantees of press freedom, some reserve powers could usually be invoked by a state in extreme situations, and the modern period has produced numerous examples where the temporary breakdown of civil order, or the actions of terrorists, or the fear of crime, or the pursuit of some minor war, or an issue of government confidentiality, has reawakened controversy about press freedom and its limitation. In general, authorities everywhere have shown a consistent inclination to want to manage the news, even if they stop short of censorship. They usually have more opportunity for control in the case of regulated broadcasting than with the printed press.

4   There has been a continued debate in many countries over another issue of control, concerning *morals, decency and portrayals of sex. crime and violence*. While direct censorship and legal limitations have diminished in proportion to more relaxed moral standards in most societies, there remain limits to media freedom on grounds of the protection of minors from undesirable influences (see, for instance clauses in the European Community Television Directive governing cross-border transmission). This issue has become further complicated by similar claims on behalf of women who may either be portrayed in degrading circumstances or risk becoming the object of media-induced pornographic violence.

5   A long-standing expectation that media should contribute to education, culture and the arts has come increasingly into conflict with actual or perceived imperatives of the media marketplace, under conditions of heightened competition for audiences. The term *'commercialism'* has many meanings, but in one influential view it stands opposed to a number of key social-cultural values. Commercialization has been associated with manipulation, consumerism, lack of integrity, lack of originality and creativity.[24] It is said to lead to homogeneity and neglect of minorities who do not provide profitable audience or advertising markets. In West Europe, a key feature of public policy for electronic media has always been to keep commercial influences under firm control.[25]

6   At different levels of social life, from village to nation-state, a claim has increasingly been heard on behalf of *cultural autonomy* or integrity, which is also threatened by current media industrial trends. In brief, it is argued that media are ceasing to reflect the culture and the circumstances of their intended publics and may undermine the local language and cultural identity, as a result of the transnational flow of content.[26] The problem of cultural dependence is most acute for poorer, less developed countries, but it also arises for other reasons for countries which are under the influence of a foreign media flow (for example Canada and some small European countries).

The outcome of political struggles over these different issues can be found in many laws and regulations. In most European countries, for instance, there are laws limiting press concentration and cross-ownership and in some places subsidy systems exist in order to encourage diversity. There are also widespread regulations applied to television which require political balance and general neutrality of news. Other regulations call for attention to minorities and to different regions and localities. The national cultural integrity may be protected by import quotas, controls on foreign ownership of media and positive measures to stimulate home production of media. The European Community has regulations of a similar kind for its member states. In varying degrees, efforts are made to apply controls on morally or culturally sensitive content.[27] While no two countries are the same and the regulatory climate and regime is often changing, we can argue with conviction that the media operate nearly everywhere within frameworks of normative expectation or actual accountability which imply a set of set of quite familiar principles for dealing with the issues raised.

Principles of Structure and Performance: An Interpretative Overview

It is a risky step to advance from the description of such conflicts and of the regulations and interventions which they have generated to a general statement of the principles involved. There are many reasons for caution. The principles exist in so many specific variants, in such sensitive terrain, often with deep historical and cultural roots, that no single short account can be satisfactory. In addition, the outcome of such an exercise has the appearance of constituting something like a coherent and comprehensive set of standards for the media, when no such thing exists in any society and if it did it would probably be inconsistent with fundamental freedoms. It also tends to advance a claim for more control of the media even if this is not the explicit wish or intention. There is still a lot of disagreement about the standards presented below and they are not all fully consistent with each other. They also apply in different ways to different media phenomena. Some, for instance, relate to structure and organization (such as concentration of ownership) others to actual service and performance (such as diversity as a choice for consumers).

Despite these reservations, it seems worth while trying to summarize the most commonly accepted ideas, if only to provide a starting-point for criticism and discussion.[28] Where relevant, the normative ideas are discussed both in terms of what they call for in respect of media structure and performance and also in terms of the benefits they should deliver for society – the 'public interest', as discussed above. The discussion is structured according to five main headings: freedom; diversity; information quality; social order and solidarity; and cultural order.

Freedom

Overuse has made this term difficult to discuss in any fresh way, but it has an obvious claim to be considered as the basic principle of any theory of public communication, from which other benefits should flow. Nevertheless, there are many versions of freedom and the word does not speak for itself. In the institutional arrangements and in the public-interest discourse referred to above, freedom of communication calls for:

- (very clearly) absence of censorship, licensing or other controls by government so that there is an unhindered right to publish and disseminate news and opinions and no obligation to publish what one does not wish to;
- (also clearly) the equal right and possibility for citizens of free reception of (and access to) news, views, education and culture (this is part of what has come to be known as a 'right to communicate');
- (less clearly) freedom for news media to obtain information from relevant sources;
- (less clearly) absence of concealed influence from media owners or advertisers on news selection and on opinions expressed;
- (desirable, but optional) an active and critical editorial policy in presenting news and opinion and a creative, innovative and independent publishing policy in respect to art and culture.

These prescriptions assume that the only legitimate interests to be served are those of communicators (whoever has some public message to transmit) and of citizens (all those who want to attend). It is the freedom of these two parties which is paramount. There are several potential conflicts and inconsistencies embedded in these requirements. First of all, freedom of public communication can never be absolute, but has to recognize limits sometimes set by the private interests of others or by the higher collective good of a society. Secondly, there is a potential conflict of interest between owners or controllers of media channels and those who might want access to the channels but have no power (or legal right) to secure it (either as senders or as receivers). Thirdly, there may be an imbalance between what communicators want to say and what others want to hear: the freedom of one to send may not coincide with the freedom of another to choose. Finally, it may be necessary for government or public power to intervene to secure some freedoms which are not, in practice, delivered by the unfettered system.

Although no ideal state of communication freedom can be attained, the public benefits expected of freedom in a democratic society are more easy to state and involve less inconsistency.[29] Most important are:

- the systematic public scrutiny of those in power and an adequate supply of information about their activities (this refers to the 'watchdog' role);
- the stimulation of an active and informed democratic system and social life;
- the chance to express ideas, beliefs and views of the world;
- the continued renewal and change of culture and society.

Diversity

This term has been almost equally emptied of clear meaning through overuse, but it stands very close to freedom as a key concept in any discussion of media theory. It presupposes, most generally, that the more the different channels of public communication there are, carrying the maximum variety of (changing) content to the greatest variety of audiences, the better. Put like this, it seems rather empty of any value direction, or prescription about *what* should actually be communicated. Indeed, this is a correct interpretation, since diversity, like freedom, is neutral with regard to content. It is a valuation only of variety,choice and change in themselves. Nevertheless, diversity applied to media systems and content does become more specific in its normative requirements and the following are the main elements:

- Media should *reflect* in their structure and content the various social, economic and cultural realities of the societies (and communities) in which they operate in a more or less proportional way.
- Media should offer more or less equal chances of *access* to the voices of various social and cultural minorities which make up a society.
- Media should serve as a *forum* for different interests and points of view in a society or community.
- Media should offer relevant *choices* of content at one point in time and also *variety* over time of a kind which corresponds to the needs and interests of their audiences.

Again, we can point to some inconsistencies and problems in these requirements. The degree of diversity that is possible is limited by media channel capacity and by editorial selections which have to be made. The more that media are *proportionally* reflective of society, the more likely it is that small minorities will be effectively excluded from mass media, since a small proportion of access will be divided between many claimants. Similarly, catering properly for dominant and consistent expectations and tastes in mass media limits the chance to offer a very wide choice or much change. However, the full range of many different media in a society can help to compensate for deficiencies of 'traditional' *mass* media.

While diversity is sometimes regarded as an end in itself, it is often perceived to result in other benefits. These include:

● opening the way for social and cultural change, especially where it takes the form of giving access to new, weak or marginal voices;
● providing a check on the misuse of freedom (for example where the free market leads to concentration of ownership);
● opening the opportunity for minorities to maintain their separate existence in a larger society;
● limiting social conflicts by increasing the chances of understanding between potentially opposed groups and interests;
● adding generally to the richness and variety of cultural and social life.

Information quality

While the expectation that media should provide information of reasonable quality has more a practical than a philosophical or normative foundation, it is hardly less important in modern thinking about media standards than the principles of freedom or diversity. Freedom and diversity do not necessarily produce more informative public communication. Informational requirements have a dual origin – relating to the desirability of an informed society and a skilled workforce on the one hand and, on the other, of a body of citizens who are in a position to participate in the choice of leaders and in democratic decision-making.[30] Some of the expected benefits are self- evident, while others are subsumed under freedom and diversity requirements. The main 'information quality' standards which are encountered in policy, prescriptions and codes of practice can be formulated as follows.

● Media (especially press and broadcasting) should provide a *full* supply of relevant news and background information about events in the society and the world around.
● Information should be objective in the sense of being accurate, honest, true to reality, reliable, separating fact from opinion.
● Information should be balanced and fair (impartial) reporting alternative perspectives in a non-sensational, unbiased, way.

Several potential difficulties are embedded in these norms, especially because of uncertainty about what constitutes an adequate or relevant supply of information and about the very nature of 'objectivity'.[31] More serious are the possible inconsistencies with claims of media freedom (which permits error) and diversity (which emphasizes the multiplicity of reality). We can also note that such criteria are more appropriate to the totality of media information in a society, rather than to any particular channel or topic.

Social order and solidarity

The issues of structure and performance which belong under this heading are those which relate to the integration and harmony of society, as viewed from different perspectives. On the one hand, there is a rather consistent tendency on the part of those in authority to look to public communication media for at least tacit support in the task of maintaining order. On the other hand, pluralistic societies cannot be conceived as having a single dominant order which has to be maintained and mass media have mixed and divided responsibilities, especially with reference to alternative social groups and subcultures and to the expression of the conflicts and inequalities of most societies. Problems also arise over how far the media can go in their support for potential subversion (as it may seem from the 'the top'). The relevant principles concerning the media are mixed and scarcely mutually compatible, but can be expressed in something like the following way.

- In respect of the relevant public which they serve (at national, local level, or as defined by group and interest), the media should provide channels of inter-communication and support.
- The media may contribute to social integration by paying concerned attention to socially disadvantaged or injured individuals and groups.
- The media should not undermine the forces of law and order by encouraging or symbolically rewarding crime or social disorder.
- In matters of national security (war, threat of war, foreign subversion, terrorism) the freedom of action of the media should be restrained by considerations of national interest.
- On questions of morals, decency and taste (especially in matters of the portrayal of sex, violence and use of language), the media should in some degree observe the reigning norms of what is broadly publicly acceptable and avoid causing grave public offence to many.

It is quite clear that the application of all the above prescriptions and proscriptions is very much subject to local and temporal definition, varying according to details of the case and point of view. The norms apply very differently to different kinds of media. Even so, it does appear that some normative controls in this area, formal or informal, are inescapable.

Cultural order

Although in many countries as well as in international fora there have been heated discussions about the possible cultural responsibilities of mass media, there is little agreement and less action in relation to such matters. Even so, although the norms involved are not usually very compelling and are selectively applied, there is some consistency about the principles involved, where cultural policies are urged on the media. The main elements are as follows:

- Media content should reflect and express the language and contemporary culture (artifacts and way of life) of the people whom they serve (nationally, regionally, locally).
- Some priority should be given to the educational role of the media and to the expression and continuity of the best in the cultural heritage of a country.
- Media should encourage cultural creativity and originality and the production of work of high quality (according to aesthetic, moral, intellectual, professional criteria).

The very uneven application of these normative principles in any form of control reflects both the primacy of freedom and also the strength of commercial imperatives. Principles of cultural performance are likely to be advanced as desirable, but not enforceable. There is rarely sufficient consensus on what criteria of cultural quality mean. Almost the only demonstrable criterion is that relating to cultural *relevance* (to the audience, especially in respect of localism and language). The more that media (for instance public broadcasting institutions) are subjected to policy in the interests of the public as a whole, the more likely that cultural criteria will be invoked as a guide to performance. Sometimes, national and economic self- interest can lead to support for some of the cultural principles described.

The Current Status and Range of Application of Normative Theory

Aside from the shrinking sector of public broadcasting, most media operate on a day-to-day basis with little conscious regard for the norms described above. The desirable goals are reached or not, the evils avoided or not, according to the workings of particular media market circumstances. These include the pulls and pushes of organizational circumstance; professional ethics; and the creative goals and routine decisions of those who work in the media. There are more immediate rules of law, ethics or good practice which are more likely to preoccupy people in the media on a day-to-day basis.[32] Only occasionally is it necessary for those within or outside the media to reflect systematically on the application of one or more of the principles outlined. Only rarely, if ever, would consideration be given to the whole range of ideas which has been summarized.

The set of principles outlined is simply one attempt to describe a universe of discourse which is available within the 'Western', liberal pluralist tradition as it has developed during the last forty years or so. It cannot be said to represent a consensus on what the media should or should not do 'in the public interest' (as defined above), although an attempt has been made to avoid extreme or controversial propositions. What may well be controversial is the degree to which a given principle is relevant to a given situation or medium. In any case, the freedom principle provides a let-out from most obligations, short of extreme antisocial forms of publication. The application of any given principle has also to be established in a relevant political forum, before it can have any weight or consequence.

The changes in the media described earlier have not yet fundamentally changed the *content* of the norms described but they have affected their relative force and the priorities amongst them. The increasing number of alternative channels of public communication has, in particular, reduced the need for seemingly 'dominant' media (such as the national newspaper press or broadcast television) to fulfil some perceived public role. There is a diminished fear of media monopoly, despite concentration tendencies, because the potential for competition is greater. More media channels appear to promise more diversity, although the quality of that diversity is far from assured.

Several of the norms outlined have come to be invoked most recently in debates about the future of public broadcasting and about the standards to be applied in television or radio operating licences. Some of the norms are also still relevant to judging whether press concentration, or cross-media ownership, works against the public interest. There is also continued pressure for media with apparent influence in cultural, social and political matters to show a degree of self-regulation. Some of the standards discussed are relevant to this matter.

We can expect that as media institutions are reshaped in former Communist states of Central and Eastern Europe, models will be sought in

Western Europe, perhaps even some coherent media 'philosophy' to
replace one that has been discarded. No doubt some will find this in an
unfettered libertarianism, which promises to open windows and dispose
of the trappings of paternalism and control. Others will find continued
value in a modified version of the former doctrines of social(ist) responsibility. The universe of ideas described above offers something to both
parties, although it tends to over-represent the responsibilities of mass
media and implicitly diminish the libertarian viewpoint. No general
recommendation can be made. It will be up to the people and to those
who frame the new institutions to decide what they want, what is viable
and what can be afforded. Social theory of the media does not have to be
subordinate to commerce, but it does have to take account of economic
reality.

Notes

1 See e.g. J. Lichtenberg (ed.), *Democracy and the Mass Media* (Cambridge:
   Cambridge University Press, 1990).
2 M. Ferguson, *Public Communication: The New Imperatives* (London/Newbury
   Park, Calif.: Sage, 1990), p. ix.
3 H. Hardt, *Social Theories of the Press* (Beverly Hills, Calif./London: Sage,
   1979).
4 e.g. R. H. Turner (ed.), *On Social Control and Collective Behavior* (Chicago:
   University of Chicago Press, 1967); M. Janowitz, *The Community Press in an
   Urban Setting* (Glencoe, Ill.: Free Press, 1952).
5 R. Hutchins, *A Free and Responsible Press: Commission on Freedom of the Press*
   (Chicago: University of Chicago Presss, 1947).
6 M. A. Blanchard, *The Hutchins Commission, the Press and the Responsibility
   Concept,* Journalism Monographs, 49 (1977).
7 F. S. Siebert, T. Paterson and W. Schramm, *Four Theories of the Press*
   (Urbana: University of Illinois Press, 1956).
8 D. McQuail, *Mass Communication Theory* (London: Sage, 1983).
9 J. Merrill, *The Imperatives of Freedom* (New York: Hastings House, 1971).
10 W. A. Hachten, *The World News Prism: Changing Media, Clashing Ideologies*
   (Ames: Iowa State University Press, 1981).
11 J. H. Altschull, *Agents of Power.* (New York: Longman, 1984).
12 R. G. Picard, *The Press and the Decline of Democracy: The Democratic Socialist
   Response in Public Policy* (Westport, Conn.: Greenwood Press, 1985).
13 I. de Sola Pool, *Technologies of Freedom* (Cambridge, Mass.: Belknap Press,
   1984).
14 J. Tomlinson, *Cultural Imperialism* (London: Pinter, 1991).
15 G. Murdock, 'Redrawing the map of the communication industries', in M.
   Ferguson (ed.), *Public Communication: The New Imperatives* (London: Sage,
   1990), pp. 1–15.

16 D. McQuail and K. Siune (eds), *New Media Politics* (London: Sage, 1986); K. Siune and W. Truetzschler (eds), *Dynamics of Media Politics* (London: Sage, 1992).
17 See J. G. Blumler (ed.), *Television and the Public Interest* (London: Sage, 1992).
18 W. H. Melody, 'Communication policy in the global information economy', in M. Ferguson (ed.), *Public Communication: The New Imperatives* (London: Sage, 1990), pp. 16–39.
19 D. Mcquail, *Media Performance* (London: Sage, 1992).
20 B. H. Bagdikian, *The Media Monopoly*, 2nd edn (Boston: Beacon Press, 1988).
21 R. G. Picard, M. McCombs, J. P. Winter and S. Lacy (eds), *Press Concentration and Monopoly* (Norwood, NJ: Ablex, 1988).
22 U. Kivikuru and T. Varis (eds), *Approaches to International Communication* (Helsinki: Finnish Unesco Commission, 1985).
23 K. Nordenstreng, *The Mass Media Declaration of UNESCO* (Norwood, NJ: Ablex, 1984).
24 J. G. Blumler, 'The new television market place: imperatives; implications; issues', in J. Curran and M. Gurevitch (eds), *Mass Media and Society* (London: Edward Arnold, 1991), pp. 194–215; Blumler, *Television and the Public Interest*.
25 McQuail and Siune, *New Media Politics*.
26 P. Sepstrup, 'Research into international television flows', European Journal of Communication, 4 (1989), pp. 393–408; C. W. Thomsen (ed.), *Cultural Transfer or Electronic Imperialism* (Heidelberg: Carl Winter Universitätsverlag, 1989).
27 Blumler, *Television and the Public Interest*.
28 For a fuller treatment, see McQuail, *Media Performance*.
29 See e.g. J. Curran, 'Mass media and democracy: a reappraisal', in J. Curran and M. Gurevitch (eds), *Mass Media and Society* (London: Edward Arnold, 1991), pp. 82–117.
30 J. Keane, *The Media and Democracy* (Cambridge: Polity Press, 1991).
31 J. Westerstahl, 'Objective news reporting', *Communication Reseach*, 10 (1983), pp. 403–24; R. A. Hackett, 'Decline of a paradigm? Bias and objectivity in news media studies', *Critical Studies in Mass Communication*, 1 (1984), pp. 229–59.
32 P. Meyer, *Ethical Journalism* (New York/London: Longman, 1987).

12

Electronic Networks, Social Relations and the Changing Structure of Knowledge

William Melody

The conditions of freedom of thought are in danger of being destroyed by science, technology, and the mechanization of knowledge.

Harold Inns, *The Bias of Communication*

Introduction

In recent times the subject of the information society has captured the imagination not only of technologists and social scientists, but also the lay public. Seldom in our history has a subject attracted such attention and generated such volumes of literature, yet yielded so little critical insight and understanding of its real long-term implications. The combination of wonderment about the unfolding technical possibilities and aggressive promotion by the sellers of equipment and services has created an impression that the new communication and information technologies and the services they can provide (CITS; that is, the application of microelectronics to computing and telecommunication functions) have a magical quality. One is led to believe that a healthy injection of CITS will solve a firm's, a society's and the world's economic, social and political problems. People are invited to submit themselves to the authority of these technologies.

Yet, if history has taught us anything it is that new technologies will not solve old social problems. They may significantly change power relations in society in favour of those who control and benefit from the new technologies. But there is no magic embodied in new technologies that will suddenly transform the nature of social and institutional relations in beneficial ways. In fact, new problems usually are created. This essay raises some empirically based conceptual issues pointing towards a better understanding of how CITS are being applied to change communication relations in society and the structure of what we call knowledge.

In the grander scheme of things, we are all involved in a massive social experiment with CITS. The laboratory is most of the developed countries. The main decisions to adopt these technologies already have been taken and are in the process of being implemented. Newly industrializing and developing countries are being urged to participate by the transnational corporations and their host countries that would benefit from the increased sales of equipment and services.[1] Nevertheless, there are substantial areas of policy discretion relating to the design, speed and direction of implementation of these technologies, as well as the economic, social and cultural considerations that are reflected in policy decisions.

The Communication Core of Institutions

The functioning of any society depends upon information, and the efficient and effective communication of it among society's members. Information is generally interpreted as a 'stock' concept, a store of knowledge and values. Communication is a 'flow' concept, reflecting the process of transmission and exchange of knowledge and values, which itself creates information influencing knowledge and values. 'Information' and 'communication' provide different analytical perspectives on essentially the same phenomena. An examination of the information characteristics of any society must focus on its communication characteristics. New communication networks are often the driving force behind the generation of vast quantities of information.

In the broadest sense, the social, cultural, political and economic institutions in any society are defined in terms of the characteristics of the shared information within and among those institutions.[2] In the narrower economic sense, it has been recognized generally that the most important resource affecting the economic efficiency of any economy, industry, production process or household is information and its effective communication.[3] Now that entire industries and major sectors of technologically advanced economies are devoted to information – the search for it, the creation of it, the manufacture, storage, classification, summarization, selection, editing, interpretation, hoarding, purchase, sale, and broadcast of it – the economic and social characteristics of information have been recognized as an area in which precious little is known.

Yet it is apparent that the characteristics of information define the state of knowledge that underlies all economic and social systems. They affect the nature of economic markets and the structure of industry. They affect the internal structure of organizations ranging from corporations to government agencies, political parties, universities, labour unions, libraries and volunteer groups. They affect the formation of social and cultural networks; the nature of work and leisure; the role and definition of education; the structure, content and effective control of the mass media; and the information environment through which public opinion is formed.

The character of all institutions is significantly influenced by the state of information. Institutions are created from the development of a need or desire to share information, thereby cultivating patterns of interaction, that is, communication or information exchange. Institutions become structured in particular ways to achieve desired internal and external information flows. The institutional structure changes when, for whatever reason, the communication processes and information flows are changed. Institutions die when the incentive or the ability to maintain the information flows and communication links ceases. Institutions can be described according to their informational characteristics, and one way to study institutional change is to focus directly upon an institution's changing information and communication structure.

Equally significant is the fact that institutions also generate information for the external environment that is employed by organizations and individuals for decision making. For any particular institutional structure in society, there will be an associated information and communication structure that will influence how that society functions. Some institutional structures will provide stronger incentives for the creation and diffusion of information than others. Moreover, the type and quality of information is likely to change as a result of changes in institutional structure. If institutional change is desired, it may be necessary to change the information structure as a prerequisite to, or as an essential aspect of, effective institutional change.

The importance of information flows and communication patterns to the establishment and maintenance of particular institutions has been well understood since earliest times. Trade routes and communication links were deliberately designed to maintain centres of power and to overcome international comparative disadvantages. Britain still benefits substantially from its historically established communication links with its former colonies, long after the empire's formal demise. Universal telephone service was adopted as a policy objective in many countries to encourage economic and social interaction within the country as a way of promoting national unity. The European Community is attempting to foster a new

European identity by promoting increased communication and information exchange as a basis for stimulating increased trade among its member countries and completing the single European market.

Essentially the information and communication sector of a technologically advanced society consists of: microelectronics; computer hardware, software and services; telecommunication equipment and services; the mass media and a plethora of new database and information services; as well as the more traditional forms of information and communication such as libraries, publishing and postal service. Stimulated by rapid and continuing technological change, this sector has experienced a high rate of economic growth in recent years. Moreover, the direct economic effects are compounded by the fact that major parts of this sector provide important infrastructure services or enabling functions that affect the operation and efficiency of almost all other industries, including manufacturing and agriculture, as well as government agencies and most other institutions.

Many analysts believe that information gathering, processing, storage and transmission over efficient telecommunication networks will provide the foundation upon which technologically advanced nations will close the twentieth century as so-called information societies, that is, societies that have become dependent upon complex electronic information and communication networks and which allocate a major portion of their resources to information and communication activities.[4]

Innis, McLuhan and Smythe

Leading scholars who have examined the implications of communication technologies for society include Harold Innis, Marshall McLuhan and Dallas Smythe.[5] Innis's work grew out of his study of the economic and political history of Canada, and how this was influenced significantly by the communication (primarily transport and trade) relations between Canada and Europe, Canada and the US, and within Canada.[6] This analytical perspective later was applied to the study of the development of ancient and medieval societies to show relations between changing systems of communication, changing structures of institutions in society, changing forms of political and social power, and changing priorities and values of how knowledge was defined and structured. Innis saw knowledge not simply as an abstract process of accumulation, but more like a kaleidoscope that changed with changing underlying technological and institutional arrangements. Societies employing oral discourse as the technology of communication were different from those based upon writing, print, or the electronic media. The type of information that was valued, researched, taught, learned and given a high priority on the agenda of society was affected significantly by the technology of communication. The definition and structure of what was regarded as knowledge in different societies changed, and the changes were associated with changes in the dominant communication technologies.

Innis died in 1952 and did not pursue his analysis of electronic media in any depth. But a junior colleague at the University of Toronto did – Marshall McLuhan. Whereas Innis approached his study of communication technology from a long-term systemic, societal perspective, McLuhan focused on the particular interrelation between the individual and the communication technology. McLuhan saw television, for example, as a sensory medium likely to stimulate involvement and imagination in a common shared experience, and was to be contrasted to the print media with its linear, sequential logic and its bias toward rationalism and individualism. The medium was the message because it determined the nature of personal communication.

There is little overlap in the work of Innis and McLuhan that would enable one to apply direct comparative analysis of their respective examinations of similar issues. Innis's unit of analysis was societies and civilizations; McLuhan's was the individual. But they reached quite different general conclusions. McLuhan saw the new communication technologies as 'extensions of man', tools for overcoming all kinds of problems (for example, by turning the world into a 'global village'). He never seriously addressed the implications for society's economic, political, social and culture institutions. For McLuhan, it was primarily a private affair between the individual and the communication medium.

Innis, on the other hand, saw the aggregate impact of the new communication technologies as providing solutions to some inherited problems, but also creating many serious new problems at the same time. He observed more than 40 years ago:

> We can perhaps assume that the use of a medium of communication over a long period will to some extent determine the character of knowledge to be communicated and suggest that its persuasive influence will eventually create a civilization in which life and flexibility will become exceedingly difficult to maintain and that the advantages of a new medium will become such as to lead to the emergence of a new civilization.[7]

Applications of new communication technologies have the potential to change society in quite fundamental ways. Significant alterations of information flows and patterns of communication can bring significant changes in economic, political, social, and cultural relations. Innis was concerned that modern communication technologies tended to depersonalize human intercourse and to impose ever more rigid constraints upon the creativity of human thinking.

Unlike Innis and Mcluhan, Dallas Smythe actually undertook detailed examinations of the new electronic communication technologies, including both television and telecommunication. The focal point for his research was neither the individual nor civilizations, but the institutions directly involved in introducing and managing the technologies, that is, the corporations and government agencies. He addressed the specific conditions under which the technologies were developed and applied, and their implications for different groups in society. His approach was much less that of detached observation of what new technologies tend to stimulate, promote, or make theoretically possible, than an analysis of how and why those who implement new technologies make the key policy decisions, justify those decisions and monitor the consequences.

Smythe exposed the contradictory character of new technologies and the tendency of those in power to expect people to magically adapt to new technologies rather than designing technologies to serve the real needs of people. He worked to develop the institutional conditions necessary to place 'needs before tools', as he frequently observed.[8]

Smythe's work on the mass media has certain direct parallels with that of Innis. His mass media research documented the power of the mass media to restrict independent thinking, channel public opinion and assemble viewing and listening audiences for advertisers, and its implications for consumer choice, free speech, democracy and human rights. He concluded that communication can and should be a force for liberating human creativity, not for regimenting it; but this would happen only if new technologies were applied to promote institutional changes that would accommodate increased public participation in social affairs. With a background understanding of Innis's contributions on communication technologies and the changing structure of societies, it is possible that informed policy development within a framework of Smythe's institutional analysis may provide a foundation for institutional change that will permit some of McLuhan's speculations to be tested.

Some Characteristics of Information

In reality, of course, all societies have been information societies. The most significant change between technologically advanced society and the oral tradition of the Greek city-state – still practised by some native cultures today – is not in the role of information in society, but in the way that information processes are institutionalized. The dominant form of information creation and exchange has shifted from oral discourse flowing outside the bounds of formal market arrangements to the establishment of information generating, storage and transmission institutions, the commodification of information and its exchange through markets. Perhaps the most significant change is not the volume of information, but the structure, the distribution, the institutions, and the dependence.

The information society of the twenty-first century will be far from a uniform, homogeneous condition. Moreover, the optimal rate of technological change is not necessarily the fastest, as many governments and corporations have learned painfully in recent years. The hard realities of the market cannot be ignored, but the particular values and priorities of individual societies need not be ignored.

Information is often regarded as something equivalent to a natural resource: a motherlode of objective, unbiased facts to be sought out by diligent search. For example, this view underlies such concepts as 'freedom of the press' in Western democracies. Although the press has been recognized as having biases of its own that influence the direction of its search, the information that is found, and how it is interpreted, there is a classification of information that can be analysed usefully as having the characteristics of a primary resource.

The stock of knowledge in society at any one time, that is, the skills and education of the populace, the detailed factual information relating to such things as the working of production processes, the inter-relationships and interdependencies of different sectors of the economy, etc., collectively represent a primary resource of society. The value of this stock of knowledge to society depends upon how pervasively it is spread throughout society, and upon the institutions for maintaining, replenishing and expanding the stock of knowledge, that is, its education and training system, and research generating new knowledge. Economic and social benefits come in the form of improved decision-making of all kinds throughout the economy.

Once information has been generated, the cost of replicating it is very much lower than the cost of generating it in the initial instance. The consumption of information by one user does not destroy it, as occurs with almost all other resources and products. The information remains to be consumed by others, the only additional costs being those associated with bringing the same information and additional consumers of it together under conditions where it can be consumed, that is, learned. And once a given level of penetration is reached, a multiplier effect comes into play with many types of information, as the information is spread throughout society by informal communication processes outside the formal processes of learning and training. Hence, although the costs of adding to the stock of knowledge may be very great, there are generally significant economies in spreading that information throughout society, and to other societies if the incentive exists to do so. The implications of this economic characteristic of relatively low cost replication of information can be extremely beneficial under some circumstances such as the spreading of knowledge throughout society, for example, information about AIDS. But it can create special problems and difficulties under other circumstances, for example, for a smaller society attempting to protect its culture from being engulfed by the spread of information and values from a dominant neighbour.

In the new age of information, much of the new information that is generated has its greatest economic value in scarcity rather than in widespread distribution. For example, information that has become important as a resource input to industrial, commercial and professional activities is specialized information sought to provide 'inside' or superior knowledge of the behaviour of consumers, suppliers, competitors, government decision-makers, etc. In essence, in imperfect economic markets, this inside information for private consumption strengthens the negotiation or market power position of the organizations or individuals that have access to it. Such information may or may not be costly to obtain, but its economic value clearly lies in its scarcity, that is, in the monopoly of information. Once such information becomes generally known to all interested parties, its economic value dissipates drastically.[9]

Specialized information services for the private consumption of a restricted clientele are springing up almost daily. They range from special research studies of the details of international markets for transnational corporations to confidential assessments of the negotiating strength of a specific customer, competitor, trade union, or government. They include remote sensing satellite data identifying the detailed swimming patterns of schools of fish, and pinpointing the location of mineral resources and the progress of crop growth in distant countries.

Many governments already have taken steps to attempt to restrain the march of information markets into the details of people's personal lives and to regulate the conditions of access to certain kinds of data banks, for example, credit, medical and tax files.[10] The pursuit, sale and use of information in accordance with the incentives of the marketplace clearly cannot be totally unrestricted. But the production characteristics of (1) the relatively high costs of establishing most database services; and (2) the relatively low costs of extending the market for services already created; provide a powerful tendency toward centralization and monopoly on an international basis. Thus, competitive forces in many information markets are likely to be rather weak. This, in turn can be expected to raise important issues of national and international government policy.[11]

Towards an Information Economy?

The rapid rise of information markets is made possible primarily by the interaction of advances in computer and telecommunication technologies. Advances in the computer industry have pushed back the intensive limit of the potential information market by reducing the costs of generating more and more kinds of data. Advances in telecommunication have pushed back the extensive geographical limit to encompass national and global markets. However, it is important to distinguish the economic implications of the new technology facility systems that provide the infrastructure within which information is generated and processed, and over which it travels, that is, the hardware, and the information services themselves, that is, the information content that is provided over the facility systems.

What are the implications of markets without geographical limits, and an enormous expansion of information in the so-called information economy? The conventional economic theory of markets would suggest that more information and better communication can only improve the functional efficiency of markets. It should lead to expanded competition and an increased role for the market in allocating resources in society. More considered analysis, with the experience of the last two decades, raises questions about this oversimplified analysis. In particular, it raises the possibility that improved information and communication networks may be fundamentally altering the structure of markets so that, at least in many instances, they function less efficiently and play a less significant role in allocating resources.

With respect to knowledge and understanding, it is not at all clear that the new CITS have led to an improved condition. Studies of transnational corporations have shown that those corporations with the most sophisticated and complex decision-making systems employing enormous volumes of information make no better decisions than firms making similar decisions with less information. Studies have shown that stockbrokers, with access to many more sources of information for their stock purchase and sale decisions, have made no better decisions in the stock market than individuals who have not had access to modern sophisticated information sources. In light of the great expansion of information, most corporations have reduced their planning horizons because their ability to forecast the future has substantially declined, despite all of this additional information. With substantially improved statistical data and descriptive information about the workings of the economy, our understanding of the economic system is substantially poorer than it was in the 1950s. Are the new information and communication technologies introducing more complexity, instability and uncertainty into our economic and social systems than the increased information will permit us to understand and control?[12]

Moreover, the benefits of these technologies are not likely to be distributed uniformly across markets. Certain segments of society are likely to be made poorer in both absolute and relative terms. The structure of markets in many industries may be less competitive, not more. These new technologies permit many markets to be extended to the international and global level. But it is the largest national and transnational corporations and government agencies that have the greatest need for, and the ability to take full advantage of, these new opportunities. For them the geographic boundaries of markets are extended globally, and their ability to administer and control global markets efficiently and effectively from a central point is enhanced. These changes have been a significant factor in stimulating the wave of mergers and takeovers involving the largest transnational corporations in recent years. The diseconomies of size and scope provided by increasing administrative costs and reduced effectiveness of information processing and communication in very large organizations can be reduced substantially by the application of information and communication technologies.

The manner in which these technological developments are being implemented creates possibilities for creating significant barriers to entry for all but the largest firms, thereby accelerating tendencies toward concentration. In fact, in many industries smaller firms are likely to find themselves disadvantaged because of the new technological developments. For example, telecommunication systems in many countries are being redesigned to meet the technically sophisticated digital data requirements of high-volume, multiple-purpose, global users, that is, the integrated services digital network, or ISDN. For traditional, simpler communication requirements, such as basic telephone services, the upgraded system will serve quite well, but at substantially increased cost to smaller users. Unless there is public policy intervention, the telecommunication option available to small, localized, and even regionalized businesses are not likely to reflect their unique needs. Rather, their range of choice among services and prices on the common telecommunication network is likely to be dictated by the global needs of the largest firms and government agencies. In similar fashion, the terms and conditions for access to many new data banks provide substantial benefit to high-volume transnational corporations, but prohibitive cost to small domestic companies, particularly in developing countries.

In most major industries the new competition that has developed from the globalization of markets is intensified oligopolistic rivalry among transnational corporations. The firms that can now leap across market boundaries are already dominant firms in their respective product/service and geographical markets. Their entry has a major impact on the structure of the supply side of the market just entered, which stimulates a major strategic response from the established dominant firm(s). This is not dynamic competition responding to the invisible hand of market forces as assumed in economic theory, but rather a type of medieval market jousting, an oligopolistic rivalry for the control of market territory. The rivalry is directed to obtaining a long-run position of market entrenchment and dominance in particular foreign national submarkets.

In attempting to achieve these long-term dominant market positions, the transnational corporations are often assisted by governments of their respective host countries. Many governments adopt policies and positions that assist their respective transnational corporations, and even participate in international marketing. Thus the oligopolistic rivalry among transnational corporations involves a strong element of nationalism and direct government involvement on both the demand and supply sides of the market exchange.

Taken collectively, these changes introduce new elements of risk and uncertainty into the economic system. But the greater the geographical coverage of a transnational corporation, the more risk and uncertainty can be diversified, although not for the particular production locations dependent on them. Indeed, major structural imbalances in regional economic development have been documented in several countries.

Historically, the current revolution in telecommunication technology can be compared in certain respects with the effect of the introduction of the telegraph upon the structure of markets in the last century. In a detailed study of these developments in the United States, Richard DuBoff concluded: 'the telegraph improved the functioning of markets and enhanced competition, but it simultaneously strengthened forces making for monopolization. Larger scale business operations, secrecy and control, and spatial concentration were all increased as a result of telegraphic communications.' He added that 'increasing market size helped "empire builders" widen initial advantages which at first may have been modest.'[13]

It is apparent that decision-making in our society at all levels – governmental, corporate and individual – is becoming increasingly dependent on highly complex information and communication systems. The information acquires value because the decision-making systems in society are being structured so as to be dependent upon highly specialized information delivered over complex, high-technology networks. As the dependence becomes greater, the economic value of the information becomes greater because the opportunity cost for following any alternative path becomes greater.

From Information Society to Information Overload

For centuries the written record of the most important information in society was safeguarded by monks. Societies, at least as judged in today's terms, were characterized by information scarcity. The demand for information greatly exceeded its supply. Both the spreading of established information to wider sectors of society and the accumulation of new information tended to enhance knowledge and understanding. This might be characterized as the acquisitive phase of information accumulation.

Because demand far outran supply, and the costs of replication were extremely high, books were enormously valuable. This information was guarded carefully. The most valuable books were chained to an immovable object. But the monks did much more than physically guard the information. They controlled access to it by making decisions with respect to who could read what books for how long, thereby imposing an information class system upon society. But perhaps even more significant was the fact that they taught selected people how to read, and they read the books to other selected groups that did not know how to read. Even for those who could read, the monks provided the appropriate contextual interpretation of the information. In sum, they exercised a high degree of monopoly of knowledge because of their unique position as gatekeepers to the information. The monks were information professionals who exercised an extremely important and powerful role in their societies.

In the course of my lifetime, I have experienced the transition from a condition of information scarcity to one of information surplus. It used to be that professional people were expected to be able to review personally all of the important information in their field and make their own judgements with respect to relevance and significance. But now that is not possible. As if the explosion in books, journals, newsletters and related print material were not enough, now this is being supplemented by a rapidly growing body of electronic information sources that may ultimately dwarf the information available in print. The sheer volume of supply of information vastly exceeds that which can be individually assessed.

But this information is merely the raw material – some people would say data – for the creation of useful information products and services. If this raw material is to be useful, it must be structured and processed to meet particular objectives. Indeed, without a compass to guide one through this sea of incomprehensible decontextualized information, one can easily drown in a flood of incomprehension. In quantitative terms, too much information may be worse than too little because it is more likely to create confusion and suspend independent thought.

One sees evidence of this problem in a variety of ways. The large consulting firms, which advise corporations and governments with respect to major decisions, used to define their role as bringing more information to bear on decisions so that they were enriched, that is, 'more informed'. However, the consultants do not justify their role in these terms any more. Now they are in the information destruction business. They justify their role by advising managers as to the 90 per cent of the available information that can he destroyed or ignored because it is not the key information for the decisions to be taken. Now the consultants point to the relevant information and protect decision-makers from the wave of unhelpful information that threatens to engulf them.

Moreover, studies of corporate decisions have been made comparing decisions taken by corporations that employ all of the latest information technology and all available databases with decisions taken by other firms that are not making full use of the information technologies and available databases; they have not been able to demonstrate that the resulting decisions are any better. In fact, a significant characteristic of decision-making in the information society is that as more information has become available to guide decision-makers, the planning horizon for decisions has been shortened because of a growing inability to make good forecasts. The dynamic character of information technology has created an environment in which the additional information has not been adequate to overcome the increased uncertainty created.

It is clear that data and raw information require context and meaning to be understood. Once again, society needs a professional class to guide it to the relevant information. Today we call this class 'information professionals'. But the functions that are required, although still in their evolutionary phase, are not all that different from those of the old monks. The new electronic monks will not be guarding the scarce information; but they will be guiding users to the relevant information. The old monks may have been defending the information storehouse; the new electronic monks will provide the compass to guide users through the ocean of information. But in each case, it is the monk who stands at the gateway to the information that will lead to knowledge and understanding.

By fulfilling this important function, the information professional will exercise major control over access to information. But access alone will not be enough. The information will need to be understood in context and interpreted. Thus the information professional will be undertaking the modern-day equivalent of reading and interpreting the information, placing it in context and explaining it. As our society becomes more and more dependent upon electronic information systems, and the sheer volume of information continues to grow at very rapid rates, it will become more and more dependent upon the guidance of information professionals.

This new role becomes very evident when one examines the functions of libraries, not in terms of their historic role, but rather in terms of the potential role in an information society. I realized the real value of my librarian when one day a journal that I had never heard of appeared on my desk with a note saying, 'I thought you would be interested in this.' I was. It was directly relevant to my research. My librarian had become sufficiently knowledgeable about my needs and interests to anticipate and make certain judgements with respect to my needs. This was fine. It was a pure benefit because I continued to exercise my full range of judgement and discretion. But over the years I have came to rely more heavily on my librarian and my postgraduate students to assist my review of the literature. For a portion of the literature, I rely on them to draw my attention to items that I ought to know about. I have voluntarily restricted my discretion and judgement so that I can concentrate on the relevant literature, that is, what they choose to call to my attention. By these and other related activities, more and more gatekeepers are selected to guide us to the relevant information and allow us to ignore most of it.

The functions of a gatekeeper can readily be expanded. If my librarian and my postgraduate students learn even more about my information needs, they can virtually take over the function of deciding what professional information I need and what I will ignore. Not only could my own role in gatekeeping be reduced to insignificance, but my judgement with respect to my information needs would be replaced by theirs. I would have my own specialized information professionals. They would be my human expert system.

If my information professionals are deciding what I need, on occasion they may need to explain to me why they think I need it. Circumstances will arise when it will be convenient and efficient for them to perform necessary interpretive, collating and comparative functions. At least for certain types of data and information, they may be better prepared to do this than I am. By playing this activist role, the information professional becomes extremely valuable and powerful. At this level of involvement, the power of the information professional begins to approach that of the old monks in terms of control of the dissemination of information ideas and knowledge.

If most of society is wallowing in a sea of incomprehensible information, will it be any better off than if it wallowed in a sea of ignorance? It will depend in part on our ability to acquire a much better understanding of the role of information and communication in societies that are increasingly penetrated by electronic communication networks.

Understanding Social Implications

The major difficulty in studying the social implications of any new technology is overcoming the overwhelming tendency to focus primary
attention on the technology itself, rather than the social implications. With
respect to CITS, there has been a great emphasis upon the technology, and
as yet comparatively little emphasis on the implications of the information
that flows and will flow over new electronic networks. In CITS, the focus
of attention for social research should be on the 'C' and the 'I', more than
the 'T'. It should be focused on needs and demands, not on the stimulation of artificial uses.

This fascination with the technology in many experiments has contributed to a lack of clear specification of purpose or the establishment of
appropriate criteria for evaluating the results. What is the criterion by
which one should judge the validity or success of a social experiment? Is it
simply public acceptance and use of the new technologies, as seems to be
the case in many studies? If this is all, then is such experimentation not
really social, but merely part of the promotion and marketing of the new
technologies?

Presumably the social experiments are to obtain a better understanding
of what the social implications might be of a widespread adoption of the
technologies. This must require that close attention be paid to the study of
information and communication patterns within and among social networks. One part of such a study must examine the new networks established and used as a result of the availability of the new technologies. But
equally important – and totally overlooked in the great majority of
research to date – is an examination of the information and communication networks being used prior to the introduction of the new technologies. Without knowing the prior information flows and communication
relations, one has no base case against which to compare the new, changed
relations resulting from the implementation of the new technologies. The
failure to pay adequate attention to the base conditions often results in a
simple documentation of purported benefits of the new technologies to
those particular users who have benefited. This approach to social
experimentation can also draw the researcher into the role of myopic
promoter of the technology.

The term 'technology' has been defined as 'creative destruction'. The
definition captures the essential dialectical character that is documented in
the work of Innis and Smythe. New technology creates new opportunities,
but it destroys some currently existing opportunities in the process. The
beneficiaries of widespread adoption of the new technology will not be
hesitant to undertake research and marketing programmes promoting the

new opportunities created. Much less likely to be understood are the implications of the currently existing opportunities that would be displaced or downgraded. It is only through a comparative assessment of new information and communication networks created, against those networks displaced or modified, that one can begin to understand the social implications of changing technologies and to assess the long-term impact on society's institutions and its institutional relations.

For example, university libraries in many countries have increased access to computerized databases in recent years. This has increased the total volume of accessible literature. Senior professors working on funded research projects have benefited substantially. But in many cases the libraries have cut back on their physical holdings. Students, who cannot afford to use the computerized databases in their research, have often suffered a reduction in service. Current discussion in library circles includes the possibilities of access charges to reading rooms and additional surcharges for copying which will magnify the differential access to information resources.

The plethora of new database and information services now being developed will expand the opportunities for those with specialized and higher-level professional qualifications and relatively high incomes. In the process – and for the most part quite inadvertently – some traditional public markets and social services will be disadvantaged. The correlation between an improving quality and variety of telecommunication services and a declining quality and variety of postal services – a clear trend in most developed countries since the 1970s – is not accidental, and carries significant social implications that are not yet fully understood. It is important to emphasize that the impact upon the less educated and the poorer classes of society will not be restricted to the displacement of social and public services. The greater impact may well be in the restructuring of information and communication networks and markets in ways that will deny them access.

Attempts to assess the long-term social implications of technological change in the information and communication field are made especially difficult because of the complex methodological problems associated with network analysis. New information and communication networks grow over time as a result of learning, adaptation through changes in personal habits, and accompanying changes in institutional relations. Newly created networks have different characteristics than mature, fully developed networks. Small networks have characteristics different from those of large networks. Rarely can new, small networks be treated as a sample, or a miniature of a large, mature network. For future research it is important that rigorous attention be paid to the limitations of existing methodologies of social network analysis which at present reduce the usefulness of some potential research in this field.[14]

There is an accompanying need to focus greater attention upon the long-term institutional changes likely to be associated with the new technologies. Most social experiments have been so short-term that they cannot capture enough data and other observational information to reflect any clear trend of institutional change. Yet changes in organizational structure and institutional relations may be more significant than the technology in influencing information flows and communication patterns. Unfortunately, most social experiments end up evaluating the insertion of immature new technologies into an inherited institutional structure that has not yet adapted to the new conditions, that is, a wholly artificial environment. A significantly improved understanding of the long-term implications of these new technologies will only come when social experimentation is made part of permanent, ongoing research and development programmes designed to monitor the implications of societal change on a long-term basis.

Towards a More Informed Public?

In the CITS literature, an important question that typically is not addressed is, what will be the universal information needs of the general public in the information society? If society is going through a transformation to a condition where information takes on increasing importance, then presumably there will be a definable set of public information needs essential to the maintenance of participatory democracy.[15] This information will be necessary for individuals to function effectively as workers, managers, consumers, and knowledgeable and responsible citizens.

This is an area that will have to be explored in detail as the information society becomes more pervasive. Inasmuch as the information society may promote increased isolation of families and individuals, and a reduced role for communal activities, both the information requirements of public services and the public requirements for information services may have to increase. And with significantly expanded quantities of information, important new roles for gatekeeping, selection, abstracting and assessing information will be created. The resolution of these important developments may well define the new role of the public library in the information society.

The information society will be characterized by ever increasing quantities of 'information', but will there be more knowledge?[16] If the information is essentially short-term instrumental and functional, will it expand knowledge, or will it substitute for knowledge? It has been observed that education is what is left after you have forgotten what you learned. And cognitive science has well established that people do have a limited capacity for information processing. If the populace is pre-occupied with ephemeral, instrumental information, what will be left when it has been forgotten? Will this tend to reduce knowledge comprehension and understanding? Will people be taught to be smart but not wise, and clever but not intelligent? Will they respond with efficiency, but not understanding? Will they know how, and not why?

The education of people occurs in part through the intake of information by listening, reading and observing, that is, receiving information. But intellectual emancipation only comes with talking, writing and participation, that is, the development and application of one's critical capabilities. Awareness and understanding arise from the cultivation of the skill, and the provision of opportunities for expression.

If the information society requires the use of substantial amounts of instrumental information, delivered to passive receivers (perhaps between television programmes!), then it may well act counter to the objective of developing an educated and knowledgeable populace. In at least some respects, dependency on complex information networks and databases may be a barrier to the pursuit of knowledge.

There is now a major research task to which our education, public library and related institutions must attend. Historically, these institutions have assumed the responsibility for expanding the information and knowledge accessible to the population at large. The introduction of CITS is bringing about a major restructuring of institutional relations in society – not just economic relations, but political, social and cultural relations as well. This will make it possible, and in some cases desirable, to bring certain kinds of information directly into the marketplace. But in conjunction with these new information services, our public information institutions must redefine their roles in meeting public information requirements in the evolving information society. This requires an assessment of what these needs are, as well as the best methods for delivering them so that access is as universal as possible. Given the very restricted budget conditions for public services for the foreseeable future, it will also require attention to the problem of cost recovery in a manner that will provide the minimal restrictions on public access. These are all areas where the contributions of social experimentation and other research approaches will be needed over the next decade.

Conclusion

In the information society of the twenty-first century, the structure of both information and knowledge will change, as will the structure of the relationship between them, in both beneficial and detrimental ways. Smythe would remind us that we are not on a treadmill of technological determinism, waiting to be pushed in one direction or another by the next round of new technology.[17] The course of events will be influenced significantly by the major policies of governments, transnational corporations, and other powerful institutions. And through these policies, the direction of technological adaptation can at least be influenced in significant ways. The primary difficulty now is that most governments and transnational corporations, despite great volumes of information, have insufficient knowledge and understanding to fashion coordinated, comprehensive policies. Developing the information, the knowledge and the policies will be a major challenge for the foreseeable future not only for them, but also for students and researchers in the field.

Notes

1 M. Jussawalla and D. M. Lamberton (eds), *Communication Economics and Development* (New York: Pergamon, 1982).

2 G. Newman, 'An institutional perspective and information', *International Social Science Journal*, 28 (1976), pp. 466–92; W. H. Melody, 'Information: an emerging dimension of institutional analysis', *Journal of Economic Issues*, Special Paradigm Series, XX1 (1987), vol. 3.

3 M. U. Porat, ' Global implications of information society', *Journal of Communication*, 28 (1978), pp. 70–80.

4 D. Bell, *The Coming of Post-industrial Society: A Venture in Social Forecasting* (New York: Basic Books, 1973).

5 H. A. Innis, *The Bias of Communication* (Toronto: University of Toronto Press, 1951); and *Empire of Communication*, rev. Mary Q. Innis (Toronto: University of Toronto Press, 1972; first publ. 1950); M. McLuhan, *The Gutenberg Galaxy: The Making of Typographic Man* (Toronto: University of Toronto Press, 1962); *Understanding Media: The Extensions of Man* (New York: McGraw Hill, 1964); and *The Global Village: Transformation in World Life and Media in the 21st Century*; D. W. Smythe, *Dependency Road: Communications, Capitalism, Consciousness and Canada* (Norwood, NJ: Ablex, 1981).

6 W. H. Melody, L. Salter and P. Heyer (eds), *Culture, Communication, and Dependency: The Tradition of H. A. Innis* (Norwood, NJ: Ablex, 1981).

7 Innis, *Empire and Communication*.

8 V. Mosco, M. Pendakur and J. Wesko (eds), *Illuminating the Blindspots: Essays in Honor of Dallas Smythe* (Norwood, NJ: Ablex, 1993).

9 C. Antonelli (ed.) *The Economics of Information Networks* (Amsterdam: Elsevier, 1991); K. E. Boulding, 'The economics of knowledge and the knowledge of economics', *American Economic Review*, 46 (1966), pp. 1–13.

10 W. H. Melody (ed.), *The Intelligent Telecommunication Network: Privacy and Policy Implications of Calling Line Identification and Emerging Information Services*, Proceedings of a CIRCIT Conference (Melbourne: CIRCUIT, 1992).

11   H. I. Schiller, *Who Knows: Information in the Age of the Fortune 500* (Norwood, NJ: Ablex, 1981).
12   W. H. Melody (ed.), 'The information society: unveiling some contradictions', *Media, Culture and Society*, 7:3 (1985).
13   R. DuBoff, 'The telegraph and the structure of markets in the United States, 1845–1890', *Research in Economic History*, 8 (1983), pp. 253–77.
14   R. Mansell, *Whose Intelligent Network? A Political Economy of European Telecommunication* (London: Sage, 1993); M. A. Ruggles, *Personal Information Flows and Boundaries in the Intelligent Network*, CIRCIT Policy Research Paper 28 (Melbourne: CIRCIT, 1992).
15   W. H. Melody, 'Communication policy in the global information economy: whither the public interest?', in M. Ferguson (ed.), *Public Communication: The New Imperatives. Future Directions for Media Research* (London: Sage, 1990), pp. 16–39.
16   F. Machlup, *Knowledge: Its Creation, Distribution, and Economic Significance* (Princeton, NJ: Princeton University Press, 1980–4).
17   Smythe, *Dependency Road*.

13

Communication and Development

Majid Tehranian

Communication and development became the focus of theoretical attention only in the post-Second World War period. As a result of rapid diffusion of the mass media into the less developed countries (LDCs), social scientists began to consider the media as possible engines of cultural diffusion and economic development. The pioneers in this first phase were Daniel Lerner, Wilbur Schramm, Lucian Pye, David McClelland, Everett Rogers, and Frederick Frey.[1] In a second phase, in part inspired by the dependency theories of development and underdevelopment, a more critical approach on the role of the media was adopted. The main theorists included Rogers, Schiller, and an increasing number of Third World scholars such as Freire, Beltran, Tehranian, and others.[2] In the third phase, in response to the rapid technological breakthroughs in telecommunication and information processing, the theoretical debates have taken three distinct new turns. First, theories of information society and information economy have posited a new evolutionary stage in history dubbed as 'post-industrial'.[3] Second, in response to the growing international gaps in income and information, the LDCs have rallied around Unesco's MacBride Report,[4] calling for a new world information and communication order (NWICO) with a dual emphasis on freedom as well as equality cum balance in information flows. Third, the critical and neo-Marxist theorists have increasingly turned to theories of post-structuralism and postmodernism for explicating the conditions of a media-saturated and information-intensive, postindustrial world.[5]

This three-way theoretical split roughly corresponds to the Cold War division of the world into the First, Second, and Third worlds of development. However, in the post-Cold War era, the three worlds can no longer be defined spatially in terms of Western Europe and North

America, the Sino-Soviet bloc, and the so-called Third World of Africa, Asia, and Latin America. The ethnic, regional, and class divisions within the countries also are rupturing into the open. For instance, India (a nation of over 850 million) may be viewed as three distinctly different but interlocking 'nations' at three different stages of development, including: (1) an underdeveloping agrarian and semi-urban population of about 350 million; (2) a developing industrial population of about 100 million placing India among the top ten industrial countries; and (3) a struggling middle class of about 400 million torn between the seductions of an industrial society and the fetters of caste, class, ethnic, and religious warfare. The United States, a country of about 250 million, is also increasingly divided between a super-rich population of about 5 per cent, a struggling middle and lower class of about 75 per cent, and an underclass of about 20 per cent characterized by functional illiteracy, drug addition, high crime rate, malnutrition, poor health, unemployment, and unemployability.[6] Although the United States ranks highest in per capita income and communication development and sixth in overall human development among the industrial countries, it also rates as one of the highest in human distress and weakening social fabric.[7] This suggests that American society is deeply torn along five major social fault-lines, including class, racial, gender, generational, and regional divisions. Aggregate national communication and development indicators thus might reveal in international comparisons as much as they conceal in intranational disparities.

Production of theoretical knowledge on communication and development is similarly following a more complex pattern, reflecting the increasing levels of differentiation of the world into interwoven patterns of centres and peripheries that defy simple spatial boundaries. Following three decades of theoretical and research productivity at the centres (mainly in the United States) generated by Cold War rivalries and USAID funding, the field went into decline in the 1980s.[8] Reflecting this decline, an African scholar declared it dead in the mid-1980s.[9] In a subsequent autopsy, an international group of scholars brought together by the Asian Mass Communication Research and Information Center (AMIC) found the subject still alive but in need of resuscitation.[10] The worldwide appearance of several journals mostly or exclusively devoted to the problems of development communication also indicates that the field is alive and expanding.[11] It now has proliferated into a diversity of fields such as political economy;[12] popular culture;[13] rural development;[14] news flows;[15] and peace and security.[16]

Without attempting to review the foregoing history in detail, this essay focuses on three sets of critical issues: the definitional, theoretical, and policy problems of development communication. In conclusion, the essay poses what appears to be the major theoretical and policy challenges and opportunities facing the field.

Problems of Definition: Some Conceptual Quagmires

Communication and development are both concepts without precise boundaries and therefore in need of some operational definition. In this essay, communication is viewed as the process of exchange of meaning by verbal and non-verbal signs operating through cosmologies, cultures, contents, and conduits. This definition avoids media-centrism by including the ideological formations, the cultural expressions (both verbal and visual), the content of messages, as well as the conduits of communication from primary (interpersonal), to secondary (organizational), and tertiary (mediated) channels. It therefore places the role of the modern media of communication, important as it might be, in the larger context of human communication. The earlier literature of development communication, however, put a central emphasis on the media to the neglect of interpersonal and organizational networks of communication, including such vital links as the traditional and religious networks.

Development is defined here as the process of increasing capacity of a social system to fulfil its own perceived needs at progressively higher levels of material and cultural well-being. This view differs somewhat from the evolutionary concepts of development which consider the process as universal, inevitable, and wholly positive. Employing an organic metaphor, evolutionary development suggests progressively higher levels of differentiation and complexity as well as integration and order. Such concepts primarily focus on the progressive rise in a set of universally applied economic, social, or cultural indicators such as per capita income, industrial output, urbanization, literacy, life expectancy, or TV sets per 1,000 of population. Without rejecting the quantitative measurements, the proposed definition problematizes them by raising a question as to whether they can be universally applied without attention to the uniqueness of particular circumstances. It thus shifts the burden of proof for development from the exogenous categories of achievement to the endogenous perceptions of development. In many LDCs, a rapid rise in some development indicators such as gross national product and per capita income has often entailed environmental pollution, income maldistribution, and serious social and psychological dislocations. Recent studies of development indicators are attempting to correct the excessive emphasis on physical output in favour of a greater stress on the human dimensions of development.[17] If we consider such factors as literacy, life expectancy, Gini coefficient (indicator of income distribution), and access to health and educational facilities, nations significantly rank differently from the traditional hierarchies of per capita income.[18]

Concepts are often better understood in terms of their opposites. The opposites of communication are silence or noise, while decay may be considered as the opposite of development. Silences are essentially of two kinds, communicative and non-communicative. When there is virtually no contact between two persons, peoples, or cultures, the silence can be considered as signifying nothing. However, silences become meaningful when they are administered as a conscious effort to convey approval, disapproval, or neglect. Noises may be considered as analogous to electrical statics in the environment, often disrupting the flow of meaningful messages – 'sounds and furies signifying nothing'. Decay suggests the declining capacity of a system to fulfil its own perceived needs. Economic decay suggests declining productive capacity. Social and political decay suggest the declining capacity of a national system to respond to its citizens' perceived needs. When rising expectations considerably outpace rising income (the situation that prevails in many LDCs), frustration, aggression, and political repression may follow. Repression is often exercised when political mobilization has outstretched the institutions of political participation. Under such conditions, political decay may be defined as the failure of the political system to channel expectations into channels of political communication and consensus building. Since 'democracy' has become a broadly shared aspiration in the modern world, it may be argued that its fulfilment vitally depends on public communication on the goals of development and is severely retarded by noise and distortion. By contrast to other forms of rule, democracy is government by discussion and consensus-building. In this fashion, communication, development, and democracy present profoundly intertwined theories and practices.

Abraham Lincoln's classic definition of democracy as government *of* the people, *by* the people, and *for* the people can be usefully applied to these concepts of communication and development. Development *of* communication may be defined as expanding the channel capacity of the communication system. Development *by* communication might mean employing that capacity to provide social services such as tele-education, tele-medicine, tele-libraries, tele-banking, etc., alongside the traditional services. Development *for* communication might be interpreted to mean power-free and dialogic communication between the state and civil society so that public policy decisions are based on communicative rather than instrumental rationality. Thus defined, development communication means increasing levels of economic democracy (productive employment), political democracy (access and participation), social democracy (expanding opportunities), and cultural democracy (pluralism of meaning).

The Theoretical Problems

Ever since the eighteenth century European Enlightenment, the concept of development has constituted an overarching metanarrative of modern discourse appearing throughout the world in a variety of ideological guises such as nationalism, liberalism, Marxism, and religious messianism. The Idea of Progress, anchored on human rationality and perfectibility, has had a spellbinding effect on the history of the last two centuries. However, we may be coming to the end of that optimistic road. It has taken two devastating world wars, a long Cold War, and the disillusionments of a post-Cold War state of world disorder to put the concept of inevitability of progress on trial. The critiques of the idea, however, have taken many forms. Some have rejected it altogether, others have attempted to modify it, still others have proposed alternative concepts. The discourse on development has thus been rich in content and variety. The following three sections review three sets of theoretical debates that reflect the historical, ideological, and paradigmatic levels of discourse on modernization, corresponding to the surface, subsurface, and deeper levels of the global discourse on development.

Modernity and its Discontents

Theory-building on communication and development has faced some insurmountable problems. The root of the problem appears to be historical in nature. Can there be a general theory of communication, development, and democracy to explicate the diverse historical experiences of so many different nations? The stark reality is that nations of the world stand at so many different stages of development. Their rates of progress towards universally defined indicators of development are also varied. In fact, the last three UN Development Decades have witnessed a growing gap among nations. As a UNDP study reports,

> In 1960, the richest 20% of the world's population had incomes 30 times greater than the poorest 20%. By 1990, the richest 20% were getting 60 times more. And this comparison is based on the distribution between rich and poor *countries*. Adding the maldistribution within countries, the richest 20% of the world's people get at least 150 times more than the poorest 20%.[19]

The same report suggests that restricted or unequal access to global markets costs developing countries some $500 billion annually – about ten times what they receive in foreign assistance. The same pattern of lopsided distribution is also reflected in media ownership: some 10 per cent of the world population owns some 90 per cent of the world media.[20] Despite this relative deprivation, the less costly media such as transistor radios, television, and audio-video cassette recorders (VCRs) along with Western programmes have rapidly penetrated the LDCs in absolute numbers.

Faced with the demonstration effects of mass consumption standards in advanced industrial societies, effectively transmitted through global media, the LDCs have resorted to three different strategies of defence *vis-à-vis* the world capitalist system: (1) Hyper-modernization and Assimilation; (2) Counter-modernization and Dissociation; and (3) Selective Modernization and Participation. In the mean time, the more developed countries (MDCs), entrapped by the rising problems of hyper-industrialism, have themselves shown two distinctly different critical reactions against modernization: (4) De-modernization and De-industrialization, and (5) Post-modernization and Accommodation. The entire Enlightenment project of modernization has thus come into theoretical and practical question through these five reactive discourses and practices.

Hyper-modernization strategies are typical of the latecomers to the industrial revolution. It is often characterized by two different types of discourse, separatist and assimilationist. In the cases of Germany under Hitler, Italy under Mussolini, Japan in the inter-war period, the USSR under Stalin, and China under Mao, the dominant theme of their crash industrialization programmes was how to build, defend, or expand separatist fortresses under siege by the more advanced industrial West. In the case of periphery countries such as Japan in the post-war period, Iran under the Shah, and the Philippines under Marcos, the dominant theme was one of trying to catch up with the West within a compressed period of time by imitating its ways. Assimilation into the world capitalist system is often the result of such strategies. Both strategies are, however, characterized by a zealous commitment to the Idea of Progress. In their critiques of liberalism, totalitarian ideologies thus became more Catholic than the Pope, more committed to industrialism than the industrial West. By contrast, Counter-modernization is a strategy of dissociation from what is perceived to be the sinful ways of modernity – too much greed, too many disparities, too few benefits, losing the soul while not necessarily gaining the world. It is a reaction typical of the earlier stages of industrialization, the period of primitive accumulation. It can take either naturalist or messianic forms. In its naturalist forms, it may be considered as a Rousseau effect. In its messianic forms, it may be considered as a Khomeini effect. It was Jean-Jacques Rousseau, the Romantic French philosopher, who first formulated a naturalist response to the Enlightenment project. 'Man was born free, but he is everywhere in chains,' he

declared in *The Social Contract*.[21] Rousseau's proposals were to return to
nature, to the original innocence, to the unity of the General Will of the
political community rather than the fragmented Will of All in representative governments. The American Transcendentalists showed some of
the same reactions. The Russian Narodniks also demonstrated similar
romantic tendencies towards a return to the land and soul of Russia. In
the Third World, however, Counter-modernization is deeply tied to anti-
colonialism, anti-urbanism, and anti-secularism. Gandhi and Khomeini
provide the two best-known and radically different faces of the same set
of reactions. Recapture of a historic past, based often on authentic religious or national traditions, is the motivating force. Proposals for self-
reliant and indigenous forms of development are the strategies for the
future.

Selective Modernization and Participation (in the world capitalist system) constitutes the third major reaction to the challenges of modernization in the Third World. As exemplified by the development strategies of
Korea under its post-war military regime, China under Deng (since 1976),
and Iran under Rafsanjani (since 1989), this strategy combines relative
economic freedom with strong political dictatorship. The state thus hopes
to launch an economic revolution with a combination of market incentives and government regulation. There are strong indications that Russia
and some of the Eastern European countries might be taking a similar
road towards constructing market economies. Selective participation in
the world capitalist system, if carefully planned, can provide opportunities
for capital and technology transfer without unduly appending the national
economy to foreign sources of control.

By contrast, the reactions to modernity in the post-industrial West have
ranged from De-modernization to Post-modernization. While De-
modernization seems to be characteristic of the stage of late-industrialism
leading often to de-industrialization, Post-modernization represents a
range of strategies from cultural accommodation to cultural guerrilla
warfare against the dehumanizing effects of hyper-industrial, information
societies. De-modernization was best crystallized in the counter-culture,
flower revolutionary movements of the 1960s – a 'soft revolution',[22] led
by the middle-class intellectual revolutionaries who were at once the
beneficiaries and critics of the industrial system. Its slogan of 'I am a
human being – do not bend, staple, or mutilate me' captured much of the
sentiments of a youthful revolt against the stupendous and anonymous
technostructures of modern industrial society reducing the individual to
an IBM card in a huge and impersonal information processing machine.
Its cultural weapons of rock music, free speech, anti-war demonstrations,
communes, and drug experimentation, for a while, scandalized respectable bourgeois society. However, much of the movement's cultural

innovations have been gradually incorporated into the more pluralist cultural patterns of post-industrial societies. In fact, the process of incorporation has given a new lease of life to the cultural industries exploiting the artistic talents of rock musicians, film directors, and multi-media producers.

In the mean time, the failure of the De-modernization movements to produce any structural changes in the capitalist system has led to Post-modernization as a new cultural revolt. Following the student revolts of 1968 in the United States and Europe and their failure to bring about significant political change, the strategy of the new cultural revolt is anti-politics. While the intellectual origins of postmodernism are rooted in the De-modernization protests of the 1960s, its cultural relativism and political nihilism are uniquely its own. A postmodernist critique of society and politics, in the words of the postmodernist high priest Michel Foucault, 'leaves no room for power to hide'. It unmasks all ideological pretensions as self-serving conceits. Epistemologically, postmodernism is founded on a tradition of sociology of knowledge that considers all reality as socially constructed and therefore subject to social negotiation. This tradition, however, can take two distinctly different theoretical and practical turns. In the works of Habermas and Giddens,[23] it has led to theories of communicative action and structuration in which democratic discourse and human agency can combine to change the social structure in more desirable directions. In the works of Foucault and Derrida, however, such optimism does not seem warranted. The structures of postmodern society appear to be of such mindless force and pervasiveness that the only recourse is a deconstructionist strategy in order to voice the despair of the individual in self-mocking expressions of cultural and political criticism without necessarily offering positivist alternatives.

Development as the meta-discourse of the modern world has thus come under severe doubts and criticisms from numerous quarters. While the concept continues to be the operative principle for most of the ruling global institutions (including the transnational corporations, the World Bank, the International Monetary Fund, and the United Nations system), its legitimacy has been seriously challenged at two political and cultural extremes, namely the fundamentalist religious revolts calling for a return to the purity and simplicity of pre-modern life and the de-modernist and postmodernist revolts against the tyrannizing and dehumanizing effects of modernity. However, neither revolt has yet succeeded in dethroning modernity. On the contrary, evidence suggests that modernity and its material rewards continue to be desperately sought after in the deprived parts of the world still struggling to achieve the conditions of basic nutrition, housing, health, and education. The central question still appears to be one of *how* and not *why* to develop. Communication about development is, therefore, as important today as development of communications. As Patricia Waught has put it aptly,

> To argue at a theoretical level that all assertions are the fictions of incommensurable language games is to deny the fact that most people do, indeed, continue to invest in 'truth effects.' If we continue to invest in 'grand narratives,' such narratives can be said to exist. Grand narratives can be seen to be ways of formulating fundamental human needs and their 'grandness' is a measure of the urgency and intensity of the need. They are unlikely, therefore, simply to die, though they may need to be profoundly transformed. I suspect that Postmodernism will increasingly come to be seen as a strategy for exposing oppressive contradictions in modernity, but I would wish to resist the idea that we have all embraced it as an inevitable condition. We can work with it, I would suggest, in some contexts shaping our behavior through universal emancipatory ideals, in others recognizing the lurking cultural imperialism potentially involved in any such position and thus drawing on the postmodern as a strategy of disruption. Freud argued that maturity is the ability to live with hesitation, ambiguity and contradiction. Perhaps to grow up is to live suspended between the modern and the postmodern, resisting the temptation for resolution in one direction or the other.[24]

Four Normative Theories

Development and communication are both normative concepts; they suggest desirable processes of social change. It is no surprise therefore that theories of development communication also are normative and often ideological in orientation. In its first four decades, development communication as a field of study was clearly polarized by the Cold War ideological battles into the two liberal and Marxist schools of thought.[25] The liberal theories have argued for a 'modernization' paradigm that tends to be idealist in perspective, emphasize individual freedom as its normative preference, assume a consensus model of social change, and focus on the nation-state as its chief unit of analysis and on the internal dynamics of the developmental process. These theories also tend to be empirical in method of research, drawing conclusions partial to market solutions and transnational corporate penetration of Third World economies. The Marxist theorists, by contrast, have largely operated on the basis of a 'dependency' paradigm that critiques the modernization theories for their failure to account for the structural factors at the national and international levels and for their pro-capitalist bias. The dependency paradigm tends to be materialist in orientation, emphasizes social equality as a normative preference, assumes a conflict model of society, focuses on the world capitalist system as its chief unit of analysis and on the centre–periphery dynamics of development. Dependency theories also tend to be critical in their research methods, arguing for structural change and social revolution (see table 13.1).[26] Modernization theories saw the role of communication in development primarily in terms of promoting modern as opposed to traditional consciousness through media participation, psychic mobility, and diffusion of innovations. By contrast, dependency theorists critiqued the capitalist strategies of development as inducing lopsided development characterized by unfair divisions of labour, unequal distributions of income, media imperialism, titillating global advertising, and social and cultural dislocations that inevitably lead to social revolutions.

In the post-Cold War era, the axis of debate seems to be shifting in a new direction focusing on a conflict between totalitarian and communitarian perspectives. The 'totalitarian' paradigm has been historically as important as the liberal and Marxist paradigms. It has given shape and legitimacy to the development policies of the Nazi, Fascist, Stalinist, and other totalitarian states. However, following the defeat of the Axis powers in the Second World War and the disgrace of Stalinism in the post-war period, totalitarian theories have not enjoyed intellectual respectability and have consequently appeared only in disguised ideological forms. Nevertheless, totalitarian political theory is vast in its reach and rich in its variety and can be studied both in its classical statements and modern renditions. This literature tends to be voluntarist in that it views history as an arena for the exercise of the human will. For this reason, Nietzsche's philosophy of Superman has been considered (perhaps unjustly) as one of the sources of inspiration for Nazism. The politicians of the right also often invoke 'law and order' as a key justification for repressive state policies. Totalitarian theories similarly focus on the primacy of 'order' as their normative preference. For this reason, Plato's *Republic* has been considered by some (perhaps unjustifiably) as the prime example of a totalitarian model of society.

Whereas Plato's republic is premised on rule by a Philosopher-King and an aristocracy of virtue, totalitarian models of ideal society are based on strict notions of social hierarchy often based on theories of racial superiority (for example, the Aryan race). However, human traits other than race have also served as the basis for totalitarian legitimacy. Any particular religious faith, ethnic origin, gender, or even academic degree (with Platonic overtones) can be privileged to serve as the basis for totalitarian domination. Witness the theocratic or patriarchal regimes, ethnic cleansing, or policies of academic credentials or presumed expertise as criteria for social privilege! Totalitarian policies therefore focus on how the collective will of any particular social group (even if a minority, as in

Table 13.1 Comparing four perspectives on communication and development

School	Philosophy	Norm	Model	Unit of analysis	Focus	Methodology
Modernization	Idealism	Freedom	Consensus	Nation-state	Internal	Empirical
Dependency	Materialism	Equality	Conflict	World system	External	Critical
Totalitarian	Voluntarism	Order	Hierarchy	Race, etc.	Will	Social engineering
Communitarian	Interdependency	Community	Construction	Culture	Emancipation	Discourse/Practice

South Africa) can impose its own vision and blueprint of an ideal and disciplined society on the rest of the population. Correspondingly, the assumption is made (as in Dostoevsky's Grand Inquisitor chapter in *The Brothers Karamazov*) that the masses of population are gravely in need of social guidance and social engineering from society's select elite. Cultural and communication policies under authoritarian and totalitarian regimes thus typically follow strict rules of censorship with respect to messages of the media.

Finally, communitarianism represents a variety of social movements for alternative modes of communication and development with a diversity of emphases. The Third World liberation movements have been primarily concerned with the need for emancipation from the economic, political, cultural, and psychological dependencies of colonialism and neo-colonialism. The Civil Rights movement in the United States concerned itself with the same set of problems in the context of internal colonialism. The feminist movement is primarily focused on problems of gender colonialism expanding into broader issues of how patriarchal societies also inflict violence on nature, other societies, and themselves. The environmentalist Green movement in the advanced industrial societies has called for a restoration of the community between humans and nature but is also deeply concerned with the related problems of world peace, social justice, participatory democracy. The Christian Theology of Liberation in the developing countries emphasizes social solidarity among the poor and the need for structural changes to restore the ruptured national community. Other religious traditions have also profound commitments to the primacy of community *vis-à-vis* the rights of individual or property and have inspired movements such as the Gandhian movement in India, the Sarvodaya movement in Sri Lanka, the Islamic movements calling for the revival of the *umma* (the community of the Faithful), and a recent intellectual communitarian movement in the United States led by Amatai Etzioni and others.

Although the communitarian perspective emerges from a long theoretical tradition critical of the processes of modernization and industrialization, it has proved its political potency only in recent decades. Jean Jacques Rousseau, Emile Durkheim, the American Transcendentalists (Whitman, Emerson, and Thoreau), John Ruskin, Mahatma Gandhi, Leo Tolstoy, and the intellectual leaders of the current, worldwide peace, environmentalist, and Green movements may be considered among the leading theorists of this fourth school. Insofar as this school tends to focus on the preservation of community as the highest value, it can be characterized as 'communitarian' in its main tendencies. This contrasts to liberalism's focus on 'liberty', Marxism's preoccupation with 'equality', and the totalitarian emphasis on 'order'. Although concerned with the

preservation of individual freedom, social equality, and national security/
order, communitarianism is most deeply concerned with the loss of
'community' in the modern world. The democratic slogans of the French
Revolution, *liberté, égalité, fraternité,* are thus revived by the goals of peace
with freedom, justice, community, and security.

With respect to the idealist vs. materialist debate, communitarian perspectives tend to assume an interdependency position. They thus attach
a higher value to human agency than either culturally or economically
determinist views of social change. Culture and cultural constructions of
reality, however, assume a central position in the communitarian perspectives. Restorations of one kind or another – of nature, of cultural
identity, of the lost sense of community – play a critical role in the
emancipatory projects of communitarian movements. In contrast to the
emancipatory projects of liberalism, communism, or totalitarianism, this
is not to be achieved through the physical or structural violence of economic accumulation, class struggle, or exercise of national will. Rather,
emancipation is primarily considered as a spiritual and internal process
leading to its external manifestations in social peace and social cooperation for common objectives.

Liberalism, communism, and communitarianism may be considered as
the three faces of the general democratic movement that has characterized
world history during the past two centuries. Ranging from Fascism to
Nazism, Stalinism, Maoism, and their contemporary Third World varieties, totalitarian formations provide complex responses to the dislocating
processes of democratization by imposing centralized, bureaucratic domination in the name of racial superiority, proletarian solidarity, national
security, or religious piety. Capitalist, communist, and communitarian
ideologies thus have the potential to slip into a totalitarian mould when
circumstances call for them to do so. Nazism in Germany was a reaction
against the liberal democratic regime of the Weimar Republic, Stalinism
put an end to the party democracy of early Bolshevism, Khomeinism
provided powerful religious justification for repressing political opposition
in a multi-ethnic and multi-religious society.

Five Operational Models

In addition to normative and ideological rivalries, the global discourse on
communication and development has also been profoundly influenced by
five competing metaphors of social change. To explicate social system
transformations, these metaphors have characterized the social system in
terms of *supernatural, mechanical, organic, cybernetic,* and *linguistic* models.
Whereas the normative perspectives tend to be concurrent, reflecting the

concurrence of conflicting social interests, the transition from one set of metaphors and models to another has signalled major paradigm shifts in the social science discourse. Social sciences have a tendency to follow in the footsteps of the paradigm shifts in the natural sciences, and the change in metaphors and models reflects these 'scientific revolutions'.[27] The first metaphor represents a pre-scientific cosmology, while the next three metaphors point to views of society, respectively, as mechanism, organism, or a cybernetic information processing system. With the rise of linguistic metaphors, social theory is attempting to emancipate itself from naturalistic towards humanistic assumptions. By contrast to natural sciences, the discourse of social science is characterized by strong normative assumptions and debates directly bearing on social policy. That is why, parallel with the scientific paradigm shifts, the policy debates appear as never-ending, focused on such normative issues as freedom vs. equality, equity vs. efficiency, order vs. community, conservatives vs. reformers vs. revolutionaries. This corresponds to what Giddens calls 'double hermeneutics' or 'duality of social structure'.[28] Human agents are part of the social system they observe. By their interpretations of the system and actions based on those interpretations, they intervene in the processes of structuration.

Table 13.2 provides a synopsis of the paradigm shifts in the pre- and post-scientific discourse with particular reference to theories of communication and social change. The table is clearly suggestive rather than exhaustive; its full explanation requires a longer piece than the present essay.[29] Briefly stated, the shift from pre-scientific to mechanical, organic, cybernetic, and linguistic metaphors and models corresponds to the transition from traditional and pre-scientific world views to the paradigm shifts in natural sciences from Newtonian physics to Darwinian evolutionary theory, to the rise of computer technologies, cybernetics and General Systems Theory, and finally to a transition from information theory to communication theory as reflected in the rise of semiotics, poststructuralism, and postmodernism. It is significant to note that some major contemporary social theorists such as Habermas, Foucault, Derrida, and Giddens have employed linguistic and communication metaphors as integrating principles in their theoretical constructions.

Although the table draws sharp distinctions, it is important to note that new paradigms in natural as well as social sciences never completely abandon the contributions of their predecessors. By employing a new set of metaphors and models, however, they shift the focus of attention to new conceptual maps, capturing some hitherto neglected aspects of reality. In the process of incorporating the older ideas into their new theoretical vision, they also hopefully achieve a higher level of explanatory power. Behavioural models of communication and social change can explain

Table 13.2 Communication and development: Supernatural, mechanical,

Supernatural	*Mechanical*	*Organic*
Development models		
Revelation:	Instrumentation:	Differentiation:
Following the commandments of Revelation (the Bible, the Koran) to attain moral and material progress/perfection.	Perfecting the machinery of society by social engineering to achieve maximum efficiency, order, and output. (Watson, Skinner)	Diffusion of higher, modern values and techniques to achieve higher levels of differentiation, order, and complexity accompanied by higher levels of income, literacy, media exposure, physical mobility, and political participation. Stage theories posit evolutionary change/mutations. (Comte, Durkheim, Marx, Rostow)
Communication models		
Metaphysical systems of world religions communicated through Divine Revelation.	Behavioural, stimulus–response, or hypodermic needle models of communication. (early mass media effects research as reviewed by Klapper)	Diffusionist models of communication of modern values, ideas, and techniques from higher to lower cultures, more developed to less developed societies. (Lerner, Schramm, Rogers)
Common assumptions		
Metaphysical rationality Invisible causality Moral universality Divine determinism Human responsibility Divine guidance and Human striving to reach perfection (salvation, nirvana)	Mechanical rationality Linear causality Machine universality Machine determinism Algorithmic process Change within mechanical structures	Organic rationality Evolutionary causality Species universality Evolutionary determinism Processes of genetic mutation from lower to higher species

organic, cybernetic and linguistic metaphors and models

Cybernetic	Linguistic
Rationalization:	Emancipation:
Information monitoring, processing, and feedback to obtain greater speed, efficiency, and accuracy in the mapping of the environment to match its complexity for making social, economic, and political decisions. (Bertalanfy, Wiener, Boulding)	Deconstructive and communicative action to achieve power-free communication and an emancipation of the human life worlds from the grammar of society embedded in the abstract and anonymous hierarchies of power. (Habermas)
Transmission-belt models of communication: e.g. Shannon–Weaver information theory: Sender, Message, Channel, Noise, Receiver, Feedback *or* the Lasswellian model of Who Says What to Whom through What Channels with What Effects. (Shannon and Weaver, Miller, Lasswell)	Semiotic models of society as a web of signs, signifiers, and signified supplying texts and discourses subject to a diversity of interpretations and meanings by their authors and readers. (Saussure, Eco, Derrida, Foucault)
Cybernetic rationality Multilinear causality Punctuated evolution Probabilistic Multifinality Change within information-bound cybernetic structures	Symbolic ir/rationality Hermeneutic causality Cultural specificity Multiple meanings Change through human agency, communicative action and structuration

certain types of rudimentary phenomena (such as memory learning based on trial and error and corrective behavioural change). For higher levels of learning, such as explanatory understanding and innovative problem solving, there is need for greater theoretical mapping to arrive at higher levels of explanatory power.[30] Such theoretical formulations need not abandon the behavioural, stimulus–response, insights which have, in fact, led to the invention of effective learning machines teaching the rudimentary principles of most disciplines.

Table 13.2 also provides a key to the common assumptions and strategies of social change implied in each paradigm. The supernatural paradigms, of which the traditional religious views are prime examples, often believe in the primacy of the invisible over the visible world. Visible society thus has to conform to the commands of God's Revelation as it provides spiritual and moral guidance for human action. Starting in the seventeenth century, the scientific paradigms dispense with such metaphysical views of society and human action; they provide a succession of alternative metaphors and models that explain 'reality' in material rather than metaphysical terms. The mechanical paradigm views society primarily in terms of the regularity and predictability of a machine. The Newtonian 'clock of the universe' or 'the mechanics of law' represent some of its better-known metaphors. The organic paradigm sees society in terms of the rationality of an organic system. The typical metaphors are 'the *body* politic', or 'the *head* of the state'. While conservative organic theorists (such as Parsons) focus on the homeostatic attributions of the social organism, revolutionary organic theorists (such as Marx) draw attention to the genetic mutations on the historical stage (for example, the qualitative jumps from feudalism to capitalism and socialism). The cybernetic theorists, by contrast, employ the metaphor of an intelligent, information processing terminal in order to portray society as a complex, adaptive, information-bound, feedback-generating, self-correcting apparatus. Their typical metaphors are 'institutional memory' and 'social networks'. Cybernetic theorists therefore employ input–processing–output–feedback models of the economy, society, and polity.

Linguistic metaphors and models of the social system, however, take serious issue with the rationality assumptions of the mechanical, organic, and cybernetic paradigms. If there is any rationality in society, it is the linguistic rationality of a loose grammar allowing almost infinite variations within the same fundamental rules and yet open to a variety of subjective interpretations. As language allows poets to innovate, so do societies grudgingly allow social innovators to go beyond the rules to achieve their purposes. Societies evolve therefore as languages do, so the metaphor suggests. Society is viewed as a text, history as a context. Readers bring to the social text and context their own meaning systems.

There is therefore no objective social reality apart from the interplay of subjectivities. Linguistic metaphors and models thus negate the meta-narratives of a logos or telos in society while celebrating epistemological pluralism.

These five ways of seeing society also imply different theories and strategies of development. At the risk of oversimplification, the central process of social change in each world view may be said to consist of *revelation* in the supernatural models, *instrumentation* in the mechanical models, *differentiation* in the organic models, *rationalization* in the cybernetic models, and *emancipation* in the linguistic models. Although individual theorists are typically preoccupied with multiple themes, the main foci of each paradigm suggests a different strategy of social change.

In the supernaturalist *Weltanschauung*, society must conform to an invisible world and its God-given rules of individual and social conduct. The strategy of social change is therefore primarily one of moral exhortation and purification. In the mechanical world views, social engineering and technological manipulation is the basic approach in order to optimize the functioning of an efficient social machine. In the organic world views, the evolutionary process reigns supreme. Processes of differentiation and integration of social systems are thus the main foci of analysis. While the conservatives emphasize gradualist and incremental change through social diffusion of knowledge and techniques, the revolutionaries call for structural change through historical mutations by midwifing social revolutions. In the cybernetic world view, rationalization of the system as a whole rather than in parts becomes the central issue. This can be achieved best through increasing the capacity of the system for self-monitoring and mapping of the environment for self-correction and self-transformation. Linguistic paradigms, by contrast, are mostly characterized by a normative bias for emancipation of the human spirit from the rationalized, routinized, and bureaucratized webs into which modern industrial society entraps its members. While some theorists are more optimistic about their prospect than others, the general thrust is towards the deconstruction of ideological mystifications of power, the strengthening of critical consciousness in society, and the enlargement of the public sphere through communicative action for mutual understanding of the life worlds.

Converging Theories and Models

Ideational formations (including theories) may be thus considered to consist of two interlocking elements, cosmological and ideological. While the cosmological element tends to be culture-bound, the ideological element is interest-bound. This view of ideational formations sharply contrasts with the orthodox liberal and Marxist views of ideology. Although the orthodox positions have been considerably modified in the neo-liberal and neo-Marxist views of ideology, the lingering view of ideology as a camouflage that needs to be unmasked remains. Whereas modernization theory provides a *stress* theory of ideology, the dependency school offers an *interest* theory.[31] In the modernization literature, ideology is essentially considered as *pathology* – a disease that transitional societies catch. In dependency literature, ideology tends to be dismissed as *fraud* – a false consciousness perpetrated by the ruling classes to mystify the realities of the class struggle. In both schools, ideology is considered as a passing historical phenomenon that will wither away once the rational discourse of modern science and technology overtakes 'the irrationalities and distortions' of ideological discourse. In the modernization paradigm, this happens as transitional societies achieve the full status of modernity.[32] In the dependency paradigm, the false consciousness of the ideological discourse becomes unnecessary once social classes have been altogether abolished in a classless communist society.[33]

Ideological formations will persist, however, because they are part of the human condition. Human experiences are perceived and framed through conceptual categories that are socially constructed. These social constructions of reality are time, space, culture, and language-bound or, in brief, epistemically determined. The dichotomy between material and ideational can thus be brought into question. Human understanding of the material world should be property viewed as mediated through ideational constructions that mutually interact with the changing material conditions. Ideological constructions are thus viewed as deeply steeped in the cultural traditions.[34] In this perspective, culture is viewed as a verb, not a noun. An epistemic community is constantly engaged in the processes of actively negotiating those visible and invisible bonds of meaning that tie it together. The society's verbal and non-verbal modes of communication are the tools through which these negotiations take place, and ideologies constitute those competing world views and hegemonic projects that attempt to unify a society towards a set of common values, norms, and behavioural pursuits.

This calls for a culture-specific understanding of ideational formations. In this sense, tradition and modernity would be considered as part of the inner tensions of a single cultural system in the process of transformation. By contrast, theories of discontinuity in historical change have been handicapped by a number of flaws. By drawing sharp distinctions between tradition and modernity or feudalism and capitalism, the orthodox liberal and Marxist theories have neglected the needs for cultural continuity. By dichotomizing tradition and modernity as mutually exclusive categories, the processes of modernization have often been

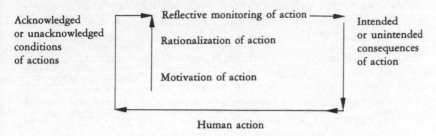

Figure 13.1   Giddens's stratification model of human agency
Source: Adapted from Giddens, Constitution of Society, p. 5

considered as a zero-sum game. The more modern a society becomes, so the orthodox theories maintain, the less traditional it is. However, historians have for long considered it 'a commonplace that tradition is constantly modernized and modernity is constantly traditionalized'.[35] No wonder that Britain and Japan, the pioneers of modernization in Europe and Asia, also continue to present the most traditional societies in those two continents. By over-emphasizing the universal aspects of the transition to modern society, the theories have thus underestimated the uniqueness and resilience of cultural traditions in the processes of social change.

The processes of human communication may be thus viewed as a series of multiple, interlocking, layers of consciousness, rationality, narratives, and communication genres that can be correlated with the discursive practices as shown in table 13.2. Human agency may therefore be operating through 'multiple hermeneutics' rather than a simple 'double hermeneutics'. This model is drawn from Anthony Giddens's stratification model of human agency (see figure 13.1) and should be, therefore, understood in conjunction with his arguments:

> The reflexive monitoring of activity is a chronic feature of everyday action and involves the conduct not just of the individual but also of others. That is to say, actors not only monitor continuously the flow of their activities and expect others to do the same for their own; they also routinely monitor aspects, social and physical, of the contexts in which they move. By the rationalization of action, I mean that actors – also routinely and for the most part without fuss – maintain a continuing 'theoretical understanding' of the grounds of their activity. . . . While competent actors can nearly always report discursively about their intentions in, and reasons for, acting as they do, they cannot necessarily do so of their motives. Unconscious motivation is a significant feature of human conduct.[36]

Table 13.3 Layers of consciousness, discourse, narrative and agency

Consciousness and rationality	Discursive practices	Narratives	Communication genres
Practical	Monitoring of action	Surface narrative	Conversation, news, rumour, gossip, information
Instrumental	Rationalizing of action	Subsurface narrative	Ideology, advertising, propaganda, public relations
Critical	De/constructing of action	Deep narrative	Cosmology, mythology religion, visual and performing arts, literature, philosophy, science
Communicative	Inter-acting	Intersubjective, democratic narratives	Discursive regimes

Source: Adapted from Tehranian, 1991

Table 13.3 correlates the layers of human communication with their corresponding layers of discursive practices, narratives, and communication genres. By practical consciousness is meant those routinized layers of awareness that a given language, culture and perceptual style pass on from generation to generation. The discursive practice most closely associated with this type of consciousness may be considered to be the reflective monitoring of action. When asked to report on our activities, we often tend to produce a simple and surface narrative of our motivations (for example, 'I refused to take the exam because I was ill'). This is the type of explanation that often appears in ordinary conversation or news stories.

By instrumental consciousness is meant those layers of consciousness that are more purposive, aiming at the achievement of certain objectives or the fulfilment of certain plans or projects. The discursive practice most closely associated with this type of consciousness may be considered to be rationalization of action. Rationalization has a triple sense here. In a Weberian sense, this means devising the most rational methods of reaching an objective. In a Freudian sense, this means covering up our real motives. In a Marxian sense, it might mean an ideological apparatus that generalizes particular interests in terms of the more generalized and socially legitimate interests. This type of explanation presents a narrow set of interests in terms of broader interests (for example, 'I refused to take the exam because I wanted to protest against the school conditions'). The explanation refers to a subsurface narrative that needs to be articulated or deciphered. This type of social explanation is often the stuff of ideologies and ideological struggles, but it is also typical of the more narrowly focused types of instrumental and persuasive communication, namely advertising and propaganda.

Critical consciousness means a layer of consciousness that monitors the routine monitoring of social action and its rationalizations in order to unmask their hidden meanings and to hypothesize alternative normative structures. This type of consciousness is perhaps best associated with the kind of constructions and deconstructions of reality that are embedded in mythology, religion, philosophy, literature, the arts, and sciences. This type of consciousness begins with the radical questioning of the origins and end of life, including the nature of truth, beauty, and goodness. The narratives behind these types of explanations are of the deepest kinds that only a critical approach can attempt to deconstruct.

Communicative consciousness is, by contrast, closely associated with the social and interactive nature of human beings. 'Interacting' is therefore the central feature of the discursive practice in this mode of consciousness. As Habermas has argued, this mode of interaction requires a high degree of equality and communicative competence among the participants.[37] Habermas's 'power-free communication' may be impossible in the real word, but to the degree that its conditions are met, negotiations of meaning can take place on an equal footing to realize a truly communicative action. The prevalent discursive regimes determined by existing power and communication configurations, however, enhance or constrain the possibilities of communicative rationality and action.

The four normative theories of development discussed above (namely modernization, dependency, communitarian, and totalitarian) have each gone through enormous changes as a result of changing material conditions in the world and their accompanying paradigmatic changes. Nevertheless, the perennial tension among the complementary and contradictory norms of order, freedom, equality, and community continue in the processes of modernization and democratization. While modernization by its very nature requires order and homogenization, democratization demands freedom, equality, community, differentiation, and pluralism. While the transition from metaphysical to mechanical, organic, cybernetic, and linguistic metaphors has challenged the normative theories to revise and adapt, their axial principles of order, freedom, equality, or community have appeared again and again in a variety of reconfigurations (including theology of liberation and religious fundamentalism) to mobilize social support on behalf of their own culturally and politically specific programmes. To understand these configurations more specifically, it is useful to focus now on the development and communication policy problems.

The Policy Problems

To consider the role of communication in development policies, we may begin with the proposition that society can be usefully viewed as a process of communication and control for hegemonic domination. Figure 13.2 portrays the economy, polity, society, and culture as social institutions of communication and control of power, exchange, norms, and meaning. In this model, the developmental functions of communication and control are proposed to be economic accumulation, political legitimation, social mobilization, and cultural integration. In the processes of modernization, these processes become the arena for the conflict of competing development world views, ideologies, and discourses.

The current global information revolution seems to have significantly contributed to four concurrent and contradictory revolutionary processes in the world. These processes may be labelled as the Developmental, Information, Control, and Democratic Revolutions. Beginning with the rise of capitalism in the modern world, the Developmental Revolution may be considered as the oldest of the four. Through the transnational corporations, this revolution has now reached the farthest corners of the globe. It has led to a transnationalization of the world economy at the centres, including Western Europe and North America as well as the metropolitan centres of Africa, Asia, and Latin America. Global advert-

The Developmental Revolution
Economy
Communication and control of exchange
Accumulation

The Democratic Revolution
Society
Communication and
   control of norm
Mobilization

The Information Revolution
Culture
Communication and
   control of meaning
Integration

The Control Revolution
Polity
Communication and control of power
Legitimation

Figure 13.2   Four global revolutions: institutional loci and processes

ising and information-processing have served as electronic highways in the integration of the world market economy.

The Information Revolution may be considered as the second oldest global revolutionary process to start with the invention of print technology. The more recent technological innovations in electronic media have, however, further accelerated this revolutionary process. The widespread diffusion of the print and electronic media throughout the world has had contradictory consequences. On the one hand, it has created a global 'pop' culture dominated by Western cultural exports. On the other hand, however, it has led to the deepening of national and ethnic consciousness in the remotest and most oppressed populations of the world. The print technology played a critical role in the rise of nationalism and revolutionary movements of the eighteenth and nineteenth centuries.[38] The small media of communication (transistor radio and audio-cassettes, mimeographing, copying machines, video-cassettes, portaback video cameras, and personal computers) are making an equally powerful impact on revolutionary and reformist social movements (witness Iran, South Africa, Eastern Europe, and the former Soviet Muslim republics).

The Control Revolution also is of modern origins.[39] This revolution consists of the rise of the modern bureaucratic state and corporation, the use of census statistics (note the etymology of the word!) and computerized information-processing, the modern systems of taxation, intelligence, and credit information-gathering, and the abuses of such information for monitoring and manipulating the citizens' behaviour. In the totalitarian regimes of the twentieth century, however, this revolution achieves its most sinister forms when combined with the instruments of state terror. In the Orwellian world, it signals its most compelling warning. In the current technological revolution in information storage, processing, and retrieval, it presents its greatest potential for mischief in an information-perfect world![40]

Information technologies, however, seem to have a Janus-like dual face. Historically, they have contributed to both democratic and counter-democratic trends in society. Hence the promises of a Democratic Revolution alongside the perils of a Control Revolution. The Democratic Revolutions in the modern world, however, seem to have taken at least three distinctly different roads, including capitalism, communism, and communitarianism. Figure 13.3 redraws the conventional half-circle, political spectrum into a full circle in order to place these three democratic ideologies in juxtaposition to the totalitarian one. The Blues, Reds, Greens, and Blacks are the symbolic colours of each of these ideologies. The circle suggests that there are many possible intermediate positions, as exemplified by the pragmatic and fundamentalist Greens, the social democratic and revolutionary socialist parties, as well as right and left

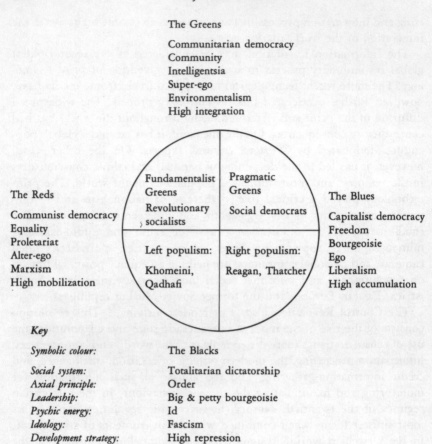

The Greens

Communitarian democracy
Community
Intelligentsia
Super-ego
Environmentalism
High integration

	Fundamentalist Greens	Pragmatic Greens	
The Reds	Revolutionary socialists	Social democrats	The Blues
Communist democracy			Capitalist democracy
Equality			Freedom
Proletariat	Left populism:	Right populism:	Bourgeoisie
Alter-ego			Ego
Marxism	Khomeini,	Reagan, Thatcher	Liberalism
High mobilization	Qadhafi		High accumulation

Key

Symbolic colour:	The Blacks
Social system:	Totalitarian dictatorship
Axial principle:	Order
Leadership:	Big & petty bourgeoisie
Psychic energy:	Id
Ideology:	Fascism
Development strategy:	High repression

Figure 13.3   The political spectrum: a conceptual map
Source: Tehranian, *Technologies of power*

populists. The Blues, the capitalist democratic forces, have been historically led by the industrial bourgeoisie championing the cause of individual
freedom and free enterprise. The Reds, the communist democratic forces,
have been led by the revolutionary working class championing the cause
of social equality. Despite their ideological differences, however, the Blues
and the Reds share in the same rationalist, secular, technological, and
scientific perspectives. They may be thus viewed as the Ego and Alter-ego
of the modern world. By contrast, the Greens and Blacks are the critics of
this modern world view and seek their inspirations either in the highest
ideals of religious traditions or in the darkest recesses of primordial
identities (race, nationality, religion). They may be thus viewed as the
forces of Super-ego and Id in the contemporary human psyche.

Table 13.4 Alternative communication and development strategies: a matrix of policies

Internal development policies External communication policies	High accumulation	High mobilization	High integration	High repression
Association	Iran (Shah) India (Gandhi II & III) Philippines (Marcos) Egypt (Sadat) Turkey (Ataturk)	Philippines (Aquino)	India (Gandhi I)	S. Africa Iraq (Hussain)
Dissociation	USSR (Stalin) PRC (1956–66)	USSR (1917–27) PRC (1949–56, 1966–76) Vietnam (1940–73)	Burma Albania Japan (Tokugawa)	Iran (Ayatollah)
Selective participation	Saudi Arabia PRC (1976–present) NICs Japan (Meiji) Egypt (Mubarak) Pakistan (Zia)	Algeria (1954–62) Indonesia (1945–65) Malaysia (1945–65) Egypt (Nasser) Pakistan (Bhutto I & II) Iran (Bazargan)	Tanzania	Spain (Franco)

India: Gandhi I refers to Mahatma Gandhi; Gandhi II refers to Indira Gandhi; Gandhi III refers to Rajiv Gandhi.

PRC (People's Republic of China): 1949–56 refers to the early revolutionary period; 1956–66 refers to the Great Leap Forward; 1966–76 refers to the Great Proletarian Cultural Revolution; 1976–present refers to the Modernization Period.

NICs (Newly Industrializing Countries) refers to South Korea, Singapore, Taiwan and Hong Kong.

Pakistan: Bhutto I & II refers to Zulfaghar Ali Bhutto and his daughter, Benazir Bhutto.

USSR: 1917–27 refers to the periods of War Communism and New Economic Policy before the rise of Stalin and Stalinism.

Source: Tehranian, 'Communication, peace, and development'

Each ideology also represents an alternative path to modernization; it proposes a different set of development priorities and strategies. The capitalist road tends to opt for high accumulation strategies of development, while the communist road has emphasized the high-mobilization strategies. As critics of both capitalism and communism, the Greens have stressed the need for the protection of the environment and social solidarity, hence, a high integration strategy. The totalitarian dictatorships, by contrast, see the need for law and order on behalf of some hierarchical society as the paramount virtue. They are prepared, therefore, to purse a high repression strategy of modernization to achieve these goals.

Table 13.4 pairs these four internal development strategies with three external communication policies – Association, Dissociation, and Selective Participation. Association policies are typical of the states following an open door policy *vis-à-vis* international capitalist penetration (for example the Philippines, Iran under the Shah, Indonesia under Suharto, and Egypt under Sadat and Mubarak). Dissociation policies typify countries that have gone through a social revolution and see a need for a period of consolidation of power (such as the Soviet Union under Lenin and Stalin, China under Mao, Iran under the Ayatollah). Selective Participation often characterizes those regimes that have passed the earlier stages of a national liberation or a social revolution and are able and willing to negotiate mutually beneficial terms for international cooperation on relatively equal terms (for example, the Soviet Union under Khruschev and after, China under Deng, etc.).

This theoretical perspective views development as a dialectical process of social change, involving the struggles for capital accumulation, social mobilization, cultural integration, and political legitimation, illustrated in figure 13.4.[41] Briefly stated, the processes of capital accumulation generate social mobilization (i.e. physical mobility from rural to urban areas, horizontal and vertical social mobility, and psychic mobility in terms of multiple social roles). In turn, the processes of social mobilization generate the need for reintegration of society along certain new common values, norms, and identities. This calls for political legitimation along newly developed hegemonic projects that coalesce around competing ideologies and discourses. Development processes have historically shown a cyclical pattern of movement from high accumulation to high mobilization and high integration strategies. The intensity and duration of these cyclical swings clearly vary from country to country. Generally, the more democratic systems allow for political feedback and participation. This in turn softens the blows of the cyclical upheavals. If we define discourse as the symbolic processes of exchange of meaning to negotiate reality, the coding and decoding systems in this process assume a central position in developmental processes. Public discourse, whether mediated or un-

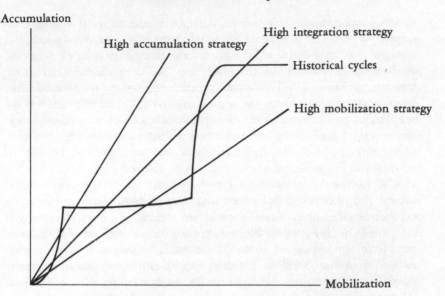

Figure 13.4   Development strategies and historical cycles
Source: Tehranian, 'Communication, peace, and development'

mediated, may thus be viewed as the social struggle for the definitions of reality and hegemonic interventions to replicate, reform, or transform it.

Conclusion

During the past three UN Decades of Development, the world has witnessed some stunning successes and failures in the less developed countries. The new industrializing countries (NICS) of South Korea, Hong Kong, Taiwan, and Singapore have joined the ranks of the industrial world within a generation. They have out-Japanized Japan. Other NICS, such as Indonesia, Malaysia, and Thailand, are following the same market strategy of export-led development policies and seem to be on the brink of take-off into self-sustained growth. China presents yet another stunning success story of the same strategy with annual growth rates of about 10 per cent even since 1978 when the modernization policies were set into motion. On the other hand, much of Africa and parts of Asia and Latin America continue to languish in desperate poverty and often negative growth.

The role of communication in these successes and failures has been a matter of intense theoretical controversy. The modernization school has steadfastly held that the introduction of modern media has: (1) assisted national integration; (2) provided linkages to the national and international markets; (3) stimulated domestic demand for modern goods and services; (4) mobilized resources for development; and (5) diffused modern values and techniques in such areas as family planning, nutrition, hygiene, agricultural and industrial production, and rural and urban life. By contrast, the dependency school has argued that the penetration of the less developed countries by the Western media has: (1) exacerbated their conditions of social, economic, political, cultural dependency; (2) undermined their national identity in favour of consumerism and internalized colonialism; (3) privileged the economic and cultural interests of an urban and Westernized elite against the vast majority of rural populations; (4) encouraged, through global advertising, conspicuous consumption at the expense of social investments in education, health, and infrastructure; and (5) failed to support development projects instead of perpetuating repressive and rapacious elites. The communitarian school of 'another development' has called for the media to be employed instead as instruments for endogenous rather than exogenous development by focusing on: (1) participatory modes of communication and development relying on both traditional and modern media; (2) horizontal rather than vertical communication channels; (3) appropriate technology rather than costly and complex high technology; (4) rural rather than urban biased programming; and (5) preservation of indigenous cultural and national identity and pride.

Historical evidence suggests, however, that there are no panaceas, no blueprints for development applicable for all times and all places. However, successful countries seem to have gone through the historical cycles of high accumulation, high mobilization, and high integration. A subsistence agricultural economy, for instance, cannot usefully follow a neoclassical, market strategy for its development, relying exclusively on market incentives for saving and investment. Low levels of income generate low savings and investment; fragmented or concentrated land tenure systems provide little incentive for investment in agriculture; lack of infrastructure discourages investment in industry. A high-accumulation strategy would release labour and capital through land reform, force savings through government confiscations, and stimulate the economy through taxation and investment. Such strategies are often undertaken by authoritarian governments employing totalitarian ideologies and persuasion techniques. If successful, however, high-accumulation strategies lead to high mobilization and the need for redistribution of income and investment in social services. The communication strategy in this phase often employs horizontal rather than vertical channels, voluntary associations and networks rather than the one-way mass media messages. In the mean time, the dislocating effects of both accumulation and mobilization create the need for national integration and unity. The role of communication in this phase of development is critical. Without the use of a lingua franca and a body of common historical memories, myths, and literature, it would be extremely difficult for a nation to absorb the disintegrating effects of the developmental process. It is no historical accident that countries with relatively homogeneous populations such as Britain, Japan, and Korea have found it easier than others to mobilize their resources for development. However, the developmental processes themselves also create the need for inventions of new languages, myths, and literature. Communication has thus served as both the cause and the effect of development.

The historical lessons of the past three Decades of Development seem to have influenced theories of communication and development to move: (1) from determinism to indeterminacy and human agency; (2) from idealist or materialist conceptions of development to interdependency; (3) from mechanical, organic, cybernetic to linguistic metaphors and models; (4) from emphasis on physical development to human development; (5) from internal or external foci to the interactions between the internal and external factors in the development process; (6) from need for technology transfer to need for technological leap-frogging; and (7) from the centrality of the mass media to the importance of interpersonal and alternative communication networks.

Notes

1   Daniel Lerner and Lucille W. Pevsner, *The Passing of Traditional Society: Modernizing the Middle East* (Glencoe, Ill.: Free Press, 1958); Wilbur Schramm, *Mass Media and National Development* (Stanford, Calif.: Stanford University Press, 1964); Lucian W. Pye (ed.), *Communications and Political Development* (Princeton, NJ: Princeton University Press); David C. McClelland, *The Achieving Society* (New York: Van Nostrand, 1961), Everett Rogers, *Diffusion of Innovations* (New York: Free Press, 1962); Frederick Frey, 'Communication and development', in I. S. Pool (ed.), *Handbook of Communication* (Chicago: Rand McNally, 1973).
2   Everett Rogers, *Communication and Development: Critical Perspectives* (Beverly Hills, Calif.: Sage, 1976); Herbert I. Schiller, *Communication and Cultural Domination* (New York: International Arts and Sciences Press, 1976); Paolo Freire, *Pedagogy of the Oppressed*, trans. Myra Bergman Ramos (New York: Herder & Herder, 1972); Luis Ramiro Beltran, 'Farewell to Aristotle', Unesco, 1980. Majid Tehranian, 'Development theory and communication policy: the changing paradigms', in G. J. Hanneman and Melvin Voigt (eds), *Progress in Communication Sciences*, vol. 1 (Norwood, NJ: Ablex, 1979);

Majid Tehranian, Farhad Hakimzadeh, and Marcello Vidale (eds), *Communication Policy for National Development: A Comparative Perspective* (London: Routledge, 1977).

3   Daniel Bell, *The Coming of the Post-Industrial Society: A Venture in Social Forecasting* (New York: Basic Books, 1973); Marc Porat, *The Information Economy* (Washington, DC: US Office of Telecommunications, 1977).

4   Unesco, *Many Voices, One World: Communication Society Today and Tomorrow* (Paris: Unesco, 1980).

5   David Harvey, *The Condition of Post-Modernity: An Inquiry into the Origins of Cultural Change* (Cambridge, Mass./Oxford: Blackwell, 1990); Patricia Waught (ed.), *Post-Modernism: A Reader* (London: Edward Arnold, 1992).

6   Donald L. Barlett, *America: What Went Wrong?* (Kansas City): Andrews, 1992).

7   United Nations Development Program [UNDP], *Human Development Report 1992* (New York/Oxford: Oxford University Press, 1992. pp. 127, 188, 189, 194.

8   Rohan Samarajiwa, 'The murky beginnings of the communication and development field: Voice of America and "the passing of traditional society"', in N. Jayaweera and Sarath Amunugama (eds), *Rethinking Development Communication* (Singapore: Asian Mass Communication Research and Information Centre, 1987).

9   Charles C. Okigbo, 'Is development communication a dead issue?', *Media Development*, 4 (1985).

10 Neville Jayaweera and Sarath Amunugama, *Rethinking Development Communication* (Singapore: Asian Mass Communications Research and Information Centre, 1987).

11 These include *Media Development* (London), *Media Asia* (Singapore), *Communication and Development Review* (Tehran, now defunct), *Chasqui* (Quito), *Journal of Development Communication* (Kuala Lumpur), *Third Channel* (Seoul), and *Asian Journal of Communication* (Singapore).

12 Cees J. Hamelink, *Cultural Autonomy in Global Communications: Planning National Information Policy* (New York/London: Longman, 1983); Jayaweera and Amunugama, *Rethinking Development Communication*; Majid Tehranian. 'Communication, peace, and development: a communitarian perspective', in F. Korzenny and S. Ting-Toomey (eds), *Communicating for Peace* (Newbury Park, Calif.: Sage, 1990); Hamid Mowlana, *Communication, Technology and Development*, Reports and Papers in Mass Communications, 101 (Paris: Unesco, 1988).

13 Georgette Wang and Wimal Dissanayake (eds), *Continuity and Change in Communication Systems* (Norwood, NJ: Ablex, 1984); Deanna Robinson, Elizabeth B. Buck, and Marlene Cuthbert, *Music at the Margins: Popular Music and Global Cultural Diversity* (Newbury Park, Calif.: Sage, 1991).

14 Emile G. McAnany (ed.), *Communication in the Rural Third World: The Role of Information in Development* (New York: Praeger, 1980).

15 Andrew Arno and Wiman Dissanayake (eds), *The News Media in National and International Conflict* (Boulder, Colo.: Westview Press, 1984); Johan

Galtung and Richard Vincent, *Global Glasnost* (Creskill, NJ: Hampton Press, 1992).
16 Katherine Tehranian and Majid Tehranian (eds), *Restructuring for World Peace: On the Threshold of the 21st Century* (Creskill, NJ: Hampton Press, 1992).
17 Caracas Report on Alternative Development Indicators, *Redefining Wealth and Progress* (Indianapolis: Knowledge Systems, 1990); United Nations Development Program [UNDP], *Human Development Report 1990/1991/1992* (New York/Oxford: Oxford University Press, 1990, 1991, 1992).
18 UNDP, 1992, pp. 127–9.
19 Ibid., p. 1.
20 Unesco, *Many Voices*.
21 Jean-Jacques Rousseau, *The Social Contract* (New York/Harmondsworth, Middlesex: Penguin, 1968).
22 Peter Berger, *Facing up to Modernity: Excursions in Society, Politics, and Religion* (New York: Basic Books, 1977).
23 Jürgen Habermas, *The Theory of Communicative Action*, 2 vols (Boston: Beacon Press, 1983–6); Anthony Giddens, *The Constitution of Society: Outline of the Theory of Structuration* (Berkeley, Calif./Los Angeles: University of California Press/Cambridge Polity Press, 1984).
24 Waught, *Post-Modernism*, p. 2.
25 Magnus Blomstrom and Bjorn Hettne, *Development Theory in Transition: The Dependence Debate and Beyond: Third World Responses* (London: Zed Books, 1984); Alvin So, *Social Change and Development: Modernization, Dependence, and World System Theories* (Newbury Park, Calif.: Sage, 1990).
26 For a lively debate between the Marxist and the communitarian theorists, see Herb Addo et al., *Development as Social Transformation* (Boulder, Colo.: Westview Press, 1985), particularly chs. 7 and 8.
27 Thomas S. Kuhn, *The Structure of Scientific Revolutions*, 2nd edn (Chicago: University of Chicago Press, 1962).
28 Giddens, *Constitution of Society*.
29 See Tehranian, 'Development theory and communication policy'.
30 Morris I. Biggs, *Learning Theories for Teachers*, 2nd edn (New York: Harper & Row, 1971), pp. 340–1.
31 C. Geertz, *The Interpretation of Cultures: Selected Essays* (New York: Basic Books, 1973).
32 Lerner and Pevsner, *Passing of Traditional Society*; Daniel Bell, *The End of Ideology: On the Exhaustion of Political Ideas in the Fifties* (Glencoe, Ill.: Free Press, 1960).
33 In the celebrated words of Marx, '*Religious* distress is at the same time the *expression* of real distress and the *protest* against real distress. Religion is the sign of the oppressed creature, the heart of a heartless world, just as it is the spirit of an unspiritual situation. It is the *opium* of the people . . . The abolition of religion as the *illusory* happiness of the people is required for their *real* happiness. The demand to give up the illusions about its condition *is the demand to give up a condition which needs illusions*.' – Karl Marx, 'Toward

the critique of Hegel's Philosophy of Right', in L. S. Feurer (ed.), *Marx and Engels: Basic Writings on Politics and Philosophy* (New York: Doubleday, 1959), pp. 262–6; emphasis in the original.

34 Geertz, *Interpretation of Cultures*.

35 P. Von Sivers, 'National integration and traditional rural organization in Algeria, 1970–1980: background to Islamic traditionalism', in S. A. Arjomand (ed.), *From Nationalism to Revolutionary Islam* (Albany: State University of New York Press, 1984), p. 96.

36 Giddens, *Constitution of Society*, pp. 5–6.

37 Habermas, *Theory of Communicative Action*.

38 Elizabeth Eisenstein, *The Printing Press as an Agent of Change: Communications and Cultural Transformations in Early-Modern Europe* (Cambridge/New York: Cambridge University Press, 1979).

39 James R. Beniger, *The Control Revolution: Technological and Economic Origins of the Information Society* (Cambridge, Mass.: Harvard University Press, 1986).

40 Majid Tehranian, *Technologies of Power: Information Machines and Democratic Prospects* (Norwood, NJ: Ablex, 1992).

41 See Majid Tehranian, 'Communication, peace, and development: a communitarian perspective', in F. Korzenny and S. Ting-Toomey (eds), *Communicating for Peace* (Newbury Park, Calif.: Sage, 1990).

Index

Adorno, Theodor 28, 45
advertising
    as social communication 130–1
    television 176–9
agency 2, 7, 9, 15
    see also Giddens
Althusser, Louis 27, 201
Altman, Robert, *The Player* 217
Ang, Ien 5, 14, 16–17
animals, communication with 89
    see also Uexkuell
Aronowitz, Stanley 228
Ashmore, Malcolm 79
audience research 15–16
    measurement 204–5
    see also New Revisionism
Austin, John 90

Bakhtin, Mikhail, heteroglossia 227
Barthes, Roland 178
Bateson, Gregory 5, 90
Baudrillard, Jean 176, 178–9, 199, 216
    Consumer Society 178
    The System of Objects 178
    Toward a Critique of the Political Economy
        of the Sign 178
Bauman, Zygmunt 209
Becker, Howard 7
Beltran, Luis 274
Berger, Peter and Luckmann, Thomas
    86
Boden, Deirdre 12–13
Boorstin, Daniel 53
Brokow, Tom 224
Burke, James 69

capitalism
    and chaos theory 207–9

and modernity 196–7
and postmodernity 193–211
Carey, James 10, 14, 16, 194, 197–8
    Communication as Culture 198
Carothers, J. C. 52
Cartesian dualism 81
Chandler, Alfred, *The Visible Hand* 4
chaos theory 205–7
    and capitalism 207–9
Chaytor, H. L. 53
Chomsky, Noam 141
CITS (communication and information
        technologies and services) 21, 254–
        5, 262, 268, 270
classical sociology 6, 27, 173–4
    see also Durkheim; Marx; Weber
Clifford, James 211
Collins, James 4, 14, 16–17
conversation(al) analysis 12–13, 140–63
    and history 143–5, 162–3
    see also discourse analysis;
        ethnomethodology
Coppola, Francis F., *Bram Stoker's*
    Dracula 222, 225–6
co-presence 98
    see also Giddens; Goffman
Covello, Vincent 113
culture and communication studies 197–
    8
    in Britain 227
    see also Carey
Curran, James 199–202
critical theory 202
cybernetics 22, 188
    second order 10, 79
        see also Maturana; Wiener

Danton, Robert 2

databases 179–84, 269
  privacy threats 15, 179–80
  multiplication of subjectivity 181–4
  as super-panopticon 184
  traces of subjectivity 181, 184
  see also Foucault, panopticon;
    information economy; post-
    structuralism
de Certeau, Michel, *The Practice of
  Everyday Life* 210
deconstruction 186–7
  see also Derrida
democracy 7
  defined 277
  democratization 286, 297
Derrida, Jacques 176, 186–7, 281, 285
development communication 21–3,
  196–7, 274–303
  commutarian theory 23, 285–6
  defined 276–7, 282–6
  dependency theory 196–7, 274, 282–
    3, 302
  diffusion of innovations theory 196,
    274, 283, 301–2
  as Enlightenment grand narrative 278,
    281–2
  information society theory 274, 297
  strategies 22–3, 279–81
  totalitarian theory 283
  uneven geographical patterns 21–2,
    274–5, 301
  see also Rogers
Dewey, John 4, 7
DiMaggio, Paul 219–21
discourse analysis (critical) 11–12, 107–
  24
  cognition and society 113–14, 122–4
  reproduction of dominance 109–10,
    113–24
  ethnic and racial discrimination 113–
    24
  see also discourse structures; social
    cognition; social representation
discourse structures in news reporting
  11, 117–22
  see also discourse analysis; social
    cognition; social representation

Drucker, Susan 69
DuBoff, Richard 264
Durkheim, Emile 27, 285
Dostoevski, Fedor 285

Eco, Umberto, "media squared", 14, 216
effects research 10–11, 195
  see also persuasion
Eisenstein, Elizabeth 53
electronic culture 57–8, 66–9, 72–3,
  174–6
electronically mediated communication
  5, 12, 173, 184–7
  e-conferences 185–6
  e-mail 185
  hypertext 185
  telephone 149–61
  writing 184–7
  see also Derrida; interaction; mode of
    information; poststructuralism
Ellis, John 218
ethnomethodology 141–3, 153
  adjacency pairs 142
  cooperation 156
  recording devices 141, 143–4, 149–
    50
  reflexiveness of talk 153–4, 161
  silences, pauses 156–7
  topic negotiation 156–7
  transcription 141, 164
  turn-taking and sequential structure
    142–3, 150, 157, 162–3
  see also Garfinkel; Goffman; Sacks

Fellini, Federico, *La Dolce Vita* 224
feminism 285
Fiske, John 16, 201
  Television Culture 201
Foucault, Michel 10, 42–3, 176, 182–4,
  281, 287
  Discipline and Punish 42
  panopticon 10, 42–3, 182–4
Frankfurt School 3, 7, 9, 27–9, 45, 187
  see also Adorno; Habermas; Horkheimer;
    Marcuse
Frey, Frederick 274
Friere, Paulo 274

Garfinkel, Harold 141
gatekeeping 20, 265, 267
Geertz, Clifford 207
Giddens, Anthony 3, 79–82, 92–102,
 154, 281, 286–7, 293–4
 double hermeneutic 93–4, 97, 101,
  287
 knowledgeable human agency 10, 81–
  2, 86, 91–2, 94, 102, 293–4
 linguistic turn 95
 mutual knowledge 86, 96–7
 practical consciousness 89, 92–3
 unintended consequences of action 82
 validity vs ethical concerns 100–2
 see also co-presence
Ginzberg, Carlo, *The Cheese and the
 Worms* 216
Giroux, Henry 228–9
Goffman, Erving 5, 9, 29, 99, 101, 162
 The Presentation of Self in Everyday Life
  101
Goody, Jack 8, 52
Gouldner, Alvin 41
Gramsci, Antonio 201
Gumbert, Garry 69
Gutenberg, J. 33

Habermas, Jürgen 9, 28–30, 41–2, 45,
 281, 287, 295
 *The Structural Transformation of the Public
  Sphere* 28–9, 41–2
Hall, Stuart 15
Hardt, Hanno 6
Hart, Roderick 69
Havelock, Eric 8, 52
Hayles, Katherine 206
Hegel, G. W. F 173–4
Heidegger, Martin 83, 89
hermeneutics 9, 29
 appropriation of media products 45
Herrenstein, Barbara 226
Horkheimer, Max 45

ideology 27–8, 200, 291–2
information 255, 259–61
information economy 19–21, 255–7,
 260–4, 266

and decisionmaking 262–4
information as commodity 20–1,
 259–61
 see also databases; information society;
  telecommunications
information society 19, 254, 257, 259–
 61, 270–1
 education 271
 explosion of knowledge 266–7, 270–1
 information professionals 20, 265–7
 institutions 255–7
information system theory 58–69
 see also social roles; social situations
information technology 268–70, 297
 social impacts 21
 see also CITS; telecommunications
information theory 5, 129–30
 see also Shannon and Weaver
Innis, Harold A. 8–9, 20, 29, 51–3,
 149, 194, 254, 257–9, 268
 The Bias of Communication 52
 Empire and Communication 52
interaction, varieties of 34–7, 43–4
 face-to-face 13, 34–7, 43–4
 mediated, 35–7, 44, 149–63
 mediated quasi 35–7
 see also electronically mediated
  communication; mode of
  information

Johnson, Mark 89

Katsh, Ethan 69
Katz, Elihu 16, 69
Krewski, Dan 135–6
Krippendorff, Klaus 5, 10
Kuhn, T. S., paradigm shifts 22, 287

Laclau, Ernesto 204–5
Laing, R. D. 88
language roles in communication 88–90
Lasswell, Harold 11, 128, 130
 see also message transmission theory
Lazersfeld, Paul 4
Leiss, William 5, 12–13
 Social Communication and Advertising
  130

Levinson, Paul 69
Liebes, Tamar 16
Lofgren, Lars 79
logical types, theory of, _see_ Russellian
ghost
Luria, A. R. 52

McBride Report 274
McClelland, David 274
McFerrin, Bobby 220–1
McLuhan, Marshall 8–9, 29, 51–3,
257–9
global village 194–5, 258
McQuail, Denis 6, 17–19
McQuire, William J. 137–8
Marcus, George 194
Marcuse, Herbert 28
Marvin, Carolyn 2
Marx, Karl 6, 27, 31, 101, 173–4
Marxism and communication 13
see also Marx; mode of production
Maturana, Humberto 80
Mead, George H. 7
Mead, Margaret 5, 10, 79
media roles in society 236–41
commercial 237
critical/emancipatory 237
cultural reflection and order 244,
250
portrayal of sex, violence, crime 244
professional code of ethics 238
quality of news and information 243,
248–9
social order and solidarity 249–50
state order and secrecy 243–4
media theory 8–10, 50–77
definition 50–1, 70–3
first generation 51–3
second generation 10, 58–69
shifts in media history 29, 33
see also electronic culture; Innis;
McLuhan; Ong; oral culture;
print culture; scribal culture
media trends, contemporary 17–19,
240–1
commercialization 241, 244
convergence 240

corporate concentration 240–1, 243,
245
deregulation 241
fragmentation/proliferation 240, 251
globalization 3, 44–6, 240–1
see also media roles in society
Melody, William 6, 17, 19–21
message transmission theory 5, 128–31,
137, 195–7, 207
see also Lasswell; Shannon and Weaver
Meyrowitz, Joshua 5, 10
mode of information 15, 173–4
constitution of the subject 174–6,
190–1
critique of ideology 191
see also electronically mediated
communication; Poster;
poststructuralism
mode of production 173, 189
see also Marxism
modernism 162
auteur theory 221
early 218–19
Morley, David 16, 199
Morris, Meaghan 210

networks 19–21
New Revisionism 15, 199–202
see also Ang; audience research; Curran;
Morley; Radway
Northern Exposure 218–19

Ong, Walter 8–9, 52–3
oral culture 54, 62–4, 149, 175, 257,
259
see also media theory

Park, Robert E. 7
Parsons, Talcott 6
Peirce, Charles S. 7
Perrolle, Judith 69
persuasion 10–12
see also effects research
phenomenology 83
see also Heidegger; Schutz
Plato, _The Republic_ 283
Polanyi, Michael 89

popular culture
  accounting for taste 214–30
  approaches to 214–15
  authority, evaluation 215, 218–21
  defining 215
  and post-modernism 16–17, 214, 221
  rearticulation 17, 215–18
  see also Bakhtin; Frankfurt School
Poster, Mark 14–15, 17, 202
Postman, Neil 69
post-mass media 1, 2, 5
  see also media trends, fragmentation
post-modernism 5, 14, 173, 214
  and capitalism 193–211
  and everyday life 180
  heterogeneity 207–8
  and pedagogy 226–30
  see also popular culture
poststructuralism 9, 14, 199
  constitution of the subject 175, 190–1
  linguistic turn 189
  radical semiotics 178–9, 198–9,
    203–4, 208–11
  see also advertising, television;
    Baudrillard; databases;
    deconstruction; Derrida;
    electronically mediated
    communication; Foucault; mode
    of information; Poster
power 31–2
  and action 31, 154
  forms of 31–2
  social 108–10
  symbolic 31–2
  see also Foucault
pragmatism 7–8
  see also Dewey; Park
print culture 55–7, 64–6, 148–9, 173–
  5
  early print industry 33–4
  and literacy 64–6
  and religious authority 33–4
  and rise of capitalism 33–4
  see also Gutenberg; media theory
public
  versus private 37–8, 68
  visibility 10, 38–41

public interest 6, 17–19, 235–52
  defined 241–3
public sphere 37–43
  see also Habermas; media roles in
    society
Putnam, Hilary 93
Pye, Lucian 274

Radway, Janice 16, 199, 229
rationality
  communicative 295
  instrumental, 294
  see also Habermas; Marx; Weber
recursiveness of communication theory
  5, 10, 78–102, 188
Ricoeur, Paul 9
risk communications 12, 127–38
  assessment and public policy 133
    136–7
  defined 132–3
  health hazard warnings (smoking)
    136–7
  message transmission problems
    134–5
Rogers, Everett, *The Diffusion of
  Innovations* 196
Rousseau, J. J. 176, 285
  Emile 176
Russell, Bertrand 79
Russellian ghost 79, 86, 88, 93–5

Sacks, Harvey 141–2, 163
Schiller, Herbert 274
Schramm, Wilbur 274
Schutz, Alfred 83
Schwartz, Tony 53
scribal culture 20, 54–5, 265
  see also media theory
Searle, John 90
semiotics 14, 197, 201
  see also structuralism
Sennett, Richard 41
Shannon, Claude and Weaver, Warren
  5, 129–30
  see also information theory
Shiller, Herbert 274
Smythe, Dallas 21, 257, 268, 271

social change
    metaphors of 286–91
    discontinuity 292
social cognition. 107–8, 110
    context models 111
    ideologies 112
    models of 111, 118
    social attitudes 111–12, 115–16
    social knowledge 111
    strategies 112
    see also discourse analysis
social representation 114–17
    see also discourse analysis
social roles
    in electronic cultures 66–9
    as information networks 58–62
    in oral cultures 62–4
    in print cultures 64–6
social situations 59–60
Sontag, Susan 69
Spheeris, Penelope, *Wayne's World* 217–
    18
Stratton, Jon 211
structuralism 3
    in linguistics 177–8
    see also poststructuralism; semiotics
Symbolic Interactionism 7
    see also Becker; Mead, George H.

Tehranian, Majid 6, 17, 21–3, 274
telecommunications 6, 19, 269
    competition and trade 256–7, 263–4
    see also CITS; information economy

Thompson, John 3, 5, 9–10
Toffler, Alvin 69
Tomlinson, John 196, 202
transportation metaphors for
    communication 20–1, 97–8, 194
Turkle, Sherry 69

Uexkuell, J. von 89
understanding
    centrality of 80–4, 87
    objections/pertubations/challenges to
        82–4
    see also Cartesian dualism; cybernetics;
        ethnomethodology;
        phenomenology

Van Dijk, Teun 11–13
von Foerster, Heinz 79
von Glasersfeld, Ernst 79

Wachtel, Edward 69
Wallerstein, Immanuel 193–4
    Realm of Uncertainty 193–4, 197, 209
Watt, Ian 52
Watzlawick, Paul et al. 81
Waught, Patricia 282
Weber, Max 6, 27, 31, 173–4, 294
Wiener, Norbert 188
Williams, Raymond 15
Wittgenstein, Ludwig 141

Zuboff, Shoshana 69